Religion and Nature in North America

BLOOMSBURY RELIGION IN NORTH AMERICA

The chapters in this book were first published in the digital collection *Bloomsbury Religion in North America*. Covering North America's diverse religious traditions, this digital collection provides reliable and peer-reviewed articles and eBooks for students and instructors of religious studies, anthropology of religion, sociology of religion, and history. Learn more and get access for your library at www.theologyandreligiononline.com/bloomsbury-religion-in-north-america

B L O O M S B U R Y
RELIGION IN
NORTH AMERICA

Also Available:
Islam in North America, edited by Hussein Rashid,
Huma Mohibullah, and Vincent Biondo
Religion, Science and Technology in North America,
edited by Lisa L. Stenmark and Whitney A. Bauman
Christianity in North America,
edited by Dyron B. Daughrity

Religion and Nature in North America

An Introduction

**EDITED BY LAUREL D. KEARNS
AND WHITNEY A. BAUMAN**

BLOOMSBURY ACADEMIC
LONDON • NEW YORK • OXFORD • NEW DELHI • SYDNEY

BLOOMSBURY ACADEMIC
Bloomsbury Publishing Plc
50 Bedford Square, London, WC1B 3DP, UK
1385 Broadway, New York, NY 10018, USA
29 Earlsfort Terrace, Dublin 2, Ireland

BLOOMSBURY, BLOOMSBURY ACADEMIC and the Diana logo are
trademarks of Bloomsbury Publishing Plc

First published online in 2021
This print edition first published in Great Britain 2024

Series design by Rebecca Heselton
Cover image: "Firefall." Horsetail Fall at Yosemite National Park © Cedric Letsch/Unsplash

A catalogue record for this book is available from the British Library.

Library of Congress Cataloging-in-Publication Data
Names: Kearns, Laurel, editor. | Bauman, Whitney, editor.
Title: Religion and nature in North America : an introduction / edited by Laurel
D. Kearns and Whitney A. Bauman.
Description: London ; New York : Bloomsbury Academic, 2024. | Series: Bloomsbury religion in
North America | First published online in 2021. | Includes bibliographical references and index.
Identifiers: LCCN 2023040916 | ISBN 9781350406605 (hardback) | ISBN 9781350406612 (paperback)
Subjects: LCSH: Human ecology–Religious aspects. | Human ecology–North America.
Classification: LCC GF80 .R45127 2024 | DDC 201/.77097–dc23/eng/20231013
LC record available at https://lccn.loc.gov/2023040916

ISBN: HB: 978-1-3504-0660-5
         PB: 978-1-3504-0661-2
         ePDF: 978-1-3504-0662-9
         eBook: 978-1-3504-0663-6

Series: Bloomsbury Religion in North America

Typeset by Integra Software Services Pvt. Ltd.
Printed and bound in Great Britain

To find out more about our authors and books visit www.bloomsbury.com
and sign up for our newsletters

Contents

Illustrations   vii

List of Contributors   xii

Acknowledgments   xvii

PART ONE North American Religious Traditions

1 Religion and Nature in North America: An Introduction
Whitney A. Bauman and Laurel D. Kearns   3

2 Reconciling to the Ancestors: The Spirit of Decolonization in
Times of Pandemic *Timothy B. Leduc*   29

3 Indigenous Language and Ecology *Marcus Briggs-Cloud*   45

4 The Tent of Abraham: The Emerging Landscape of Jewish,
Christian, and Islamic Ecological Traditions *Rebecca Kneale Gould
and Laurel D. Kearns*   56

5 Asian Religions and Nature in North America *Elizabeth Allison*   83

6 Environmentalism, Ecological Activism/Theology, and New
Religious Movements *Morgan Shipley*   101

PART TWO Embodiments and Identities

7 Race, Religion, and Environmental Racism in North America
Elaine Nogueira-Godsey, Laurel D. Kearns, and Whitney A. Bauman   123

8 African American Religious Naturalism in the Novel *Sula*
by Toni Morrison *Tyson-Lord Gray*   146

9 Religion, Nature, and Critical Materialisms *Courtney O'Dell-Chaib*   155

10 Bodily Beings: Sex, Sexuality, and Gender at the Intersection
of Religion and Nature *Heather Eaton*   170

11 Religion, Nature, and Disability *Roger S. Gottlieb*   187

12 Prayerful Living with Animals in the Ancestral Skills Movement
    Sarah M. Pike   201

PART THREE Themes and Issues

13 Globalization and Planetary Ethics Related to Religion and Nature
    in North America *Cynthia D. Moe-Lobeda*   213

14 Religion and Climate Change *Kevin J. O'Brien*   228

15 Petrocultures and Christianity in the United States
    Terra Schwerin Rowe   242

16 Is Extinction Religious? *Willis Jenkins*   249

17 Animals and Religion *Laura H. Hobgood*   254

18 Sacred Water of Florida: Ceremony and Spirituality in the
    Sunshine State *Victoria Machado*   270

Index   282

Illustrations

Cover Image "Firefall" Photograph by Cedric Letsch. Firefall is the natural phenomenon of Horsetail Fall at Yosemite National Park, California that may happen in February when the shadow from El Capitan and the angle of the setting sun set the edge of the falls "ablaze." Viewing this phenomenon is so popular that it damages the ecosystem, leading to some viewing spots being closed. This image from Yosemite was chosen because the creation, and use, of the park embodies the complicated, and often disturbing, colonial and religious attitudes toward "Nature" and indigenous peoples discussed throughout this book. We think the image captures that tension of what is hidden and what is illuminated in the history of religion and nature in North America.

1.1   Indigenous peoples map 5

1.2   Standing Rock Protest 7

1.3   *The Landing of Columbus* by John Vanderlyn 9

1.4   *American Progress* by John Gast, 1872 11

1.5   "Earthrise" over the lunar horizon 15

1.6   Rachel Carson 16

1.7   DDT spraying in 1995 as part of the Western spruce budworm control project 17

1.8   A mountain of damaged oil drums near the Exxon refinery 19

1.9   Members of the United Methodist Women at the 2019 Youth Climate Strike in New York City 22

1.10 Hundreds of thousands join the People's Climate March in Washington, DC in 2017 24

2.1   Hollow tree in fall 30

2.2   Seasonal representation of Herb Nabigon's Medicine Wheel 34

2.3   Tree of Life Mandala 35

2.4   Alberta tailing pond 36

2.5   Canadian Maple Leaf Mandala 39

2.6   Flying sandhill cranes 40

3.1   The Welcome Sign at the Ekvn-Yefolecv ecovillage 46

3.2   Language immersion students have daily farm responsibilities 48

3.3   No-English zones are enforced while traditional ecological education is offered to ecovillage residents 49

3.4   Strawbale wall system at the Community Center 50

3.5   Ekvn-Yefolecv cofounder and codirector Marcus Briggs-Cloud preparing for sturgeon spawn 51

3.6   Ekvn-Yefolecv cofounder and codirector Tawna Little about to offer prayer on sturgeon release day 53

3.7   Language immersion inside the aquaponics greenhouse 54

4.1   Hazon Sukkahfest, an annual retreat to celebrate the holiday of Sukkot 61

4.2   Young Evangelicals for Climate Action (YECA) at a demonstration outside of the White House in January 2020 63

4.3   Youth-led School Strikes for Climate took place globally in 2019 65

4.4   Solar panels on Woodlawn United Church in Dartmouth, Nova Scotia 66

4.5   GreenFaith activists of many different religious traditions protest Enbridge's Line 3 oil pipeline expansion in Minnesota 67

4.6   Wild Earth Spiritual Community 68

4.7   Harvest thanksgiving altar in San Antonio, Huasteca, Mexico 71

5.1   Henry David Thoreau's cabin at Walden Pond 86

5.2   Chinese workers in the Sierra 87

5.3   People leaving Buddhist church at Manzanar War Relocation Center, California 88

5.4   Green Gulch Farm, Marin County, California 90

5.5 Convergence of the Allegheny and Monongahela rivers with a subterranean river surfacing through a fountain in downtown Pittsburgh 94

6.1 Protest against Dakota Access and Keystone XL Pipelines 102

6.2 Indigenous Environmental Network 105

6.3 Julia "Butterfly" Hill in a 2006 protest tree sit 107

6.4 Tar Sands Healing Walk 109

6.5 The Scandinavian permaculture festival of 2013 112

6.6 Findhorn Foundation 114

6.7 Earth First! banner from 2001 Bluebird protest tree sit 115

7.1 A diverse crowd of well over 150,000 at the Washington, DC, People's Climate March on April 29, 2017 126

7.2 A former resident visits the "Uptop" section of Altgeld Gardens in Chicago 127

7.3 A mural in Detroit by Brandan "bmike" Odums 131

7.4 A poster advertising "Indian Territory" available for settlement, *circa* 1889 132

7.5 Vast mining operation in the Athabasca Tar Sands, Alberta, Canada 135

7.6 Veronica Kyle of Faith and Place, co-visionary and cofounder of the EcoWomanist Institute 137

7.7 A Latinx Chicago congregation on a Nature Outing through Faith in Place 138

8.1 An African American family leaving Florida during the Great Depression 147

8.2 Toni Morrison 147

8.3 African American sharecropper boy plowing 149

8.4 Social and Environmental Justice March through Harlem, New York 153

9.1 People waiting to enter the Superdome during Hurricane Katrina 161

9.2 A water protector at Standing Rock 163

9.3 Yosemite National Park 164

9.4 Theodore Roosevelt with John Muir 166

9.5 Muir Woods 166

10.1 Gender Unicorn, "Trans Student Educational Resources, 2015" 172

10.2 US Supreme Court protest for LGBTQ equality, Washington, DC, 2019 174

10.3 Promise Keepers rally in Washington, DC, 1997, which promoted godly manhood and fatherhood 176

10.4 A Missing and Murdered Indigenous Women (MMIW) Task Force rally in Minnesota 178

10.5 Ecofeminism, Ritual Venus de Primavera, part of the Tiempo de Mujeres, Festival por la Igualdad, Mexico 180

10.6 A greater sage-grouse courtship display 183

11.1 Protesters at a rally outside a courthouse 188

11.2 Author's daughter playing basketball 191

11.3 A sign indicating the location of the wheelchair ramp and entrance 194

11.4 Flint, Michigan water crisis 195

11.5 Alaska climate change erosion village refugee 196

12.1 Rabbitstick organizers' trailer 202

12.2 Handmade hunting tools 203

12.3 Hunting bows and handmade brooms at Rabbitstick 204

12.4 Skins for sale at Rabbitstick 207

13.1 Electronic waste 214

13.2 Deforestation 218

13.3 Three men braving the flood waters on a tractor in Sri Lanka 222

13.4 Voices of the Earth 224

13.5 Climate change protesters march in Paris' streets 226

14.1 Evangelical climate scientist Katharine Hayhoe, speaking about climate change 230

14.2 Aerial view of a solar power plant station in Nevada, United States 232

14.3 The Qur'an, the holiest book in Islam, which many Muslims believe contains clear directions for sustainable living 233

14.4 Water protectors and protesters march at Standing Rock to protest the Dakota Access Pipeline in 2016 236

14.5 A resident in her damaged home in Puerto Rico in the aftermath of Hurricane Maria, which struck the island in October 2017 238

15.1 Spindletop Lucas Gusher, Texas, 1901 244

15.2 Oil well pumpjacks 245

16.1 1556 painting by Aurelio Luini of the story of Noah's Ark from the book of Genesis 251

17.1 Yup'ik ceremonial mask 258

17.2 Bison at Ekvn-Yefolecv 260

17.3 Blessing of animals, First Christian Church, Alexandria, Virginia 262

17.4 Blessing of animals, First Christian Church, Alexandria, Virginia 263

18.1 Slime coated the Caloosahatchee River at Cape Coral, Florida, in July 2018 271

18.2 Headaches and nausea caused by the toxic algae bloom on the St. Lucie River caused offices to shut down 272

18.3 A mandala created in the sand at the Sacred Water Tribe ceremony, September 2018 274

18.4 Adam Ingham calls participants into reflection with the beat of a drum at the Sacred Water Tribe ceremony 274

18.5 Participants gather by Lake Okeechobee for the "Healing Our Relationship With Water" prayer ceremony 276

18.6 After the ceremony, water is returned to its source 277

18.7 Cohosts of the "Healing Our Relationship With Water" prayer ceremony 277

18.8 Flyer by clean water advocates John Moran and Rick Kilby 278

List of Contributors

Elizabeth Allison, PhD, is Professor of Ecology and Religion at the California Institute of Integral Studies in San Francisco, USA, where she founded and chairs the graduate program in Ecology, Spirituality, and Religion and created the Religion & Ecology Summit conference series. She is a member of the Advisory Group for the Yale Forum on Religion & Ecology; an editorial board member for the journal *Worldviews: Global Religions, Culture, and Ecology*; and the Secretary of the International Society for the Study of Religion, Nature, and Culture. Her dozens of scholarly articles appear in journals including *Ecology & Society*, *WIREs Climate Change*, *Religions*, *Mountain Research and Development*, *Journal for the Study of Religion, Nature, and Culture*, and in numerous edited volumes on Bhutan, religion, nature, and geography. She is co-editor of *After the Death of Nature: Carolyn Merchant and the Future of Human-Nature Relations*. A past Fulbright scholar in Nepal, she earned her PhD in environmental science, policy, and management at the University of California—Berkeley, a master's in environmental management from Yale University, a master's in religious ethics from Yale, and a bachelor's degree from Williams College.

Whitney A. Bauman is Professor of Religious Studies at Florida International University (FIU) in Miami, FL. He is also co-founder and co-director of *Counterpoint: Navigating Knowledge*, a non-profit based in Berlin, Germany that holds public discussions over social and ecological issues related to globalization and climate change. His areas of research interest fall under the theme of "religion, science, and globalization." He is the recipient of a Fulbright Fellowship and a Humboldt Fellowship, and in 2022 won an award from FIU for Excellence in Research and Creative Activities. His publications include: *Religion and Ecology: Developing a Planetary Ethic* (2014), and co-authored with Kevin O'Brien, *Environmental Ethics and Uncertainty: Tackling Wicked Problems* (2019). The third edition of *Grounding Religion: A Fieldguide to the Study of Religion and Ecology*, co-edited with Kevin O'Brien and Richard Bohannon, is due out with in late 2023. His next monograph is entitled *A Critical Planetary Romanticism: Literary and Scientific Origins of New Materialism* (2023).

Marcus Briggs-Cloud (Maskoke) is co-director of Ekvn-Yefolecv Maskoke Ecovillage. A graduate of Harvard Divinity School, he has a PhD in interdisciplinary ecology from the University of Florida. Marcus is partnered to Tawna Little (Maskoke) and they have two children, Nokos-Afvnoke and Hemokke, with whom Marcus enjoys speaking exclusively in the Maskoke language.

Heather Eaton is Professor of Conflict Studies at St. Paul University in Ottawa. She teaches and writes on issues of peace and conflict studies, particularly as they relate to ecological issues, ecofeminism, and religion and ecology in general. She has written and edited many different books and articles including *Introducing Ecofeminist Theologies* (T&T Clark, 2005); with Lauren Levesque (eds.), *Advancing Nonviolence and Social Transformation* (2016); and as editor, *The Intellectual Journey of Thomas Berry: Imagining the Earth Community* (2014).

Roger S. Gottlieb is William B. Smith Dean's Professor of Philosophy at Worcester Polytechnic Institute and the author or editor of twenty-one books of philosophy, religious studies, environmental ethics, spirituality and fiction. Three of his recent woks—the short story collection *Engaging Voices*, the novel *The Sacrifice Zone* and *Spirituality: What it Is and Why it Matters*—won Nautilus Book Awards. *Morality and the Environmental Crisis* was called by *Indepenent Publisher* magazine a "book most likely to save the planet."

Tyson-Lord Gray is a legal, religious, and environmental scholar. He holds a MA and PhD from Vanderbilt University, a MDIV from Morehouse School of Religion, a STM from Boston University School of Theology, and a JD from Elisabeth Haub School of Law. Currently, he teaches at Boston University School of Law and has held previous appointments at the University of Arkansas School of Law, NYU Stern School of Business, Pace University, and Baylor University. His research addresses social justice concerns within the areas of environmental law, food law, and cannabis law.

Rebecca Kneale Gould is Associate Professor of Environmental Studies at Middlebury College where she co-directs the Religion, Philosophy and Environment Focus. A scholar of comparative religion and American religious history by training, she works in both historical and contemporary contexts, focusing on "nature religion" in its various modalities, as well as on Jewish and Christian forms of religious environmentalism. She is the author of *At Home in Nature: Modern Homesteading and Spiritual Practice in America* (2005) as well as numerous articles and book chapters pertaining to her research including, most recently, "The Whiteness of Walden: Reading Thoreau with Attention to Black Lives" in *Thoreau in an Age of Crisis: Uses and Abuses of an American Icon* (2021), "Mind the Gap: What Ethnographic Silences Can Teach Us" in *Interpreting Religion* (2022) and, with Laurel Kearns, "Ecology and Religious Environmentalism in the United States in the *Oxford Research Encyclopedia of Religion* (2018). She is the co-creator, with Phil Walker, of the documentary short *The Fire Inside: Place, Passion and the Primacy of Nature* (2012). She lives in Vermont with her spouse and a small flock of rescue sheep.

Laura H. Hobgood is Professor and holder of the Paden Chair in Environmental Studies and Religion at Southwestern University. She has published several books, including *A Dog's History of the World* and *Holy Dogs and Asses*, along with numerous articles and book chapters focused on animals and religion. In addition to teaching, researching, and writing, Laura volunteers with her partner as a dog foster for municipal shelters and orphan squirrel rehabilitator for wildlife rescue, as well as riding a bicycle as much as possible.

Willis Jenkins lives in the Rivanna River watershed (Monacan land), where he works as Hollingsworth Professor of Ethics and chairs the Department of Religious Studies at the University of Virginia. He is author of two award-winning books: *Ecologies of Grace,* which won a Templeton Award for Theological Promise, and *The Future of Ethics,* which won an American Academy of Religion Award for Excellence. He is co-editor of several books, including the *Routledge Handbook of Religion and Ecology*, and a number of essays along intersections of religion, ethics, and environmental humanities. Jenkins co-directs the Coastal Futures Conservatory which integrates arts and humanities into coastal change research at the National Science Foundation's Virginia Coast Reserve Long-Term Ecological Research site.

Laurel D. Kearns is Professor of Ecology, Society and Religion at Drew Theological School/University in New Jersey (Lenni Lenape land). Her research is focused on religious involvement in ecological issues and movements, with a particular interest in environmental justice, climate change, and food. In addition to co-editing with Catherine Keller and contributing to *Ecospirit: Religions and Philosophies for the Earth* (2005), she has contributed chapters to volumes such as *The Oxford Handbook on Climate Change and Society; Bloomsbury Handbook on Religion and Nature: The Elements; Grounding Religion: A Field Guide to the Study of Religion and Ecology; Religions and Environments: A Reader in Religion, Nature and Ecology, The New Evangelical Social Engagement;* and *Living Cosmology: Christian Responses to Journey of the Universe.* She is a co-founder of the Green Seminary Initiative, and serves on the board of the Parliament of World Religions. Her decades-long involvement in religious environmentalism has roots in the island where she grew up, Sanibel, Florida, which recently, like many islands, was significantly impacted by climate change.

Timothy B. Leduc is Associate Professor in the Faculty of Social Work at Wilford Lawrence and author/editor of four books, including *Climate, Culture, Change* (2010), *A Canadian Climate of Mind* (2016), and *Q da gaho dęs: Reflecting on our Journeys* (2022). His Two Row work is rooted in his French canadien ancestral relations with Indigenous nations along the St. Lawrence River.

Victoria Machado is a Visiting Assistant Professor in the Environmental Studies Department at Rollins College in Winter Park, FL. She completed her PhD in 2021 at the University of Florida, where she specialized in Religion & Nature and Religion in the Americas. Her research explores the spirituality behind Florida's environmentalists. Dr. Machado is also a contributor to *Watershed Discipleship: Reinhabiting Bioregional Faith and Practice* (2016).

Cynthia D. Moe-Lobeda is Professor of Theological and Social Ethics at Pacific Lutheran Theological Seminary (PLTS), Church Divinity School of the Pacific, and the Graduate Theological Union's Core Doctoral Faculty. She is author or co-author of seven volumes, including the award-winning *Resisting Structural Evil: Love as Ecological-Economic Vocation*, and over 50 articles and chapters. Moe-Lobeda has lectured or consulted on six continents regarding faith-based resistance to systemic injustice, moral agency and hope, ethical implications of resurrection and incarnation, climate justice and climate racism, and economic justice. She is Founding Director of the PLTS Center for Climate Justice and Faith.

Elaine Nogueira-Godsey is Assistant Professor in Religion and Society at Drew University Theological School. She is a Latinx ecofeminist scholar originally from Brazil and lived in South Africa for nineteen years, during which time she completed her Ph.D. in Religious Studies from the University of Cape Town. Her expertise is in intersecting decolonial and ecofeminist methods of research and teaching that include religion, gender/sexuality, economics and race, with a focus on advancing knowledge and experience from the Global South. Among her recent publications is "A Decological Way to Dialogue: Rethinking Ecofeminism and Religion." She is currently working on her book, *Rethinking Ecofeminism and Religion: A Decological Perspective*. She co-chairs the AAR/SBL Women's Caucus.

Kevin J. O'Brien teaches courses in religion and environmental studies at Pacific Lutheran University in Tacoma, Washington. His research focuses on the intersections of ethics, climate, environment, religion, and social justice. He has published *An Introduction to Christian Environmentalism* with Kathryn Blanchard (2014), *The Violence of Climate Change* (2017) and *Environmental Ethics and Uncertainty* with Whitney Bauman (2020). He is currently working on a book about the ethics of having fossil fuel companies as enemies.

Courtney O'Dell-Chaib teaches middle and upper school Religion & Ethics at Parish Episcopal School, Dallas, TX. She has a doctorate in Religion from Syracuse University and an MA in Multicultural Women's & Gender Studies from Texas Woman's University. She is the author of "The Shape of This Wonder: Consecrated Science and New Cosmology Affects" (*Zygon: Journal of Religion and Science*, 2019) and "Biophilia's Queer Remnants" (*Bulletin for the Study of Religion*, 2017). Currently, she is developing programming for secondary students that addresses environmental trauma and anxiety.

Sarah M. Pike is Professor of Comparative Religion at California State University, Chico. She is the author of *Earthly Bodies, Magical Selves: Contemporary Pagans and The Search for Community* (2001), *New Age and Neopagan Religions in America* (2004), and *For the Wild: Ritual and Commitment in Radical Eco-Activism* (2017) and co-editor of *Reassembling Democracy: Ritual as Cultural Resource* (Bloomsbury,

2020) and *Ritual and Democracy: Protests, Publics and Performances* (2020). She has written numerous articles and book chapters on contemporary Paganism, ritual, the New Age movement, the ancestral skills movement, Burning Man, spiritual dance, California wildfires, environmental activism, climate strikes, and youth culture. Her current research focuses on ritual, spirituality, and ecology in several different contexts, including a project on ritualized relationships with landscapes after wildfires.

Terra Schwerin Rowe is associate professor in the Philosophy and Religion Department at the University of North Texas, a leading program in environmental philosophy. She received a PhD in Theological and Philosophical Studies from Drew University. She is co-director of the AAR seminar on Energy, Extraction, and Religion and on the steering committee of the academy's Religion and Ecology unit. Her most recent book is *Of Modern Extraction: Experiments in Critical Petro-theology* (T&T Clark, 2023).

Morgan Shipley (Ph.D.) is the Inaugural Foglio Endowed Chair of Spirituality and Associate Professor of Religious Studies at Michigan State University. Author of *Psychedelic Mysticism: Transforming Consciousness, Religious Experiences, and Voluntary Peasants in Postwar America* (2015) and co-editor of *The Silence of Fallout: Nuclear Criticism in a Post-Cold War World* (2013), Dr. Shipley's research explores secular spirituality, new religious movements, and individuals who increasingly identify as spiritual but not religious.

Acknowledgments

Putting together an edited volume is a process that takes on a life of its own. This project started out as part of the online resource "Bloomsbury Religion in North America," and it wasn't at all clear there would be a printed volume. We thank our editor at Bloomsbury, Lalle Pursglove, for working with us and making the case for a print version. In addition, when we started this project we had no idea that there was a pandemic looming just around the corner. Getting the online and print version out even as we struggled through a global pandemic was nothing short of a miracle: working together was a bright spot. We want to thank all the authors and editors and others involved in this publication for their hard work on this volume. Representing two generations of scholars in the field, we have worked with each other and many of the authors before, and welcome the next generation whose work we are just getting to know: together they all have enriched the field of Religion and Ecology/Religion and Nature with their contributions to this volume. Their combined voices, perspectives, disciplines, religious traditions, and range of social and geographical locations contributed to making Religion and Nature in North America reflect the rich diversity of peoples and traditions in North America. The editors particularly want to thank Beth Quick, a PhD student in Religion, Animals and Ecology at Drew Theological School for her patience as she tracked down images and copyrights, read every chapter for typos and style consistency, suggested bibliography and assisted authors in general. It was a joy to work with her, and the volume benefitted from her careful eye and research skills. Finally, we thank all of the life forms, be they partners, family, colleagues, friends, animal and plant companions—all our relations—in the beloved landscapes and complex eco-systems, the air, waters, and lands, that nurture us and make it possible to walk and think on this earth in these troubled times.

PART ONE

North American Religious Traditions

1

Religion and Nature in North America: An Introduction

Whitney A. Bauman and Laurel D. Kearns

What comes to mind when you think of the word "nature?" If you are like many, probably blue skies, mountains, rivers, whales, the ocean, trees, or a national park; for some, images of destructive storms and floods, or of bugs and scary animals. When we ask this question in courses or in groups, very seldom is the answer: me, other humans, the building I am in, New York City, my cell phone, or my computer, yet these are all nature. The field of religion and ecology or religion and nature developed to ask two primary questions: (1) How is it that some humans have written and thought themselves outside of the rest of the natural world, and what role have religious worldviews and institutions played? And, for those who have seen themselves outside, (2) how can we write and think ourselves back into the rest of the natural world? What religious/spiritual/cultural ideas and practices, groups might help? One might argue, then, there is always a descriptive and a normative element to thinking about religion and nature.

Similarly, when many people think of religion, they often think of institutions, religious texts and rituals, buildings, beliefs, codes of action (ethics/morality), and perhaps the supernatural and the unexplained. The study of religion can include all of these things, but it is also more broadly the study of how we co-create meaning in our lives and decide, hopefully, together what types of world we want to live in. As the historian of science Lynn White, Jr. (1967) observed, religious traditions have often given humans a special place in the cosmos. Western monotheisms, he argued, and in particular Christianity, suggest that humans are made in God's image or at least that they are granted some special place over the rest of the natural world (what this special place means is the subject of much debate), yet how followers of those Western traditions have acted in relation to nature has varied greatly. For White, these religious roots of "human exceptionalism" have contributed to a lot of the actions and attitudes that have led to environmental degradation on the planet today. The field of religion and ecology/nature wants to examine how meaning-making practices in the name of various religions shape human-earth, human-human, human-sacred, and human-nonhuman animal relationships and has shaped the scholarly, sometimes activist, work of all of those contributing chapters to this volume.

There are many great introductions to the study of religion and nature/ecology (see "Further Reading and Online Resources" below). We do not want to repeat what our colleagues have done in these excellent resources, so here we want to offer not so much of an introduction to the field of religion and ecology or religion and nature, nor necessarily the institutions that have built this field (including the Religion and Ecology Group of the American Academy of Religion, the Forum on Religion and Ecology at Yale [https://fore.yale.edu/], and the related Religions of the World and Ecology series, the International Society for the Study of Religion, Nature and Culture [https://www.issrnc.org/] and its related *Encyclopedia of Religion and Nature* [Taylor 2005], or the multiple religious groups and subfields who have formed organizations that promote the concern for other animals and the rest of the natural world). Again, we think this history has been done well and we do not need to repeat it here. Instead we offer a brief overview of how religions have shaped, and been shaped by, the landscapes, peoples, other animals, and the rest of the natural world in what we know of now as "North America" and what some Indigenous peoples refer to as "*Turtle Island.*"

We begin with the various European colonizers, predominantly the Spanish, the French, the Dutch, and the British, crash-landing into what they called the "New World," and its effect on Indigenous populations. They carried the idea that the land was "*terra nullius*" or empty, according to a papal bull (Bauman 2009), so that they felt justified in occupying and, eventually, taking over the North American continent, and in the process diminishing the rich cultures and flora and fauna already thriving there. Furthermore, the narrative of manifest destiny, a type of Christian salvation narrative that was imposed upon the geography of what became the United States (in particular), helped cement the European mindset that the "new worlds," which would become the Americas, and especially, with the hindsight of history, what would become known as the United States of America, was to be the torch of progress for the so-called Western and mostly Christian project of progress (Merchant 2013). Finally, this narrative of progress was, of course, not a common, shared narrative. It was not just Indigenous peoples that faired poorly but also Black enslaved people brought to North America, and their religious traditions, which included Islam, and over the course of time, a variety of immigrants viewed as cheap labor, such as the Chinese and Irish, for example, or, somewhat ironically, the descendents of Spanish colonizers in British colonial occupied lands.

After this brief history of the clash of religions, colonization, and the rest of the natural world in the centuries leading up to the industrial-fueled rapid transformation/ deformation of ecosystems and cultures, we take a look at the initial dominant "environmental" narratives of North America: conservation and preservation (these

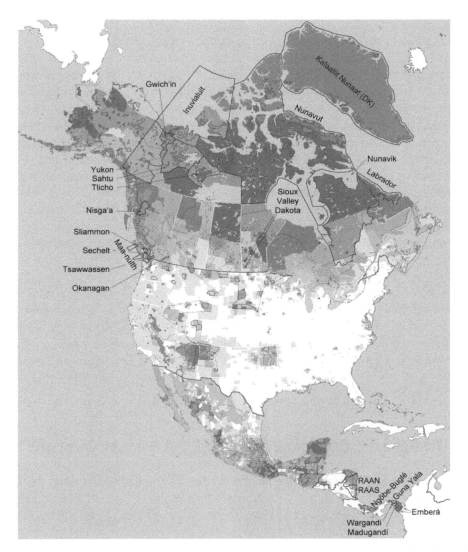

FIGURE 1.1 *Map of the population density and territories of indigenous peoples of North America at the beginning of the twenty-first century.* Source: *Fährtenleser/CC BY-SA 4.0.*

later are joined by restoration efforts). These early sources for "environmentalism" in many ways perpetuate the colonial approach to the rest of the natural world that sees "nature" as the opposite to "culture," and in need of cultivation/civilizing and saving (D. Taylor 2016; Kearns 2004). Notions of "untamed nature" became a source for the denigration of women, *queer* peoples, Indigenous peoples, enslaved and indentured servants, and changing categories of poor immigrants (as those in these categories are deemed more like animals) and, frequently, a place inhabited by evil spirits or the devil.

Yet there were also strands of religious and spiritual interpretations that read nature as the "book of nature," the first revelation of God, and a source of inspiration, or as a source for purity and reunification with one's "inner nature" away from the corrosive nature of capitalism and urban cities (which were increasingly becoming more immigrant, brown and Black, and even queer). Nature became marked as both a place of dangerous exile and of refuge (Berry 2015). Finally, the conservation and preservation movements, and in particular the development of the national park system, (such as Yosemite National Park, pictured on the cover), which furthered the practice of the removal of Indigenous peoples from their ancestral lands (Spence 2000) and their placement upon reservations (often located on land that bore no resemblance to their home lands, and that was not considered valuable or productive land). Religion was used as both a justification for these practices and as a source of resistance to these colonial and racist practices.

Finally, we want to offer a picture of a different type of religiously motivated environmentalism that focuses more on justice for people and for the rest of the natural world, and one that understands humans, and all things human, are a part of the rest of the natural world. After all, technology, the city, our agricultural and other production practices are "natural" too, albeit forms of human-mediated nature. How have ideas about "religion" and "nature" shifted because of liberation movements and thoughts, such as civil rights, feminist, queer, postcolonial, and decolonial movements, and other critical types of thinking? If we are going to think critically about "religion and nature in North America," then we need the help of these critical perspectives. We will then end this introduction with a brief discussion of what is to come in the rest of this volume.

Religions, Colonization, and "Manifest Destiny"

Who will find peace with the lands? The future of humankind lies waiting for those who will come to understand their lives and take up their responsibilities to all living things. Who will listen to the trees, the animals and birds, the voices of the places of the land? As the long forgotten peoples of the respective continents rise and begin to reclaim their ancient heritage, they will discover the meaning of the lands of their ancestors. That is when the invaders of the North American continent will finally discover that for this land, God is red.

(Vine Deloria Jr. 1973)

The story of religion and nature in North America begins with understanding that both "religion" and "nature" are handed down to us as cultural constructs that are implicated in colonial practices. The study of religion, itself, is the result mostly of European Christians coming into contact with other cultures and carving out a thing in each that they called "religion," usually made in the image of what Christianity meant in relationship to the larger "western cultures" (Masuzawa 2005). In fact, most

FIGURE 1.2 *Standing Rock Protest: "Indigenous people are still fighting to have treaty rights honored. People protesting the Dakota Access Pipeline stand with signs and banners across from San Francisco City Hall."* Source: *Pax Ahimsa Gethen/CC BY-SA 4.0.*

cultures did not separate out "religion" in the same way as Europeans began to look at Christianity during the Enlightenment. After the Protestant Reformation in Europe and the Thirty Years' War, the fact that there were multiple religious authorities within Christianity (never mind in Islam and Judaism), meant that a nonreligious or "secular" authority had to emerge as an arbiter of different truth claims and claims to power. Thus, notions of the "secular," namely, not spiritual or religious, an example of A/not A categorization (the second term is defined by the absence of the characteristics of the first), is deeply tied to these definitions of "religion." This understanding of "the secular," to be sure, is not shared globally. In fact, in places such as India, Indonesia, and for most Indigenous cultures, the idea of separating out religion from the rest of life does not make sense. Furthermore, many scholars and pundits would question how separate "religion," namely, Christianity, is from much of politics in the three countries that now lay claim to the continent of North America.

Along similar A/not A thinking, "nature" became associated with all the things nonhuman or "not culture": itself another colonial term, since many other cultures understand humans as a part of nature. "Natural scientists" became the authority on the "nature" of the natural world, while the authorities/scholars on values, meaning, and culture became what modern Westerners know as the humanities: philosophy, literature, arts, and religious studies. Further, through the long process of what we know as the "scientific revolution," nature became that which could be used as "resources" for human (read European) progress (Merchant 1990). Thus, nature became associated with "wild" or "untamed" places that could be cultivated and made civilized by certain types of humans. Nature also became paradoxically associated with both what was fallen/evil, and that which was edenic and pure (as mentioned above). For instance, in this hierarchical, racist, and patriarchal (or male-centered) structure, people of color, and women and children in general, were understood to be more "like nature" in a negative way, meaning that they were less cultured and rational than white European males. At the same time what was "natural," *heteronormativity* and patriarchy, was good and what was deemed "unnatural" was bad, because it opposed those normative structures. The story of European colonizers (white males) taking over wild, untamed lands, was one of "development," which meant bringing civilization and cultivation to the "dark and unlearned masses." At the same time, white males who were "corrupted" by the evils of urban life, needed to spend time in "nature" to find their true selves again. This double-speak or two-faced response to nature—as dark, wild, and evil on the one hand, and a source of value, revelation, and truth on the other—was crucial for colonial success (Gaard 1997). For early European colonizers, the idea that something was more "like nature," meant that it was in an untouched or ideal state. Nature sometimes was seen as a source of revelation (Stoll 2015), but more often that it needed to be cultured/cultivated and this in turn meant that lands and peoples could, and should, be colonized: the land could be cultivated and resources could be used for human ends, while the people could be civilized and educated into the truth of Western ideas, and become human resources for those more powerful. At the same time uncivilized and wild nature could be scary: storms and disease killed many before the rise of modern medicine and there were a lot of things "in the wild" that were threats to the lives of these settlers. So, when certain peoples were thought to be closer to that wild, scary, natural world, they could just as easily be thought of as "noble" or "evil" savages: who should then either be educated or tamed and/or destroyed, respectively (Bauman 2009).

Prior to the European colonization of the Americas there were, of course, other non-native settlers before the pilgrims, but these white, overwhelmingly Christian European settlers forever changed the landscape of native peoples and North America. For example, it is part of US mythology that the United States was founded on religious toleration: tell that to Native Americans and enslaved Africans, or even Quakers, Catholics, Jews, and Muslims, who were not tolerated either. Even today Native Americans are trying to help the descendents of those settlers understand how what we know of as "North America" was built upon their ancestors genocide, whether it be in Mexico, the United States, or Canada (Dunbar-Ortiz 2014). In addition, many African Americans, and the Black Lives Matter movement especially, are helping white and other Americans understand the historic and systemic racism that North America was built upon (Carter 2018). The legacies of genocide, slavery, and systemic racism still function in the nations of North America today and still produce racial and ethnic inequalities.

The early religious dissenters from England and Europe brought with them a range of understandings of both religion and nature. As Carolyn Merchant explains, they even tried to recreate their home landscapes in North America, by bringing species of plants and animals from Europe, and England in particular, to recreate those same environments in North America, often failing spectacularly (Merchant 2007). For these settlers, the land was mostly empty, and the Indigenous peoples were either knowing guides or savages in the otherwise "empty" lands. As mentioned earlier, the idea of empty lands or *terra nullius* was a colonial and religious concept that enabled the takeover of so-called empty lands, despite the fact that there were long histories, cultures, and even urban areas in the Americas. Due to the displacement and genocide of native peoples throughout the Americas through the intentional introduction of diseases and through wars, the lands were made into the "empty" land the colonializers desired (LaDuke 1999). By most estimates 90 percent of the Native American populations were killed off by European colonizers, be they Spanish, French, Dutch, or British.

Many of the rest were driven to or placed on less desirable lands, which we will discuss in the next section (Gilio-Whitaker 2020). There was little recognition of the religious liberty of these Indigenous Americans, and disdain that these native peoples were unwilling to adopt the model of agriculture and land management by the European settlers (Weaver 1996). This was in no small part because it was a clash with European religious beliefs, and their failure to see how intergral the landscapes and all therein were to their own cultural lifeways (see Briggs-Cloud chapter in this volume).

FIGURE 1.3 The Landing of Columbus *by John Vanderlyn (installed in the Capitol Rotunda in Washington, DC in 1847). Public Domain.*

Manifest Destiny and Slavery

The clash between colonial ideas about religion and about nature also extended to those people from various African countries who were enslaved and brought to North America by the European colonizers. Some readers might be confused by how so-called Christians or so-called reasonable people could condone the genocide of Native Americans and the enslaving of Africans, but those Christians came with a hertiage of religious wars, supressions of pagan religions, anti-Semitism, crusades against Muslims, and colonial expansions around the globe that labeled those who were non-Christian, or not the right kind of Christian, as less valuable. This, again, is at least in part to do with the systemic engrained racist colonial mentality grounded in a religious worldview. This mentality, which has been named patriarchy, hetero-patriarchy, white supremacy, logocentrism, and simply colonialism and racism, works on what environmental feminist philosopher Val Plumwood calls the "logic of colonization" in *Feminism and the Mastery of Nature* (1993). First you have a value hierarchy, or "great chain of being" that stretches from a Male God, often associated with Reason and Light, to wealthy light colored men, to their wealthy counterparts, to women, other people of color, and slaves, to animals, and to the earth and minerals (See Eaton chapter in this volume). Then you have a set of characteristics that are associated with good and bad, such as male and female, white and black, spirit and body, light and dark, culture and nature, reason and emotion, etc. These are "exclusionary dualisms" that force bodies into being categorized as one or the other (Plumwood 1993). This is what might be called a sociocultural ideology that is mapped onto the bodies of the planet.

In such a racist and sexist hierarchy: men are understood as more reasonable and valuable than women, lighter skinned peoples are seen as more valuable than darker skinned peoples, and upper-class people are more valued than the poor, and always lingering behind these two assumptions is the great divide between humans and animals or humans and the rest of the natural world (Ruether 1994). Humans are "above" nature, and those that fail to act in such a way as this "above" is understood are considered to be "below" or more "like the animals" (Johnson 2015). This is why women, slaves, and native peoples get associated with animals and as sources of evil simply because they don't act and appear as dominant males. See Hobgood chapter in this volume.) Some argue that the boundaries created between humans and animals are the linchpin for sexisms, racisms, and ethnocentrisms (Ko 2019). In other words, if humans are set apart from the rest of the natural world, then who and what gets counted as the ideal human matters a great deal. If the moral and ethical boundaries of concern end at humanity, then what happens to those who the dominant eurocentric group do not consider fully human in the colonial framework (see Moe-Lobeda chapter in this volume)?

If we add to this racist, colonial, sexist, and all-around violent mentality (which was grounded in the "religion" and the "science" of the modern Western world) a narrative component of progress, and then map that on to the westward push across North America on the part of European colonizers, (or what is referred to as manifest destiny, that the land was part of the promised land for Christians), then we get a pretty good picture of the way colonial understandings of "religion" and "nature" shaped individual bodies and collective geographies of the United States. Certain bodies were enslaved, others were placed on reservations and into "re-education" programs, certain freed slaves became indentured servants, and many immigrants were recruited to provide additional labor for this westward expansion, such as Chinese men, while white and male bodies were given free land west of the Mississippi, as torch bearers of the "angel of progress" (see Merchant 2007).

It is important to note that within the category of "white" there have also been hierarchies, so that, at times during this history, for example, the Irish, Italian, eastern European, and Spanish descendents, were seen as not white, often because of their religion, as Catholics were devalued in much of the United States, but not in Mexico (nor in parts of the lands taken from it, such as Texas, New Mexico and California), and Quebec, Canada. Further complexifying this portrait is recognizing the diverse strands of Christianity and Asian influences (see Allison, and Gould and Kearns, chapters in this volume) that often played "counter notes" to the song of Western progress, even while participating in them (see Rowe chapter in this volume). There have, of course, been dissident non-racist, non-sexist, non-colonizing traditions of

FIGURE 1.4 *John Gast,* American Progress, *1872. Photograph by George A. Crofutt. Public Domain.*

"religion" and understandings of what "nature" is throughout this whole history as well, which we discuss briefly below, but for now, it is important to lay out how this colonial understanding of "religion" and "nature" became foundational to the early environmental movements of North America known as the conservation and preservation movements.

Conservation and Preservation: A Colonial History of Environmentalism in North America

If you have ever wondered why environmentalism in North America has until recently been considered a "white" concern, or why it has not been connected with issues of social justice, or why some Christians seem to have a fear that environmentalism leads to worship of nature or some sort of dark paganism, there are some historical reasons for this, as well as issues of what is defined as environmentalism (B. Taylor 2009). In part, the early conservation and preservation movements in North America (though not only in North America) were based upon those colonial concepts of "religion" and "nature" that we discussed above. Adding in the British/US acquisition of lands colonized by the French and Spanish, provides even more complexity to this picture of North America, particularly noting that Mexico, which included a lot of the western / southwestern United States at that time, remained heavily dominated by Spanish colonial influences, and Canada remained connected to Britain, while the province of Quebec continued the close association with France (Leduc 2016).

Religion, and from the perspective of North American colonizers this meant mostly some form of Christianity, was associated with human history, and nature was mostly relegated to the backdrop on which that human history played out. Nature was often viewed (as mentioned above) as a blank slate or empty lands (*terra nullius*), or as inert or dead matter (Merchant 1990) that awaited, in Lockean terms, human culture and labor to cultivate, utilize, or civilize it. Although there were always subcurrents who viewed it as valuable in itself, nature from this Lockean sense was raw material or resource for the projects of human beings (read, the project of progress for modern Western human beings). This may help explain what we referred to earlier as the paradoxical colonial mentality toward nature as in need of cultivating/dominating *and* in need of remaining wild. If so-called wild nature is the fodder for the progress of manifest destiny, and masculinity is defined by the frontier mentality of "man against nature," then what happens when all wild places begin to disappear? For this reason, the reasoning goes, there needs to be protected wild places, without human presence, so that (initially European) men can go into nature to reconnect with their masculinity. This, by the way, was the reason that the Boy Scouts of America were formed: to prevent wealthy European males in urban areas from becoming too "soft" (Mortimer-Sandilands and Erickson 2010).

For indigenous North Americans, this understanding meant that they were removed from their landscapes and placed on reservations in part to then form national parks, reflecting the racism tinged preservation views of John Muir and others (Spence 2000). From the dominant colonial settler perspective, there is no conservation or preservation of natural places with people living in and on these natural places, although many eastern US conservation efforts did include people continuing to live in those areas. The wild places (which were not so wild after all) had to be protected from human use, so that some humans could come and enjoy them for spiritual gain, mental rejuvenation, sport, hunting, and other recreational uses. Of course, removing native peoples from their ancestral lands is tantamount to cultural genocide (Dunbar-Ortiz 2014). For most Indigenous communities, culture is landscape, the religious "text" is the region they find themselves in. Linguistic and cultural references are tied to local places. From a monotheistic mentality, religion, and culture, of which religion is a part, can be practiced anywhere so it was just assumed this was true about "other" peoples and their cultures (if the colonizers even recognized native cultures, which often they did not).

The idea of categories of nature in need of taming or civilizing also helped to justify the enslavement of Black people in the United States. They were seen as more "like animals," in need of cultivating and civilizing. In addition, Black men in particular were to be feared due to their wild lust for white women, and Black women were to be feared due to their sexual entrapment of white men—these tropes remain active today. There were also the "civilized" understandings of Black men in the form of Uncle Tom, and the "civilized" Black woman in the form of "Mammy," whose "purpose" was to take care of white folk. In all these cases the ideological structure that placed white people as "closer to god" and Black and brown and Indigenous peoples as "closer to nature," remained in place. Yet, Black peoples had thriving nature spiritualities that included rural and urban appreciation for how humans were a part of nature and depended upon the rest of the natural world (White 2016). In fact, the woods and wilderness became a refuge for many Black and Indigenous peoples escaping slavery, led by "naturalists" such as Harriet Tubman, just as some wild areas were refuges for forcibly removed native peoples because white Europeans thought those places were uninhabitable or inhospitable (Glave 2010). It has become clear that we can speak of an "African American" naturalism (see Gray chapter in this volume), that is, perhaps, a mixture of nature-based spirituality coming from ancestral African traditions, the reality of farm and rural life of most early Black peoples brought to North America, and eventually the justice/civil rights traditions of the African American Christian community in North America (Harris 2017). For these reasons an African American environmentalism in North America is one that most often connects critical issues of embodiment and justice with those of environmentalism (Cone 2000). In fact there is a growing "intersectional" understanding of environmentalism today (Gaard 2017; Intersectional Environmentalist 2021). For indigenous, and North Americans of color, the concepts of both "religion" and "nature" as constructed by the European colonizers were used to maintain white supremacy and keep nonwhite "others" in place. Such abuses of religion and nature were targeted in many new religious movements, and the civil rights, feminist, and indigenous peoples movements.

Modern Environmental Movements

We could explore many events that kicked off the modern environmental and environmental justice movements, and the study of "religion and nature" in North America. These are not mutually exclusive events and processes, however, there were tensions between white European environmentalism, long-existing Indigenous lifeways and activism, and the environmental justice/toxics movements (Zimring 2015), and religious actors have played roles in naming and negotiating those tensions. There were, of course, differences and tensions between the activism of these movements and the study of "religion and ecology" or "religion and nature." In this chapter we want to outline some of those differences, and why tensions may have existed between them, and in the next section we will end this introduction with a brief nod to the type of intersectional, planetary environmentalism that is emerging today (See Nogueira-Godsey, Kearns, and Bauman chapter in this volume).

Environmental Movements in North America

We could begin our discussion of the "modern" environmental movement with the concern over nuclear holocaust after the Second World War, or even with the Earth Rise image taken by Apollo 8, which was the first photo ever of the earth from outside the earth. These events did indeed spill into the heightening of concern over how humans and human technologies (particularly Western industrial ones) affect the rest of the natural world. The radiation experienced by humans and other life-forms after atomic bombs were dropped during the Second World War combined with the recognition of the virtually eternal need to deal with the radioactive nuclear waste, led to slogans such as "No nukes is good nukes." The image of the earth from outer space became (though not unproblematically) (Garb 1985) an image for the fragility and unity of life on the planet that did have a profound impact, for instance, on the work of Thomas Berry (Berry and Tucker 2009). For the first time, humans could see through popular media that all of life, across the globe was contained within what appears to be a fragile blue planet, floating in space. That image became almost synonymous with the early, modern environmental movements.

We would like to suggest that there is one person, however, one woman in particular that should be credited with really providing the fuel for the modern environmental movement, even leading to the creation of the EPA and the first Earth Day under President Nixon: Rachel Carson (See also Allison chapter in this volume).

Carson was a soft-spoken, rational scientist, but the wonder of the rest of the natural world, in particular the sea, did not escape her. She was influenced by philosopher Albert Schweitzer's "Reverence for Life" ethic, which was in many ways a precursor to E.O. Wilson's understanding of biophilia (Kellert and Wilson 1995). Both the reverence for life and biophilia were meant to signal the orientation of human beings to have connections with and value the rest of the natural world. Such connections,

FIGURE 1.5 *This photo of "Earthrise" over the lunar horizon was taken by the Apollo 8 crew as they orbited the moon on December 24, 1968, showing Earth for the first time as it appears from deep space.* Source: *William Anders/NASA. Public Domain.*

however, are "taught" out of us over time as we become adults in the industrialized, modern Western world. The question then becomes, how might we be able to gain that reverence, love, and wonder for the rest of the natural world again (Sideris 2017; Swimme and Berry 1994; Wilson 2006). Carson believed that engagement with the natural world produced such wonder, yet not to the extent that it excluded good science. In fact, for Carson, wonder demands good science to care for that which is wonderful: nature. Her 1962 book, *Silent Spring*, took on big agri-business and argued (among other things) that human pesticides and industry, in general, were destroying the rest of the natural world—this critique still stands. In one example, that of the pesticide DDT, she convincingly argued that the buildup of this toxin led to the thinning of bird shells, and drastically reduced numbers of chicks. She then imagines that if this continues there will come a spring where no new life will be born, and thus it will be silent.

Carson was ridiculed by the mostly male scientific community for this, much of which was funded by big agricultural businesses (which basically turned the chemical warfare industry into agricultural chemicals after the Second World War).

FIGURE 1.6 *Rachel Carson.* Source: *United States Fish and Wildlife Service. Public Domain.*

In the end, Carson died of breast cancer, one of the causes of which is, sadly, toxins in the environment. The point is that, for Carson, environmentalism is not only about wild places devoid of humans but also how we live our lives and the ways in which industrial living in cities and changing farming practices in rural communities have ripple effects throughout the ecosystems. At around the same time that the environmental movement was beginning to swell around Carson's groundbreaking work, among other things, there was another important movement happening: the civil rights movement.

Civil Rights and Environmental Justice in North America

Though they are connected, early on, the modern environmental movement and the movement known as "environmental justice" were separate and not necessarily mutually supportive. This had to do largely with issues related to racism and the racist and colonial undertones of the earlier conservation and preservation movements, some of which continue (D. Taylor 2016). Though there were exceptions to the rule, in general, the ideas that connect race and nature, and the Euro-Western ideal of the

FIGURE 1.7 *DDT spraying in 1995 as part of the Western spruce budworm control project. The use of DDT was largely banned in the United States due to Carson's work in* Silent Spring. *Source: USA Forest Service. Public Domain.*

human as a white male, discussed above, conceptually led to the ideas that white men should control/educate/enlighten/rule over people of color and the rest of nature. This was aided by the increasing technocratic nature of the biggest environmental organizations and their reliance on people with certain degrees in fields dominated by white men (this is changing slowly). The creation of the national park system, suffused with religious/spiritual, and racist, motivations, and the ideas that urban peoples who were wealthy enough should spend time in this "wild nature" to reconnect with their true selves, excluded Black people, other people of color, and often the poor from this type of nature recreation that led to concern for the environment (Finney 2014). Finney and others (Clay 2011) stress it is important not to think that black and brown environmental concerns are only environmental justice concerns about people and urban areas.

In addition to these overtly and systemic racisms, the Indigenous rights, civil rights, women's rights, and labor movements in the United States were focused on justice for people (not necessarily to the exclusion of the rest of the natural world). Martin Luther King Jr. did, after all, talk about the problems of industrialism and globalization, and the exposure of garbage men to hazardous materials. And, Rachel Carson was aware that waste sites and places where chemicals were "dumped" were in poor communities and communities of color. She also recognized the problems of industrial chemicals in agriculture and that there was little to no protection for agricultural workers. In their embrace of environmental issues as justice issues, the Indigenous rights movement (in particular here those aspects that were against nuclear waste siting), the labor movement (in particular around issues of agricultural labor), the civil rights movement, and the anti-toxics movements (often led by women), all fed into a form of environmentalism that began to take serious account of issues of human justice as well (Cone 2000), as did the growing religious environmental movement, for instance, embodied in the National Council of Churches Eco-Justice Working Group (Kearns 2004).

These crucial issues became seen as environmental in what we now call the Environmental Justice (EJ) movement. Though we could talk about "environmental justice" as part of human colonial history and the ways in which empires treated conquered peoples and their lands, we will focus here on the Environmental Justice movement's beginnings in the United States. There were many events that fed this movement. The human rights based movements mentioned above were all tributaries to the EJ movement in North America. Starting in the early 1980s, several legal arguments helped to solidify the movement. In a watershed moment in Houston, Texas, Linda McKeever Bullard won a case, *Bean v. Southwestern Waste Management*, against the citing of waste facilities based upon race. The case hinged on the 1964 Civil Rights Act. Title VI of the Act prohibited the use of federal funds to discriminate based on race, color, and national origin. She successfully argued that the citing of waste facilities was disproportionately in communities of color, and that because the waste management company received federal funding, this was a violation of Title VI (Bullard 1993). Many similar cases followed and Robert Bullard would become a key sociologist documenting these patterns (Bullard 2000).

In 1982, during a protest against a PCB landfill in Warren County, North Carolina, a predominantly Black community, the United Church of Christ (UCC) Reverend Benjamin Chavis described the placement of the landfill with the phrase "environmental racism." Following intense activism that included many UCC ministers, in 1987 the UCC published the landmark report *Toxic Wastes and Race in the United States* (for more on this history, see Kearns 2014). Their research showed a statistically significant correlation, if class was held as a constant, between the siting of toxic waste facilities and the racial makeup of those host communities of color than in white communities. The First National People of Color Environmental Leadership Summit in 1991 brought together Indigenous and people of color environmental organizers who outlined the seventeen Principles of Environmental Justice (National People of Color Environmental Leadership Summit 1991), with many participating out of their own spiritual and religious motivations. Yet the literature often did not mention the role of religion in the motivation of many activists, for instance, in fighting "Cancer Alley," the Mississippi River region primarily from Baton Rouge to New Orleans, Louisiana. This is a region where petrochemical refineries and plastics

FIGURE 1.8 *A mountain of damaged oil drums near the Exxon refinery.* Source: *Environmental Protection Agency. Public Domain.*

manufacturing create a significant toxic burden on people and the land (Cole and Foster 2001). This, combined with all of the runoff from industrial agriculture further upstream, builds up in the waters and soils, and cancer rates there are much higher per capita than the rest of the nation. This region is inhabited by mostly poor Black, and Cajun, people. The texts and cases are too numerous to mention, but a couple of important aspects of the EJ movement should be noted.

First, though the movement's early public figures were all male, this was a movement led predominantly by women of color, such as Charlotte Keys and Hazel Johnson (McKittrick 2006). These were the women taking care of their children and relatives, who noticed birth defects and cancers, etc., in the communities where they lived. They were the ones who connected the dots between landfills, industrial factories, and higher rates of birth defects and cancers. Second, it wasn't until 1990, when Richard Moore of the Southwest Organizing Project sent a letter, signed by 100 Indigenous, Latinx, Black, and people of color leaders, to the "Big 10" environmental organizations that these organizations and mainstream, modern environmentalism began to take more seriously an intersectional approach to environmentalism. Finally, as with religious environmentalism and the study of it, there is a gap between the scholarship on the Environmental and Environmental Justice movements, and with acknowledging the role of religious/spiritual motivation and organizations (Kearns

2014). Ideally these two things are always connected but that does not always play out. In the next section we turn to the development of the study of "religion and nature" in North America.

The Study of Religion and Nature in North America: The Emergence of a Field

Looking back on the study of religion and nature, most scholars begin with Lynn White, Jr.'s brief essay on "The Historical Roots of Our Ecologic Crisis" in 1967. In this essay, White, a historian of science, argued that the Christian idea of humans' dominion over the rest of the natural world (being made especially in the image of God) has helped to fuel *human exceptionalism*. White was not alone in his critique. A similar analysis of the crisis of values and the damaging impact of Western worldviews was made by Seyyed Hossein Nasr in *The Encounter of Man and Nature: The Spiritual Crisis of Modern Man* (1968). Earlier, members of the Frankfurt School and other German scholars who had fled Germany under Nazism, such as the theologian Paul Tillich, had raised concerns about technology and Christian values. In *Traces on the Rhodian Shore* (1967), Glacken traced how Platonic ideas that the really real is eternal, unchanging, and nonmaterial leads to ideas that bodies and the material world are not as important as spirits and transcendent ideals. Aristotelian ideas of teleology help move us into linear understandings of progress, and this becomes associated with progress through science and technologies that humans use to transform the world into a new paradise (but mainly for human beings, and even then, just some human beings). These Greek influences shaped much of the development of Christianity. Ideas of impermanence of the material world and salvation as transcending the material world, prevalent in many forms of North American Christianity, are found in other traditions, and these ideas help to support the idea that the material world can be transformed by humans to make it "better" for humans. Since that time, many others have made this story of religion and the environment a more complex story (see Ellingsen 2016; Glave and Stoll 2006; Gottlieb 2009; Gould and Kearns 2018; Kearns and Keller 2007; D. Taylor 2009).

Obviously, such transformations have helped to create the environmental crises we are experiencing now. Although there were concerned Christian theologians and ethicists since the beginning of the twentieth century, such as Walter Rauschenbusch, Walter Lowdermilk (a soil scientist who wrote the 11th Commandment concerning stewardship), Paul Tillich, and Joseph Sittler (Pikhala 2017), it was the 1970s and 1980s, in response to White, that some religious scholars (for more details, see Gould and Kearns chapter in this volume) such as Rosemary Radford Ruether (1975) began to ask more directly how religious traditions have contributed to environmental problems and what resources religions might have to support environmental thinking and acting in the world. This project accelerated with the founding of the Forum on Religion and Ecology by Mary Evelyn Tucker and John Grim. They organized a set of ten conferences and subsequent volumes on religion and ecology that really set the stage for the field of "Religion and Ecology." Influenced by the work of the Passionist Priest and historian of religions turned "geologian" Thomas Berry (2009), they began to look at the different world religions for how they might support a more holistic understanding of human beings as part of the evolutionary and cosmological stories.

In addition to this type of scholarship, too numerous to cover here, there also emerged in the 1960s and 1970s what today is called "religious naturalism" (or Robert Corrington's [2013] ecstatic naturalism). Religious naturalism and those who promote religious naturalist ideas and scholarship (see Branch and White chapters in our companion volume, Religion, Science, and Technology in North America, 2024) argue that perhaps the world's religious traditions were formulated in such a different context that it would be impossible for them to address things like globalization and climate change today (as did Ruether [1994] about ecology in general). While they may offer resources for environmentalism, many religious naturalists would argue that we need thinking that reflects our current cosmological, evolutionary, and ecological contexts (White 2016). So, thinkers such as Loyal Rue and Ursula Goodenough (2000), as well as Thomas Berry (Berry and Tucker 2009), argue that we can develop a "spirituality" for the planet from the stories and ideas based upon the natural sciences.

Today, there are many academic groups that analyze "religion and ecology" and religion and nature: some of which draw from these two main ways of thinking about religion and the rest of the natural world, and others that are some combination of these or critical of both in some way. Or said differently, environmentalism and religious involvement in its many forms in North America is changing, and along with it understandings of what "religion" and "nature" are and how they are related.

Contemporary Critical, Intersectional Environmentalisms

As will be discussed in many of the chapters in this volume, environmentalism is not just about "the nonhuman world." Environmentalism and various understandings of nature tell us a lot about who we humans are as well. This is not just because humans are part of the natural world, undoubtedly we are; but rather because each of our embodiments shape the way we experience the worlds in which we live. On the one hand, we mean our mere physical embodiment: human beings experience the world differently than say a fly or a turtle. The world of nature we experience also depends on where we are born and live: someone in the arctic circle experiences nature differently than someone in the San Francisco Bay Area or Mexico City. It is also important to note that our experiences of nature are not static or singular and that they change over time and as we move through different regions. On the other hand, whether we are male, female, trans, or gender queer; whether we are Black, white, Asian, Indigenous, Latinx, or mixed race; whether we are straight, gay, bi, lesbian, or queer: each of these ways of being in the world are shaped by the languages, cultures, politics, and economics in which we live and these shape our understandings of nature.

From an intersectional environmental approach, it is important to take race, class, gender, sexuality, and ability (among other things) into account when thinking about environmental and religious issues (Intersectional Environmentalist 2021). In North America (and in other places) poor people of color and Indigenous peoples experience environmental ills at a disproportionate rate from wealthy white people, for instance, and these ills made them particularly susceptible to the COVID-19 pandemic of 2020–21. Due to racist hetero-patriarchal structures and biologies, women are often the ones who are most affected by the pollution of local places and pass on the toxins to their children in the womb and through breastfeeding (Steingraber 2003), they are the ones that first notice the increased rates of birth defects and cancers in their own communities. These types of intersectional environmentalism mean that there is no "direct" experience of "nature," and that we should constantly examine the ways in which our understandings of humans and the natural world shape and affect different bodies differently (Alaimo 2010; see also Gottlieb chapter in this volume). As more and more people take to the streets to protest climate change or fossil fuel pipelines, the intersectionality of the movement is clearly evident.

The emerging discourses around queer environmentalisms also help us to think differently about human-earth relations. Even though modern, Western sciences

FIGURE 1.9 *Members of the United Methodist Women at the 2019 Youth Climate Strike in New York City. Courtesy of Karen Mancinelli.*

have often been thought of as universal, rational, and reductive, some queer theorists engaging with the sciences are arguing that evolution, ecology, and even quantum physics are, in a word, queer. Evolutionary theory, for instance, drastically challenged the background Christian, Platonic, and Aristotelian understandings of biology. Whereas much of the Western worldview, for over two thousand years, thought that different bodies and even individuals had different forms and essences, the theory of evolution changed all of that. According to evolutionary theory, there are no universal forms or essences, but rather different bodies emerge out of the same evolutionary process. In addition, because there is so much diversity in the animal and plant world when it comes to sex and reproduction, shouldn't the same hold for the human world? This is what Joan Roughgarden (2013), among others, argues in *Evolution's Rainbow*. Ecology is also queer in that it suggests our bodies, all bodies, are porous "communities" made up of the other life around us: the air we breathe, the food we eat, and the microbiome in our guts, are all part of the community that make up each individual being. We are not, then, distinct, solid, unchanging individuals, but rather porous subjects. Others such as Karen Barad (2007) have argued about the queer nature of the quantum world and the indeterminancy of reality: that reality is not given, but emergent in each moment of the evolving process.

Other scholars have begun to speak of this radical entangled life on the planet that is multiple, mixed, and "queer," in terms of a "new materialism" (Bauman 2018). From a "new materialist" perspective, all of reality is interrelated, living, and has agency (see O'Dell-Chaib chapter in this volume). We are each acted upon by the rest of the planetary community even as we act upon it. From this perspective, something like "climate change" might be understood as an organism of which we are a part. We do not just act to solve the problem of climate change, but we are changed by climate change and are a part of the larger planetary community. These "new materialisms" draw from old forms of animisms and romanticisms, and from new ways of thinking in science that suggest that the earth and all therein, in fact all of matter in the universe, is somehow alive and active rather than dead. One implication of this is that we are not fully in charge of managing the world, as some forms of "*stewardship ethics*" might imply, but rather that we are part of a chaotic, emergent system. Whatever environmentalism means in light of this, it probably ought to be based much more on a "kinship ethics" or "planetary citizenship" ethics (Bauman 2014) rather than a stewardship ethics. (See Shipley chapter in this volume).

Finally, at the edges of our thinking here and the edges of humanity, if we are part of the evolving planetary community, and if we are porous and entangled with other bodies around us, then we might also want to think about a "posthuman" environmentalism (Haraway 2016). Not all post-humanities are the same; indeed some only look toward the time when humans are more cyborg than animal, more synthetic than biological, so that our consciousnesses can live on eternally in some type of microchipped based reality. This would be a form of posthumanism that doesn't take into account the entire planetary community. The posthumanity we are speaking of takes into account our entanglement with the evolutionary process of other life and bodies on the planet, on the one hand, and that we are entangled with the technologies that make up and mediate our experiences of the world, on the other. Technology, nonhuman nature, and humans exist all together in this evolving process, and if we are not just going to recreate the entire planet in the image of humanity, then we ought to start thinking about a future in which we evolve beyond ourselves along with the planetary community. From this perspective, might we be able to think about planetary technologies that promote the flourishing of the entire planetary community and not just the human, especially in crises provoked by anthropocentric global warming for more on climate change (see O'Brien, this volume)

The chapters in this volume trace some of these shifts, in thinking about nature from the context of North America. First, we will look at the history of religious traditions and nature/environmentalism in the North American continent (Indigenous, Western monotheisms, Asian, new religious movements). Then, we move on to look at some of the intersectional approaches to environmentalism—race, gender and sexuality, economics, critical theories. And, finally, we look at some important environmental issues and how religions are, or might, respond to them—climate change, animals, extinction, sustainable living, water. Far from comprehensive, what follows should be an entryway in to the complex and growing reflections on "Religion and Nature in North America."

FIGURE 1.10 *Hundreds of thousands join the People's Climate March in Washington, DC in 2017.* Source: *Mark Dixon/CC BY 2.0.*

Further Reading and Online Resources

Bauman W., R. Bohannon, and K. O'Brien, eds. (2017), *Grounding Religion: A Field Guide to the Study of Religion and Ecology*, New York: Routledge.

Gottlieb R., S. ed. (2006), *The Oxford Handbook on Religion and Ecology*, New York: Oxford University Press.

Hart J., ed. (2017), *The Wiley Blackwell Companion to Religion and Ecology*, Hoboken, NJ: John Wiley & Sons.

Hobgood L. and W. Bauman, eds. (2018), *The Bloomsbury Handbook of Religion and Nature: The Elements*, London: Bloomsbury.

Jenkins W. (2009), *Berkshire Encyclopedia of Sustainability*, vol. 1, *The Spirit of Sustainability*, Great Barrington, MA: Berkshire Publishing.

Jenkins W., M.E. Tucker, and J. Grim, eds. (2017), *Routledge Handbook of Religion and Ecology*, New York: Routledge.

References

Alaimo S. (2010), *Bodily Natures: Science, Environment, and the Material Self*, Bloomington: Indiana University Press.

Barad K. (2007), *Meeting the Universe Halfway: Quantum Physics and the Entanglement of Matter and Meaning*, Durham, NC: Duke University Press.

Bauman W. (2009), *Theology, Creation, and Environmental Ethics: From Creatio Ex Nihilo to Terra Nullius*, New York: Routledge.

Bauman W. (2014), *Religion and Ecology: Developing a Planetary Ethic*, New York: Columbia University Press.

Bauman W., ed. (2018), *Meaningful Flesh: Reflections on Religion and Nature for a Queer Planet*, Santa Barbara, CA: Punctum Books.

Berry E. (2015), *Devoted to Nature: The Religious Roots of American Environmentalism*, Berkeley: University of California Press.

Berry T. and M.E. Tucker (2009), *The Sacred Universe: Earth, Spirituality, and Religion in the Twenty-First Century*, New York: Columbia Press.

Branch G (2024), "Creationism, Evolution, and Public Education," in W. Bauman and L. Stenmark (eds), *Religion, Science and Technology in North America: An Introduction*, New York: Bloomsbury Academic.

Bullard R. (2000), *Dumping in Dixie: Race, Class, and Environmental Quality*, New York: Routledge.

Bullard R., ed. (1993), *Confronting Environmental Racism: Voices from the Grassroots*, Cambridge, MA: South End Press.

Carson R. ([1962] 2002), *Silent Spring*, 40th anniversary edn., Boston: Houghton Mifflin.

Carter C. (2018), "Blood in the Soil: The Racial, Racist, and Religious Dimensions of Environmentalism," in W. Bauman and L. Hobgood (eds.), *The Bloomsbury Handbook of Religion and Nature the Elements*, 45–61, New York: Bloomsbury Publishing.

Clay E. (2011), "How Does It Feel to Be an Environmental Problem? Studying Religion and Ecology in the African Diaspora," in W. Bauman, R. Bohannon II, and K. O'Brien (eds.), *Inherited Land: The Changing Grounds of Religion and Ecology*, 148–70, Eugene, OR: Wipf & Stock.

Cole L. and S. Foster (2001), *From the Ground Up: Environmental Racism and the Rise of the Environmental Movement*, New York: New York University Press.

Cone J. (2000), "Who's Earth Is It Anyway?," *Cross Currents*, 50 (1–2) (Spring/Summer): 36–46.

Corrington R. (2013), *Nature's Sublime: An Essay in Aesthetic Naturalism*, Lanham, MD: Lexington Books.

DeLoria V., Jr. (1973), *God Is Red*, New York: Penguin Books.

Dunbar-Ortiz R. (2014), *An Indigenous Peoples' History of the United States*, Boston: Beacon Press.

Ellingson S. (2016), *To Care for Creation: The Emergence of the Religious Environmental Movement*, Chicago: University of Chicago Press.

Finney C. (2014), *Black Faces, White Spaces: Reimagining the Relationship of African Americans to the Great Outdoors*, Durham: University of North Carolina Press.

First National People of Color Environmental Leadership Summit (1991), "Principles of Environmental Justice." Available online: http://www.ejnet.org/ej/principles.html (accessed May 2, 2021).

Gaard G. (1997), "Toward a Queer Ecofeminism," *Hypatia*, 12 (1): 114–37.

Gaard G. (2017), *Critical Ecofeminism*, Lanham, MA: Lexington Books.

Garb Y.J. (1985), "The Use and Misuse of the Whole Earth Image," *Whole Earth Review*, 45: 18–25.

Gilio-Whitaker D. (2020), *As Long as Grass Grows: The Indigenous Fight for Environmental Justice, from Colonization to Standing Rock*, Boston: Beacon Press.

Glacken C.J. (1967), *Traces on the Rhodian Shore: Nature and Culture in Western Thought from Ancient Times to the End of the Eighteenth Century*, Berkeley: University of California Press.

Glave D. (2010), *Rooted in the Earth: Reclaiming the African American Environmental Heritage*, Chicago: Lawrence Hill Books.

Glave D. and M. Stoll, eds. (2006), *To Love the Wind and the Rain: African Americans and Environmental History*, Pittsburgh, PA: University of Pittsburgh Press.

Goodenough U. (2000), *The Sacred Depths of Nature*, Oxford: Oxford University Press.

Gottlieb R.S. (2009), *A Greener Faith: Religious Environmentalism and Our Planet's Future*, Oxford: Oxford University Press.

Gould R.K. and L. Kearns (2018), "Ecology and Religious Environmentalism in the United States," in J. Corrigen (ed.), *Oxford Encyclopedia of Religion and America*, Oxford: Oxford University Press. Available online: https://doi.org/10.1093/acrefore/9780199340378.013.445.

Haraway D. (2016), *Staying with the Trouble: Making Kin in the Cthulucene*, Durham, NC: Duke University Press.

Harris M. (2017), *Ecowomanism: African American Women and Earth Honoring Faiths*, Maryknoll, NY: Orbis Books.

Intersectional Environmentalist (2021). Available online: https://www.intersectionalenvironmentalist.com (accessed May 17, 2021).

Johnson E. (2015), *Ask the Beasts: Darwin and the God of Love*, New York: Bloomsbury.

Kearns L. (2004), "The Context of Eco-theology," in G. Jones (ed.), *Blackwell Companion to Modern Theology*, 466–84, Malden, MA: Blackwell Publishing.

Kearns L. (2014), "Environmental Justice," in R. Bohannon (ed.), *Religions and Environments: A Reader in Religion, Nature and Ecology*, 297–312, London: Bloomsbury Press.

Kearns L. and C. Keller, eds. (2007), *Ecospirit: Religions and Philosophies for the Earth*, New York: Fordham University Press.

Kellert S.R. and E.O. Wilson (1995), *The Biophilia Hypothesis*, Washington, DC: Island Press.

Ko A. (2019), *Racism and Zoological Witchcraft: A Guide to Getting Out*, New York: Lantern Books.

LaDuke W. (1999), *All Our Relations: Native Struggles for Land and Life*, Cambridge, MA: South End Press.

Leduc T.B. (2016), *A Canadian Climate of Mind: Passages from Fur to Energy and Beyond*, Montreal and Kingston: McGill-Queen's University Press.

Masuzawa T. (2005), *The Invention of World Religions: Or How European Universalism was Preserved in the Language of Pluralism*, Chicago: University of Chicago Press.

McKittrick K. (2006), *Demonic Grounds: Black Women, Geography, and the Cartographies of Struggle*, Minneapolis: University of Minnesota Press.

Merchant C. (1990), *The Death of Nature: Women, Ecology, and the Scientific Revolution*, New York: Routledge.

Merchant C. (2007), *American Environmental History: An Introduction*, New York: Columbia University Press.

Merchant C. (2013), *Reinventing Eden: The Fate of Nature in Western Culture*, New York: Routledge.

Mortimer-Sandilands C. and B. Erickson (2010), "Introduction," in C. Mortimer-Sandilands and B. Erickson (eds.), *Queer Ecologies: Sex, Nature, Politics, Desire*, 1–50, Bloomington: Indiana University Press.

Nasr S. (1968), *The Encounter of Man and Nature: The Spiritual Crisis of Modern Man*, London: George Allen and Unwin.

Pikhala P. (2017), *Early Ecotheology and Joseph Sittler*, Studies in Religion and Environment 12, Zurich: LIT Verlag.

Plumwood V. (1993), *Feminism and the Mastery of Nature*, New York: Routledge.

Roughgarden J. (2013), *Evolution's Rainbow: Diversity, Gender, and Sexuality in Nature and People*, Berkeley: University of California Press.

Ruether R. (1975), *New Woman, New Earth: Sexist Ideologies and Human Liberation*, New York: Seabury Press.

Ruether R. (1994), *Gaia and God: An Ecofeminist Theology of Earth Healing*, New York: Harper One.

Sideris L.H. (2017), *Consecrating Science: Wonder, Knowledge, and the Natural World*, Oakland: University of California Press.

Spence M. (2000), *Dispossessing the Wilderness: Indian Removal and the Making of the National Parks*, rev. edn., Oxford: Oxford University Press.

Steingraber S. (2003), *Having Faith: An Ecologist's Journey to Motherhood*, New York: Berkley.

Stoll M. (2015), *Inherit the Holy Mountain: Religion and the Rise of American Environmentalism*, Oxford: Oxford University Press.

Swimme B. and T. Berry (1994), *The Universe Story: From the Primordial Flaring Forth to the Ecozoic Era—A Celebration of the Unfolding of the Cosmos*, San Francisco: Harper One.

Taylor B. (2009), *Dark Green Religion: Nature Spirituality and the Planetary Future*, Berkeley: University of California Press.

Taylor B., ed. (2005), *The Encyclopedia of Religion and Nature*, 2 vols., New York: Continuum.

Taylor D. (2016), *The Rise of the American Conservation Movement: Power, Privilege, and Environmental Protection*, Durham, NC: Duke University Press.

Tucker M.E. and J. Grim (1998–2003), *Religions of the World and Ecology (Series)*, Cambridge, MA: Harvard University Press.

United Church of Christ Commission for Racial Justice (1987), *Toxic Wastes and Race in the United States: A National Report on the Racial and Socio-Economic Characteristics of Communities with Hazardous Waste Sites*, New York: United Church of Christ Commission for Racial Justice.

Weaver J., ed. (1996), *Defending Mother Earth: Native American Perspectives on Environmental Justice*, Maryknoll, NY: Orbis.

White C.W. (2016), *Black Lives and Sacred Humanity*, New York: Fordham University Press.

White C.W. (2024), "Religious Naturalism," in W. Bauman and L. Stenmark (eds.), *Religion, Science and Technology in North America: An Introduction*, New York: Bloomsbury Academic.

White L., Jr. (1967), "The Historical Roots of Our Ecological Crisis," *Science*, 155 (3767): 1203–1207.

Wilson E.O. (2006), *The Creation: An Appeal to Save Life on Earth*, New York: W.W. Norton & Company.

Zimring C. (2015), *Clean and White: A History of Environmental Racism in the United States*, New York: New York University Press.

Glossary Terms

Heteronormativity A term used in queer studies, highlights the ways in which cultures, religious practices and ideas, laws, economics, and other institutions are set up to favor heterosexuality as normative over any other sexuality.

Human exceptionalism This is the idea that humans are exceptions to the rest of the natural world and can use the rest of the natural world as means toward human projects and goals.

Queer A term that has been taken back by "queer theorists" and members of the LGBTQ (lesbian, gay, bisexual, transgender, and queer/questioning) community to highlight that there really is no "normal." Rather, what we think of as "normal" is constructed over time. Ecology is also queer in that it suggests our bodies, all bodies, are porous "communities" made up of the other life around us.

Stewardship ethics An ethics of stewardship is derived from monotheistic traditions that suggest humans are caretakers or managers of the rest of the natural world. Though many religious forms of environmentalism based in monotheisms have rallied around "stewardship," it has also been critiqued by many for still holding humans above the rest of the natural world.

Turtle Island The name given by a range of First Peoples and Native Americans, particularly those of the Iroquois or Haudenosaunee confederacy to the land of North America. In their creation stories, Sky Woman falls and lands on the back of a turtle that supports the land that Sky Woman and a range of animals help to create, which then becomes home.

2

Reconciling to the Ancestors: The Spirit of Decolonization in Times of Pandemic

Timothy B. Leduc

On the point that is a ten-minute canoe paddle away, the birch, maple, and oak are ablaze with the beautiful reds, oranges, and yellows of fall. Even as the sun shines on this warm fall day, I can feel the cool air that has replaced the summer heat of a month ago and will soon bring winter. Something about this annual cycle seems timeless, unmoved by the climate of change and pandemic swirling around our modern lives. The words of Thomas Berry echo: "when autumn comes the fruits appear, the birds depart, the leaves fall, darkness settles over the land … This ever-renewing sequence of sunrise and sunset, of seasonal succession, constitutes a pattern of life, a great liturgy, a celebration of co-existence" (1999: 177).

In our changing times, the ancient mystery of the cycling blue-green orb on which we live is showing us how its vital spirit works far from the eyes of humans. These patterns, and the ways of nature oblivious to human desires for control, became more evident to many during the COVID-19 pandemic, as air became less smoggy, allowing natural beauty to be visible, and animals become more visible in urban areas. Across the planet, greenhouse gas emissions finally showed a marked reduction reflecting the momentary constriction of industrial activities across the planet that was sensed by many living beings as a space of regenerative potential.

As the summer closed, the stories of cleaner air and waters contrasted with the dark realities of global *climate change*. A record number of hurricanes appeared in the Atlantic Ocean. Forest fires across the west set ablaze the smoggy skies, with smoke bringing a haze to large swaths of Turtle Island (North America). To the south the Amazon rainforests burned at unprecedented rates, while the comparatively new corporate giant Amazon.com posted record profits as the easiest place for isolated people to get virtually anything they desire. With systemic injustices making the vulnerable more vulnerable, and air pollution exacerbating health inequalities, the pandemic also haunted us with the continuation of colonial abuses against Indigenous and Black peoples, women of color, their children, and the earth. There is so much *numinous* mystery in all this, which I sense most intimately upon the lands where I live.

Not all headlines were about the pandemic and climate change. The focus in Canada was on a host of Indigenous protests concerning the national government's decision to build pipelines across sovereign Indigenous territory. The traditional chiefs of the Wet'suwet'en nation in British Columbia announced they had "unanimously opposed all pipeline proposals and have not provided free, prior, and informed consent to Coastal Gaslink/TransCanada" (Unist'ot'en 2020). Not far from where I was teaching truth, reconciliation, and Indigenous healing to aspiring social workers in southern Ontario, the Mohawk communities of Tyendinaga and Kahnawake enacted their support by stopping one of Canada's busiest rail corridors. Thousands in cities joined the protests that called for a change in the way colonial governments and institutions relate with Indigenous nations and the land.

Under the cloak of the pandemic's spreading uncertainty, Canadian politicians worked on plans to reignite the economy in predictable ways such as speeding up oil pipeline development across Indigenous lands. From fish and fur to forests, minerals and energy (hydro and oil), resource extraction connects Canadian identity to its origins as a colonial nation whose wealth depends on providing resources to the more industrialized nations of Europe and the United States (Innis 1999: 401; for a look at these issues in a United States context, see Whyte 2018). These colonial roots of

FIGURE 2.1 *Hollow tree in fall. Photograph by the author.*

ongoing land disputes became more visible as the energy projects intersected with Indigenous protests about worker camps on remote lands and the threat of spreading disease. Arising from the land were deep ancestral patterns.

There is an addictive impulse driving these colonial-Indigenous relations that Anishinaabe healer Herb Nabigon depicts in the title of his book *The Hollow Tree*, which he says is "a metaphor for what Western culture has become, an empty shell" where individual desires rule over communal needs (2006: xvii). The experience of addiction followed by its healing through cultural reconnection is what allowed Nabigon to see this hollowness within and then to recognize the same pattern in the colonial culture that impacted his life. Residential school, severance from family and culture, uprooting from land relations, and the intergenerational trauma of these losses fueled an addiction that brought his life into a death spiral. His Elders advised him that he was at a moment of choice: "You can either pick up your sacred bundle or you can die from drinking" (2006: 33).

With a climate of uncertainty swirling around us, we seem to be collectively facing a similar moment of choice when the earth asks whether we can reaffirm ways of living with the mystery of life. As Nabigon writes:

> Two paths are available to us. One is a dark anxious way. Those who exclusively or persistently follow it see the Earth as a resource to be exploited … On this path their nurturing Mother will become the dark Mother and destroy them. The other option is the Medicine Wheel path … All those who embark upon this path hold the land in truth. Their every act is of leadership and their every service is directed towards Mother Earth, Sky Nation, or Spirit World.
>
> (2006: 58)

I was teaching with Nabigon's book in an Indigenous *Wholistic Healing* course for social workers as the pandemic halted face-to-face classes with three weeks remaining in our term. I co-teach the course with the *Haudenosaunee* Elder Norma Jacobs whose cultural knowledge of land-based healing offers students a living relation with Indigenous traditions like Nabigon's. I bring experiences as a social worker in northern Indigenous communities and two decades of learning with Indigenous knowledge holders about my responsibilities as someone whose mother is French Canadien and father carries French Canadien relations to Haudenosaunee and Wendat communities. As most of the students are also settlers of diverse origins, we complement the reading of Nabigon with Vine Deloria Jr.'s book on Carl Jung because of his assertion that Jung's ideas are the closest in the Western healing tradition to an Indigenous approach—though they need decolonizing, as does social work, academia, and most of us.

Isolated to the bubbles of our most intimate relations and virtual sharing, the voices of Nabigon, Deloria, and Jung ever more starkly highlight the mysterious recurrence of patterns related to unresolved colonial violence that have the power to cut across an individual life or the generations of a nation. The words of Anishinaabe Elder Mary Deleary in the 2015 Canadian *Truth and Reconciliation* Commission report reverberate: "Our relatives who have come from across the water, you still have work to do ... The land is made up of the dust of our ancestors' bones. And so to reconcile with this land and everything that has happened, there is much work to be done" (2015: 9). A resonant understanding can be read in Jung's sense of individuated maturity as requiring the "reconciliation of the ancestral with the present" (cited in Deloria 2016: 149). The ancestors are always with us, whether we carry them in our genes, our cultural stories, or in the broader Indigenous sense of our bodies and culture being spiritually interwoven in Mother Earth.

Though the sacred teachings I sense in the fall colors of these lands have their own ancestry, there is a spirit of land connection that can be found wherever we live; all you need to do is open to the mystery held in the unique land relations that interweave the seasons of our life. By engaging Nabigon, Jung, and others, we are given a way to approach the numinous dimensions of the climatic choices before us. There is so much mystery in what it means to choose to serve Earth and Spirit, and that seems to be what the present conflicts around identity, systemic violence, and cultural *appropriation* are asking us each to struggle with.

The Hollow Spirit of Colonialism

Tending a fire on a lake a few hours north of Toronto, the uncertainty around keeping up modern appearances in the face of COVID-19 evaporates in the quiet of night. There is nothing to do here but stop and allow my eyes to be drawn in by a dark sky pierced with stars so numerous and awe-inspiring, and yet often forgotten in the light pollution of my urban life. Here I feel the true source of the Thanksgiving Address I have learned from Indigenous Elders such as Norma Jacobs and writers like Robin Wall Kimmerer (2013: 105–17). In this tradition, each gathering starts with gratitude for the relations our lives depend on. It is a ceremony that Thomas Berry says epitomizes Indigenous understandings of "the universe primarily as celebration," adding that "the human might be identified as the being in whom the universe celebrates itself and its numinous origins" (1999: 19).

A slight wind whispering through the changing fall leaves stills me into a deeper sense of where I am. In the silence, I hear Nabigon's words: "After I sat down and reviewed my life, I wrote down the gifts that the Creator gave me ... I felt good because I accepted how vulnerable and weak I am without the life givers" (2006: 70). This is how he talks of his introduction to gratitude as central in his choice to heal. Drawing a connection from Nabigon's individual life to the cultural scale of *colonialism*, Berry and many others propose that modern society is in need of relearning such gratitude if we are to have a sustainable future. But moving in that direction will entail remembering how this human responsibility was curtailed by a colonial culture that saw the land and Indigenous peoples as needing "to be conquered" (Berry 1999: 41). With these ancestral acts, the mysterious reverence for this night sky and land receded into the shadows for a time.

In the *Anishinaabe* stories of Nabigon, it is told that their Elders foresaw the arrival of the European ship and the need for a swift response. Seeing that their spiritual tradition known as the "Midewiwin Way was in danger of being destroyed," the sacred bundles and "scrolls that recorded the ceremonies" were gathered and buried, and thus "hidden out of sight but not out of memory" (Benton-Banai 2010: 91). The subsequent centuries saw a succession of colonial resource wars, epidemics of European diseases, Christian missions, and the founding of the colonial nations of the United States (1776) and then Canada (1867), which in the past century outlawed Indigenous ceremonies and undermined Indigenous lifeways. While cultural displays of gratitude for creation went into deeper hiding, the colonial nations simultaneously extended their relentless grasping for lands now primarily seen as resources.

Though Nabigon's story is unique, the colonial hollowness he describes has afflicted many Indigenous people. A key moment in his uprooting occurred when he was taken to a Residential School at nine years old, a story repeated time and again in both Canada and the United States. The intention of the schools is epitomized in the 1920 description by then Deputy Minister of Indian Affairs, Duncan Campbell Scott: "our object is to continue until there is not a single Indian in Canada that has not been absorbed into the body politic" (cited in Truth and Reconciliation Commission 2015: 2). In 2008, the Prime Minister of Canada apologized for the schools and initiated a Truth and Reconciliation Commission that in 2015 published its report. In its words: "The Canadian government pursued this policy of cultural genocide because it wished to divest itself of its legal and financial obligations to Aboriginal people and gain control over their land and resources" (Truth and Reconciliation Commission 2015: 1–2).

These colonial actions impacted Nabigon and many others who came to internalize feelings of inferiority related to the racism experienced, often leading to a rejection of their culture. In the absence of these roots, an alcohol addiction unfolded in his teenage years that slowly unravelled many of his relations. As he writes, "My father ... gave me a choice: I could either sober up or I could leave. Naturally, I chose the latter alternative because I certainly did not want to quit drinking" (2006: 14). In the lead-up to his father's ultimatum, Nabigon's addiction had deteriorated to the point of losing his arm after falling asleep, drunk, along a railway. Leaving his father, family and culture behind initiated an intensifying of his addictive behaviors over a number of years until he hit bottom, and once there his Elders offered him another choice: "pick up your sacred bundle or you can die" (33).

Over the past few decades, Indigenous teachings have been brought out of hiding to support cultural renewal and offer a different view on our climate of uncertainty. It was these teachings that Nabigon was introduced to at a treatment center that combined the Alcoholics Anonymous program with the Indigenous healing traditions of a Medicine Wheel that is, he writes, "a part of the daily rituals and ceremonies dating as far back as the early Stone Age" (2006: 58–60). And so with Elder guidance he entered the *Medicine Wheel* starting in the east where one learns about the renewal given by the daily rising sun and annual return of spring. Here one learns of good feelings and values such as kindness, caring, and gratitude. But when that connection is disrupted,

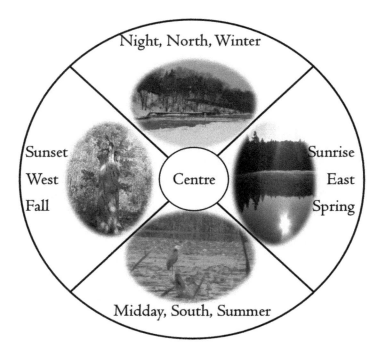

FIGURE 2.2 *Seasonal representation of Herb Nabigon's Medicine Wheel. Photograph by author; to see his representation of the Medicine Wheel with its inclusion of teachings around associated Values, see Nabigon (2006: 58–74).*

then the east is where we struggle with "feelings of inferiority" (62). Four days on the land brought up memories of how alcohol led to aggression that masked his sense of inferiority. In this way, he learned about how "suffering is part of the healing" (76), but in doing so he also came to see that Mother Earth centers and balances the circle. "Our dependency upon Nature should never be forgotten" (72–3).

Like others, the synchronistic impacts of colonialism meant that Nabigon became distanced from Anishinaabe culture and land relations. His healing journey also brings to the surface Western cultural patterns that cut across Canada in a host of ways. For example, the growth of Canadian social work is connected to residential schools and a subsequent child welfare system that is still composed of more than 50 percent Indigenous children (see Blackstock 2009; Leduc 2018), as well as the ensuing intergenerational trauma that leads to Indigenous overrepresentation in sectors such as addictions and prisons. More than that, social work is mired in modern assumptions that marginalize any sense of land being connected to the profession's colonial growth, or, following Nabigon, that land can be actively engaged in healing. It is in this context that it is helpful to read Deloria as he decolonizes Jung.

"When I began drawing the *mandalas* [sacred circles]," Jung says he began to see that "all the paths I had been following [...] were leading back to a single point—namely, to the mid-point. It became increasingly plain to me that the mandala is the [...] path to the center, to individuation" (1989: 196). Deloria recognizes the vital connection between Jung and the Medicine Wheel as a guide to holistic healing in Indigenous traditions. For Nabigon, *fasting* around this circle brought him to reflect on the fundamental question, "Why am I here?" (2006: 84). In a similar sensibility, Jung writes that "we count for something only because of the essential we embody, and if we do not embody that, life is wasted" (1989: 325). Healing entails coming to our center in a holistic circle that reaches out to our relations.

Despite the relational potential of Jung's thought, Deloria shows how he is caught in colonial assumptions such as a hierarchical evolutionary framework that fosters "detrimental, derogatory, or condescending views" of Indigenous people (2016: 34). This critique resonates with ecofeminists who outline a system of intersecting dualities in Western culture (e.g., male/female; white/Indigenous; society/nature) that have fostered hierarchical violence against the most marginalized (e.g., Plumwood 1993; Rowland 2002; Shiva 1993). In Canada, and the United States, the intersectional nature of this violence is epitomized in the experience of Indigenous women, who are the traditional center of their matrilineal cultures and have thus suffered the brunt of colonial impacts, as documented by Canada's *National Inquiry on Murdered and*

FIGURE 2.3 *Tree of Life Mandala. This is a Western representation of the Tree of Life circle. Jung drew his own Tree of Life mandala that is viewable on various websites. Courtesy of Ali Selmi/Getty Images.*

Missing Indigenous Women and Girls (2019; see Lawrence 2003). It is a testament to Deloria's balanced scholarship that he takes time to decolonize Jung's assumptions in the hopes of fostering a conversation.

Beyond the sense of circular wholeness, Deloria also sees fertile ground in Jung's diagnosis of modern society being in search of a lost soul. An unbalanced rational consciousness was for Jung spreading like a dark shadow, doing "violence to natural forces" that are now opening our unconscious to this "outbreak of intense spiritual suffering" (1933: 240). What Nabigon helps us to see is that this modern imbalance is being maintained by an addiction that supports individual or collective irresponsibility in the face of what is arising. People caught in an addiction are guided by unconscious beliefs, with the most prominent being the sense that they are in control and can resist the addictive substance. In the words of Gabor Maté, these behaviors are "meant to calm anxiety—an unease about life itself, or about a sense of insufficient self [inferiority] [...] described as '*brain lock*'" (2009: 353–4). The addictive lock escalates as we socially isolate from loved ones, like Nabigon with his father.

We can read these *Hollow Tree* dynamics in relation to colonial patterns that continue to paralyze Liberal Canadian politics which oscillate between taking leadership around the Paris Climate Treaty (2016) but fighting Indigenous-environmental protests of pipelines—all the while touting the Truth and Reconciliation process. The international agreement to cut carbon emissions and keep global climate changes below a rise of 2°C over the next century is contradicted by a seemingly pragmatic capitalist response

FIGURE 2.4 *Alberta tailing pond. The waste from extracting bitumen is here shown being deposited into a tailing pond.* Source: *Francis Black/Getty Images.*

to building pipelines from the Albertan oil sands. Similar tensions came to confront the United States, who initially signed the agreement under President Obama, and then withdrew under President Trump. Troubling the Canadian (and American), balancing act is its replication of colonial patterns, a point reflected in a Paris Climate Treaty that saw American and European delegations advocate to cut any reference to Indigenous rights as binding; a ghostly reminder of the 1783 Paris Peace Treaty that defined the borders of the United States and Canada without mentioning the lands of Indigenous peoples.

Just as individual addicts become more isolated, antisocial, irrational, and angry, our fossil fuel energy addiction is extending the modern separation from creation. On a collective scale, pipelines, bitumen extraction, fracking, and offshore development are analogous to those dark corners where an addict goes as they try to maintain ways that are hitting bottom. Summing up our situation, Berry concludes that "the traditional Western civilization must withdraw from its efforts at dominion over the Earth. This will be one of the most severe disciplines in the future, for the Western addiction to economic dominance is even more powerful than the drive toward political dominance" (1999: 195).

Reflecting on the clear sky as the flames of the fire subside, I feel myself as part of a mystery that is so beyond me. Just as with Nabigon, the climatic uncertainties of our time are showing us a different world than that which once seemed a given. There is so much mystery in the interconnection of our individual lives, nations, and the collective moment to deep ancestral patterns that seem to be calling us to some kind of transformation. If Nabigon wanted to live, he would have to remember his sacred connections and "transform that hollow tree into the sacred tree it was meant to be" (2006: xvii). A comparable choice is collectively before us, and it is to learning about that task that we now turn.

Becoming a Fall Tree

With the dawn, the liquid reflection of magnificent reds, oranges, yellows, and greens that line the shores covers more than half the lake, drawing me into the peace of gratitude. It is thanks to the privilege of working in a university and teaching with an Indigenous Elder that I take time to be with these fall changes that Nabigon learned about on his third fast in the west door of the Medicine Wheel. It is here that we come to the humility of "understanding our sacred place within creation [...] I am mortal. You are mortal. Death is inevitable" (Nabigon 2006: 66–7). This is "the ancestor's path home," a humble path of wisdom and spiritual strength that is modeled by Elders who live a balanced and "honest life [that] is a spiritual reward in itself."

The stilling reflection of these trees leads me to recall Nabigon describing the tree as "the symbol of honesty in our tradition," and how when he goes to the forest his behavior is reflected back to him through them. As he writes, "if I strive for an honest life, and progress with honesty, I will find a straight tree and that tree will be me

[...] Nature teaches us how to behave and how to conduct our lives" (Nabigon 2006: 101–12). When we approach the world with the intention of taking time to learn, then the trees can teach something that is deep within us and also in our relations.

To the modern mind, such relational learning seems irrational; as it did at first to Nabigon whose impression of the Indigenous cultural relation "to Nature was extremely negative [...] My mind and heart were cold. I did not know how to receive the Elders, or how to listen." It is not simply that colonialism undermines a sense of self and cultural integrity, but also fosters in these clear cuts a rational disconnection from living relations: family, community, culture, land, and spirit. By fasting on the land and then coming into the *sweatlodge* with his Elders, Nabigon learned to listen again. It is from this path that he eventually came full circle to pick-up his sacred bundle and give what he has received in the fall splendor of an Elder.

Following the Medicine Wheel fasts, Nabigon also offers a "brief description" of the sweatlodge (2006: 83), with his word choice of "brief" signaling for us the vital issue of appropriating cultural practices. Appropriation is a continuation of the colonial addiction to taking. As Cindy Baskin writes: "Appropriation is not only hurtful; it is also dangerous. Some non-Indigenous peoples include versions of our ceremonies and rituals, such as the sweatlodge" (2011: 10–11). One result of this misuse has been cases where people have died from not using the ceremonies with respect for the tradition. But appropriation also speaks to a disrespect of the mystery from which ceremonies arise and evolve in the integrity of a cultural tradition.

It is here that Deloria also proves helpful as he quotes Jung: "the more limited a man's field of consciousness is, the more numerous the psychic contents (images) which meet him" (2016: 164). This sense of "a discrete system of thought" as valuable to self-awareness is for Deloria important, though he opens Jung to an Indigenous worldview "in which Spirits are not mental images projected outwards but have real power in the physical world" (164). In other words, these ceremonies are "a discrete system" for fostering relations in a mysterious world. A ritual fast around the Medicine Wheel calls "the directional powers to participate in the event [...] [and] does not symbolize" (192–3). Rather than abstract symbols of a modern mind that can "become over-familiar" and thus worn out, ceremony opens space for us to relate with the spirit teachings carried in each direction.

Appropriation extends the violation of land and spirit through taking that which others have earned with their lives. Paired to this external violation is an internal devaluing of one's own ancestral traditions as having value. Looking at a Western culture where people were starting to pick-up aspects of Eastern spiritual practices such as meditation and yoga, Jung asked whether it is possible to "put on, like a new suit of clothes, ready-made symbols grown on foreign soil [...] We are surely the rightful heirs of Christian symbolism, but somehow we have squandered this heritage" (1933: 25–8). Whether it be the current extremes of a Christian fundamentalism that harkens back to the surety of colonial missions or a kind of liberal secularism that rationalizes everything, the lack of a spiritual practice that can renew relations with a changing creation was for Jung another dimension of the modern soul dis-ease.

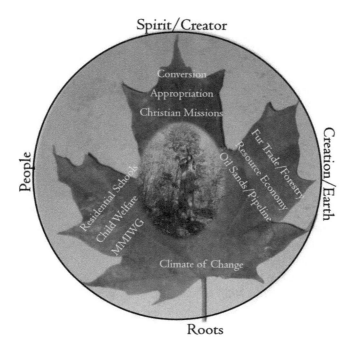

FIGURE 2.5 *Canadian Maple Leaf Mandala; this mandala draws upon the insights of Nabigon's Medicine Wheel and the Jungian Mandala to represent the interconnected issues that confront Canada's colonial approach to land and Indigenous peoples, as reflected on in this chapter. Photograph by the author.*

After Norma Jacobs guides our class through the Thanksgiving Address, we ask the students to learn about the values of this ceremony through engaging each of these land relations over the course. But they are to do so through words and sensibilities that connect to their cultural grounding rather than parroting an Indigenous approach. Just as with Berry earlier, we are to learn how these values might change our approach to social work, religion, or more generally, living, but do so without appropriating specific practices. The words of Baskin are helpful: "How do non-Indigenous in the helping professions take up Indigenous ways of helping, then? The answer lies in concentrating on Indigenous worldviews" for the values they model rather than picking up cultural practices (2011: 11). Spirit is found through embodying values such as gratitude, humility, kindness, and caring, but we each need to find our unique way.

As the sun rises higher in the sky, the cool northwesterly wind reminds me of an approaching winter filled with uncertainty. An economy that cannot slow down, schools filled with masked children, a pandemic's second wave, and the next climatic event. I can almost hear a decolonized Jung describing our collective sufferings as "cracks, fissures, doorways into what might be called the inside of the world" (Tacey 2013: 126). We have approached such a doorway through the healing stories of Nabigon, thus giving us a glimpse of the ancestral spirits that are inside the patterns of our addictions as we struggle with historic injustices, appropriation, equity, privilege, and identity. To take up what we have been given while opening out to the gifts of so many relations is our challenge, and to do so in the midst of the mystery that is the coming winter.

Conclusion: Winter Is Coming

Kar-r-r-o-o-o, kar-r-r-o-o-o ..., a polyphony from above draws my eyes to a flock of sandhill cranes flying across the lake. Sleek straight necks and white wings slice through the sky as they, with other marsh birds, prepare for the next leg in their migration journey that started hundreds of kilometers north of here on the tundra and which will end in the American Midwest. These seasonal patterns have been cycling from times much deeper than the colonial and modern periods, and this timelessness is part of the sacred mystery held in Nabigon's Medicine Wheel as fall gives way to winter.

It was in his final fast in the North that Nabigon learned about how the "north wind [...] is a master of movement," and thus reminds us "that every action has a

FIGURE 2.6 *Flying sandhill cranes.* Source: *Vicki Jauron, Babylon and Beyond Photography/ Getty Images.*

consequence, a caring one or one that promotes fear" (2006: 70). The isolating nature of this fear was highlighted for him from his time living in Toronto, for it was here that he "drifted away from thinking about Nature. I was concerned with survival, but most of all I was concerned with how I was going to get my next drink." In those acts, he also drifted into the isolating values of not caring, inferiority, jealousy, and control. Approaching such a winter season in this city is always a season of cold and slowing relations, but with COVID-19 we will be more distanced and isolated than usual. Sometimes our waiting game with this pandemic feels like Nabigon's experience; survival until we can continue with modern addictions in ways that are essentially unchanged. Something more transformative is being called for.

Many students feel pulled toward the beauty of something in Indigenous traditions that has been missing; a way of being that starts by fostering connections with Nature. As Nabigon explains: "My culture embraces universal values that are treasured by all peoples of the world [...] all major cultures and religions. However, the traditional Native culture expresses these values in a unique way. All of our values are expressed through Nature, and then Nature teaches us how to behave" (2006: 102). There is much value in relearning to root our ways of living in Nature. We know there are positive health effects of being intimate with forests, water, and mud (see Capaldi et al. 2015; Kimmerer 2013: 236; Williams 2016), but Indigenous land ceremonies highlight the potential reciprocity of nurturing connections to this healing energy as we become, in Deloria's words, "active participants in this wholeness" (2016: 155). But we need to find ways of rooting our uniquely limited, yet mysterious, lives into this wholeness.

Hearing the *kar-r-r-o-o-o* fade into silence, I feel thankful for just being here. Every relation reminds me of the world we live in, even as the stressors of navigating our climate of uncertainty wrap us in a ball of tension. Colonialism is a spiritual breach of our individual, ecological, and biospheric connection to the regenerative source of life. And yet these spectacular fall changes suggest we can find support as we migrate to a different way of living. The stark ancestral patterns of our time are like a beacon to what needs changing if we are to reconnect with the life-giving values of Mother Earth. This is what Nabigon describes as a holistic healing process that re-roots us in the spiritual core of our identities, and which opens us out, in the words of his Elders, to "serve each other [...] If we recognize each other's spirit and humanity we begin to empower each other" (2006: 84). It is in this way that we can renew our lives on this mysterious earth where beautiful fall colors inevitably let go to winter winds, becoming compost for spring.

Further Reading and Online Resources

Absolon K. (2019), "Reconnecting to Creation: A Spirit of Decolonizing," in N.J. Profitt and C. Baskin (eds.), *Spirituality and Social Justice: Spirit in the Political Quest for a Just World*, 43–64, Toronto: CSP Books.

Bernstein J.S. (2005), *Living in the Borderland: The Evolution of Consciousness and the Challenge of Healing Trauma*, New York: Routledge.
Leduc T.B. (2016), *A Canadian Climate of Mind: Passages from Fur to Energy and Beyond*, Montreal and Kingston: McGill-Queen's University Press.
Nabigon H. (2006), *The Hollow Tree: Fighting Addiction with Traditional Native Healing*, Montreal and Kingston: McGill-Queen's University Press.
Turner F. (1986), *Beyond Geography: The Western Spirit against the Wilderness*, New Brunswick, NJ: Rutgers University Press.

References

Baskin C. (2011), *Strong Helpers' Teachings: The Value of Indigenous Knowledges in the Helping Professions*, Toronto: Canadian Scholars' Press.
Benton-Benai E. (2010), *The Mishomis Book: The Voice of the Ojibway*, Minneapolis: University of Minnesota Press.
Berry T. (1999), *The Great Work: Our Way into the Future*, New York: Bell Tower.
Blackstock C. (2009), "The Occasional Evil of Angels: Learning from the Experiences of Aboriginal Peoples and Social Work," *International Indigenous Journal of Entrepreneurship, Advancement, Strategy, and Education*, 1 (1): 1–24.
Capaldi C.A., H. Passmore, E.K. Nisbet, J.M. Zelenski, and R.L. Dopko (2015), "Flourishing in Nature: A Review of the Benefits of Connecting with Nature and Its Application as a Wellbeing Intervention," *International Journal of Wellbeing*, 5 (4): 1–16.
Carson R. ([1962] 2002), *Silent Spring*, Boston: Houghton Mifflin.
Deloria V., Jr. (2016), *C. G. Jung and the Sioux Traditions: Dreams, Visions, Nature, and the Primitive*, New Orleans: Spring Journal Books.
Innis H.A. ([1930] 1999), *The Fur Trade in Canada: An Introduction to Canadian Economic History*, Toronto: University of Toronto Press.
Jung C.G. (1933), *Modern Man in Search of a Soul*, Boston: Houghton Mifflin.
Jung C.G. ([1961] 1989), *Memories, Dreams, Reflections*, New York: Vintage Books.
Kimmerer R.W. (2013), *Braiding Sweetgrass: Indigenous Wisdom, Scientific Knowledge and the Teachings of Plants*, Minneapolis, MN: Milkweed Editions.
Lawrence B. (2003), "Gender, Race, and the Regulation of Native Identity in Canada and the United States: An Overview," *Hypatia*, 18 (2): 3–31.
Leduc T.B. (2016), *A Canadian Climate of Mind: Passages from Fur to Energy and Beyond*, Montreal and Kingston: McGill-Queen's University Press.
Leduc T.B. (2018), "'Let Us Continue Free as the Air': Reconciling Social Work Education to Indigenous Lands," *Journal of Social Work Education*, 54 (3): 412–25.
Maté G. (2009), *In the Realm of Hungry Ghosts: Close Encounters with Addictions*, Toronto: Vintage Canada.
Nabigon H. (2006), *The Hollow Tree: Fighting Addiction with Traditional Native Healing*, Montreal and Kingston: McGill-Queen's University Press.
National Inquiry into Missing and Murdered Indigenous Women and Girls (2019), *Reclaiming Power and Place: The Final Report*. Available online: https://www.mmiwg-ffada.ca/wp-content/uploads/2019/06/Final_Report_Vol_1a-1.pdf (accessed March 13, 2021).
Otto R. (1924), *The Idea of the Holy: An Inquiry into the Non-Rational Factor in the Idea of the Divine and Its Relation to the Rational*, London: Oxford University Press.
Plumwood V. (1993), *Feminism and the Mastery of Nature*, New York: Routledge.

Rowland S. (2002), *Jung: A Feminist Revision*, Cambridge, UK: Polity Press.
Shiva V. (1993), *Monocultures of the Mind*, London: Zed Books.
Tacey D. (2013), *The Darkening Spirit: Jung, Spirituality, Religion*, New York: Routledge.
Truth and Reconciliation Commission of Canada (2015), *Executive Summary Report*.
    Available online: http://www.trc.ca/websites/trcinstitution/File/2015/Exec_
    Summary_2015_06_25_web_o.pdf (accessed October 10, 2020).
Unist'ot'en (2020), *Wet'suwet'en Supporter Toolkit 2020*. Available online: https://
    unistoten.camp/supportertoolkit2020/ (accessed March 13, 2021).
Whyte K. (2018), "Settler Colonialism, Ecology and Environmental Injustice," *Environment
    & Society: Advances in Research*, 9: 129–48.
Williams F. (2016), "This Is Your Brain on Nature," *National Geographic Magazine*, January.
    Available online: https://www.nationalgeographic.com/magazine/article/call-to-wild
    (accessed March 13, 2021).

Glossary Terms

Anishinaabe An Indigenous culture and nation "spread from the Atlantic Coast, all along the Saint Lawrence River, and throughout the Great Lakes region" (for a fuller description, see Benton-Banai 2010: 1).

Appropriation A colonial process by which particular cultural practices (e.g., ceremonies, prayers) of a violently marginalized group (e.g., Indigenous peoples) are brought into the dominant political culture in a way that decontextualizes their ancestral roots and minimizes their challenging potential to the dominant worldview. It is a dimension of colonial taking that is related to land. See Colonialism below.

Brain lock A term that Gabor Maté uses to describe the feedback pattern of addictive behaviors as they play out in our brain neurology. In his words, "the stuck neurological gears that cause thought to be acted out before the action can be stopped" (Maté 2009: 353–4).

Climate change Our global and local climates are always changing, from the deep past into the present there have been cycles of climate changes that lead to glaciations and warmings not unlike our annual seasons but on a vaster time frame. When we talk about climate change today, we are referring to a kind of anthropocentric or, to be more specific, industrial shift in the climatic patterns of the earth through the mediation of greenhouse gas emissions related primarily to fossil fuel use.

Colonialism "For over a century, the central goals of Canada's Aboriginal policy were to eliminate Aboriginal governments; ignore Aboriginal rights; terminate the Treaties; and, through a process of assimilation, cause Aboriginal peoples to cease to exist as distinct legal, social, cultural, religious, and racial entities in Canada" (Truth and Reconciliation Commission 2015: 1).

Decolonization A process of truth-telling and learning about colonialism and its impacts that starts with a positioning of ourselves in these violent systems/histories, and from there recognizing where change can be fostered based on our positioning as means for allying with Indigenous communities.

Fasting A practice associated with various religious and spiritual traditions that require the practitioner to not ingest food and drink and/or do particular behaviors for a designated period of time related to the ceremony. More recently, fasting has also been connected with various nonreligious health diets. In the context of this chapter, fasting is discussed as part of an Indigenous traditional approach to healing on the land.

Haudenosaunee This name translates as "People of the Longhouse" and describes the pre-colonial confederacy that brought together six Iroquois-speaking nations (Mohawk, Oneida, Onondaga, Cayuga, Seneca, Tuscarora) in a peace treaty on the lands related to New York State. Following the American Revolution, some of those nations who supported the British (Canada) relocated north of the Great Lakes and Saint Lawrence River.

Mandala The sacred circles that Jung learned about through Buddhism, which seemed indicative of the kind of psychological wholeness that his clients were searching for, and that he also saw in his own healing process. In his words, "all the paths I had been following … were leading back to a single point—namely, to the mid-point. It became increasingly plain to me that the mandala is the … path to the center, to individuation" (Jung [1961] 1989: 196).

Medicine Wheel "An ancient tool used by our ancestors to explain our world view. It also helped them organize their medicines, animals, birds, and plants in a systematic fashion. It helped them to understand life in accordance with nature as we understand it today" (for a fuller description, see Nabigon 2006: 116–17).

Numinous Awe-inspiring experiences like those of the changing colors in fall, prodigious expanse of a night sky, or even burning forests can be understood as bringing us into relation with an experience of the sacred. Rudolf Otto (1924) gives us a way to distinguish the different qualities of such experiences. He explains that while the concept of the "holy" tends to confirm our understandings/beliefs of where we

fit in the world, the numinous takes the form of a prodigious energy that breaks in upon our beliefs, rationality, and expectations with an unsettling impact, a numinous energy "can only be evoked, awakened in the mind; as everything that comes 'of the spirit' must be awakened" (Otto 1924: 7). It is in this sense that our climate of change can be seen as a series of numinous awakenings.

Sweatlodge "A divine gift from the Creator. The purpose of the lodge is to purify our mind, body and spirit through this form of prayer […] First Nations people say the sweatlodge represents the womb of our birth mother, Mother Earth, and the universe" (see Nabigon 2006: 83–91, for further discussion on the cultural teachings and values that he feels comfortable sharing).

Truth and Reconciliation "To some people, reconciliation is the re-establishment of a conciliatory state. However, this is a state that many Aboriginal people assert never has existed between Aboriginal and non-Aboriginal people. To others, reconciliation, in the context of Indian residential schools, is similar to dealing with a situation of family violence. It's about coming to terms with events of the past [Truth-telling] in a manner that overcomes conflict and establishes a respectful and healthy relationship among people, going forward" (Truth and Reconciliation Commission 2015: 6).

Wholistic Healing An approach to wholistic healing is "foundational to helping approaches within Indigenous worldviews," and usually takes into account "the four aspects of a person" (physical, mental, emotional, spiritual), the individual's grounding in family/community/culture, and the individual's relation to an interconnected creation (Baskin 2011: 108).

3

Indigenous Language and Ecology

Marcus Briggs-Cloud

I used to think that the most critical issue Maskoke People face was language loss as our ancient, yet threatened, language was projected to fall silent by the year 2040. I thought language revitalization was the sole work to be done to restore wellness among our People. In trying to think about how to measure success, that monolithic thinking came to an abrupt halt upon awakening to the reality that successful language revitalization work is contingent upon numerous interconnected factors that address systemic issues through a holistic lens. To see a real reversal of language loss, we have to altogether change the way we live.

Within our Maskoke medicinal traditions, practitioners sing prescribed formulas and blow into plant concoctions, which results in an efficacious healing substance to be consumed by members of the community (Howard 1984). These medicine traditions are required components of Maskoke Posketv (often referred to as Green Corn Dance) ceremonies that renew our relationship to the natural world around us. Our prophecies tell us that if we cease conducting our Posketv ceremonies, thereby allowing our sacred fires to go out, Maskoke People will perish. No language means no ceremony; and no ceremony means no Maskoke People. So, ultimately the silence of the Maskoke language equals the disappearance of the Maskoke People.

It started when I began noticing that endangered language communities globally were addressing the pervasive issue of obsolescence by importing nouns/concepts from the settler-colonial society around them and crafting new words to convey those nouns/concepts. I started thinking more critically about the philosophical underpinnings of such a practice in my own Maskoke context, on grounds that by the time we import into our lexicon over three thousand words that are inherently premised on postindustrialization capitalist ideology, we have deviated significantly from the unique bioregionally derived traditional ethos that our ancestors left to us. Our Indigenous worldview that is inextricably tied to the natural world, was being flipped upside down; therefore, such a practice begs the question "why not just speak English?"

FIGURE 3.1 *The Welcome Sign at the Ekvn-Yefolecv ecovillage. You can visit the intentional eco-community's website at https://www.ekvn-yefolecv.org/. Shared with permission from Ekvn-Yefolecv.*

For example, grammatically, the terms *Vhakv* and *Vhake* are derivatives of the infinitive verb *haketv*, which means "to become." They descend from the same philosophical source, that is, the natural order. Possessing only one different letter (the final letter), both terms are ecological in origin. Maskoke cultural "law" emerges by way of replicating phenomena in the natural order within the contiguous Maskoke bioregion, hence derivation from the word *haketv* "to become [like the natural world]," hence the word *hake*, in its autonomy, conjures an active verb mode of mirroring another entity, whereas uttering its nominalized form *hakv* converts the meaning to elucidate a societally solidified perception of the biogeographical ecosystem. The first letter "*v*" serves as a locative prefix marker, placing the noun in vertical parallel attachment to another entity. Thus, in this case, abidance of *vhakv* (law) means to attach Maskoke People to the bioregional natural order through obligatory observance and biomimicry of local nonhuman ecology. Maskoke People then implement and promulgate, in worldview and praxis, cultural regulations based on the observed natural order; albeit these are human arbitrary constructions to accommodate Western scientific pursuits, ecosystems are self-regulating. Therefore, when not subject to anthropogenic harm, ecosystems maintain balance, which is the ultimate goal of Maskoke society.

Both accommodating the settler-colonial apparatus either by inserting so much English or the alternative option, by composing an abundance of vocabulary to dump into our lexicon (as opposed to gradually incorporating a handful of new words with each generation as our ancestors did) felt like an unjust compromise of our indigeneity. I started thinking more radically about a theory of change, concluding that we would have to recreate the society in which our language once historically functioned best; a society premised on intimate relations with the natural world. In other words, instead of constantly trying to fit the language into our lifestyle, we must commit to changing our lifestyle while allowing the language to be our guide in that transition to more ecologically just and equitable lifeways. From this consciousness emerged the vision to build an ecovillage.

Our ancestors were forcibly removed from what are commonly/colonially known as Alabama and Georgia, to lands 1,100 kilometers away, known today as Oklahoma and Florida (Ethridge 2003). In light of this diaspora of forced removal, it became spiritually evident that we needed to assemble an intentional community of like-minded Maskoke folks descended from our homelands who are interested in returning for the purpose of both the biophysical stewardship and ceremonial renewal of the land our ancestors cared for since time immemorial. On January 12, 2018, we reclaimed a parcel of our ancestral homelands in what is colonially and commonly known as Central Alabama. Because we were traditionally an agrarian society, our contemporary communities must be centered on agricultural practices to provide the host activities for our ancient lexicon to thrive in the most authentic Maskoke way, and more notably to regain the ability to engage agriculture in culturally competent ways.

This is all part of our regular discernment of ways in which we can walk the talk! My late uncle, a language speaker, used to say "why do we hand our children over to white people to be schooled [...] they are our children and our responsibility to teach." We have never had the space to address that question, until now. For instance, we have to build from scratch a decolonial language curriculum for our immersion students (across age groups); design and implement regenerative agricultural approaches; explore ways to ensure many forms of health for ecovillage residents; develop plans to function as a carbon-negative community; generate revenue from non-extractive, economy-based ventures so the ecovillage can be sustained; navigate and maintain harmony among diverse personalities using traditional conflict resolution mechanisms to retain the ecovillage's population, overcome inclinations to inflict lateral violence, learn natural building construction, relearn the ecology of our traditional homelands and try to piece together our traditional canon of stories that provide the foundation for understanding significant ecological places/spaces/species, and the list goes on. Simply trying to save a language from extinction has necessitated the creation of a new/old society (Charleston 2015). We are not so naïve to believe that our ecovillage is somehow exempt from globalization or the climate crisis, but it is just insular enough to retain our language and culture with exponentially more integrity than we have had

FIGURE 3.2 *Language immersion students have daily farm responsibilities. Shared with permission from Ekvn-Yefolecv.*

the chance to do since we were displaced from our traditional homelands 182 years ago. We are building resilience for our grandchildren's grandchildren's grandchildren.

Indigenous language revitalization work must not contribute to ecological destruction, so our community had to start thinking about how we materialize an ecovillage in non-extractive ways. For instance, we founded a language immersion program, wherein NO English is spoken, and quickly began crafting a decolonial lens to penetrate our common tendencies in succumbing to conventional Western ways in which we school our children—such as not building lesson plans around disposable materials that soon end up in a landfill and contribute to methane gas emissions that warm the planet. Additionally, elder language bearers often have diabetes and hypertension, thus, decolonizing our diets became imperative as we slowly reclaimed traditional food systems knowledge from various sources (Henry et al. 2018). This has not happened without resistance from our elders who love soda-pop and spam. We are also learning what it means to eat "traditional foods" in an era of climate crisis wherein our food choices also impact all peoples' livelihoods. This causes us to reflect on what it means when we say "vnokeckv etemocet fullēt owēs" (we go about having love for one another) to extend to all peoples, especially the most vulnerable peoples of the planet.

FIGURE 3.3 *No-English zones are enforced while traditional ecological education is offered to ecovillage residents. Shared with permission from Ekvn-Yefolecv.*

The objective is not to return to a Clovis Indian era of living but rather to incorporate low-tech integrated regenerative systems that provide a good quality of living while demonstrating reverence for Earth and all living beings. For instance, we are building our community completely off-grid with a couple of nickel-iron battery solar systems, rainwater catchment, living roofs, composting toilets, rocket mass heaters and other masonry heaters, barrel and cob ovens, geothermal HVAC systems, natural building construction such as strawbale wall systems with earthen plaster coating and earthen floors, perlitecrete trenches and stem walls for annualized thermal inertia, and small-scale biodigesters that produce methane gas used for cooking from buffalo manure (see below) and food scraps.

To address the chronic illness among our elder language bearers, we are reintroducing healthy animal proteins that coevolved with our genotypes, and growing heirloom crops that are planted and harvested by everyone in the ecovillage community (Whyte 2018). As a part of our regenerative agriculture work, we steward a herd of buffalo, a culturally significant species to our People, and we made a conscious choice to implement holistic management (intensive rotational grazing) to improve soil health. This approach is labor-intensive and requires a relationship with the buffalo, as opposed to conventional farming practices that lead to soil degradation and dependence on imported chemical fertilizers, which has its own set of negative ecological repercussions. Another feature of this work includes our ongoing creation of silvopasture for carbon sequestration

FIGURE 3.4 *Strawbale wall system at the Community Center. Shared with permission from Ekvn-Yefolecv.*

and an improved small-scale hydrological cycle. We are culturing and releasing lake sturgeon, another culturally significant species to our People, back into the watershed from which they were extirpated in the 1950s due to the erection of hydroelectric dams that prevented them from returning to their natal spawning areas (Scott 1951). Our facility includes a closed-lake aquaponic system that does not abuse the aquifer. Others are attracted to the harvests of these efforts, so we generate income from farmers markets and an onsite farm stand, and we are in the process of building an off-grid regenerative integrated systems eco-learning conference/retreat center with a farm-to-table restaurant and museum.

Ekvn-Yefolecv Maskoke Ecovillage, the catalyst for profound transformation, is enabling us to once again be a full-time Indigenous People instead of compartmentalizing our lives by making asymmetrical concessions to accommodate the rhythms of Western society (LaDuke 1999). For example, we are able to hold traditional ceremonies in accordance with lunar calendar scheduling, rather than making concessions to settler-colonial notions of time and capitalist workforce demands. The entire world must learn to slow down and simplify human lifeways. Green technologies alone are not the answer; rather, it must be coupled with an entire lifestyle drawdown. Ekvn-Yefolecv rejects capital and material accumulation and is an income-sharing community wherein

FIGURE 3.5 *Ekvn-Yefolecv cofounder and codirector Marcus Briggs-Cloud preparing for sturgeon spawn. Shared with permission from Ekvn-Yefolecv.*

residents receive a modest stipend for performing rotating duties, in addition to receiving healthy meals and a thirty-seven square meter off-grid timber-framed home for residence. All residents of the ecovillage receive the same $400 monthly stipend rate regardless of Western levels of education or ability to perform a more laborious task than another. We promote our traditional Maskoke Etvlwv egalitarian lifeways and the concept that the community can be collectively content through living simply and being fulfilled by fluency in our language and the ability to live our culture daily. Living more simply involves regular interrogation of material uses. For instance, as we were compiling an energy budget, it became apparent that certain technologies would not be possible to deploy. Some residents of Ekvn-Yefolecv formerly enjoyed using an Instant Pot to cook with, but it requires one thousand watts to run a twenty-minute session. The typical settler-colonial mainstream response would be "how much more solar battery storage will we need to run the Instant Pot and a toaster and ...?" Our response is simply "we don't need an Instant Pot or a toaster or ....!" This is all part of slowing down our lives, which makes us open to the medicine growing stronger in our lives.

Cutting firewood to operate a barrel oven or rocket mass heater is more time-consuming than turning on a grid-tied thermostat, but our masonry heaters are 80 to 90 percent more energy efficient than conventional combustion heaters—so it is good to the earth—and individuals burn lots of calories and strengthen core muscles by harvesting and splitting firewood. Although the timber framing technique we employ is not Maskoke tradition, it coincides with our philosophical worldview concerning regeneration. Ecovillage residents select trees from the on-site forest based on species population densities in a basal area, and then, performing traditional ceremony protocols with each single tree before harvesting, we fell, skid, debark, and mill the timbers on-site. Next, we create natural joinery using mortise and tenon and wooden pegs, which reduces hardware needs in the structures. The entire process, from forest to frame, decreases embodied energy requirements, such as eliminating the need for extracted precious metals and fossil fuel and carbon emissions that would have been required in ordering and transporting equipment and timber from off-site. All of these aforementioned practices demand immense body energy expenditure and a lot of time, but that means less time to participate in capitalist consumerism. It is also what is necessary, in a spirit of reciprocity, to be in good relationship with the natural world.

Admittedly, minimalist living, income sharing, swimming with sturgeon, and inhaling bison breath, even cleaning composting toilets, all sound like utopian lifeways, but engaging Maskoke folks in this project has not been without immense ambivalence. Some community members have wrestled with a difficult-to-identify issue as they came to realize that even though the revitalization philosophy sounded "right," their apprehensions stemmed from correlating such a lifestyle to childhood impoverished living conditions. We were all taught to pursue the American capitalist dream, which leaves only minimal time to actively engage traditional Maskoke language and cultural identity. Recognizing that the ecovillage lifestyle may be simple and associated with living "poor," a number of Ekvn-Yefolecv residents instead choose to perceive it as legitimate liberation from oppression because they have agency in choosing to live this way, and see the genuine good quality of life in this paradigm. We are all coming to find profound healing we did not anticipate; just being on the land and having hands in the soil is healing to our spirits as we are regularly encouraged by our ancestors' presence and know they are happy we are home.

Because heteropatriarchy has inflicted much pain in the world (Smith 2020), Ekvn-Yefolecv seeks to dismantle it within the community as part of this healing. The most sacred food in Maskoke society is corn, a gift from Corn Woman, for which profound sacrificial thanks is given during annual renewal ceremonies called Posketv. Since this sacred food was left to the People by a female, the descendent agriculturalist caretakers of this crop were females. These responsibilities also inherently bestowed great importance on the value of women as caretakers of something sacred. Settler-colonialism deeply severed this connection, allowing for heteropatriarchy to infiltrate our society. Indian agents sought to dismantle traditional gender structures within Maskoke society, thereby removing women from agricultural responsibilities and domesticating them in a manner identical to European lifeways (Hawkins 2003). Under the new heteropatriarchy paradigm, Maskoke men began to view society through a European lens of productivity, wherein women were not perceived as primary contributors (Shiva 2016). Ekvn-Yefolecv seeks to decolonize our practices by supporting the women of the community in their journey to reclaim these roles, especially in agricultural leadership.

FIGURE 3.6 *Ekvn-Yefolecv cofounder and codirector Tawna Little about to offer prayer on sturgeon release day. Shared with permission from Ekvn-Yefolecv.*

Since women are often the most significant transmitters of language, we recognize that it is only when Indigenous women are socially empowered at the community level, namely, with a richness of traditional knowledge, and furthermore intentionally equipped with language fluency skills, will revitalization efforts be destined for success. Intermittently, we will continue lying to ourselves that a realistic resurgence of Indigenous languages is possible so long as patriarchy perpetually permeates our communities. Therefore, deliberately investing in our daughters, nieces, and granddaughters with good teachings is key to the survival of our languages.

In conclusion, if one wants to revitalize the Maskoke language, not only does one have to speak to children exclusively in the language from their preverbal stage onward, but also one has to: know how to grow heirloom corn and pumpkins for community physical health and save seed; generate revenue from regenerative agriculture and be content with a modest financial return; clean poop from a composting bucket to supply the food forest with nutrients instead of wasting potable water to send your poop to an unknown place; toast acorns you harvested in the woods with language immersion school kids on the most incredibly energy-efficient homemade rocket stove that required you to harvest fallen wood from the forest to burn; cease mansplaining and invest in women as the key to intergenerational language transmission; mourn the loss of a sturgeon when she dies of unpredicted biological factors; and honor a buffalo with song and dance upon harvest to nourish an elder language bearer. Additionally, one has to quit frivolously buying short-term-use plastics; turn to the sun each morning and give thanks for the day and for its energy to power your LED lights through photovoltaic panels; thank Earth for the clay with which you make nontoxic earthen plaster for your straw bale walls; and finally, abandon a harmful energy intensive individualistic paradigm and embrace interdependent collectivistic societal living premised on the cultivation of abundant love and compassion! Although this daily life is laborious and exhausting, it means less opportunity to participate in oppressive capitalist structures and enables us to more genuinely embody who we are as Maskoke People. In twenty-five years, Ekvn-Yefolecv Maskoke Ecovillage may be the rare place on the entire planet where one can go to hear the Maskoke language spoken fluently in a community. Through this holistic paradigm, we project that in two generations, having raised children as a full-time Indigenous People, Maskoke language will be the primary language spoken at the ecovillage, and our residents will be spiritually and physically healthy persons who inherited a resilient non-extractive, small-scale society in the midst of a climate crisis. We hope to serve as a replicable archetype for other communities to implement in their own culturally responsive contexts centered on intimate relations with the natural world wherein our unique languages and cultural lifeways thrive once again.

FIGURE 3.7 *Language immersion inside the aquaponics greenhouse. Shared with permission from Ekvn-Yefolecv.*

Further Reading and Online Resources

Ekvn-Yefolecv (2021), "Home." Available online: https://www.ekvn-yefolecv.org/ (accessed May 2, 2021).
Gilio-Whitaker D. (2020), *As Long as Grass Grows: The Indigenous Fight for Environmental Justice, from Colonization to Standing Rock*, Boston: Beacon Press.
Global Ecovillage Network (n.d.), "About." Available online: https://ecovillage.org/ (accessed May 2, 2021).
Kimmer R. (2015), *Braiding Sweetgrass: Indigenous Wisdom, Scientific Knowledge and the Teachings of Plants*, Minneapolis, MN: Milkweed Editions.
Nelson M. and D. Schilling (2018), *Traditional Ecological Knowledge: Learning from Indigenous Practices for Environmental Sustainability*, New York: Cambridge University Press.

References

Charleston S. (2015), *Coming Full Circle: Constructing Native Christian Theology*, Minneapolis, MN: Augsburg Fortress Publishers.
Ethridge R. (2003), *Creek Country: The Creek Indians and Their World*, Chapel Hill: University of North Carolina Press.
Hawkins B. (2003), *The Collected Works of Benjamin Hawkins, 1796–1810*, Tuscaloosa: University of Alabama Press.
Henry R., A. LaVallee, N. Van Styvendale, and R.A. Innes, eds. (2018), *Global Indigenous Health: Reconciling the Past, Engaging the Present, Animating the Future*, Tucson: University of Arizona Press.
Howard J.H. (1984), *Oklahoma Seminoles Medicines, Magic and Religion*, Civilization of the American Indian Series, Norman: University of Oklahoma Press.
LaDuke W. (1999), *All Our Relations: Native Struggles for Land and Life*, Cambridge, MA: South End Press.
Scott D.C. (1951), "Sampling Fish Populations in the Coosa River, Alabama," *Transactions of the American Fisheries Society*, 80 (1): 28–40.
Shiva V. (2016), *Staying Alive: Women, Ecology, and Development*, Berkeley, CA: North Atlantic Books.
Smith A. (2020), "Heteropatriarchy and the Three Pillars of White Supremacy: Rethinking Women of Color Organizing," in C. McCann, S. Kim, and E. Ergun (eds.), *Feminist Theory Reader*, 141–7, New York: Routledge.
Whyte K. (2018), "Food Sovereignty, Justice and Indigenous Peoples: An Essay on Settler Colonialism and Collective Continuance," in A. Barnhill, T. Doggett, and A. Egan (eds.), *Oxford Handbook of Food Ethics*, 345–66, Oxford: Oxford University Press.

4

The Tent of Abraham: The Emerging Landscape of Jewish, Christian, and Islamic Ecological Traditions

Rebecca Kneale Gould and Laurel D. Kearns

Preface: Dwelling in the Tent of Abraham

While geopolitical history of the last two millennia might have us think otherwise, *spiritual* history, by contrast, teaches us that Jews, Christians, and Muslims are part of one common family. The sacred texts, stories, and rituals of the "Abrahamic traditions" tell us—as the very term indicates—that these people of faith share common spiritual ancestors—through Abraham and his sons—whose stories convey particular values and character traits that later became central to the teachings of Judaism, Christianity, and Islam. Among these were: concern for the suffering of others, an ethic of always "welcoming the stranger," and a commitment to sharing scant resources among those who needed them (Waskow et al. 2007). In contemporary theological terms, these underlying values might be called compassion, radical hospitality, and justice.

Why begin this examination of the meanings of "nature" with these myths about the welcoming tent of Abraham? In a religious studies context, the term *myth* more broadly refers to the cultural stories that communities tell about themselves, expressing the ethics, values, and principles that they hold dear. Pondering the power of ancient myth is essential for any discussion of nature, environment, and religion because these myths call attention back to the essential principles and lived ethics of a given tradition.

Of course, the evidence for the welcoming "tent of Abraham" is decidedly mixed. For instance, the majority of Muslims who first came to North American shores, came as enslaved persons, while anti-Semitism (and resistance to it) erupted as early as the founding of the first synagogues in the seventeenth century (GhaneaBassiri 2010). Given the extent to which colonialism, slavery, and Christian missionizing have been so deeply intertwined, it is impossible to speak honestly of North American history—and "nature"—without reckoning with the domination, oppression, stolen lands, and stolen people that are woven into that history with legacies that continue to reverberate today (Gilio-Whitaker 2020; Glave and Stoll 2006) (see Bauman and Kearns chapter in this volume). Nevertheless, the mythic power of the welcoming tent of Abraham persists against these long-standing odds.

In ecological contexts, for example, we find interfaith organizations, discussed below, where Jews, Muslims, and Christians work together to address our most urgent challenges: the climate crisis, environmental injustice, species extinction, and the future of sustainable food and water systems. This work means uniting across theological and cultural differences and toward the common good, forging alliances that bring hope in these life-threatening times (Gould 2007). Others, however, are working primarily *within* their own communities (such as the Catholic Climate Covenant [n.d.] or KairosCanada [n.d.]), simultaneously strengthening the eco-justice commitments and spiritual growth that the current times demand. Before delving into the on-the-ground ecological work that is flowering today, it is helpful first to examine some underlying theological and cultural principles (often ignored, threatened, or distorted from within and without) that are shared across these pluralistic faith communities (Foltz et al. 2003; Hessel and Ruether 2000; Tirosh-Samuelson 2002).

Conceptual Foundations I: The Oneness of God and the Dangers of Idols

The Oneness of the Divine

At key moments in any Jewish prayer service, the congregation will collectively call out the *Shema*, often translated in English as "Hear, O Israel, the Lord is our God, the Lord is One." This translation, however, obscures the layered meanings of the original Hebrew where the letters YHWH are commonly thought to indicate forms of the verb "to be," as well as evoking *ruach* (spirit, wind, Divine Breath) (Keller 2003; Waskow 2020). Whether understood traditionally, or more experimentally, the *Shema*'s clear emphasis is on the final word: One (*ehad*). The implication is that no matter how many names and metaphors may be applied to God, God ultimately eludes all definitions and manifestations (McFague 1993; Mevorach 2017).

Across the three faith traditions, God is sometimes understood to be "in all" (*immanent*), sometimes "beyond all" (*transcendent*) and sometimes a combination of both (Chryssavgis 2017; Cobb and Griffin 1976; Troster 1998). Christian Protestant founders saw God even in the tiniest grain of rice (Martin Luther), or in the "face of every creature" (John Wesley) (Dahill and Martin-Schramm 2016). Correspondingly, in Islam, the spiritual importance of Divine Oneness (*tawhid*) is also clearly evoked and emphasized in multiple suras of the Qur'an.

The Idols of Our Times

Hand in hand with the significant emphasis on the Oneness of the Divine come corresponding warnings in the sacred texts of all three monotheistic traditions: "do not worship idols or false gods." Such warnings include regular, dramatic, and sometimes punishing reminders of the uniqueness and oneness of God. How is the core concept of Divine Oneness (and the corresponding warning against idolatry) relevant to our current ecological discussions? In broad terms, it constitutes an emphatic assertion of *the connectedness of all life*, very much akin to the assertion of connectedness that lies at the core of environmental science and of biocentric, ecological thinking. This shared concept of connectedness suggests that despite significant distinctions in worldview, *both* biocentric and theocentric perspectives have similar capacities to respect and preserve the broad web of life and to hold *anthropocentrism* in check.

Within the Abrahamic traditions, the case against idolatry has its own particular ecological relevance: nothing should be valued above God, the creative force that brought all life into being. Thus, many ask: "In what ways does our worship of 'false gods' threaten the mutual flourishing of all life?" Their answers include: consumerism, the false god of the market (unrestrained capitalism), and the pursuit of "success" at all costs (*Laudato Si* 2015). These "idols" become manifest in our addiction to fossil fuels, our neglect of neighbors and the planet, and our blindness to the welfare of future generations, threatening our fate and the fate of the earth (Loy 2003; McFague 2008; Waskow 2000).

Conceptual Foundations II: The Goodness of Creation, the Book of Nature and the Call to Stewardship

"And God Saw That It Was Good"

The Hebrew Bible (much of which reappears in the Christian Old Testament) begins with two striking stories of creation. The first story, the *Priestly* version, reveals a Divine Force that literally speaks creation into being out of unformed raw material

(Bauman 2009). Tellingly, however, God does not simply "place" fully formed plants and animals as figures on an earthly stage, but rather asks the earth and waters *themselves* to "bring forth," to cocreate vegetation and all manner of creatures (Genesis 1:11–12). This ancient story reflects, in a mythic sense, what biological science later reveals: that Abrahamic creation stories offer fascinating foundations for contemporary eco-theological conversations about ongoing "creation" and the process of evolution (Johnson 2015; Keller 2008; Ward-Lev 2019). Such links compellingly argue against popular representations of "belief in creation" and "belief in evolution" as mutually exclusive worldviews.

The second, much older, creation story (commonly called the J/Yahwist story) portrays an ideal garden in need of tending, and tells of the human (*adam*, "earthling") being molded from arable soil (*adamah*, earth) explicitly to "work and keep" the land (Bernstein 2005; Hiebert 2000). While *both* creation stories emphasize that humans are insufficient without the rest of creation on which they utterly depend, the older story is notable for directly stating that caring for the earthly garden is the very *reason* that humans were created at all (Genesis 2:15). The Qur'an echoes this sentiment, similarly emphasizing the profound human–soil connection by describing humans as being solely a mixture of clay and Allah's creative power (23:12–14). Elsewhere in Islamic sacred literature, we are reminded that not only are humans inherently *of* the earth but also that the earth itself is rightly seen as a *mosque*, a sacred space in which all humanity and all life forms dwell (Sahih Bukhari, 335; Abdul-Matin 2010).

But what of the troubling terms "dominion" and "hold sway over" in the first Genesis story (1:28) that some claim is justification for human domination over the natural world (Bernstein 2021; Scully 2003)? What of the clear hierarchies of life forms that appear in the sacred literatures of all three traditions, exalting humans as the seeming "crown of creation?"

Focusing on themes of domination and hierarchy in these stories has led to interpretations of the Abrahamic traditions as anthropocentric, a not unreasonable claim given the history of the *use* of dominion ideas as justification for the exploitation of nature (Thomas [1983] 1991; White 1967). Nevertheless, sacred texts, interpretive commentaries, and centuries of theologizing reveal a consistent refrain that pushes back: the need to keep human hubris in check and an overarching concern for the fate of humanity and all living beings (Moe-Lobeda 2013; Nasr 1968). Those advocating for the "greening" of their traditions warn that humans need to recognize their tendencies to step outside ecological and social limits, and to act "like God" (Schorsch 1992). These theological messages augment more direct statements of creation's goodness, such as God recognizing God's initial creative acts as "good," songs and poetry in which the natural world *itself* is praising the divine, and injunctions for people, animals, and the land to rest in regular cycles of sabbath that are prevalent in *Jewish environmentalism*.

The Book of Nature

In the Abrahamic traditions, the goodness of our planetary home is not simply an assertion of value limited to the first moments when the Divine Presence (*Allah*, God, YHVH, *Elohim*) brings all life into being. Rather, there is a consistent *reassertion* of the profound goodness of creation that emphasizes the extent to which humanity and the Divine remain in an ongoing relationship of cocreating. Moreover, the natural world is understood to be a continual source of wisdom and instruction for humanity.

Nowhere is the concept of "nature as teacher" more highly developed than in the Christian concept of "the Book of Nature": the idea that creation is the first revelation to be read to understand God. In a broad sense, this idea is also present in the Islamic notion of *ayat* (see glossary terms) and in Jewish understandings of "the Torah as a commentary on the world, and the world as a commentary on Torah" (a guiding phrase for the eco-Jewish organization Hazon [2019]).

The Puritan practice of "reading" the Book of Nature, best exemplified in the work of Jonathan Edwards, was particularly pronounced. Weather events, disease, and "success" in settlement were all seen as signs of God's favor or disfavor and a form of "covenantal reply" (Cherry 1980; Edwards 1948). The Book of Nature idea participates in a broader biblical trope that Christian colonial settlers brought with them to what *they* called "the New World": the dualistic vision of the "virgin" landscape as both a wilderness to be tamed and a Garden of Eden to be freely enjoyed by the settlers, a tension that would remain (Merchant 2003). This double-sided trope—in which the colonial project of settlement and missionization (often under the premise of the Catholic Doctrine of Discovery) was interpreted and justified as an essentially religious act—also frequently portrayed Indigenous peoples as "wild men," forces of nature, who should be "tamed" or driven from their land (LaDuke 1999).

The problematic legacies of the Garden-Wilderness trope remain lively today, playing out differently across North America, and continuing to inform the denial of Indigenous land rights, unrestrained resource extraction and land degradation, and the general privatization and poisoning of water, except what is deemed "useful" for human progress (Center for Earth Ethics n.d.; De La Torre 2021; Gilio-Whitaker 2020; Noqueira-Godsey 2021; Pagan 2020). Nevertheless, the view of nature as being both the Garden of Eden and a spiritual book to be read also succeeded in promoting a *habit of attentiveness to nature* that served both the development of Enlightenment science, and an overall attitude of respect and awe for the natural world (Gould 2005; Kimmerer 2018; Stoll 2015). Moreover, from Ralph Waldo Emerson, Margaret Fuller, and Henry David Thoreau in the nineteenth century to, more recently, Howard Thurman, Annie Dillard, Alice Walker, Homero Aridjis, Barry Lopez, Mary Oliver, Robin Wall Kimmerer, and Terry Tempest Williams (among many others) one can see the persistence of the idea that the natural world can—and should—be consulted for spiritual insight and inspiration. Despite the complex legacies of the "Book of Nature" idea, the ecological power of this concept continues to reverberate, not only in the work of religious leaders and theologians but also in the work of many beloved nature writers such as those listed above.

The Human as Khalifa (Steward)

In the North American context, an increasingly "green" conversation is emerging in the Muslim world. Diverse forms of Islamic/Muslim environmentalism echo similar theological reorientations in eco-Jewish and eco-Christian preaching, writing, and activism (Foltz, Denny, and Bararuddin 2003). For "greener" Muslims, the idea that nature is full of "words" and signs, *ayat*, from Allah calls attention to the manifold ways in which protection of nature is divinely commanded (Gade 2019).

This protective task is that of the *khalifa*, Allah's "vice-regent," a key concept in Muslim environmental work (Koehrsen 2021; see the Canadian group, Khaleafa [n.d.]). Groups such as Green Muslims not only embody the concept of *khalifa* but, in so doing, also promote women's leadership and youth involvement in Islamic environmental work (Abdul-Matin 2010; Hancock 2018). Others, including the Islamic Society of North America (ISNA), promote "greening Ramadan" (*ISNA n.d.*) as a logical extension of humanity's vice-regent role.

A wide range of interpretations of the concept of stewardship are also a part of the many "Christianities" and "Judaisms" present in North America. Evangelical Christians

FIGURE 4.1 *Hazon Sukkahfest, an annual retreat to celebrate the holiday of Sukkot ("the Feast of Booths") a traditional, autumnal pilgrimage festival, at Isabella Freedman Jewish Retreat Center (Falls Village, CT). It is meant to honor the time when the ancient Israelites wandered in the desert following the Exodus from Egypt. The holiday's agricultural roots are likely considerably older and many Jewish communities now emphasize the ecological dimensions of celebrating the harvest and dwelling close to the land in the outdoor Sukkah ("booth").* Source: *Hazon/used with permission.*

and their Orthodox Jewish counterparts tend to embrace this biblically rooted idea that intertwines with the "exceptional" status of humans as *imago Dei/ b'tzelem Elohim*, made "in the image of God" (Dewitt 2006). The risk of such conceptual capaciousness, however, is that the term "stewardship" can be easily distorted. In contrast, more liberal Protestants, Catholics, and Jews are often ambivalent about stewardship for different reasons, challenging the often patriarchal, hierarchical, and anthropocentric assumptions folded into the *imago Dei* and *kalifah/steward* concepts. They seek more egalitarian language to capture humans' responsibility for the natural world. Nevertheless, stewardship as a "big tent concept" remains a compelling way to counter the abuses of "dominionship" in the midst of the life-threatening environmental crises we currently face.

Eco-Religion on the Ground

So what does the "lived religion" of ecological commitments look like in North America for Jews, Christians, and Muslims? These "on the ground" initiatives can be grouped into a typology of eco-religious responses: stewardship, "eco-justice" (joining together traditional "environmental justice" and "justice for all creation") and religiously grounded nature spirituality (Jenkins 2008; Kearns 1996). As religious environmentalism has grown, these three typologies of *praxis* have correspondingly diversified, overlapped, and become occasions for debate, while new "types" have arguably emerged (Baugh 2020). For instance, "justice" efforts often invoke the language of stewardship and spirituality, while stewardship work is often attuned to injustice, and eco-feminist/eco-womanist concerns can be found in all three (see Eaton chapter in this volume). Examples of such "on the ground" actions given here include: developing ecologically just food systems (stewardship), confronting the climate crisis and its constituent elements of pollution and urban heating (justice), and creating ways for individuals and communities to connect to nature directly without having to "hide" their Muslim, Christian, or Jewish identities, which some see as threatening, or irrelevant, to ecological action (spirituality). Of course, individuals, small groups, non-governmental organizations (NGOs), and entire denominations have launched a wide range of innovative actions that combine these foci in varied ways (Ellingson 2016; Lothes Biviano 2016; Lysack 2014; McDuff 2010; Schade and Bullitt-Jonas 2019). The examples we give below are simply *representative cases*, windows onto a much wider world of vibrant and creative, religiously-based ecological action.

Stewardship

As discussed earlier, the understanding of humans as stewards or *khalifa* appeals most to those who rely on scriptural/textual foundations, and who are often more traditional in their theological views. In the realm of Christian environmentalism, this has tended to mean those who are more evangelical or biblically oriented. Groups that use the term "stewardship" can have different and competing views, using terms such as "wise use" (dating back to the language of forester Gifford Pinchot) to mask the impact of extractive practices. For example, climate skeptic/denier groups such as the Cornwall Alliance for the Stewardship of Creation (2013) advocate fracking, oil-drilling, and mining for the "gifts" that God has hidden in the earth for human use (see Kearns 2013; Veldman 2019). Such utilitarian interpretations have led other, "greener" evangelicals, such as the Evangelical Environmental Network (Creation Care n.d.), to adopt the term "creation caretakers" to clarify their stance. Often the language of "creation caretaking" and stewardship is combined with an emphasis on individual actions (for example, Green Deen n.d.) and on care/love of the neighbor (Leviticus 19:18; Luke 10:29–37), or the Qur'an's reminder that all creatures are "communities like you" (6:38), expanding the familiar concept of "neighbor" to include all who dwell upon the earth.

Stewardship in the arena of food and agriculture is hardly surprising given the extent to which food is *the* place where all of us "meet" nature in a direct, embodied way. Moreover, for people of faith, food plays a central role in formal religious ritual (such as Communion/the Eucharist), in marking religious identity (eating only kosher or *halal* foods) and in binding a community together through post-ritual gatherings (such as "coffee hour" after church or Ramadan *iftars*). Many Christians have asked if the bread and wine of Communion can truly be considered sacred if the grapes are grown in pesticide-laden

FIGURE 4.2 *Young Evangelicals for Climate Action (YECA) at a demonstration outside of the White House in January 2020.* Source: *Luke Overstreet/YECA/used with permission.*

fields, endangering the health of creatures, workers, and consumers alike (Ayers 2013; Wirzba 2018). Similarly, Muslim and Jewish leaders have sought to expand the concepts "eco-kosher" and "eco-halal" to raise consciousness about sustainable farming practices, practices that minimize harm to animals, workers, and the land's biotic community, while maximizing climate benefits (Arumugam 2009; Waskow 2000).

Given the significant impact that meat production (and consumption) is having on the global climate crisis—not to mention the animal cruelty involved in factory farming—some are actively making the case for vegetarianism or veganism as an authentic way to bring long-standing spiritual and ecological values into everyday eating practices (Clough 2018; Schwartz 2001). Books such as *Vegangelical* (King 2016), podcasts such as *Food and Faith (2018–)*, and organizations such as CreatureKind, JewishVeg, and the Vegan Muslim Initiative all focus on what it means to be a "good steward" in a time of climate crises and at an historical moment when the cruelty of raising and slaughtering animals for meat is increasingly under scientific and ethical scrutiny. At the same time, more orthodox Christians, Muslims, and Jews have pushed back against these efforts, claiming that eating certain kinds of meat is central to religious practice (such as the *Eid al-Adah*, "Feast of the Sacrifice," marking the end of the *hajj*). In such instances, the request from activists is to lessen the amount of meat consumed because of its carbon impact; others focus on reducing food waste for the same reason (watch a Greening Ramadan webinar, see ISNA 2017).

Justice

As is already evident in the discussion of food and stewardship, justice concerns are inherently present in religiously-based environmental work. Activists in all three traditions ask questions concerning the just treatment of agricultural/meat workers and of animals (including insects/bees killed from spraying pesticides, or habitat loss from clearing forests to raise cows) (Ayers 2013; Kasaam and Robinson-Bertoni 2014). Food activists also ask why so much food is wasted (also a contributor to climate change) while people go hungry, and *who* has access to healthy food or land to grow it. The latter two issues have been of great concern among Black religious leaders, and the work of Faith in Place (Kyle and Kearns 2018) and the Black Church Food Security Network (n.d.) provide excellent examples (Carter 2021).

The term "eco-justice" is often used to include all living beings, whereas environmental justice primarily refers to the unequal impacts on humans of pollution, growing desertification, increased temperatures, or rising ocean levels. Today, eco-justice and environmental justice unite under the common umbrella of climate justice, particularly for members of frontline communities who are the most affected. For instance, the air pollution that contributes to trapping greenhouse gases and a warming planet also contributes to the negative health effects of those who live near emitting facilities, an issue that reflects what the COVID-19 pandemic has also made clear, the stark, exacerbating effects of unequal access to clean air (Kearns 2018; see O'Brien chapter and Nogueira-Godsey, Kearns and Bauman chapter in this volume).

Concern for the disproportionate burden caused by pollution and toxic wastes that falls upon people of color and those who are poor has been a central issue for many religious activists dating back to before the well-known 1987 United Church of Christ *Toxic Wastes and Race* report (for the history, see Creation Justice Ministries n.d.); and the 1991 Principles of Environmental Justice where the environment was famously defined by Dana Alston as "where we live, work and play" (Alston 2018). Because justice (welcoming the stranger/care for one's neighbor) is an ancient, central concern of the Abrahamic faiths, many now ask: "What is our responsibility for the safe disposal of hazardous waste, or for the poisoning effects of fossil fuel extraction and expanding consumption, especially when these activities also contribute to global warming?"

Any focus on "global weirding," as the evangelical climate scientist Katherine Hayhoe names it (see her Global Weirding videos n.d.), leads to fundamental questions about the nature of nature. Humans are now "uncreating" the creation, acting "like God" in exerting so much power, demonstrating the very human hubris against which the ancient texts warn (Rasmussen 2012; see also Moe-Lobeda chapter in this volume). Such a stance enacts the "dominion as domination" misinterpretation of Genesis that has consistently held sway in Western culture, severely challenging the future survival of species and peoples. Hundreds of thousands of young people—including those in the communities most affected—have taken to the streets in protest over this robbing from the future.

FIGURE 4.3 *Youth-led School Strikes for Climate took place globally in 2019.* Source: *CityofStPete/CC BY-ND 2.0.*

Because the climate crisis threatens us all, the work to raise awareness and response is often interfaith—we only have one planet, and we must work together. The interfaith organizations Interfaith Power & Light, Earth Ministry, *La Foie et le Bien Commun*/Faith and the Common Good (n.d.), and GreenFaith (n.d.) have had a significant focus on climate action and climate justice. Moving well beyond encouraging houses of worship to use energy efficient light bulbs, these organizations have helped congregations to get "energy audits," to install solar panels on their roofs, and to purchase and advocate for renewable energy and a fossil fuel-free future.

Focusing on the reduction of fossil fuel usage can be challenging in Muslim circles because of preexisting social and political ties with oil-producing Middle Eastern states, but GreenFaith Muslim activists were leaders in the 2015 Islamic Declaration on Climate Change (United Nations 2015). Going even further, GreenFaith activists have staged actions at all the COP United Nation meetings regarding the Paris Climate Agreement, joined Indigenous leaders at pipeline protests to emphasize the need to keep fossil fuels in the ground, protested at financial institutions that profit from fossil fuels, and urged denominations/religious institutions to divest from making money from the fossil fuel industry. These concerns for the justice implications of climate and environmental degradation are also well expressed in most denominational programs, such as the United Methodist Caretakers of Creation (n.d.) or the US Catholic Bishops Environmental Justice Program (n.d.), the Mexican response to the *Indigenous Pastoral*

FIGURE 4.4 *Solar panels on Woodlawn United Church in Dartmouth, Nova Scotia.* Source: *Paulo O/CC BY 2.0.*

FIGURE 4.5 *GreenFaith activists of many different religious traditions protest Enbridge's Line 3 oil pipeline expansion in Minnesota. The pipeline brings tar sands oil, one of the dirtiest forms of fuel, from Alberta, Canada where it has ruined tribal lands.* Source: *Courtesy of Greenfaith.org.*

(Tiedje 2018), and the various religious statements on climate change from the 1990s to the present (see Yale Forum on Religion and Ecology n.d.). As Pope Francis's historic encyclical *Laudato Si* (2015) illustrates so well, justice concerns strike at the very heart of our socioeconomic systems and religious attitudes, calling for profound structural transformations in how we live our lives.

Spirituality

If the work of stewardship evokes humans' responsibilities as the "vice-regents" of God and the call to eco-justice represents humans' responsibilities to their human and more than human neighbors, the cultivation of a "greener" spirituality refers most explicitly to humans' direct, embodied experience of the natural world and the ethical commitments that then emerge. Of course, North American nature spirituality has its *own* history, a history marked by the turn *from* traditional, institutional (usually Christian) religiosity and toward nature itself as the center of meaning and authority, a history that has different racialized narratives (Albanese 1991; Berry 2015; Finney 2014; Gould 2005; Robinson 2021; B. Taylor 2009). From the 1990s onward, however, new spiritually rooted programs have come to the fore, inviting people of faith into direct experience of the natural world in wilderness, pastoral, agricultural, and even urban and suburban contexts (Loorz 2021). Organizations such as the Wild Church Network,

FIGURE 4.6 *Wild Earth Spiritual Community.* Source: *Beth Norcross, the Center for Spirituality and Nature used with permission.*

the Center for Spirituality and Nature, Torah Trek, TEVA, or Wilderness Torah, have quite literally *grounded* their spiritual work in immersive nature experience often making space for the expression of climate grief in a pastoral context (for more, see The BTS Center; Loorz 2021). In so doing, they have bridged the older gaps between "secular" nature spirituality and the "indoor bias" (and ecological neglect) of traditional religious programming (Comins 2007).

The "re-wilding" of Christianity, Judaism and Islam are direct and indirect expressions of theological conversations that have laid the groundwork. The discourse of "Creation Spirituality" is but one example. Initiated by Father Thomas Berry (Tucker and Grim 2016) and Matthew Fox (1991)—whose work is also indebted to the ecofeminist theologian Rosemary Radford Ruether (1975, 1992)—"Creation Spirituality" seeks to overturn the "other-worldly" and anti-science dimensions of the Christian tradition. Berry emphasizes the inherent sacredness of the cosmos and the common genesis story for all found in the "universe story" of evolution, while Fox reinvigorates and reinterprets the ancient idea of "the Cosmic Christ" (that Christ is incarnate in the whole cosmos). Both approaches—while subject to incisive critique (Goodall and Reader 1992; Sideris 2017)—have enabled a simultaneous embrace of science, spirituality and earth-based *praxis*. Creation Spirituality has also played a significant role in the sustainable agricultural and eco-liturgical innovations of a wide swath of "Green Nuns" who have redefined their vows to be deeply attentive to present and future ecological challenges (S.M. Taylor 2009).

In the same way that stewardship and eco-justice work may result in individual experiences of spiritual renewal, eco-spirituality often invokes the language of stewardship and justice, while emphasizing the need for contemplative time in nature as the experiential basis for that work (Christie 2016). Renewal in nature cultivates an appreciation of beauty and an openness to awe, long understood as "religious" by some and can lead to more impassioned levels of ecological commitment (Hessel-Robinson and McNamara 2011). In a Christian context, programs emphasizing immersion in (and celebration of) God's creation can also help to challenge long-standing theological notions of "fallen" nature that militate against Christian ecological action, particularly in conservative Christian contexts.

Whether joining a communal Passover in the (Southern California) Desert, giving praise for the *ayat* of the blossoming fruit trees in a local park, or singing Psalms to the accompaniment of a rushing river, having a direct, embodied experience of the natural world in a context where one can also be fully and openly Muslim, Christian, or Jewish is a potentially transformative experience and one that can lead to broader ecological commitments.

Tensions

As already noted, there are always tensions in religiously-based ecological work. Given the extent to which Christian colonial actions and worldviews shaped North American history, it is not surprising that the primary tensions today are Christian legacies. These can be seen in the tension between concern for this world and holding a primarily "other-worldly" orientation: focusing on "the next life" or on the spiritual in a disembodied, strictly transcendent way. Those who focus more on "the next life" and future reward often argue that it is human well-being, and not the well-being of all creation, that is of primary concern.

While this anthropocentric focus is present in all three traditions, what is particularly problematic is the Christian concept that nature is "fallen," or is *meant* to decline as part of an "end-times" scenario where global destruction precedes the return of Christ (Doran 2017). Such views map onto a general distrust of materiality (of both the body and "the world"), which, in turn, shapes concepts of nature. "Fallen" nature then becomes something to be distrusted, tamed, fixed, and controlled in ways that benefit only humans, even when evidence for care for nature is woven throughout sacred texts (Wallace 2018).

This colonial conception of nature in need of taming, lives in tension with an understanding of North America as a garden, a fecund and abundant New Eden. Within the Garden of Eden motif lies the tension between the "garden" being primarily for human thriving and the garden as fragile and in need of protection (Merchant 2003). Movements to conserve, preserve, and restore the "garden," while beneficent in intent, often involve arguments about an "original" state of nature—or at least a restoration to a thriving eco-system (Van Wieren 2013)—a state that can never really be determined.

These tensions haunt the significant divide within Christianity over acceptance of anthropogenic climate change and the dire need for climate change mitigation and adaptation. The contrasting skepticism and denial, often fueled by those with material interests in a petroleum dominated culture (see Rowe chapter in this volume), appear to align with certain theological worldviews, but even more salient are political, racial, and religious identity. In a PRRI survey in 2014 (Jones, Cox, and Navarro-Rivera 2014), white evangelicals/Pentecostals, white mainline protestants, and white Catholics in the United States shared similar lower levels of climate concern, whereas Jews, Hispanic Catholics, Black Protestants (theologically similar to white evangelicals), and Muslims (lumped into "non-Christian religions") expressed nearly twice the levels of concern (Green the Church n.d.; Kearns 2018).

For all those who seek to find the divine presence in nature, however named, to read the *ayat* written in the more-than-human world, there are those who accuse them of giving in to "pagan" influences and "worshiping creation." This focus on God as only transcendent (and not also immanent) has long been fueled by cultural forces that suppress Indigenous understandings of nature (see Briggs-Cloud chapter in this volume), while fostering a utilitarian focus on all of nature being "meant" for human use. Yet the argument for a singularly transcendent God strikes many as ironic, particularly within a Christian context where the *incarnation* of the Divine in a human body (Jesus, the Christ) is the absolute core of Christian theology.

If the more than human world is infused with the sacred, then, as Jewish, Muslim, and Christian environmentalists all argue, it must be treated with respect and restraint, with an attitude not of entitlement, but of gratitude. While "gratitude practice" lies at the heart of the Abrahamic faiths, this focus on gratitude is sometimes especially emphasized by those who also are shaped by the Indigenous heritages of North America (Kimmerer 2013; Woodley 2012) (see Leduc chapter in this volume).

Finally, as suggested earlier, there exist tensions among the three ideal "types" of eco-religious response outlined above. Some focus more on changing ideas, others on personal actions, and others on political action and structural change, and the literature suggests that changed perspectives do not necessarily lead to changed behavior (Taylor, Van Wieren, and Zaleha 2016). Additionally, the anthropocentrism of stewardship and environmental justice views, however muted, runs up against the views of those who focus on the preservation of wilderness as a spiritual respite from human concerns. Correspondingly, a primary focus on those humans impacted by environmental threats (due to race, class, gender, age, ability, and geographical location) may seem to leave little room for protection of animals or particular bioregions. Despite these prevailing tensions, Christians, Muslims, and Jews are creatively bridging such divides, seeking to care for all.

FIGURE 4.7 *Harvest thanksgiving altar in San Antonio, Huasteca, at a gathering in a Teenek community related to the Huasteca Indigenous Pastoral, which notes that the "seeds of the corn cob" symbolize the coming together of Indigenous religions, identities, languages and Catholicism in search for social liberation and justice.* Source: *Kristina Tiedje/used with permission.*

Conclusion

The terms "Nature," "North America," and "Abrahamic Traditions" each bears the weight of centuries of complex and often contested meanings. When yoked together, the complexity deepens. Furthermore, *how* these meanings are interpreted and conveyed depends greatly on *who* is telling the story. An evangelical Christian elder from Mexico might put these three terms in conversation with each other quite differently than a college-age, progressive Canadian Muslim involved in the First Nations' Idle No More movement.

As is true for all religious traditions, Judaism, Christianity, and Islam are themselves ever changing, transforming themselves across space, time, and cultures, often engaging in internal conflict and debate. In the twenty-first century, the ecological crises we face are unprecedented, already destroying both nature and myriad histories of the human-nature encounter. The present situation requires immediate, sociocultural transformation and religion has always played a central role in such moments of crisis and change. The Abrahamic faiths provide a range of varied, highly creative responses to this crisis, all emerging under "the Tent of Abraham," a tent where the stranger is welcomed, the hungry are fed, the creation is valued and the dispirited are renewed, an ancient ethos that demands our attention today.

Further Reading and Online Resources

Jenkins W., ed. (2010), *Berkshire Encyclopedia of Sustainability*, vol. 1: *The Spirit of Sustainability*, Great Barrington, MA: Berkshire Publishing Group.

Ostrow M. and T.K. Rockefeller (2007), [Documentary] *Renewal: Stories from America's Religious Environmental Movement*, USA: Fine Cut Productions. Available online: http://renewalproject.net/ (accessed September 26, 2021).

Taylor B., ed. (2010), *Encyclopedia of Religion and Nature*, New York: Continuum. Available online: https://doi.org/10.1093/acref/9780199754670.001.0001.

United Nations Environment Programme (UNEP) and Parliament of the World's Religions (2020), "Faith for Earth: A Call for Action," Nairobi: UNEP. Available online: https://parliamentofreligions.org/faith-earth-call-action (accessed September 26, 2021).

Yale Forum on Religion and Ecology (n.d.). Available online: https://fore.yale.edu/ (accessed September 26, 2021).

References

Abdul Matin I. (2010), *Green Deen: What Islam Teaches about Protecting the Planet*, San Francisco: Berrett-Koehler.

Albanese C.L. (1991), *Nature Religion in America: From the Algonkian Indians to the New Age*, Chicago: University of Chicago Press.

Albrecht J. (2011), *Muslim American Environmentalism: An Emerging Environmental Movement in America and Its Implications for Environmentalism and Muslims in America*, Sunnyvale, CA: Lambert Academic Publishing.

Alston D. (2018), "Moving Beyond the Barriers, the First National People of Color Environmental Leadership Summit Proceedings," in C. Wells (ed.), *Environmental Justice in Postwar America*, 178–9, Seattle: University of Washington Press.

Arumugam N. (2009), "Sustainability: The Eco-Halal Revolution," *Patheos*, December 4. Available online: https://www.patheos.com/blogs/altmuslim/2009/12/the_eco-halal_revolution/ (accessed July 28, 2021).

Ayers J. (2013), *Good Food: Grounded Practical Theology*, Waco, TX: Baylor University Press.

Baugh A. (2020), "Nepantla Environmentalism: Challenging Dominant Frameworks for Green Religion," *Journal of the American Academy of Religion*, 88 (3) (September): 832–58.

Bauman W. (2009), *Theology, Creation, and Environmental Ethics: From Creatio Ex Nihilo to Terra Nullius*, New York: Routledge.

Bernstein E. (2005), *The Splendor of Creation*, Cleveland, OH: Pilgrim Press.

Bernstein E. (2021), "The Bible Does Not Validate Endless Exploitation and Domination of the Environment," *Tikkun Magazine*. Available online: https://tinyurl.com/Dominon-is-not-Exploitation (accessed October 10, 2021).

Berry E. (2015), *Devoted to Nature: The Religious Roots of American Environmentalism*, Berkeley: University of California Press.

Black Church Food Security Network (n.d.). Available online: https://blackchurchfoodsecurity.net/ (accessed September 26, 2021).

Carter C. (2021), *The Spirit of Soul Food: Race, Faith, and Food Justice*, Champaign: University of Illinois Press.

Catholic Climate Covenant (n.d.). Available online: https://catholicclimatecovenant.org/ (accessed September 26, 2021).

Center for Earth Ethics (n.d.). Available online: https://centerforearthethics.org (accessed October 12, 2021).

Center for Spirituality and Nature (n.d.). Available online: https://www.centerforspiritualityinnature.org/ (accessed October 11, 2021).

Cherry C. (1980), *Nature and Religious Imagination: From Edwards to Bushnell*, Philadelphia: Fortress Press.

Christie D. (2016), "Nature Writing and Nature Mysticism," in W. Jenkins, M.E. Tucker, and J. Grim (eds.), *Routledge Handbook of Religion and Ecology*, 251–8, London: Routledge.

Chryssavgis J. (2017), "The Face of God in the World: Insights from the Orthodox Christian Tradition," in J. Hart (ed.), *The Wiley Blackwell Companion to Religion and Ecology*, 273–85, Oxford: John Wiley & Sons.

Clough D.L. (2018), *On Animals: Volume II: Theological Ethics*, London: Bloomsbury Publishing.

Cobb, J. and D. Griffin (1976), *Process Thought: An Introductory Exposition*, Philadelphia, PA: Westminster Press.

Comins M. (2007), *A Wild Faith: Jewish Ways into Wilderness, Wilderness Ways into Judaism*, Woodstock, VT: Jewish Lights Publishing.

Cornwall Alliance for the Stewardship of Creation (2013), "The Biblical Perspective of Environmental Stewardship: Subduing and Ruling the Earth to the Glory of God and the Benefit of Our Neighbors." Available online: https://cornwallalliance.org/landmark-documents/the-biblical-perspective-of-environmental-stewardship-subduing-and-ruling-the-earth-to-the-glory-of-god-and-the-benefit-of-our-neighbors/ (accessed September 26, 2021).

Creation Care (n.d.). Available online: https://creationcare.org/ (accessed September 26, 2021).

Creation Justice Ministries (n.d.). Available online: https://www.creationjustice.org/history.html (accessed October 11, 2021).

CreatureKind (n.d.). Available online: http://www.becreaturekind.org/ (accessed September 26, 2021).

Dahill L. and J. Martin-Schramm, eds. (2016), *Eco-Reformation: Grace and Hope for a Planet in Peril*, Eugene, OR: Wipf & Stock Publishers.

De La Torre M. (2021), *Gonna Trouble the Water: Ecojustice, Water, and Environmental Racism*, Cleveland, OH: The Pilgrim Press.

DeWitt C.B. (2006), "Stewardship: Responding Dynamically to the Consequences of Human Action in the World," in R.J. Berry (ed.), *Environmental Stewardship: Critical Perspectives—Past and Present*, 145–58, London: T&T Clark International.

Doran C. (2017), *Hope in the Age of Climate Change: Creation Care This Side of the Resurrection*, Eugene, OR: Cascade Books.

Earth Ministry (n.d.), "Mission, Vision, and Values." Available online: https://earthministry.org/about/ (accessed September 26, 2021).

Edwards, J. (1948), *Images or Shadows of Divine Things*, ed. P. Miller, New Haven, CT: Yale University Press.

Ellingson S. (2016), *To Care for Creation: The Emergence of the Religious Environmental Movement*, Chicago: University of Chicago Press.

Faith and the Common Good/La Foie et le Bien Commun (n.d.). Available online: https://www.faithcommongood.org/ (accessed September 26, 2021).

Faith in Place (n.d.). Available online: https://www.faithinplace.org/ (accessed September 26, 2021).

Finney C. (2014), *Black Faces, White Spaces: Reimagining the Relationship of African Americans to the Great Outdoors*, Chapel Hill: University of North Carolina Press.

The Fire Inside (n.d.), [Film] Available online: http://fireinsidefilm.com/ (accessed September 26, 2021).

Foltz R., F. Denny, and A. Bararuddin, eds. (2003), *Religions of the World and Ecology*, vol. 9: *Islam and Ecology: A Bestowed Trust*, Cambridge, MA: Center for the Study of World Religions, Harvard Divinity School.

Food and Faith (2018–), [Podcast]. Available online: https://foodandfaithpodcast.podbean.com/ (accessed September 26, 2021).

Fox M. (1991), *Creation Spirituality: Liberating Gifts for the Peoples of the Earth*, New York: Harper.

Gade A.M. (2019), *Muslim Environmentalisms: Religious and Social Foundations*, New York: Columbia University Press.

GhaneaBassiri K. (2010), *A History of Islam in America*, Cambridge: Cambridge University Press.

Gilio-Whitaker D. (2020), *As Long as Grass Grows: The Indigenous Fight for Environmental Justice, from Colonization to Standing Rock*, Boston: Beacon Press.

Glave D.D. and M. Stoll, eds. (2006), *To Love the Wind and the Rain: African Americans and Environmental History*, Pittsburgh, PA: University of Pittsburgh Press.

Global Weirding with Katharine Hayhoe (n.d.) https://www.youtube.com/channel/UCi6RkdaEqgRVKi3AzidF4ow (accessed June 24, 2023).

Goodall M. and J. Reader (1992), "Why Matthew Fox Fails to Change the World," in I. Ball, M. Goodall, C. Palmer, and J. Reader (eds.), *The Earth Beneath: A Critical Guide to Green Theology*, 104–19, London: SPCK.

Gould R.K. (2005), *At Home in Nature*, Berkeley: University of California Press.

Gould R.K. (2007), "Binding Life to Values," in J. Isham and S. Waage (eds.), *Ignition: How a Grassroots Movement Can Stop Global Warming*, 119–33, Washington, DC: Island Press.

Gould, R.K. and L. Kearns (2018), "Ecology and Religious Environmentalism in the United States," in J. Corrigan (ed.), *Oxford Encyclopedia of Religion and America*, 604–46, Oxford: Oxford University Press.

Green Deen (n.d.). Available online: https://www.greendeen.org (accessed September 26, 2021).

GreenFaith (n.d.). Available online: www.greenfaith.org (accessed September 26, 2021).

Green Muslims (n.d.). Available online: http://www.greenmuslims.org/ (accessed September 25, 2021).

Green the Church (n.d.). Available online: https://www.greenthechurch.org (accessed September 25, 2021).

Hancock R. (2018), *Islamic Environmentalism: Activism in the United States and Great Britain*, Routledge Advances in Sociology, New York: Routledge.

Hazon (2019), "Mission & Vision." Available online: https://hazon.org/about/mission-vision/ (accessed September 25, 2021).

Hessel T. and R.R. Ruether (eds.) (2000), *Religions of the World and Ecology*, vol. 3: *Christianity and Ecology: Seeking the Well-Being of Earth and Humans*, Cambridge, MA: Harvard University Press.

Hessel-Robinson T. and R.M. McNamara, eds. (2011), *Spirit and Nature: The Study of Christian Spirituality in a Time of Ecological Urgency*, vol. 163, Eugene, OR: Wipf and Stock Publishers.

Hiebert T. (2000), "The Human Vocation: Origins and Transformations in Christian Traditions," in T. Hessel and R.R. Ruether (eds.), *Religions of the World and Ecology*, vol. 3: *Christianity and Ecology: Seeking the Well-Being of Earth and Humans*, 135–54, Cambridge, MA: Harvard University Press.

Interfaith Center for Sustainable Development (n.d.). Available online: https://www.interfaithsustain.com (accessed September 25, 2021)

Interfaith Power & Light (n.d.). Available online: https://www.interfaithpowerandlight.org/ (accessed September 25, 2021).

Islamic Society of North America (ISNA) (2015), "The Green Masjid Project." Available online: https://isna.net/wp-content/uploads/2020/04/isnagreenmasjid.pdf (accessed June 23, 2023).

Islamic Society of North America (ISNA) (2017), "Webinar: Greening Ramadan," YouTube, May 26, 2017. Available online: https://www.youtube.com/watch?v=VSOT3yPJ8U0&t (accessed June 23, 2023).

Islamic Society of North America (ISNA) (n.d.-a). Available online: https://isna.net/ (accessed September 26, 2021).

Islamic Society of North America (ISNA) (n.d.-b), "Green Ramadan." Available online: https://isna.net/greenramadan/ (accessed June 23, 2023).

Jenkins W. (2008), *Ecologies of Grace: Environmental Ethics and Christian Theology*, Oxford: Oxford University Press.

JewishVeg (n.d.), "Home." Available online: http://www.jewishveg.org (accessed June 23, 2023).

Johnson E. (2015), *Ask the Beasts: Darwin and the God of Love*, London: Bloomsbury.

Jones R., D. Cox, and J. Navarro-Rivera (2014), "Believers, Sympathizers, & Skeptics: Why Americans Are Conflicted about Climate Change, Environmental Policy, and Science," Public Research Religion Institute, November 21. Available online: http://goo.gl/KR64Rc (accessed September 26, 2021).

Kairos-Faithful Action for Justice (n.d.), "Home." Available online: https://www.kairoscanada.org/ (accessed September 26, 2021).

Kassam Z. and S.E. Robinson (2014), "Islam and Food," in D.M. Kaplan and P.B. Thompson (eds.), *Encyclopedia of Food and Agricultural Ethics*, 1282–91, Dordrecht: Springer Netherlands.

Kearns L. (1996), "Saving the Creation: Christian Environmentalism in the United States," *Sociology of Religion*, 57 (1): 55–70.

Kearns L. (2013), "Green Evangelicals," in B. Steensland and P. Goff (eds.), *The New Evangelical Social Engagement*, 157–73, New York: Oxford University Press.

Kearns L. (2018), "Conspiring Together: Breathing for Justice," in L. Hobgood and W. Bauman (eds.), *The Bloomsbury Handbook of Religion and Nature: The Elements*, 117–32, London: Bloomsbury Publishing.

Keller C. (2003), *The Face of the Deep: A Theology of Becoming*, New York: Routledge.

Keller C. (2008), *On the Mystery: Discerning God in Process*, Minneapolis, MN: Fortress.

Khaleafa (n.d.). Available online: http://www.khaleafa.com/ (accessed September 25, 2021).

Kimmerer R.W. (2013), *Braiding Sweetgrass: Indigenous Wisdom, Scientific Knowledge and the Teachings of Plants*, Minneapolis, MN: Milkweed Editions.

Kimmerer R.W. (2018), "Mishkos Kenomagwen, the Lessons of Grass: Restoring Reciprocity with the Good Green Earth," in M.K. Nelson and D. Shilling (eds.), *Traditional Ecological Knowledge: Learning from Indigenous Practices for Environmental Sustainability*, 27–56, Cambridge: Cambridge University Press.

King S.K. (2016), *Vegangelical: How Caring for Animals Can Shape Your Faith*, Grand Rapids, MI: Zondervan.

Koehrsen J. (2021), "Muslims and Climate Change: How Islam, Muslim Organizations, and Religious Leaders Influence Climate Change Perceptions and Mitigation Activities," *Wiley Interdisciplinary Reviews: Climate Change*, 12 (3): e702. Available online: https://doi.org/10.1002/wcc.702.

Kyle V. and L. Kearns (2018), "The Bitter and the Sweet of Nature: Weaving a Tapestry of Migration Stories," in M. Krasny (ed.), *Grassroots to Global: Broader Impacts of Civic Ecology*, 41–64, Ithaca, NY: Cornell University Press.

LaDuke W. (1999), *All Our Relations: Native Struggles for Land and Life*, Boston: South End Press.

Laudato Si (2015). Available online: https://www.laudatosi.va/en.html (accessed October 11, 2021).

Loorz V. (2021), *Church of the Wild: How Nature Invites Us into the Sacred*, Minneapolis, MN: Broadleaf Press.

Lothes Biviano E. (2016), *Inspired Sustainability: Planting Seeds for Action*, Maryknoll, NY: Orbis Books.

Loy D. (2003), "The Religion of the Market," in R.C. Foltz (ed.), *Worldviews, Religion, and the Environment: A Global Anthology*, 66–76, Belmont, CA: Wadsworth.

Lysack M. (2014), "Stepping Up to the Plate: Climate Change, Faith Communities and Effective Environmental Advocacy in Canada," in R.G. Veldman, A. Szasz, and R. Haluza-Delay (eds.), *How the World's Religions Are Responding to Climate Change: Social Scientific Investigations*, 157–73, New York: Routledge.

McDuff M.D. (2010), *Natural Saints: How People of Faith Are Working to Save God's Earth*, Oxford: Oxford University Press.

McFague S. (1993), *The Body of God: An Ecological Theology*, Minneapolis, MN: Augsburg Fortress Publishers.

McFague S. (2008), *A New Climate for Theology: God, the World, and Global Warming*, Minneapolis, MN: Fortress Press.

Merchant C. (2003), *Reinventing Eden: The Fate of Nature in Western Culture*, New York: Routledge.

Mevorach I. (2017), "The Divine Environment (al-Muhit) and the Body of God: Seyyed Hossein Nasr and Sallie McFague Resacralize Nature," in J. Hart (ed.), *The Wiley Blackwell Companion to Religion and Ecology*, 301–14, Oxford: John Wiley & Sons.

Moe-Lobeda C. (2013), *Resisting Structural Evil: Love as Ecological-Economic Vocation*, Minneapolis, MN: Fortress Press.

Nasr S.H. (1968), *The Encounter of Man and Nature: The Spiritual Crisis of Modern Man*, London: George Allen and Unwin.

Nogueira-Godsey, E. (2021), "A Decological Way to Dialogue: Rethinking Ecofeminism and Religion," in E. Tomalin and C. Starkey (eds.), *The Routledge Handbook of Religions, Gender and Society*, New York: Routledge.

Pagán M. (2020), "Cultivating a Decolonial Feminist Integral Ecology: Extractive Zones and the Nexus of the Coloniality of Being/Coloniality of Gender," *Journal of Hispanic/Latino Theology*, 22 (1): Article 6. Available online: https://repository.usfca.edu/jhlt/vol22/iss1/6 (accessed September 26, 2021).

Primavesi A. (1991), *From Apocalypse to Genesis: Ecology, Feminism, and Christianity*, Tunbridge Wells, UK: Burns and Oates.

Rasmussen L.L. (2012), *Earth-Honoring Faith: Religious Ethics in a New Key*, New York: Oxford University Press.

Reuther R.R. (1975), *New Woman, New Earth: Sexist Ideologies and Human Liberation*, New York: Seabury Press.

Ruether R.R. (1992), *Gaia & God: An Ecofeminist Theology of Earth Healing*, New York: HarperCollins.

Robinson T. (2021), "He Talked to Trees! 'Thinking Differently' about Nature with Howard Thurman," *Spiritus: A Journal of Christian Spirituality*, 21 (1) (Spring): 1–19.

Schade L. and M. Bullitt-Jonas, eds. (2019), *Rooted and Rising: Voices of Courage in a Time of Climate Crisis*, Lanham, MD: Rowman & Littlefield Publishers.

Schorsch I. (1992), "Learning to Live with Less," in S. Rockefeller and J. Elder (eds.), *Spirit and Nature: Why the Environment Is a Religious Issue*, 25–38, Boston: Beacon Press.

Schwartz R.L. (2001), *Judaism and Vegetarianism*, New York: Lantern Publishing & Media.

Scully M. (2003), *Dominion: The Power of Man, the Suffering of Animals, and the Call to Mercy*, New York: Macmillan.

Sideris L. (2017), *Consecrating Science: Wonder, Knowledge, and the Natural World*, Berkeley: University of California Press.

Stoll M. (2015), *Inherit the Holy Mountain: Religion and the Rise of American Environmentalism*, New York: Oxford University Press.

Taylor B. (2009), *Dark Green Religion: Nature Spirituality and the Planetary Future*, Berkeley: University of California Press.

Taylor B., G. Van Wieren, and B. Zaleha (2016), "The Greening of Religion Hypothesis (Part Two): Assessing the Data from Lynn White, Jr, to Pope Francis," *Journal for the Study of Religion, Nature & Culture*, 10 (3): 306–78.

Taylor S.M. (2009), *Green Sisters: A Spiritual Ecology*, Cambridge, MA: Harvard University Press.

TEVA (n.d.). Available online: www.hazon.org/teva (accessed September 26, 2021).

Thomas K. ([1983] 1991), *Man and the Natural World: Changing Attitudes in England 1500–1800*, London: Penguin UK.

Tiedje K. (2018), "Articulating Indigenous Ecologies: The Indigenous Pastoral in the Huasteca, Mexico," in E. Berry and R. Albro (eds.), *Church, Cosmovision and the Environment: Religion and Social Conflict in Contemporary Latin America*, 195–224, New York: Routledge.

Tirosh-Samuelson H. (2002), *Religions of the World and Ecology*, vol. 8: *Judaism and Ecology: Created World and Revealed Word*, Cambridge, MA: Center for the Study of World Religions, Harvard Divinity School.

Torah Trek (n.d.). Available online: http://www.torahtrek.com/ (accessed October 11, 2021).

Troster L. (1998), "The Blessings of Holiness," in E. Bernstein (ed.), *Ecology and the Jewish Spirit*, 200–6, Woodstock, VT: Jewish Lights Publishing.

Tucker M.E. and J. Grim (2016), *Thomas Berry: Selected Writings on the Earth Community*, Maryknoll, NY: Orbis Books.

United Church of Christ Commission for Racial Justice (1987), *Toxic Wastes and Race in the United States: A National Report on the Racial and Socio-Economic Characteristics of Communities with Hazardous Waste Sites*, New York: United Church of Christ Commission for Racial JusticeAvailable online: https://www.ucc.org/what-we-do/justice-local-church-ministries/justice/faithful-action-ministries/environmental-justice-ministries/ (accessed June 23, 2023).

United Methodist Caretakers of Creation (n.d.). Available online: https://www.umccreationcare.org/ (accessed October 11, 2021).

United Nations (2015)," Islamic Declaration on Climate Change," August 18. Available online: https://unfccc.int/news/islamic-declaration-on-climate-change (accessed September 26, 2021).

US Catholic Bishops Environmental Justice Program (n.d.). Available online: https://www.usccb.org/issues-and-action/human-life-and-dignity/environment/environmental-justice-program (accessed October 12, 2021).

Van Wieren G. (2013), *Restored to Earth: Christianity, Environmental Ethics, and Ecological Restoration*, Washington, DC: Georgetown University Press.

Vegan Muslim (n.d.), "Home." Available online: http://www.veganmuslims.com/ (accessed September 26, 2021).

Veldman R.G. (2019), *The Gospel of Climate Skepticism*, Berkeley: University of California Press.

Walker P. (2013), [Documentary] *The Fire Inside: Place, Passion, and the Primary of Nature*, USA: Small Circle Films.

Wallace M.I. (2018), *When God Was a Bird*, New York: Fordham University Press.

Ward-Lev N. (2019), *The Liberating Path of the Hebrew Prophets: Then and Now*, Maryknoll, NY: Orbis Books.

Waskow A. (1982), *Seasons of Our Joy: A Handbook of Jewish Festivals*, Toronto: Bantam Books.

Waskow A., ed. (2000), *Torah of the Earth: Exploring 4,000 Years of Ecology in Jewish Thought*, vol. 1, Woodstock, VT: Jewish Lights Publishing.

Waskow A. (2020), *Dancing in God's Earthquake: The Coming Transformation of Religion*, Maryknoll, NY: Orbis Books.

Waskow, A., J. Chittister, and S.S. Chishti (2007), *The Tent of Abraham: Stories of Hope and Peace for Jews, Christians, and Muslims*, Boston: Beacon Press.

White L. (1967), "The Historical Roots of Our Ecologic Crisis," *Science*, 155 (3767): 1203–7.

Wild Church Network (n.d.), "Home." Available online: https://www.wildchurchnetwork.com/ (accessed September 26, 2021).

Wilderness Torah (n.d.). Available online: https://wildernesstorah.org/ (accessed September 26, 2021).

Wirzba N. (2018), *Food and Faith: A Theology of Eating*, Cambridge: Cambridge University Press.

Woodley R. (2012), *Shalom and the Community of Creation: An Indigenous Vision*, Grand Rapids, MI: Wm. B. Eerdmans Publishing.

Worldviews (2015), Special Issue, "Religion, Disability, and the Environment," 19 (1). https://www.jstor.org/stable/i40156083.

Yale Forum on Religion and Ecology (n.d.), "Climate Change Statements from World Religions." Available online: https://fore.yale.edu/Climate-Emergency/Climate-Change-Statements-from-World-Religions (accessed September 26, 2021).

Young Evangelicals for Climate Action (n.d.). Available online: https://yecaction.org (accessed October 11, 2021).

Glossary Terms

Anthropocentrism Worldviews that are primarily human (anthro) centered. In environmental terms (particularly in religious and philosophical discourse), anthropocentric perspectives are typically contrasted with *bio*centric perspectives where nature is given moral consideration according to its *intrinsic value*, as opposed to its availability simply as resource for human use (*utilitarianism*). The term can be confused with androcentrism, which means male centered, but an eco-feminist critique would highlight the connection between the two. Of course, all perspectives can be said to be anthropocentric to a certain degree in that views of the world are created from within human cultures. Ecological anthropocentrism, then, is better understood when placed on a continuum where attitudes toward nature can be described and evaluated as more or less anthropocentric. Thus, valuing the natural world for its aesthetic beauty (and arguing for the preservation of nature on aesthetic grounds) could be said to be "anthropocentric" in that the human desire for beauty informs the valuation of nature. Nevertheless, such a view is considerably *less* anthropocentric than a view that regards nature simply as a resource for economic gain and material comfort, such as food, medicines, building materials, or fuel, or as a mere "stage" upon which the human drama is acted out. From the mid-nineteenth century onward, the Abrahamic faiths have been criticized on ecological grounds for being notably anthropocentric (relative, say, to Buddhism, Hinduism, and Indigenous traditions), particularly in terms of theological concepts that elevate the role of humans as being at the top of the Great Chain of Being, made in the image of God (*imago Dei*/*b'tzelem Elohim*) and commanded by God to rule over the natural world. Equally, anthropocentric is the notion that all of nature is a gift from God for humans to use, and only has value in terms of its utility or value to humans, namely, nature does not have intrinsic value. Scholars and religious thinkers have pushed back against this criticism, however, arguing for the special responsibilities that humans have as stewards of creation and as the only species that has the power to create or destroy the planet on which they dwell, and that creation is of value separate from humans. Many decades of scholarship and activism has brought more nuance to the question of whether or not Judaism, Christianity, and Islam are fundamentally anthropocentric. On a theological level, however, these traditions are more accurately *theocentric*, not anthropocentric, with God (*theo*) being the ultimate focus of human action. Theologically rooted environmental ethics stresses this theocentric orientation, arguing that God cares for all of God's creations and expects humanity to extend this ethic of care to all life. All adherents, however, have to wrestle with the material reality that no matter how they think about it, humans have altered the workings of eco-systems and the planet in deep and destructive ways that demand human action.

Ayat Originally a sociopolitical term denoting spiritual leaders deemed to be the successors of Muhammad (in English, "the caliph"). The Islamic term ayat simultaneously denotes: (1) one of the 6,236 verses of the Qur'an, (2) a miracle, (3) a moral, and (4) an instructive, or simply beautiful, "sign" of God's presence in the natural world (a particular mountain, bird, flower, or stream all may manifest as ayat). With its rich interlayering of meanings, ayat is worthy of note because it emphasizes the extent to which nature, sacred texts, ethics, and Divine action are all conceptually interwoven.

Several concepts are frequently emphasized in Islamic/Muslim environmentalism, beginning with *tawhid*, the affirmation that "there is no God but God." *Tawhid* describes the interconnectedness of all things in God, celebrating the unity of all creation as an expression of God. The idea of *mizan*, the balance and harmony found throughout the universe, similarly speaks of God's presence. Additionally, the concept of *ayat*—any one of the 6,236 verses of the Qur'an—is also applied to creation, which is filled with *ayats*, signs of God's presence.

These core concepts combine to emphasize both the goodness of creation, and that humans are called by God to serve as *khalifa*, vice-regents, or stewards, of the earth. In this understanding, care for the creation is a religious duty, part of *maslahah*, or public service, prioritizing the good of the community over individual interests. With these concepts in mind, it is easy to see how climate change, pollution, and species extinction—all of which diminish God's presence and disrupt the *mizan*—would be considered *haram*, forbidden. While the concept of *haram* is generally used in contrast to *halal* (permitted foods), Muslim environmentalists have expanded the idea of *halal* to address animal welfare and suffering, as well as related agri-business concerns such as the ethical treatment of both workers and the soil.

Many "green" Muslim groups also use halal to discuss the relationship between food waste and greenhouse gas emissions, focusing especially on the iftars (feasts) that break the daily fasts during Ramadan. Historically, because one is blessed by being generous, iftars are marked by both surplus and waste (hence the genesis of the creative concept of *leftars*, iftars made of leftovers!). Such practices of waste-reduction are also tied to hadith about the Prophet's admonition not to waste water during *wudu*, the ritual washing before prayers. Here again, an ancient principle is expanded into a broad warning against excess. In the face of a capitalist economy that encourages overconsumption, the prohibition against usury (*riba*) is also used to chasten unearned profit at others' expense, including the creation.

The greening of mosques is another significant area of activism (for more, see ISNA 2015), especially in the realm of energy reduction, where wastefulness is allied with the notion that "all the earth is a mosque" and should be treated as such. Finally, the ancient concept of *harim* lands (protected areas) is increasingly being used in contemporary land conversation efforts.

As with any religious tradition, new/ old interpretations of sacred writings are often resisted. A critique of fossil fuel consumption lies in tension with the central focus on petroleum production of many Islamic states. Others claim that environmentalism is a Western imposition. As in Judaism and Christianity, Islam contains theological concepts that can be deployed to argue that climate degradation is part of God's plan, or that an omnipotent God will always protect the earth. Perhaps stronger, however, is the foundational commitment to care for your neighbor in just ways, a promising motivation to fight for environmental justice.

Jewish environmentalism A movement with roots in the ancient commandment, "Justice, Justice, shall you pursue" (Deuteronomy 16:20; Exodus 23:8). The pursuit of justice has always been considered central to Jewish practice (as the repetition of "justice" implies), with some ancient texts supporting the view that protesting against evil is as important as religious observance. From this emphasis on justice comes the long-standing notion of *tikkun olam* ("repair of the world") as being central to ethical Jewish life. Since the 1970s, the notion of *tikkun olam* has been cast in particularly environmental terms, with a focus on the physical, ecological repair that the earth itself urgently requires.

Judaism's environmental focus was first birthed in the most progressive streams of Judaism (Reform, Reconstructionist and Renewal), and was notably encouraged by Rabbi Zalman Schacter-Shalomi (1924–2014), the founder of the Jewish Renewal movement. In 1988, Ellen Bernstein founded *Shomrei Adamah* ("Keepers of the Earth"), the first North American Jewish environmental organization, although it was preceded by the Shalom Center (1983) whose peace and justice work has always had a strong environmental component. From the 1990s onward, the Coalition on the Environment and Jewish Life (COEJL), Hazon, Canfei Nesharim (offering an orthodox perspective), and most recently, Dayenu: A Jewish Call to Climate Action, among others, have all sought to make explicit the inherent connection between Jewish identity and environmental commitment. Research has shown that the rise in Jewish environmentalism has brought some disaffected Jews "back to Judaism" in terms of community engagement and diverse forms of observance, particularly among young people.

Jewish environmental initiatives have included: re-enlivening the agricultural roots of the Jewish Holidays (first articulated in Arthur Waskow's *Seasons of Our Joy* [1982]), emphasizing "neglected" holidays such as *Tu B'shavat* (the Jewish New Year for the Trees) and bringing new ecological vision to cyclical calendric observances such as *shmita*, the sabbatical year when land lies fallow, debts are forgiven, and food is redistributed to those in need. Other innovations include developing environmental interpretations of ancient ethical principles (such as *Bal Taschit* "Do Not Destroy") and, most importantly, emphasizing the urgency of *tikkun olam* work in the face of the growing climate crisis. Jewish activist work has included protest and civil disobedience, particularly in response to the unequal harms caused by fracking and the building of fossil-fuel pipelines across Indigenous lands. As with their Christian and Muslim counterparts, Jewish environmentalists have advocated for and participate in interfaith initiatives, particular in the realm of climate justice work.

Jewish critics of Jewish environmentalism have expressed concerns about whether environmental work should be considered a priority when anti-Semitism and "assimilationism" continue to be significant issues for many North American Jews. Their critiques have focused on the question of whether Jewish communities have "bigger things to worry about" than the fate of the earth. While acknowledging the unique challenges that Jewish communities face, Jewish environmentalists have responded that if there is not a sustainable environment in which to live, other traditional "Jewish" concerns will no longer be relevant.

The Priestly Story The story of creation that is narrated in the book of Genesis (1:1–2:4a), which contrasts—in substance, style, and tone—with the second, older, story of creation found in Genesis 2:4b–25, the "J" or Yahwist story. These two stories both offer rich resources for pondering Jewish and Christian perspectives on the God-human-nature relationship, but the tales themselves are strikingly divergent. Understanding "the creation story" as being, in fact, two creation stories gives us a window into the diversity and complexity of the potentially "ecological" messages in Genesis.

The scholarly names given to these two stories come from a long history of biblical criticism, known as Source Criticism, which has theorized four distinct—although often overlapping—narrative strands running through the first five books of the Hebrew Bible/Christian Old Testament. While the exact nature of the sources (a single text, a multiauthored text, an assemblage of oral traditions) is unknown and their precise dating is a matter of scholarly debate, the broad claims of Source Criticism are generally accepted by biblical scholars. These sources are: J (Yahwist, with J representing the English name "Jehovah" that was derived from the Hebrew letters of the divine name YHVH), E (Elohist), P (Priestly), and D (Deuteronomist). The J and E sources come from the southern and northern kingdoms of ancient Israel, likely beginning as oral traditions. They are most easily identifiable through the different names used for God—YHVH, the sacred name of God revealed to Moses (J source) and Elohim (E source)—but are also marked by other distinctions, including differences in the historical, political, and theological themes that are emphasized. The Priestly Source, by contrast, is a "younger" source, one that draws on aspects of J and E, while also promoting the interests of the priests, thereby expressing a more "elite" view. The extent of "pre-exilic" and "post-exilic" material in P is still debated, nevertheless, the Priestly Source certainly reflects the conditions of the Babylonian Exile (586 BCE), such that the language of "subduing" in Genesis 1 may reflect not only the harshness of the desert landscape but also the longings of the Judean people to overcome their condition of exile.

In the opening chapter of Genesis, the creation story is told in regal tones, emphasizing hierarchy and portraying a transcendent God who calls the world into being through the spoken words "let there be." The "dominion" role given to humanity not surprisingly reflects the authoritative role of the priests. By contrast, most of Genesis 2 consists of a story that is typical of the J source: God is portrayed in intimate, immanent and human-like terms. Moreover, God gets God's "hands dirty" in the work of creation, molding humanity from rich, arable soil and enlivening all creatures with divine breath. Here the essential work of humanity is not portrayed as dominion, but as that of a servant who must, as the Hebrew words directly state, "guard and tend" the land.

5

Asian Religions and Nature in North America

Elizabeth Allison

The Pervasive Influence of Asian Religions on American Environmental Thought

The extensive influence of Asian religions on the environmental movement in the United States is under-recognized. Scholars widely credit the European Romantic movement in literature, philosophy, and the arts for shaping American environmental thought. However, another significant stream of influence is also present. Asian thought, particularly Hinduism, Buddhism, Taoism, and Jainism, influenced early and contemporary advocates for nature. Even Romantic thought carries influences from India and Hinduism. The German idealist F.W.J. Schelling (1775–1854) drew on Eastern philosophies to develop his views on nature; Schelling lauded the "sacred texts of the Indians" over the Bible (Clarke 2006: 63); Hegel drew on the philosophies of India and China in his own work (65). A close examination of the history of Asian religions, particularly Hinduism and Buddhism, in the United States, shows how they are interwoven with the history of environmental thought. Influence from Asian religions has colored Americans' perceptions of wilderness and nature conservation most noticeably, and has also influenced approaches to foodways and the nuclear threat.

The non-dual approach of Asian religions, particularly Indian Vedanta and Zen Buddhism, has been influential on American nature advocates. As understood by their American interpreters, Asian religions offered a more holistic, integrated, and organic

---

This chapter is dedicated to the memory of Steven D. Goodman (1945–2020), Professor of Buddhism at the California Institute of Integral Studies.

perception of the human embedded in nature. Asian religions emphasize compassion for living beings, drawing on nature symbolism to depict human relations to the divine. The aesthetic sense of coherence of many Asian traditions, as well as habits of analogical thinking, appreciation of the particular, and resistance to freezing categories distinguish them from Euro-American preferences for objectivity, uniformity, determinacy, and universal logic stemming from first principles (Callicott and Ames 1989: 15).

Though Asian religions share commonalities, the traditions are distinct. Buddhism, which arose in India, traveled to Tibet, and spread throughout Asia, seeks the cessation of suffering and the attainment of nirvana through the insights and practices of the Noble Eightfold Path. Hinduism, expressed through myriad sects in India, Nepal, Sri Lanka, and other Asian countries, refers to a broad set of ideas and practices that originated in India, flowing from four sources: (1) the original inhabitants of India; (2) the Indus Valley civilization (2500 BCE–1500 BCE); (3) the Dravidian culture; and (4) the ancient Vedic religion (Williamson 2010: 18). For many Indians, religion is culturally based and thus not amenable to conversion or proselytization. However, enthusiastic study of Hindu texts and practices has influenced American culture since the time of the transcendentalists. The United States is home to both Hindus of the South Asian diaspora, and Americans of all backgrounds who have adopted Hindu-inspired practices (see Syman 2010; Willliamson 2010).

Asian thought influenced the American environmental movement from centers on the two coasts. The vicinity of Boston was the center of transcendentalism that introduced Asian thought, particularly Hinduism and yoga, to the United States. Taoism, which encourages harmony with the Tao understood to flow through all reality, and Confucianism, with a reverence for elders and a well-ordered society, arrived on the Pacific coast with successive waves of immigrants from China and Japan, as did Buddhism. From these centers of influence, Asian thought informed many leading American scholars, naturalists, and writers.

Both the Romantic movement and Asian religions bequeathed an idealist bent—a sense that human ideas about the natural world shape the way that people act—to the environmental movement, through the writings of Ralph Waldo Emerson and Henry David Thoreau, which then inspired John Muir and Aldo Leopold, widely influential in creating the preservationist movement to protect public lands and wilderness. The religious thought of India guided the noted humanitarian and physician Albert Schweitzer, who in turn influenced Aldo Leopold and Rachel Carson. Asian religions influenced deep ecologists such as Arne Naess and led to the creation of the contemporary transdisciplinary field of religion and ecology.

When the UCLA historian Lynn White Jr. published a short article in the journal *Science* in 1967 identifying the "historical roots of our ecologic crisis" as being rooted in Christianity, and calling for a turn to the "Zen Buddhism of the Beats," he was identifying a movement of thought that had been evident for more than a century already. Those fearing that environmentalism was a new religion challenging the dominance of Christianity were perhaps correct because leading environmental thinkers were so thoroughly influenced by concepts from Asian religions. If American values elevated humans over nature, property over people, and a unitary omnipotent God over animistic gods, those who critiqued the environmental movement as anti-American were correct.

Transcendentalism, Yoga, and Nature

For new Americans, the continent's vast wilderness appeared "hideous and desolate," as William Bradford proclaimed upon disembarking the *Mayflower* (cited in Nash 1973: 23–4). Industrious Americans set about shaping the new territory to their needs. Taming the wilderness was essential to Americans' self-identity: increasing perceived physical safety made taming the wilderness a moral, as well as utilitarian, duty (Nash 1973).

Asian religions arrived in North America not long after the founding of the United States. Transcendentalists, including Ralph Waldo Emerson and Henry David Thoreau, studied translations of Hindu texts, absorbing Asian philosophies into their worldviews. These same figures were instrumental in reshaping American attitudes of nature away from purely utilitarian use toward reverent appreciation.

The Reverend William Emerson, a Unitarian minister and armchair Orientalist living in Boston, helped found the *Monthly Anthology*, which published a famous Hindu play *Sacontalá; or The Fatal Ring*, in 1805. The senior Emerson introduced his family, including his son Ralph Waldo Emerson (1803–82), later a leading figure of transcendentalism, to the religion and culture of India, which Ralph Waldo continued to study at Harvard University.

Emerson's enthusiasm for Hindu texts facilitated their introduction into the United States and influenced his transcendental approach to nature: he called for solitude for the purposes of reverent contemplation in natural spaces (Christy [1932] 1972; Syman 2010). Emerson's recommendation of Hindu texts to his friend and student Henry David Thoreau motivated Thoreau's decision to retreat to Walden Pond in 1845, where he engaged in Hindu-inspired yoga—seeking union with the ultimate—through practices of asceticism, devotion, abstaining from animal products, meditation, and attunement of his senses with the forest (Christy [1932] 1972; McShane 1964; Syman 2010). Thoreau's writings influenced many subsequent environmental luminaries who shaped the way Americans view the landscape, including Frederick Law Olmsted (designer of Central Park), John Muir, and Aldo Leopold. His writings on nonviolent civil disobedience have been especially important to the environmental movement as it has relied on this method, most recently with extended protests against the Dakota Access Pipeline.

With other transcendentalists, Emerson founded *The Dial*, which published English translations of Buddhist and Hindu scriptures, in 1840. In 1857, Emerson published an unsigned poem "Brahma," which celebrated nonduality—"shadow and sunlight are the same"—and repudiated Christianity in the influential *Atlantic Monthly*. In elevating the Hindu concept of Brahman, the Absolute, *The Atlantic* was signaling a new palatability of these concepts for Americans (Syman 2010).

FIGURE 5.1 *Henry David Thoreau's cabin at Walden Pond. Source: Nick Pedersen/Getty Images.*

On the other side of the Atlantic, not long after Charles Darwin published *On the Origin of Species* (1859), the German naturalist, zoologist, medical doctor, and artist Ernst Haeckel (1834–1919), influenced by Spinoza and Goethe, who had studied Asian thought, coined the term *oekologie* (1866), in reference to his perception of the planet as a unified whole, with the diversity of organisms living together in both harmony and competition, setting the stage for the introduction of the field of ecology (Grim and Tucker 2014: 65).

Chinese Immigration, John Muir, and "Nature's Cathedral"

While Emerson and Thoreau were developing the transcendental perception of nature on the East Coast, Chinese immigrants were streaming into the West Coast to work on "Gold Mountain." The innovation of Chinese workers helped build the American West, including the transcontinental railroad that opened the region to settlement. They built Confucian and Taoist temples in San Francisco, while suffering xenophobia, harassment, and lynching. In a few decades, the prevalence of Chinese workers increased dramatically: from less than 1 percent in 1850 to more than 50 percent of gold miners in 1870 (Jiobu 1988: 34). Chinese immigrants also took on roles that

FIGURE 5.2 *Chinese workers in the Sierra.* Source: *Library of Congress Prints and Photographs Division, Washington, DC.*

supported the mining industry, providing laundry services, vegetables to supplement the miners' monotonous diets, and legendary meals (Chan 2017). Despite, or because of these contributions, the Chinese Exclusion Act of 1882 then prevented immigration until 1943.

The magnificent landscape of what is now Yosemite National Park in California's Sierra Nevada mountain range has had an outsized role in shaping American perceptions of nature. Chinese immigrants were essential in creating Yosemite National Park and, by extension, the entire national park system (Chan 2017). Lauded for their industry and ingenuity, Chinese workers built the mountain roads facilitating access to Yosemite. Chinese cooks, bakers, and laundry staff supported the operations of the Yosemite hotels, allowing urbanites enjoying the majesty of nature to appreciate the aesthetic resource worthy of preservation. Just four years after parts of Yosemite were preserved in public trust to prevent commercial exploitation in 1864, John Muir (1838–1914), the "father of American conservation," visited the area, describing his rambles across the mountains in closely observed, poetic works, bringing further appreciation to the region (Muir [1913] 1997, [1916] 2018).

Muir was the first president of the Sierra Club, founded to promote mountain recreation. His mystical writings present an expansive view of God transcending the dominant Christian streams of his time. He relied on *"extra-religious practice"* to experience the divine, similar to a Buddhist, transcendentalist, or Taoist practice (Barnett 2016; Berry 2015: 80). Treasuring a well-worn copy of Emerson's essays, Muir met his mentor when an elderly Emerson visited Yosemite in 1871. Through unstinting advocacy, Muir encouraged the establishment of the world's first national parks, Yellowstone in 1872 and Yosemite in 1890, as natural cathedrals for tourist worship, a process of purification resulting in the violent expulsion of Native Americans from their ancestral lands (Gilio-Whitaker 2020). The National Parks Act of 1916 established the National Park Service, the first in existence, inspiring the creation of park services around the world.

1940s: Aldo Leopold, Albert Schweitzer, and *Ahimsa*

Building on the spiritual nature writings of Muir and Thoreau, as well as the Hudson River School painters' appreciation of the sublime in the landscape, Aldo Leopold (1887–1948), the father of wildlife ecology, created the world's first global ecological organization, the Conservation Foundation in 1948, with Fairfield Osborn, president of the New York Zoological Society, and William Vogt (Mann 2018).

Leopold conceptualized an early environmental ethic in his most famous work, *A Sand County Almanac* (1949), which includes his observations while working with his family to restore a depleted farm in Wisconsin. Leopold advocated for extending ethics to include the nonhuman ecological substrate of life, in a process of "ecological evolution," leading to the Land Ethic that incorporates a broader definition of community to include soils, waters, plants, animals—collectively "the land." Leopold drew on the concept of a "reverence for life" developed by the humanitarian Albert Schweitzer, who was in turn was shaped by Indian thought, particularly the doctrine of *ahimsa,* or nonviolence and non-harming, found in Jainism, Buddhism, and Hinduism (Nash 1973; Schweitzer [1936] 1960: 82–3, cited in Martin 2007: 90).

FIGURE 5.3 *People leaving Buddhist church at Manzanar War Relocation Center, California.* Source: *Library of Congress, Prints & Photographs Division, Ansel Adams, photographer, LC-A35-6-M-34.*

1950s–1960s: Beat Poets "Going to the Mountains to Pray"

In the 1950s, the Beat poets, who blended Zen Buddhism and reverence for nature in their poetry, converged in the San Francisco Bay Area. Allen Ginsberg (1926–97) and Jack Kerouac (1922–69), who had read Thoreau, met Gary Snyder (1930–) in Berkeley, and sometimes studied at the newly launched American Academy of Asian Studies (AAAS), founded to bridge Eastern and Western thought, in San Francisco. The influential writings of these poets drew attention to the moral and aesthetic aspects of nature. Snyder, who spent several years studying Buddhism in Japan, is known as the "poet laureate of deep ecology," blending influences from nature and Buddhism in his writing. Snyder inspired the central character of Kerouac's *The Dharma Bums*, which depicts a generation "going up to mountains to pray" and "giving visions of eternal freedom to everybody and to all living creatures" (cited in Fields 1992: 222–3).

While the AAAS folded in 1956, some contributors reconstituted its goals in the Cultural Integration Fellowship (CIF), and then the California Institute of Asian Studies, which became the California Institute of Integral Studies (CIIS), an accredited university since 1981. CIIS emphasizes "sustainability" as one of its Seven Ideals, and incorporates ecological perspectives into its offerings through the work of faculty members including Brian Thomas Swimme, an evolutionary cosmologist who has collaborated with religion scholars John Grim and Mary Evelyn Tucker on the book and film *The Journey of the Universe* (2011); and Joanna Macy, a scholar of Buddhism, systems theory, and deep ecology. In 2013, I launched the graduate program in Ecology, Spirituality, and Religion, which weaves courses in Buddhism, Hinduism, Christianity, and other spiritual traditions together with environmental studies.

1960s–1970s: Rachel Carson, Environmental Policy, and a "Turn to the East"

As the environmental harms of industrial society became more apparent in the 1960s, advocates called for alternatives. Rachel Carson's *Silent Spring* ([1962] 1994) launched the environmental movement, warning of the hazards of toxic pesticides for humans and wildlife. Trained as a zoologist and working for the Bureau of Fisheries, Carson wrote with a lyrical appreciation for the natural world, drawing a wide readership. Following in the lineage of Emerson and Thoreau, she kept a copy of Thoreau's *Walden* by her bed and dedicated *Silent Spring* to Albert Schweitzer, cherishing a letter she received from him (Lasher 2012). Inspired by the publication of *Silent Spring*, the National Council of Churches established a Faith-Man-Nature Group in 1964, which met for the next ten years (Rockefeller and Elder 1992).

FIGURE 5.4 *Green Gulch Farm, Marin County, California.* Source: *Frank Schulenburg via Wikimedia Commons/CC BY-SA 4.0.*

Increasing dissatisfaction with the status quo was expressed in the liberation movements for feminism, civil rights, Black Power, and Free Speech during the 1960s. The search for alternatives to atomistic and mechanistic assumptions of the military-industrial paradigm contributed to increasing interest in Buddhism and environmentalism (Clarke 2006; Tarnas 1991). Shunryu Suzuki Roshi, a Japanese Soto Zen priest, established the San Francisco Zen Center (SFZC) in 1962, anchoring the study and practice of Zen Buddhism on the West Coast. SFZC grew to include two satellite sites, the Tassajara Retreat Center to the south and Green Gulch Farm to the north, placing meditators in close contact with nature.

Concern about the state of the environment led the US Congress to pass legislation to protect and preserve environmental quality, including the Clean Air Act (1963), the Wilderness Act (1964), the Water Quality Control Act (1965), the National Environmental Policy Act (1970), the Clean Water Act (1972), and the Endangered Species Act (1973), which all established a responsibility for caring for the surrounding environment. Senator Gaylord Nelson of Wisconsin originated the first Earth Day in 1970, with twenty million Americans taking part in grassroots environmental activism and education (Kline 2011).

Asian religions seemed to offer an alternative to the industrial development choking the United States. Seeking an alternative path to economic development, the German-born British economist E.F. Schumacher (1911–77) drew on the Buddhist concept of the Middle Way, learned while working in Burma, to devise "Buddhist Economics" ([1973] 1999). Schumacher's influential book *Small Is Beautiful* developed a theory of "economics as if people mattered," encouraging localization of economic development and relatively simple "appropriate technology" ([1973] 1999). President Jimmy Carter invited Schumacher to the White House as an adviser in 1977; California Governor Jerry Brown sought to apply his ideas in California (Kumar 2018: 271).

The historian Lynn White Jr. proposed Zen Buddhism as an alternative to ecologically destructive Christianity, which he called "the most anthropocentric religion the world has ever seen" (1967). The Taoist classic *Tao Te Ching* by Lao Tzu, published in English translation by Gia-Fun Feng and Jane English in 1972 with lush calligraphy and black-and-white nature photographs, appeared to offer a visceral, emotional respite from the deluge of grievous environmental news. The same year, the famed religion scholar Huston Smith published "Tao Now: An Ecological Testament," calling for a "new consciousness" to address the ecological crisis, and suggesting that Chinese Taoism, with its subtle understandings of relativity, interdependence, complementarity, and surrender of control might guide the way.

1960s–1990s: Emergence of Religion and Ecology

In the late 1960s, Thomas Berry, a cultural historian, scholar of Asian religions, and self-proclaimed "geologian" or theologian of Earth, created the History of Religions program at Fordham University. He called for interreligious cooperation to address the growing ecological crisis (Tucker, Grim, and Angyal 2019: 87, 94). Berry drew on his expertise in Asian religions, Native American religions, and Western philosophy to propose a new paradigm that would center planetary well-being in all human activity, encouraging humanity to become a mutually enhancing species on Earth because "the universe is a communion of subjects rather than a collection of objects" (Berry 1988; Swimme and Berry 1992: 243).

Ecological concerns in the study of religions emerged into public dialogue through the work of two of Berry's former graduate students, Mary Evelyn Tucker and John Grim, then professors of religion at Bucknell University, who organized a series of conferences on "World Religions and Ecology" at Harvard University between 1996 and 1998. Involving scientists, policy makers, and scholars of religion, the conference series was the first to focus on nature and ecology from the perspective of world religions (Tucker, Grim, and Angyal 2019: 144). Conferences, and subsequent books, addressed *Buddhism and Ecology* (Tucker and Williams 1997); *Hinduism and Ecology* (Chapple and Tucker 2000); *Daoism and Ecology* (Girardot, Miller, and Liu 2001); *Jainism and Ecology* (Chapple 2002); *Confucianism and Ecology* (Tucker and Berthrong 1998); and *Shinto and Ecology* (published in Japanese). Following these conferences, Tucker and Grim created the Forum on Religion and Ecology to promote understanding of the engagement of the world's religions with ecology and nature, based at Yale University since 2006. Religion and ecology, as an emerging academic field and activist force, focuses on the intersections of "historical and contemporary quests for understanding the interrelationships of humans, the Earth, the cosmos, and the sacred" (Tucker, Grim, and Angyal 2019: 144–5).

1970s–1980s: Buddhism and Deep Ecology

Following a 1971 pilgrimage to Tsheringma (or Gauri Shankar), a 7,134 meter peak in Nepal sacred to Buddhists and Hindus, the Norwegian professor of philosophy Arne Naess (1912–2009) introduced "deep ecology," drawing on inspiration from Gandhian, Buddhist, and Taoist ideas, as well as the philosophy of Spinoza, Whitehead, and Heidegger (Clarke 2006: 176; Faarlund 2015). Naess and his Norwegian colleagues were impressed with the friendliness that the local Buddhist Sherpa people extended to all others, including mountains and wild nature (Naess 1995). Observations from this trip influenced the 1972 talk Naess gave at the Third World Future Research Conference in Bucharest, in which he argued for "deep ecology" (Anker 2008; Faarlund 2015). Naess articulated deep ecology in response to the "shallow" movement focused on cleaning up the pollutants of industrialized society, the central objective of which is "the health and affluence of people in the developed countries" (Naess 1973: 95). In his deep ecology, Naess emphasized "respect, and even veneration, for ways and forms of life" echoing the values of the Sherpas he had observed in Nepal (95). Bill Devall (1938–2009) further articulated the intersections of Buddhism and deep ecology in "Ecocentric Sangha." He built from Leopold's notion of "thinking like a mountain," and Buddhist principles to articulate "a new face to the environmental crisis": "a crisis of character and cultural integrity" (Devall 1996: 183). The philosophy of deep ecology influenced radical environmental groups such as Greenpeace, founded in 1971, and Earth First!, founded in 1980, that conduct direct action in defense of natural organisms and ecosystems and subscribe to nonviolence as a central principle (Devall 1991).

Like Naess, Michael Soule (1936–2020), the "Father of Conservation Biology," and professor at the University of California—Santa Cruz, saw a resonance between Buddhism and conservation. He was a founder of both the Society for Conservation Biology (1985) and the Wildlands Network (1991). He began studying Buddhism in 1971 and observed that Buddhism and conservation biology both address "liberation, because the more we are liberated from our narrow, little selves, the more effective we can be in saving all beings" (Strand 2005).

1980s–1990s: Asian Religions, Environmental Philosophy, and Nature

Asian thought contributed to the development of the academic field of environmental philosophy. J. Baird Callicott taught the first environmental ethics course at the University of Wisconsin-Stevens Point in 1971. In the late 1980s, philosophers actively turned to Asian thought, as Lynn White Jr. had recommended, to investigate alternatives to the dominant foundations of Western philosophy. In a foundational 1987 article, the environmental philosopher Holmes Rolston asked "Can the East Help the West to Value Nature?" Environmental philosophers drew on intellectual resources in Asian traditions for rethinking the moral and metaphysical frameworks of philosophy toward a more Earth-centered paradigm (Callicott and Ames 1989).

In the 1990s, scholars of religion explored the connections of Asian religions and nature through several volumes including *Dharma Gaia* (1990), *This Sacred Earth* (1995), and *Spirit and Nature* (1992), a volume resulting from a conference held at Middlebury College in Vermont in 1990 that convened leaders from Buddhist, Christian, Islamic, Jewish, Native American, and liberal democratic traditions, along with international environmental conservationists. *Dharma Gaia* includes contributions from Beat poets and essays from leading global Buddhist thinkers such as Thich Nat Hanh, Sulak Sivaraksa, Roshi Joan Halifax, and His Holiness the Dalai Lama. Halifax, now the abbot Upaya Zen Center near Santa Fe, New Mexico, identifies deep ecology as arising out of the intersection of shamanism and Buddhism (1990: 21). In *The Fruitful Darkness* (1993), Halifax places animist experiences in the larger context of Buddhist understandings of a living Earth.

The noted Tibetan Buddhist teacher Chogyam Trungpa Rinpoche (1940–87) fled Tibet and settled in Boulder, Colorado, to found the Naropa Institute in 1974, on the model of the ancient Indian Buddhist university Nalanda (Fields 1992). By 1999, Naropa University became the only university in North America based on contemplative education, focusing on the arts, education, environmental studies, peace studies, psychology, and religious studies. Rita Gross (1943–2015), a student of Trungpa Rinpoche and a feminist professor of Buddhism, called for a Buddhist environmental ethic, arguing that population, often called the "third rail" of environmentalism, must be considered along with consumption and environmental quality, as interconnected per Buddhist notions of interdependence (Gross 1997).

Similarly drawing on Buddhist teachings on interdependence, Joanna Macy, a scholar of Buddhism and general systems theory, drew on her experiences in Sri Lanka with the Sarvodaya movement, and with Buddhists in Tibet, to develop theories and practices of sustaining motivation and resilience in the face of environmental degradation. Macy created spiritual practices that build connections between individuals and ecosystems, to strengthen and support environmental activists (Macy 1991; Macy and Brown 1998; Macy and Johnstone 2012).

1990s–2000s: Sacralizing the Landscape, *Ahimsa*, and Food

The 1990s to 2000s saw growing awareness of the influences of food choices on environmental sustainability, and increasing emphasis on local, seasonal eating. Green Gulch Farm, a branch of SFZC that provides organic produce to Greens Restaurant in

San Francisco, became a leader in the local organic food movement, contributing to reshaping the American palate and foodways. Stephanie Kaza, now Professor Emerita of Environmental Studies at the University of Vermont, studied Zen Buddhism at Green Gulch with Joanna Macy, among others. With Kenneth Kraft, she edited *Dharma Rain* (2000), a collection of primary sources exploring Buddhist teachings on the natural environment. Wendy Johnson, a founder of the organic farm and garden at Green Gulch, became a garden mentor for the Edible Schoolyard project in Berkeley in 1995, helping a new generation of students understand the sustaining power of the natural world in creating human and ecological health.

Jainism, which emphasizes *ahimsa* (non-harming) and vegetarianism, carries a worldview that resonates with environmentalism (Chapple 2007: xv). Diasporic Jains from India and East Africa, while likely numbering only in the hundreds of thousands in North America, have also contributed to more ecologically sustainable foodways, bringing their core values of vegetarianism, animal rights, and environmentalism (195). Some North American Jains view involvement with animal rights activism and environmental causes as a modern practice compelled by their faith (xxii).

The construction of Hindu temples in North America sanctifies the surrounding terrain. In upstate New York, a Hindu temple established in 1998 sits in an area that was previously the site of the Second Great Awakening in the nineteenth century (Dempsey 2006: 157). When establishing a new Hindu temple, the community will give attention to surrounding mountains, rivers, and other geological formations that may bear resonance with Indian holy sites. The convergence of three rivers in Pittsburgh, for example, resonates with the holy convergence of three rivers, the Ganges, the Yamuna, and the underground Sarasvati in India (157).

FIGURE 5.5 *Convergence of the Allegheny and Monongahela rivers with a subterranean river surfacing through a fountain in downtown Pittsburgh.* Source: *Atul Patel/EyeEm/ Getty Images.*

2000s and Beyond: Biodiversity Conservation, Climate Change, and Increasing Social Engagement

International conservation and development organizations began to take an interest in religion, publishing a series of reports on religious contributions to environmental protection, including the World Bank's *Faith in Conservation: New Approaches to Religions and the Environment* (2003) and the World Wildlife Fund's *Beyond Belief: Linking Faiths and Protected Areas to Support Biodiversity Conservation* (2005). At the Society for Conservation Biology, Tom Baugh established the Religion and Conservation Biology Group in 2007. The World Wildlife Fund was home to Dekila Chungyalpa's Sacred Earth project, a faith-based conservation project that worked globally to articulate the moral and ethical case for ecological sustainability, beginning in 2009. Chungyalpa moved to the University of Wisconsin-Madison in 2018 to lead the Loka Initiative, which links faith and ecology, and promotes interreligious dialogue on environmental issues (Center for Healthy Minds n.d.).

Since 2010, EcoSikh, an international organization, has promoted Sikh Environment Day to commemorate the enthronement of the seventh guru and to mark the beginning of the Sikh new year (EcoSikh 2013). Sikh communities across the United States plant trees, provide environmental and waste reduction education, and host rituals honoring nature.

The meditative aspects of Buddhism, Jainism, and Hinduism have been offered as ameliorative approaches to the stresses of activism in an approach called "contemplative environmentalism" (Litfin 2016; Richey and Wapner 2017). Others suggest that the study of Jain philosophy and contemplative practice can provide beneficial self-care, and offer foundational sources for developing ethical and empathic relationships with the natural world (Miller 2019). The greatest influence of Hinduism in contemporary America may be through the practice of postural Hatha yoga. Scholars and practitioners of postural yoga have identified connections between this practice, the study of other "limbs" of yoga—particularly the doctrine of *ahimsa,* or non-harming—and broader environmental behaviors (Chapple 2009; Frawley 2017; Strauss and Mandlebaum 2013: 176). The Green Yoga Association was established in 2003 to promote environmentally friendly yoga practice (Strauss and Mandlebaum 2013: 195).

Some Buddhist retreat centers and *sanghas* emphasize Earth care in their teachings. The Buddhist Peace Fellowship was the first socially engaged Buddhist group, founded in 1978 by Nelson Foster, Robert Aitken Roshi, Anne Aitken, and others. Members have addressed eco-social issues including war, the nuclear threat, prisons, and human rights. The Green Dragon Earth Initiative of Zen Mountain Monastery in New York is an effort to "address the individual, institutional, national and global degradation of our planet" (Zen Mountain Monastery 2018).

One Earth Sangha, which began in 2013 as a project of the Insight Meditation Community of Washington, DC, argues that Buddhist teachings offer a wellspring of resources for addressing ecological crises. It has catalyzed the Buddhist response to climate change, contributing to the founding of the Buddhist Climate Action Network (BCAN n.d.) and helping prepare the Buddhist Climate Change Statement to World Leaders (2015) delivered at the 2015 Paris Climate Summit. The Earth Holder Community, a network of individual and sangha initiatives throughout North America and beyond, embodies the teachings and methods of the Venerable Thich Nat Hanh's Engaged Buddhism, to awaken "inter-dependence with and love for Mother Earth" (Earth Holder Community 2021).

As the global threats of species extinction and climate change intensified in the twenty-first century, Buddhist leaders spoke out about the climate emergency (Stanley, Loy, and Dorje 2009). The Sacred Mountain Sangha invites practitioners to "join the movement for radical change" in addressing the climate emergency (Sacred Mountain Sangha 2021). Activists called on nonviolent civil disobedience to assert the need for policy change. The Reverend angel Kyodo williams, a socially engaged Zen Buddhist priest, led a busload of Buddhists to the People's Climate March in Washington, DC, in 2017 (Demont 2019). The New York Insight Meditation Center has hosted climate events and has expressed affinity with the goals of Extinction Rebellion (XR), an activist movement originating in the UK (Abrahams 2019).

The story of Asian religions and nature in the United States returns to the northeast, where Asian religions first took root on American soil. In New York City, and in numerous chapters, Sadhana: Coalition of Progressive Hindus supports living out Hindu faith values through service, provides guidance on eco-friendly *pujas* (rituals), and organizes beach cleanups to honor sacred waters (Sadhana n.d.). North of New York City, a new center for spiritual contemplation and social action arose in the shell of a former Capuchin monastery: The Garrison Institute (TGI), which was founded in 2003 to bring the wisdom of the world's contemplative traditions to pressing social issues, including environmental degradation. In 2018, TGI hosted the Pathways to Planetary Health conference to discuss strategies for global well-being, drawing on contemporary Chinese articulations of "ecological civilization" that build on Buddhist, Daoist, and Confucian traditions. Likewise, the Center for Process Studies in Claremont, California, organized a conference on "Seizing an Alternative: Toward an Ecological Civilization," in 2015, to explore the contemporary Chinese concept of "ecological civilization" in the context of religion, philosophy, justice, and governance. As these initiatives show, Asian religions and philosophies continue to infuse the American interaction with nature and the quest for sustainability with fresh perspectives.

Further Reading and Online Resources

Snyder G. (2010), *The Practice of the Wild: With a New Preface by the Author*, Berkeley, CA: Counterpoint.
Sponsel L.E. (2012), *Spiritual Ecology: A Quiet Revolution*, Santa Barbara, CA: Praeger.

Taylor B. (2009), *Dark Green Religion*, Berkeley: University of California Press.
Taylor D.E. (1997), "American Environmentalism: The Role of Race, Class and Gender in Shaping Activism 1820–1995," *Race, Gender & Class*, 5 (1): 16–62.

References

Abrahams M. (2019), "The Buddhists of Extinction Rebellion," *Tricycle: The Buddhist Review*, September 16, 2019.
Anker P. (2008), "Deep Ecology in Bucharest," *The Trumpeter*, 24 (1): 56–67.
Badiner A.H. (1990), *Dharma Gaia: A Harvest of Essays in Buddhism and Ecology*, Berkeley, CA: Parallax Press.
Barnett R.J. (2016), *Earth Wisdom: John Muir, Accidental Taoist Charts Humanity's Only Future on A Changing Planet*, North Charleston, SC: CreateSpace Independent Publishing Platform.
Berry E. (2015), *Devoted to Nature: The Religious Roots of American Environmentalism*, Berkeley: University of California Press.
Berry T. (1988), *The Dream of The Earth*, San Francisco: Sierra Club Books.
Buddhist Climate Action Network (BCAN) (n.d.), "Current Status." Available online: http://globalbcan.org (accessed January 25, 2021).
Buddhist Climate Change Statement to World Leaders 2015 (2015), Plum Village, October 31. Available online: https://plumvillage.org/articles/buddhist-climate-change-statement-to-world-leaders-2015/ (accessed January 25, 2021).
Callicott J.B. and R.T. Ames (1989), *Nature in Asian Traditions of Thought: Essays in Environmental Philosophy*, Albany: State University of New York Press.
Carson R. ([1962] 1994), *Silent Spring*, Boston: Mifflin.
Center for Healthy Minds (n.d.), "The Integration of Faith and Ecology." Available online: https://centerhealthyminds.org/loka-initiative (accessed January 25, 2021).
Chan Y.F. (2017), "Interpreting the Contributions of Chinese Immigrants in Yosemite National Park's History," *George Wright Forum*, 34 (3): 299–307.
Chapple C.K. (2002), *Jainism and Ecology: Nonviolence in the Web of Life*, Religions of the World and Ecology, Cambridge, MA: Harvard University Center for the Study of World Religions.
Chapple C.K., ed. (2009), *Yoga and Ecology: Dharma for the Earth: Proceedings of Two of the Sessions at the Fouth DANAM Conference Held on Site at the American Academy of Religion*, Hampton, VA: Deepak Heritage Books.
Chapple C.K. and M.E. Tucker, eds. (2000), *Hinduism and Ecology: The Intersection of Earth, Sky, and Water*, Cambridge, MA: Harvard University Press.
Christy A.E. ([1932] 1972), *The Orient in American Transcendentalism: A Study of Emerson, Thoreau, and Alcott*, 3rd edn., New York: Octagon Books.
Clarke J.J. (2006), *Oriental Enlightenment: The Encounter between Asian and Western Thought*, London: Routledge.
Demont J. (2019), "The Radical Buddhism of Rev. angel Kyodo williams," *Lion's Roar*, March 8. Available online: https://www.lionsroar.com/love-and-justice-the-radical-buddhism-of-rev-angel-kyodo-williams/ (accessed January 25, 2021).
Dempsey C.G. (2006), *The Goddess Lives in Upstate New York: Breaking Convention and Making Home at a North American Hindu Temple*, New York: Oxford University Press.
Devall B. (1991), "Deep Ecology and Radical Environmentalism," *Society & Natural Resources*, 4 (3): 247–58.

Devall B. (1996), "Eco-centric Sangha," in A. Kotler (ed.), *Engaged Buddhist Reader: Ten Years of Engaged Buddhist Publishing*, 181–8, Berkeley, CA: Parallax Press.

Dudley N., L. Higgins-Zogib, and S. Mansourian (2005), *Beyond Belief: Linking Faiths and Protected Areas to Support Biodiversity Conservation, The Arguments for Protection Series*, Gland, CH: Worldwide Fund for Nature.

Earth Holder Community (2021), "Home." Available online: https://earthholder.training (accessed January 25, 2021).

EcoSikh (2013), *Sikh Environment Day Report 2013*. Available online: http://www.ecosikh. org/wp-content/uploads/2013/05/Sikh-Environment-DayReport-2013.pdf (accessed October 30, 2020).

Emerson R.W. ([1836] 1990), "Nature," in R. Finch and J. Elder (eds.), *The Norton Book of Nature Writing*, 145–8, New York: W.W. Norton & Company.

Faarlund N. (2015), "The Tseringma Pilgrimage, 1971: An Eco-philosophic 'anti-expedition'," [Blog] *P2P Foundation*, March 9. Available online: https://blog.p2pfoundation.net/the-tseringma-pilgrimage-1971-an-eco-philosophic-anti-expedition/2015/03/09 (accessed October 30, 2020).

Fields R. (1992), *How the Swans Came to the Lake: A Narrative History of Buddhism in America*, Boston: Shambhala.

Frawley D. (Pandit Vamadeva Shastri) (2017), "Yoga and Nature," American Institute of Vedic Studies. Available online: https://www.vedanet.com/yoga-and-ecology/ (accessed October 27, 2020).

Gilio-Whitaker D. (2020), "The Problem with Wilderness," *UU World* Magazine, Spring. Available online: https://www.uuworld.org/articles/problem-wilderness?fbclid=IwAR0UPEbzJ-fJujrTxs8QftB1JGXjxfl0QDFqszCfSZLK0l-R-Wc00cl9LGI (accessed October 7, 2020).

Girardot N. J., J. Miller, and X. Liu (2001), *Daoism and Ecology: Ways within a Cosmic Landscape*, Cambridge, MA: Harvard University Press.

Gottlieb R.S. (1995), *This Sacred Earth: Religion, Nature, Environment*, New York: Routledge.

Grim J. and M.E. Tucker (2014), *Ecology and Religion*, Washington, DC: Island Press.

Gross R.M. (1997), "Toward a Buddhist Environmental Ethic," *Journal of the American Academy of Religion*, 65 (2): 333–53.

Halifax J. (1990), "The Third Body: Buddhism, Shamanism, and Deep Ecology," in A.H. Badiner, *Dharma Gaia*, 20–38, Berkeley, CA: Parallax Press.

Halifax J. (1993), *Fruitful Darkness: A Journey through Buddhist Practice and Tribal Wisdom*, San Francisco: HarperCollins.

Jiobu R.M. (1988), *Ethnicity and Assimilation*, Albany: State University of New York Press.

Kline B. (2011), *First along the River: A Brief History of the U.S. Environmental Movement*, Lanham, MD: Rowman & Littlefield.

Kumar S. (2018), "E. F. Schumacher, 1911–1977," in J.A. Palmer-Cooper, and D.E. Cooper (eds.), *Key Thinkers on the Environment*, New York: Routledge.

Lasher C. (2012), "The Religious Humanism of Rachel Carson: On the 50th Anniversary of the Publication of Silent Spring," *Institute of Oriental Philosophy*, 22: 193–205.

Leopold A. ([1949] 1966), *A Sand County Almanac: With Essays on Conservation from Round River*, New York: Ballentine Books.

Litfin K. (2016), "Person/Planet Politics: Contemplative Pedagogies for a New Earth," in S. Jinnah and S. Nicholson (eds.), *New Earth Politics: Essays from the Anthropocene*, 115–34, Cambridge, MA: MIT Press.

Macy J. (1991), *Mutual Causality in Buddhism And General Systems Theory: The Dharma of Natural Systems*, Albany: State University of New York Press.

Macy J. and C. Johnstone (2012), *Active Hope: How to Face the Mess We're in without Going Crazy*, Novato, CA: New World Library.

Macy J. and M. Young Brown (1998), *Coming Back to Life: Practices to Reconnect Our Lives, Our World*, Stony Creek, CT: New Society Publishers.

Mann C.C. (2018), *The Wizard and The Prophet: Two Remarkable Scientists and Their Dueling Visions to Shape Tomorrow's World*, New York: Alfred A. Knopf.

Martin M.W. (2007), *Albert Schweitzer's Reverence for Life: Ethical Idealism and Self-Realization*, New York: Routledge.

McShane F. (1964), "Walden and Yoga," *The New England Quarterly*, 37 (3): 322–42.

Merchant C. (1980), *The Death of Nature: Women, Ecology, and the Scientific Revolution*, San Francisco: Harper & Row.

Merchant C. (2002), *The Columbia Guide to American Environmental History*, New York: Columbia University Press.

Miller C.P. (2019), "Jainism, Yoga, and Ecology: A Course in Contemplative Practice for a World in Pain," *Religions*, 10 (4): 232.

Muir J. ([1913] 1997), *Nature Writings: The Story of My Boyhood and Youth; My First Summer in The Sierra; The Mountains of California; Stickeen; Selected Essays*, New York: Literary Classics of the United States: Distributed by Penguin Books.

Muir J. and W.F. Badé ([1916] 2018), *A Thousand-Mile Walk to The Gulf*, Mineola, NY: Dover Publications.

Naess A. (1973), "The Shallow and the Deep, Long-Range Ecology Movement. A Summary," *Inquiry*, 16: 95–100.

Naess A. (1995), "Interview with Norwegian Eco-Philosopher Arne Naess," in J. van Boeckel (ed.), *This Interview Was Made for the Film* The Call of the Mountain, Blankenham, The Netherlands: Stichting ReRun Producties. Available online: http://www.natureartеducation.org/Interview_Arne_Naess_1995.pdf (accessed January 29, 2021).

Nash R. (1973), *Wilderness and the American Mind*, New Haven, CT: Yale University Press.

Odin S. ([1998] 2010), "The Japanese Concept of Nature in Relation to the Environmental Ethics and Conservation Aesthetics of Aldo Leopold," in M.E. Tucker and D.R. Williams (eds.), *Buddhism and Ecology*, 55–66, Cambridge, MA: Harvard University Press. (Reprint Harper Perennial)

Palmer M. and V. Finlay (2003), *Faith in Conservation: New Approaches to Religions and The Environment*, Washington, DC: World Bank.

Palmer-Cooper J.A. and D.E. Cooper, eds. (2018), *Key Thinkers on the Environment*, New York: Routledge.

Richey J. and P. Wapner (2017), "Inner and Outer Ecologies: Contemplative Practice in an Environmental Age," *The Arrow: A Journal of Wakeful Society, Culture, & Politics*, 4 (1). Available online: https://arrow-journal.org/wp-content/uploads/2017/03/Teaching-Contemplative-Environments-2017-Vol.-4.1.pdf (accessed January 29, 2021).

Rockefeller S.C. and J. Elder (1992), *Spirit and Nature: Why the Environment Is a Religious Issue; an Interfaith Dialogue*, Boston: Beacon Press.

Rolston H. (1987), "Can the East Help the West to Value Nature?," *Philosophy East and West*, 37: 172–90.

Sacred Mountain Sangha (2021), "Declare Climate Emergency Now." Available online: https://sacredmountainsangha.org/climate-emergency/ (accessed January 25, 2021).

Sadhana (n.d.), "Our Vision." Available online: https://www.sadhana.org (accessed January 25, 2021).

Schumacher E.F. ([1973] 1999), "Buddhist Economics," in *Small Is Beautiful: Economics as if People Mattered*, Vancouver, BC: Hartley and Marks Publishers.

Schweitzer A. ([1936] 1960), *Indian Thought and Its Development*, trans. Mrs. C.E.B. Russell, Boston: Beacon Press.

Smith H. and M.D. Bryant ([1972] 1995), *Huston Smith: Essays on World Religion*, New York: Paragon House.

Sorkhabi R. (2008), "Albert Schweitzer and Indian Thought," *The Gandhi Foundation*, July 1. Available online: https://gandhifoundation.org/2008/07/01/albert-schweitzer-and-indian-thought-by-rasoul-sorkhabi/ (accessed August 5, 2020).

Stanley J., D. Loy, and D. Gyurme (2009), *A Buddhist Response to the Climate Emergency*, Boston: Wisdom Publications.

Strand C. (2005), "The Whole Package," *Tricycle: The Buddhist Review*. Available online: https://tricycle.org/magazine/whole-package/ (accessed October 30, 2020).

Strauss S. and L. Mandelbaum (2013), "Consuming Yoga, Conserving the Environment: Transcultural Discourses on Sustainable Living," in B. Hauser (ed.), *Yoga Traveling: Bodily Practice in Transcultural Perspective*, 175–200, Heidelberg, Switzerland: Springer.

Swimme B. and T. Berry (1992), *The Universe Story: From the Primordial Flaring Forth to the Ecozoic Era*, San Francisco: HarperSan Francisco.

Syman S. (2010), *The Subtle Body: The Story of Yoga in America*, New York: Farrar, Straus and Giroux.

Tarnas R. (1991), *Passion of The Western Mind: Understanding the Ideas That Have Shaped Our World View*, New York: Random House.

Tucker M.E. and D.R. Williams (1997), *Buddhism and Ecology: The Interconnection of Dharma and Deeds*, Cambridge, MA: Harvard University Press.

Tucker M.E. and J.H. Berthrong (1998), *Confucianism and Ecology: The Interrelation of Heaven, Earth, and Humans*, Cambridge, MA: Harvard University Press.

Tucker M.E., J. Grim, and A.J. Angyal (2019), *Thomas Berry: A Biography*, New York: Columbia University Press.

Tzu L., J. English, and G.-f. Feng (1972), *Tao Te Ching*, 1st edn., New York: Vintage Books.

White L. (1967), "Historical Roots of Our Ecologic Crisis," *Science*, 155 (3767): 1203–7.

Williamson L. (2010), *Transcendent in America: Hindu-Inspired Meditation Movements as New Religion*, New York: New York University Press.

Zen Mountain Monastery (2018), "Earth Initiative." Available online: https://zmm.org/our-programs/earth-initiative/ (accessed January 25, 2021).

Glossary Terms

Extra-religious practice Spiritual discipline engaged in on a frequent, regular basis that allows the practitioner to gain insight that transcends the individual self through embodied, intuitive, or prayerful means.

6

Environmentalism, Ecological Activism/Theology, and New Religious Movements

Morgan Shipley

Environmentalism and Global Religion

To best understand the rise and diversity of environmental activism associated with North American new religions, we must first outline the connection between environmentalism, theological positions, and global religiosity. In so doing, this first section offers a breakdown of both new and "old" religions in and outside the American context to capture the shared impact, aims, and in many cases, religious lineages that both shape *new religious movements* in North America and spiritually ground overlapping environmental ethos.

Although still contested today by scholars who find it too simplistic and believers who find it insulting, in 1966, historian Lynn White, Jr. argued that Christianity must assume a "burden of guilt" for contemporary environmental and ecological crises by actively desacralizing and instrumentalizing nature to meet the needs of and desire for human flourishing (White 1969: 42–7). Rather than a point of harmony and responsibility, White demonstrated how religious thinking produced the conditions and justifications to transform nature into the location for human manipulation—it changed humanity's relationship from one of mutual dependency to domination, reifying an anthropocentric (or human-centered) worldview that centralized humans' dominion *(or dominionism)* over the earth.

While White's thesis identifies the overlapping of Eurocentric religiosity and the degradation of the environment, this does not mean that (1) only the Abrahamic traditions (e.g., Judaism, Christianity, and Islam) are responsible for ecological indifference or environmental destruction; (2) that other traditions do not also create a binary between spiritual/material concerns that can lead to a privileging of the human; or (3) that religion alone bears responsibility. Rather, we must understand contemporary environmental concerns and crises as a matrix of various forces, primarily global capitalism, reliance on technology, growth of scientism and material concerns, and the rise of modern nation-states, all of which often rely on religion (as a source, cudgel, or warning) to help legitimate human needs over environmental concerns. Seyyed Hossein Nasr identifies this as a crisis of values shared across global humanity: "it is important we remember that all of us on the globe share in destroying our natural environment, although the reasons for this are different in different parts of the globe" (2007: 29). For Nasr, religion and spirituality offer the proper "traditional" "virtues" and "values" that "allowed countless generations to live in equilibrium with the world around them were at the same time conceived as ways of perfecting the soul, as steps in the perfection of human existence. These virtues provided the means for living at peace with the environment" (33).

When we consider the relationship between environmentalism and religion we must account for varying definitions of environmental responsibility, human agency, and the role of the sacred, whether this be a transcendent God or more immanent understandings, including the deification of nature. Religion, to borrow from Clifford Geertz's sociological definition, establishes moods and motivations, which in turn, outline specific worldly measures when it comes to engaging with and using our natural worlds (Geertz 1973: 93–135). In this light, religious environmentalism identifies

FIGURE 6.1 *"Protest against Dakota Access and Keystone XL Pipelines."* Source: *Pax Ahimsa Gethen/CC BY-SA 4.0 https://creativecommons.org/licenses/by-sa/4.0, via Wikimedia Commons.*

and seeks to act upon an increased understanding of environmental crises and the religious positionings and orientations that exacerbate or counteract the effects of human-made climate change.

Starting from the proposition of mutual dependency, Indigenous and *neo-pagan* beliefs that connect the spirit realm directly to our physical conditions often incorporate specific teachings regarding responsibility in relation to how all the elements of nature, including animals, are engaged and used. This spiritual entwining of human existence with the natural world manifests in both everyday reverence of the environment, as well as an unambiguous commitment to protect "land" from the excesses of human activity. Reflecting on how "Indigenous peoples have been forced into never-ending battles of resistance," Dina Gilio-Whitaker stresses how such resistance "is inextricably bound to the worldviews that center not only the obvious life-sustaining forces of the natural world but also the respect accorded the natural world in relationships of reciprocity based on responsibility toward those life forms" (2019: 13).

Ancient religions that elevated a goddess associated with the world, such as the Greek primordial goddess Gaia/Gaea, the personification of Earth, or what some Native American Indigenous traditions identify as Mother Earth, demonstrate how the continuation of human existence is predicated on appeasing and harmonizing with gods/goddesses associated with the natural world. Similarly, Hinduism's core panentheistic teaching regarding the immanence of Brahman, or the belief that an Ultimate Reality (Brahman) creates, maintains, and pervades all of existence (see the *Bhagavad Gita*, 7.19 and 13.13, and the *Bhagavad Purana*, 2.2.41 and 2.2.45), produces a general reverence for nature (or gods/goddesses associated with nature, such as Devi), as well as a dedication to nonviolence (ahimsa) and related karmic directives to take responsibility for our physical worlds (both of which we also see in Jainism and its general approach to ethical conduct and ecological concerns). A belief in interpenetration and interconnectedness grounds this understanding, and while the emphasis on the divine may change, we see this similarly reflected in a variety of Asian-based traditions, religious systems predicated on dependence, and a variety of spiritual orientations that emphasize Mother Earth (from Indigenous to neo-pagan to contemporary witchcraft).

The Buddha, for example, introduced the principle of pratitysampupada. Translated as dependent origination, this specific teaching highlights Buddhism's broader acceptance of an interconnected world at both the material and spiritual levels. To see the world as an endless chain of causation, dependency, and contingency produces a worldly orientation in which harm to others, including damage inflicted upon the earth, is also harm done to oneself. To alleviate the burden and inevitability of suffering, the Buddha taught that deep contemplation of interconnection leads inevitably to ethical actions and an empathetic responsiveness to the natural systems we, as humans, are intimately entwined with. Within twentieth- and twenty-first-century movements and expressions, this teaching grounds Buddhist responses to environmental crises. From the Dalai Lama's 2020 text, *Our Only Home: A Climate Appeal to the World*, to the "engaged Buddhism" of Thich Nhat Hanh, Buddhist environmentalism reflects how "our love and admiration for the Earth has the power to unite us and remove all boundaries, separation, and discrimination. Centuries of individualism and competition have brought about tremendous destruction and alienation. We need to reestablish true communication—true communion—with ourselves, with the Earth, and with one another as children of the same mother" (Thich Nhat Hanh 2014). Importantly, this foundational teaching of interconnection demonstrates a core sense of responsible conservationism that directs religious environmentalism: that is, belief in harmony and interconnection leads to awareness that the need to derive sustenance from the earth cannot come at the cost of depleting, polluting, or destroying the natural world.

Reflecting more and more this sense of contingency and interconnection, within monotheistic religions, religious environmentalism is expressed in new theologies that, to borrow from Christian theologian Larry Rasmussen, re-center the worship of God from the perspective of "earth community" and the need for an "earth ethics" that "argues for a dedication to earth in the manner of the sacred … with a sense of wonder that is protective of life" (2000: xii). Such dedication finds expression today in a series of public declarations, from the "Statement on Stewardship of the Environment" (1996) by the Seventh-day Adventists or the more recent policy on "Environmental Racism & Justice" (2018) adopted by the Presbyterian Church (USA), to Pope Francis's second encyclical *Laudato Si'*, the National Council of Churches USA "Resolution on Global Warming" (2006), and the World Council of Churches "Statement on Climate Justice" (2016), as well as more direct forms of advocacy and activism as we see with groups such as A Rocha USA, Blessed Earth–Serving God, Saving the Planet, the Catholic Climate Covenant, or the Blessed Kateri Tekakwitha Conservation Center.

Like Christianity, Judaism ultimately holds to *anthropocentrism*—however, from the idea of God providing "land" for the Chosen People to the principle of *tikkun olam*, or efforts to repair a broken world, Judaism holds a clear sense of responsibility to God's creation and the specific role of Jews in maintaining this covenant. For some Jewish thinkers and rabbis, and specifically those influenced by Kabbalistic tendencies, the creation of the first person indicates this commitment as the very word "man" in Hebrew derives from "adamah," meaning ground or earth. Expressed in the *stewardship* Adam and Eve assume in the Garden of Eden, this interpretation leads to the belief that Jews should be actively concerned with maintaining the elements of creation as gifted by God, which includes commitments to sustainability and environmental justice. For example, as first enunciated by Rabbi Zalman Schachter-Shalomi in the 1970s and extended by Arthur Waskow in the 1990s, the eco-kashrut (or eco-kosher) movement seeks to extend Jewish dietary laws to also address environmental concerns and promote sustainability (Katz 2011: 227). More broadly, we see this echoed in the adoption of *Tu Bishvat*, a Jewish holiday (adapted from a Kabbalistic ritual) also called *Rosh HaShanah La'Ilanot*, which literally translates as "new Year of the Trees," designed to celebrate and reflect on ecological awareness through the planting of trees.

Within Islam, the Qur'an teaches that all of existence is a gift from Allah, which includes the belief that humanity holds guardianship over the earth because, as Seyyed

Hossein Nasr summarizes, "the whole of nature is descended from higher spiritual realms" (cited in Hope and Young 1994: 182). For many, this necessitates pursuing actions that prevent the exploitation of natural resources by adhering to environmental stewardship as a *khalifa* (or trustee) of God (Qur'an 2:30). In the twenty-first century, we see this exemplified in both the notion of "Green Deen" (Deen, also Din, is an Arabic word for religion or way of life) and its corresponding belief that "the earth is a mosque, and everything in it is sacred" (Abdul-Matin 2010: 1), as well as institutional commitments, such as the Islamic Foundation for Ecology and Environmental Science (founded in 1993 by Fazlun Khalid), which seeks to raise awareness of environmental issues (see their newsletter *EcoIslam* or 2008 publication *Muslim Green Guide to Reducing Climate Change*) while also modeling specific projects in environmental conservation, including "green audits" for mosques.

Notably, the late twentieth and early twenty-first centuries experienced an increase in interfaith and pluralistic efforts that connect religious beliefs regarding environmental stewardship with more activist-oriented and advocacy projects. From the Interfaith Center for Sustainable Development's work "to promote green faith initiatives, religion-environment issues, and green religion education" (Interfaith Center for Sustainable

FIGURE 6.2 *Indigenous Environmental Network.* Source: *Frypie/CC BY-SA 4.0, via Wikimedia Commons, https://commons.wikimedia.org/wiki/File:Indigenous_Environmental_Network_2638.jpg.*

Development n.d.), to campaigns such as current efforts to influence the United States Environmental Protection Agency (EPA) to cut methane pollution by Interfaith Power & Light, whose mission is to mobilize an interfaith "religious response to global warming" (Interfaith Power & Light n.d.), these movements, projects, and efforts illustrate how the concerns of religious environmentalism offer the means to bypass orthodoxic and orthopraxical differences in favor of securing a world for believers of all faiths. In this unique way, religious environmentalism opens up space for the development of new ecological theologies and new religious movements grounded in expressions of activism predicated on the belief that human flourishing manifests by maintaining a mutually sustaining relationship with the natural world.

Ecological Activism/Theology

Theological commitments often produce believers whose conduct becomes a direct reflection of spiritual teachings regarding the environment. Theology grounds humans within a material realm and, in so doing, either portends to narratives of dependence, interconnection, and responsibility, or results in salvific idealizations that see climate change as either an illusion or necessary by-product of God's will. In addition to grounding how individual believers connect to and engage with nature, the previous section stressed how religious motivations create real-world efforts—on both the individual and institutional/social levels—to live more harmoniously and responsibly with our natural worlds. In this chapter, we will explore how ecological activism itself becomes a theology (or *ecotheology*), as well as more concrete examples of ecological activism that emerge out of theological and spiritual interpretations. Theologically, where religious environmentalism identifies how believers situate their relationship to the natural world, the move to ecological activism signifies efforts to make real the commitments imposed through religious orthodoxy and spiritual interpretations that stress the need for collective striving and wellness.

This does not suggest that religious environmentalism is unmoored from activist enterprises, which we see internationally, for example, in a 2005 project coordinated by the Islamic Foundation for Ecology and Environmental Science and CARE International to stop dynamite fishing in Zanzibar or initiate "Green Indonesia," a tree-planting campaign that reflects the notion of "Green Deen." However, to best understand commitments to environmentalism by North American new religious movements (NRMs), it is important to distinguish between the role religion assumes in advancing moral commitments to environmentalism and the development of distinctive theologies and activist networks whose very existence is predicated on active and continued stewardship of our natural worlds. Additionally, while influenced by spiritual orientations, ecotheology assumes a different position than "deep ecology." In defining "deep ecology" as "a normative, ecophilosophical movement that is inspired and fortified in part by our experience as humans in nature and in part by ecological knowledge" (Devall 1992: 52), Arne Naess distinguishes it from shallow ecology, or "the fight against pollution and resource depletion ... [seeking primarily] the health and affluence of people in the developed countries" (1973: 97). Heavily influenced by Rachel Carson's *Silent Spring*, a book often credited for helping galvanize the international environmental movement by exposing the truths, realities, and threats associated with pesticides, Naess's understanding of deep ecology represents a position from which to understand, critique, and respond to human-caused environmental crises. Echotheology, conversly, signifies religious positions that emphasize an enduring interconnection with the environment that necessitate working to ameliorate the conduct (intentional or otherwise) of humans, including activism that ranges from advocacy to direct action and civil disobedience.

What ultimately separates the two—ecotheology from theological/spiritual manifestations of environmentalism—is worldly expression, with the latter committed more to the "development of an ecological theology as a public discourse" (Lai 2017: 477)

FIGURE 6.3 *Most known for spending 738 days on "Luna," an over 1,000 years old redwood, Julia "Butterfly" Hill participates in a May 2006 tree sit to protest the proposed demolition of a 14-acre urban farm in Los Angeles, California, worked mostly by Hispanic families.* Source: UPI Photo/Jim Ruymen. Image ID: TXYBYC Contributor: UPI/Alamy Stock Photo.

and the former as modes of religious understanding that stress the dependency between humans and nature, foreground the effects of environmental degradation, and maybe most distinctly, pursue overt projects of sustainability and social expressions of environmental activism as religious/spiritual causes. Ecotheology developed from the work of Christian theologians and leaders, such as Pierre Teilhard de Chardin, Thomas Berry, or, even earlier, Francis of Assisi, Jewish philosophers Abraham Joshua Heschel, Martin Buber, and Rabbi Zalman Schachter-Shalomi, or as discussed above in relation to Islam, within the writings of Seyyed Hossein Nasr. Broadly defined, ecotheology represents critical examinations of "our patterns of living in light of the environmental and ecological challenges we face, and test the ways in which our religious traditions harm or help in coming to healing solutions" (Fortress Press n.d.).

While the field of ecotheology reflects Western notions of religiosity (the very term, "theology," speaks to this), it is imperative to recognize the distinct place Indigenous understandings and expressions assume, both by influencing how Western religious systems and believers understand their entwining with the natural world, and in worldly projects designed to make human activity more reflective of the belief that the sacred imbues all of nature, not simply humans alone. As described within the field of anthropology, North American Indigenous environmentalisms draw on traditional ecological knowledge (TEK), which in being passed down through generations in the form of spiritual narratives, myths, and stories, lead people to be "materially and spiritually integrated with their landscape" (Kimmerer 2002: 433). Concerned "with the relationship of living beings to one another and to the physical environment" (432), TEK and Indigenous religiosities not only highlight responsibility to nature but also offer an embodied approach that understands the material realm as tethered to the spiritual, and vice versa. The result is a clear dedication to act on behalf of nature, with recent contemporary examples ranging from anti-fracking activism to direct action designed to interrupt the abuse of land caused by drilling or the construction of pipelines that often cut directly through sacred land.

Founded and led by Native American activist Winona LaDuke, Honor the Earth draws from Indigenous spiritual understandings of interconnection, dependency, and stewardship to expand awareness of and increase financial support for environmental issues among the general American populace. Similarly, the Indigenous Environmental Network (IEN), a grassroots movement of Indigenous peoples founded in 1990, addresses "environmental and economic justice issues (EJ) … [by] building the capacity of Indigenous communities and tribal governments to develop mechanisms to protect our sacred sites, land, water, air, natural resources, health of both our people and all living things, and to build economically sustainable communities" (Indigenous Environmental Network n.d.). Accepting spiritual responsibility to nature similarly directs the social justice activism of the Standing Rock Sioux tribe, who along with members of—and allies to—nearly one hundred more tribes from across the United States and Canada (including IEN), turned to direct action to resist the construction of the Dakota Access Pipeline. Initiated in April 2016 by Native American youth through the "ReZpect Our Water" campaign, the protest became a forerunner of twenty-first-century activism

FIGURE 6.4 *Tar Sands Healing Walk. Source: Photograph by taylorandayumi via Creative Commons/licensed with CC BY 2.0.*

and spiritual resistance aimed at recognition, pluralism, and Indigenous sovereignty within a distinctly ecological narrative of engaged stewardship.

Clearly indebted to both Indigenous and ancient wisdom traditions that expressed connection with "Mother Earth," nature, or Gaia, various modern neo-pagan groups, as well as new religious movements, reflect what scholar of religion Bron Taylor describes as "*dark green religion*," which he defines in ecotheological terms as "religion that considers nature to be sacred, imbued with intrinsic value, and worthy of reverent care" (2010: ix). While the specific form, type, and expression vary, what connects "dark green religions" together is both the depth of reverence for nature as well as a clear imperative to act on behalf of the environment. As Taylor notes, dark green religion "motivates a wide array of individuals and movements that are engaged in some of the most trenchant environment-related struggles of our time" (2010: ix–x), resulting in both individual activism motivated by nature-based spirituality, as well as new religious movements predicated on sustained stewardship of a natural world they actively worship.

Of those individual activists steeped in dark green religion, Julia Butterfly Hill, "who made the national news for her two-year sit in a coastal redwood [located in Humboldt County, California] called 'Luna,' believed her action was justified because 'majestic ancient places, housing more spirituality than any church, were being turned into clear-cuts and mudslides'" (Pike 2004: 33). In analyzing her motivation, Sarah Pike emphasizes Butterfly Hill's belief that "the woods and humanity ... [are] part of 'the Universal Spirit'," an understanding that characterizes how, spiritually, many "environmentalists act from the conviction that humans are part of a web of life that includes trees and animals. Destruction of other living beings, they say, destroys us all" (Pike 2004). Reflecting also on Butterfly Hill, as well as others, such as Alisha Little Tree, Graham Innes, and a small collection of activists operating out of Headwaters Redwood Forest Reserve in Northern California in the late 1990s, Taylor emphasizes how the move to direct action results from "experiencing the earth's sacred energies or lifeforce, or communication with nonhuman beings," and the corresponding need to revitalize and maintain this spiritual connection (2010: 95–7).

Ecotheology, Activism, and New Religious Movements

The most direct manifestations of dark green religion, ecotheologies, and nature-based spiritual activisms are found within a variety of neo-pagan, New Age, and women's spirituality movements that have developed primarily in the United States and the United Kingdom since the 1960s, a period defined by deep individual journeys for religious belonging and understanding, including the founding of unique new religious movements dedicated to nature reverence and/or environmental responsibility. The development of the Gaia Theory by James Lovelock and Lynn Margulis, along with the emergence of PaGaian Cosmology, speak to an entwining of spiritual orientations, acceptance of interconnection, and nature worship. Maybe more importantly, these orientations identify a relationship between scientific discourses and the needs of and for environmental stewardship. PaGaian Cosmology (Livingstone 2008), which "brings together a religious practice of seasonal ritual based in a contemporary scientific sense of the cosmos and female imagery for the Sacred" (PaGaian Cosmology n.d.), reflects the broader claims of the Gaia Theory, namely, that our worlds function through interactions—both organic and inorganic—that maintain the balance necessary for continued survival. As evolutionary biologist, futurist, and lecturer on Gaia Theory Elisabet Sahtouris proposes, the well-being and flourishing of humanity must occur within a mutually sustaining relationship with the larger ecosystems of the earth and cosmos (Sahtouris and Lovelock 2000).

Such belief leads not only to a direct worshipping of nature, as we see, for example, with the Church of All Worlds, but also an emphasis within neo-pagan, New Age, and witch-based groups to "act as caretakers and stewards of the land" (Pike 2004: 33). Founded by American Neopagan Morning Glory Zell, the Church of All Worlds venerates the Greek god Pan as the personification of the "natural cosmos. Our word pantheism," Zell continues, "is derived from that idea, that all Nature is God and that God is all

Nature" (1994: 12–13). Inspired similarly by the belief that nature is imbued with spirit and sacredness, Circle Sanctuary, a "non-profit international Nature Spirituality resource center and legally recognized Nature Spirituality church" that "honor[s] the Divine through Nature preservation and fostering Community through celebrations, ceremonies, education, outreach and other ministries," is engaged "in environmental education, prairie habitat restoration, woodlands and wetlands conservation, and other Nature preservation endeavors" (Circle Sanctuary n.d.). Lothlorien, a neo-pagan retreat in southern Indiana "envisioned as a magical place where spiritual beings are free to roam and accessible to humans who treat the land properly," demonstrates, to borrow from scholar of neo-paganism and the New Age, Sarah Pike, how "nature sanctuaries are one of the ways that Neopagans put their religious ideas into practice, because they are set up to facilitate the relationships between humans and other sentient beings" (2004: 33). While demonstrating the contingent overlapping of neo-pagan and New Age groups, the veneration of nature, and concerns for environmental degradation, others go further, connecting this specific understanding of "green religion" with activist projects that range from direct action to experiments in alternative and more responsible ways of being.

As historian of American religion Catherine Albanese develops, "the New Age social ethic has been an environmental ethic … New age people have—in keeping with the theory of correspondence—linked the well-being of their lives to the well-being of the world" (1999: 364). From EarthSpirit, a "non-profit organization founded in 1977, dedicated to the preservation and development of Earth-centered spirituality, culture and community" (EarthSpirit n.d.), to the modern witchcraft/goddess movement of Starhawk, we encounter a base concern that directs a series of contemporary new religious movements centered in neo-pagan orthodoxies; that is, to understand the world and nature as invested with life produces not only an entirely different orientation but also necessitates efforts to make daily life a reflection of this sacred relationship and mutual contingency. Reflecting on the correlation between raising consciousness and environmental activism, Pike notes how neo-pagan priestess Vivianne Crowley and the British neo-pagan environmental group, for example, conduct "'magical healing rites at threatened natural sites' and a similar group in New York City called the 'Gaia group' focuses on 'ecological magic.' Crowley," as Pike continues, "applauds these efforts because she believes that 'earth healing rituals raise awareness of environmental issues and those who take part in them are generally encouraged to take action on the material as well as on the magical plane to further their ends'" (2004: 159).

Maybe the most sustained example of this overlapping of nature reverence and activism is found in the work of Starhawk and Reclaiming, a San Francisco-based witchcraft collective founded by Starhawk and Diane Baker in 1979, with a specific focus on social issues, including environmental and economic activism. Founded with the mission to establish a "center for feminist spirituality and counseling," the group "reclaim[ed] the Goddess, the immanent life force, the connecting pattern to all being" (Salomonsen 2002: 40–1) as a means to overturn patriarchy and advance human relationships with and responsibility to nature. Almost immediately after their founding,

FIGURE 6.5 *The Scandinavian permaculture festival of 2013.* Source: *Photograph by Øyvind Holmstad via Wikimedia Commons/licensed with CC BY-SA 3.0.*

for instance, Reclaiming joined other activists in 1981 in acts of civil disobedience to stop the opening of a nuclear power plant in Diablo Canyon, California, and in 2002, Starhawk and other neo-pagans were arrested while nonviolently protesting against the World Trade Organization (WTO) because, as Starhawk reflects, "we worship nature. The WTO is part of a global attempt to elevate profit as a value that supersedes nature or any other value" (cited in Pike 2004: 159). Starhawk and Reclaiming highlight how "patriarchal religions [e.g., the Abrahamic traditions] reinforce the domination of humans over nature just as they reinforce the domination of male over female, which has resulted in a long history of exploitation of both women and the environment" (Urban 2015: 172).

As opposed to adhering to an anthropocentric worldview of domination, Reclaiming follows Starhawk's teaching that "the world itself [is] a living being, made up of dynamic aspects, a world where one thing shape-shifts into another, where there are no solid separations" (1987: 15). On a more practical level, Starhawk and Reclaiming's commitment to social justice and environmentalism find expression in permaculture, "a branch of ecological design and environmental engineering that seeks to create self-sustaining and regenerative habitats and agricultural systems based on natural ecosystems" (Urban 2015: 173). As Starhawk summarized in a 2013 lecture to the Harvard Divinity School, as "a whole system of ecological design," permaculture is

based on the idea that, if we can observe nature, and figure out how nature is working, and work in the same way that nature works, we can actually create systems that will meet our human needs while actually regenerating the environment around us instead of destroying it ... this is the practical application of the idea that the earth is sacred.

(Starhawk 2013)

Where many religions and new religious movements accentuate orthodoxy, or proper belief, this notion of "practical application" directs the efforts of new religious movements based in *orthopraxical* conduct designed to improve human-to-human and human-to-nature relationships. While some share with neo-pagans a reverence for the environment, others understand that any teaching of interconnection includes imperatives to treat one another and the natural world more compassionately, empathetically, and responsibly. Such commitments have led to a blending of new religious movements, communal living, and environmental activism. For example, inspired by the teachings of Stephen Gaskin, whose spiritual insights highlight "a belief in the moral imperative toward altruism that was implied by the telepathic spiritual communion we experienced together" (Gaskin 2005: 11), a group of spiritual travelers founded the Farm in 1971 in Summertown, Tennessee. The Farm offered space and opportunity for the group to put into practice their shared belief in oneness and love, and a corresponding commitment to altruism and social justice. Founding the Farm, then, was not about going to "get a place to be, it wasn't to go get a farm, it was," Gaskin stresses, "to *make a difference*" (cited in Mother Earth News Editors 1980: 141; emphasis added). Realizing that values of love and imperatives of responsibility mean nothing if not expanded beyond the confines of the Farm itself, members established Plenty International in 1974, "a not-for-profit 501-c-3 organization ... created to help protect and share the world's abundance and knowledge for the benefit of all. Plenty supports economic self-sufficiency, cultural integrity and environmental responsibility in partnership with families, community groups and other organizations in Central America, the U.S., the Caribbean, and Africa" (Plenty International n.d.). A recent project in Jalacte, Belize, for instance, promotes "equity, sustainability and resilience to climate change with regards to food security" through the creation of agricultural structures, agro-forestry, and updated eco-friendly irrigation (Plenty International 2018).

We encounter a similar motivation and expression of environmental activism in two twentieth- and twenty-first-century movements, one is a British community connected to the New Age, and the other is a new religious movement centered on worldly projects as opposed to institutional coherency. Referred to as a "spiritual utopian community," and commonly cited as a core expression of the New Age, the Findhorn Ecovillage, located at the Park in Moray, Scotland, is an experimental intentional commune dedicated to modeling sustainable alternatives for living more responsibly and harmoniously with nature (Spielvogel 1985: 231–44).

The Findhorn Ecovillage reflects the collective spiritual teachings of founders Eileen Caddy, Peter Caddy, and Dorothy Maclean, the latter of whom claimed to have the ability to "intuitively contact the overlighting intelligence of plants—which she called angels, and then devas—who gave her instructions on how to make the most of their

FIGURE 6.6 *Findhorn Foundation.* Source: *Wikimedia Commons/licensed with CC BY-SA 4.0.*

fledgling garden" (Findhorn Foundation n.d.). Abiding by the corresponding recognition that "our planet is alive and aware. By communicating and working with the rest of nature humans can find and bring new and creative solutions to life," Findhorn offers workshops, retreats, and resources designed to help inspire others to "co-create" with, and live according to, "spirit" (Spielvogel 1985).

Derived from his teachings that spirituality expresses both a condition of oneness and an obligation toward lovingkindness (Shankar 1999), Ravi Shankar founded the Art of Living Foundation in 1981, an international non-governmental organization (NGO) with centers in more than 156 countries dedicated to education, meditation, and humanitarian projects. In addition to offering courses in Sudarshan Kriya, a breathing technique taught in relation to self-development and stress reduction, the foundation operates a series of social service undertakings often connected to environmentalism. For example, Project Vidarbha (in 2007) offered training in organic and zero-budget farming to farmers decimated by famine, and Mission Green Earth (in 2008) represented a partnership between the Art of Living Foundation, the United Nations Millennium Campaign, and the United Nations Environment Programme aimed at planting over 100 million trees to help reduce the effects of global warming.

While many environmentally-oriented religious groups and movements seek change through nonviolent advocacy and protests, others turn to more radical forms of direct action to challenge the modern, capitalist system bent on negating the value of life through the willful pillaging of land and environmental resources.

Bron Taylor goes so far as to argue that "radical environmentalism is best understood as a new religious movement that views environmental degradation as an assault on a sacred, natural world" (2013: 297). Based on the belief that Western ideologies—

FIGURE 6.7 *Earth First! Following the arrest of tree-sitters on July 6, a construction worker removes an Earth First! Banner from the March through July 2001 Bluebird tree sit. The tree sit was initiated to protest the construction of low-income housing in the Brown Woods area of Bloomington, Indiana.* Source: *Image ID: J4YBAK. Contributor: Jeremy Hogan/Alamy Stock Photo.*

from Eurocentric religions to neoliberal capitalism—lead inevitably to environmental destruction, radical environmentalists, such as some members of Earth First!, the Earth Liberation Front (ELF), and the Earth Liberation Army (ELA), seek both a return to and a re-sacralizing of nature, often in the form of actively defending "Mother Earth" through various expressions of economic sabotage—or *ecotage*—initiated to prevent logging or industrial pollution. As Sarah Pike summarizes, some "radical environmentalists involved in spiking trees and setting up tree sits to prevent logging in old-growth forests are likely to share the Neopagan belief that nature is imbued with spirit, and this is what fuels their activism" (2004: 33). The challenge, when considering radical environmentalism as new religion, however, emerges in relation to ends and means; in defense of nature's sacrality, what occurs when groups participate in willful violence, including the destruction of property or acts of arson that affect the very elements of nature they seek to defend?

As the twenty-first century continues to experience heightened environmental crises, religiously-based environmentalism, ecotheologies, and nature-revering new religious movements offer guidance in efforts to connect moral imperatives with actions and activisms aimed at ameliorating the effects of human-caused degradation and climate change.

Further Reading and Online Resources

Gottlieb R.S. (2006), *A Greener Faith: Religious Environmentalism and Our Planet's Future*, New York: Oxford University Press.

Gottlieb R.S., ed. (2006), *The Oxford Handbook of Religion and Ecology*, New York: Oxford University Press.

Hallman D.G., ed. (1994), *Ecotheology: Voices from South and North*, Ossining, NY: Orbis Books.

McKanan D. (2017), *Eco-Alchemy: Anthroposophy and the History and Future of Environmentalism*, Berkeley: University of California Press.

Woodhouse K.M. (2020), *The Ecocentrists: A History of Radical Environmentalism*, New York: Columbia University Press.

References

Abdul-Matin I. (2010), *Green Deen: What Islam Teaches about Protecting the Planet*, San Francisco: Berrett-Koehler Publishers.

Albanese C. L. (1999), *America: Religions and Religion*, Belmont, CA: Wadsworth.

Carson R. (2002), *Silent Spring*, Boston: A Mariner Book.

Circle Sanctuary (n.d.), "About Circle Sanctuary." Available online: https://www.circlesanctuary.org/index.php/organization/about-circle-sanctuary (accessed April 23, 2021).

Dalai Lama (2020), *Our Only Home: A Climate Appeal to the World*, New York: Hanover Square Press.

Devall B. (1992), "Deep Ecology and Radical Environmentalism," in R.E. Dunlap and A.G. Mertig (eds.), *American Environmentalism: The U.S. Environmental Movement, 1970–1990*, 51–62, New York: Routledge.

EarthSpirit (n.d.), "About Us." Available online: http://www.earthspirit.com (accessed June 1, 2021).

Findhorn Foundation (n.d.), "About Us." Available online: https://www.findhorn.org/about-us/ (accessed April 21, 2021).

Fortress Press (n.d.), "Eco-theology." Available online: https://www.fortresspress.com/store/category/287099/Eco-theology (accessed June 11, 2021).

Gaskin S. (2005), *Monday Night Class*, Summertown, TN: Book Publishing Company.

Geertz C. (1973), "Religion as a Cultural System," in *The Interpretation of Cultures: Selected Essays*, 93–135, New York: Basic Books.

Gilio-Whitaker D. (2019), *As Long as Grass Grows: The Indigenous Fight for Environmental Justice, from Colonization to Standing Rock*, Boston: Beacon Press.

Hanegraaff W.J. (1996), *New Age Religion and Western Culture: Esotericism in the Mirror of Secular Thought*, Leiden: Brill.

Hoel N. and E. Nogueira-Godsey (2011), "Transforming Feminisms: Religion, Women, and Ecology," *Journal for the Study of Religion*, 24 (2): 5–15.

Hope M. and J. Young (1994), "Islam and Ecology," *CrossCurrents* 44 (2): 180–93.

Indigenous Environmental Network (n.d.), "Our History." Available online: https://www.ienearth.org/about/ (accessed May 16, 2021).

Interfaith Center for Sustainable Development (2021), "Homepage." Available online: https://www.interfaithsustain.com (accessed April 23, 2021).

Interfaith Power & Light (n.d.), "About." Available online: https://www.interfaithpowerandlight.org/about/ (accessed April 24, 2021).

Katz E. (2011), "Ecokosher," in A. Berlin and M. Grossman (eds.), *The Oxford Dictionary of Jewish Religion*, 227, New York: Oxford University Press.

Kimmerer R.W. (2002), "Weaving Traditional Ecological Knowledge into Biological Education: A Call to Action," *BioScience*, 52 (5): 432–8.

Lai P. (2017), "Ecological Theology as Public Theology: A Chinese Perspective," *International Journal of Public Theology*, 11: 477–500.

Livingstone G. (2008), *PaGaian Cosmology: Re-inventing Earth-based Goddess Religion*, Lincoln, NE: iUniverse.

Martin J.W. (2001), *The Land Looks After Us: A History of Native American Religion*, New York: Oxford University Press.

Mother Earth News Editors (1980), "A Good Look at the Farm," *The Mother Earth News*, 62: 138–41.

Naess A. (1973), "The Shallow and the Deep, Long-range Ecology Movement. A Summary," *Inquiry: An Interdisciplinary Journal of Philosophy*, 16: 95–100.

Nasr S.H. (2007), "Religion and the Environmental Crisis," in W. Chittick (ed.), *The Essential Seyyed Hossein Nasr*, 29–39, Bloomington, IN: World Wisdom.

PaGaian Cosmology (n.d.), "Home." Available online: https://pagaian.org (accessed April 25, 2021).

Pike S. (2004), *New Age and Neopagan Religions in America*, New York: Columbia University Press.

Plenty International (2018), "Adapting Food Security to Climate Change in Jalacte." Available online: https://plenty.org/area/environmental-protection/ (accessed April 19, 2021).

Plenty International (n.d.), "About Plenty." Available online: https://plenty.org/about-plenty/ (accessed April 19, 2021).

Rasmussen L.L. (2000), *Earth Community Earth Ethics*, Maryknoll, NY: Orbis Books.

Sahtouris E. and J.E. Lovelock (2000), *EarthDance: Living Systems in Evolution*, San Jose, CA: iUniversity Press.

Salomonsen J. (2002), *Enchanted Feminism: The Reclaiming Witches of San Francisco*, New York: Routledge.

Shankar R. (1999), *Bang on the Door: A Collection of Talks*, Santa Barbara, CA: Art of Living Foundation.

Spielvogel J. (1985), "Findhorn: The Evolution of a Spiritual Utopian Community," *Journal of General Education*, 37 (3): 231–44.

Starhawk (1987), *Truth or Dare: Encounters with Power, Authority and Mystery*, San Francisco: Harper and Row.

Starhawk (2013), "Permaculture and the Sacred: A Conversation with Starhawk," YouTube, March 18. Available online: https://www.youtube.com/watch?v=zV-MsQYrW0g (accessed May 17, 2021).

Taylor B. (2010), *Dark Green Religion: Nature Spirituality and the Planetary Future*, Berkeley: University of California Press.

Taylor B. (2013), "Religion, Violence and Radical Environmentalism from Earth First! to the Unabomber to the Earth Liberation Front," in C. Muddle (ed.), *Political Extremism*, vol. 4, 297–336, Thousand Oaks, CA: SAGE Publications.

Thich Nhat Hanh (2014), "Thich Nhat Hanh's Statement on Climate Change for the United Nations." Plum Village. Available online: https://plumvillage.org/about/thich-nhat-hanh/letters/thich-nhat-hanhs-statement-on-climate-change-for-unfccc/ (accessed April 13, 2021).

Urban H. (2015), *New Age, Neopagan, & New Religious Movements: Alternative Spirituality in Contemporary America*, Oakland: University of California Press.

White L., Jr. (1969), "The Historical Roots of Our Ecologic Crisis," *JASA*, 21: 42–7.

Zell Morning Glory (1994), "Pan," *Green Egg*, 27 (104): 12–13.

Glossary Terms

Anthropocentrism A human-centered point of view that positions human beings as the only site of and for morality and ethics; an understanding that elevates humans above and beyond the environment and animals.

Dark green religion As defined by scholar of religion Bron Taylor, a "religion that considers nature to be sacred, imbued with intrinsic value, and worthy of reverent care" (2010: ix). Often deinstitutionalized, and lacking any single orthodoxy, orthopraxy, or sacred text, dark green religions identify moral, ethical, and spiritual orientations that elevate the innate value of the environment and connect religious action to projects of stewardship and activism, including direct action and civil disobedience.

Dominion/Dominionism An ideology that seeks to install Christianity as the ruling political order based on the belief that Christians hold a biblical mandate to rule over nature and control worldly institutions, particularly the government. Also referred to as dominion theology, dominionism emerges from the teaching in Genesis 1:28, which establishes a distinctly anthropocentric worldview, including humans domination over nature: "Be fruitful, and multiply, and replenish the earth, and subdue it: and have dominion over the fish of the sea, and over the fowl of the air, and over every living thing that moveth upon the earth."

Ecotage Variably understood as ecologically-based sabotage; acts of sabotage committed in defense of the environment; or sabotage-based radical environmentalism. Beyond projects of sustainability and conservation, ecotage describes a manifestation of radical environmentalism defined by acts of direct action and civil disobedience designed to interrupt a system, process, machinery, or political order in efforts to secure the vitality of nature. Examples include the deliberate destruction of whaling and fishing vessels by groups such as the Sea Shepherd Conservation Society; the sabotage of construction or logging equipment by groups like Earth First!; treespiking, which describes the practice of inserting a metal rod or nail into trees to damage saws and milling equipment; or treesitting, as with Julia Butterfly Hill's protest, to prevent deforestation.

Ecotheology Often connected to constructive theology, ecotheology centers the interrelationship between religious worldviews and spiritual understandings with human-caused environmental crises. Ecotheology highlights both a recognition of humanity's contingent relationship with nature as well as the need to take active steps to ameliorate the degradation of nature, improve sustainability, and advance ecological responsibility.

Neo-pagan/Neo-paganism A broad and collective term used to describe contemporary religious movements based in, or influenced by, premodern peoples and historical pagan beliefs and rituals. Scholar of esotericism Wouter Hanegraaff contends that neo-paganism represents "all those modern movements which are, first, based on the conviction that what Christianity has traditionally denounced as idolatry and superstition actually represents/represented a profound and meaningful religious worldview and, secondly, that a religious practice based on this worldview can and should be revitalized in our modern world" (1996: 77). Lacking any single definition or representational structure, neo-paganism ranges (to name a few) from witchcraft, goddess spiritualities, Faerie Faith, and Wicca to Ásatrú, druidism, and heathenry. Often pantheistic (belief that the divine interpenetrates all existence) and animistic (belief that the divine animates existence and/or that everything that exists is imbued with a spiritual energy), many neo-pagans venerate nature (as Gaia or Mother Earth) and correspondingly commit themselves to environmental and ecological stewardship.

New religious movement (NRM) A new religion or alternative spirituality with "modern" origins (meaning typically the mid-1800s onward), a condensed timeline (e.g., it is "younger"), and that often exists on the outside of, or counterculturally to, a society's dominant religious culture. NRMs can be both entirely novel, introducing new orthodoxies, sacred narratives, and rituals, or an offshoot—or subset—of an established religious tradition. NRMs are commonly eclectic, pluralistic, and syncretic, combining elements of both ancient and more recent religious expressions most often in response to modern crises of faith that lead people away from traditional ideologies and religious systems.

Orthopraxical Adjective form of orthopraxy, or the notion of "correct" action. Distinguished from orthodoxy, or the idea of correct belief, orthopraxical describes the agreed to and accepted practices associated with religious traditions and spiritual orientations, including rituals, worldly activity, and ethical conduct.

Stewardship Religious belief that humans assume responsibility for the world and are thus tasked for actively caring for nature and the environment. For monotheists, stewardship results from a single God who created both humanity and the world, with humans often explicitly situated as the caretakers of God's kingdom. For religions that emphasize a sacred immanence, such as Indigenous traditions, Hinduism, and neo-paganism, responsibility results from belief that the earth (or nature) itself is sacred, godly, or divine. In the twentieth and twenty-first centuries stewardship has become increasingly linked to environmentalism.

PART TWO

Embodiments and Identities

7

Race, Religion, and Environmental Racism in North America

Elaine Nogueira-Godsey, Laurel D. Kearns,
and Whitney A. Bauman

Introduction

Although many people think about racism as a prejudice or discrimination for a person on account of skin color, that is only one aspect of racism. A more complex and multifaceted form of racism is what scholars name as structural or systemic racism. The structural expression of racism has normalized racist actions, making it "simply 'natural', flowing from nature itself and the nature(s) of things" (Plumwood 1993: 4–5), so that we do not see how anthropogenic climate change exacerbates racism. It seems that both terms, "climate change" and "racism," are terms that need to be better defined in the public space. Most people do not think of themselves as racists or that they are directly contributing to the destruction of the planet's living conditions (Moe-Lobeda 2013). Racism, in the popular imagination of everyday people, is confined to discrete acts motivated by malicious intent. In reality, this is just the tip of the iceberg of what racism is and how far-reaching its effects are. In the same way that environmentalism and climate change is about much more than litter on the side of the road, or a mild winter, racism is much more than epithets and segregation. With both climate change and racism, its effects and impacts are compounding in its normalized manifestations that are a part of everyday life with deadly consequences.

Climate change has been explained by scientists as anthropogenic (see O'Brien chapter in this volume). The term "anthropogenic" refers to the fact that although the earth's climate has changed before because of natural processes, according to 97 percent of scientists studying the atmosphere, the change in climate that we experience today is a product of human influence and is "getting more dangerous" (Local Science Engagement Network [LSEN] n.d.) and requires an urgent call to action (Cook et al. 2016; NASA n.d.). Anthropogenic climate change and its negative consequences are perhaps the most overwhelming issue to have ever faced humanity. Studies from different disciplines have demonstrated that the consequences of climate change permeate every sphere of life. Yet, we still hear people saying, "I don't believe in climate change." How did climate change become a matter of faith? (see Kearns 2007; Veldman 2019). In the United States, climate change has been polarized and couched as a political issue. It is, yet based on data it is also "undeniably personal; it leaves individuals, families and communities devastated or demolished in its wake" (Nogueira-Godsey 2019a). Teaching and learning about the causes, consequences, and mitigation of climate change is fundamental to the survival of life as we know it.

What is the relationship between race, nature, and religion? At first these three concepts/terms may not seem to be inherently connected at all, but we will argue that they are. First, the predominant understanding of "nature" and "the environment" in North America has been defined mostly by white Europeans, to the detriment of peoples of color (Cordova and Moore 2007). Second, notions of race and nature have been justified on the basis of both religious and scientific or natural foundations (Keel 2018). Third, race matters in terms of environmental justice: the fact that the poorest people, and people of color, deal with most of the consequences of anthropogenic climate change and ecological degradation is something termed "environmental racism" (Bullard 2007: viii; see also Cole and Foster 2000; Taylor 2014; Yusoff 2018). Why are Black, brown, and Indigenous peoples breathing in more contaminated air than their fellow white Americans (Kearns 2018; McKittrick and Woods 2007)? Why is a person's race and ethnicity the most strongly correlated factor for their risk of being affected by a natural disaster and its aftermath (Bullard and Wright 2012)?

In this chapter, we examine the relationship between religion and environmental racism, which in its worst version is the intersection between racial dynamics and environmental destruction. We show that humanity's slow and insufficient response to address such issues are, in part, a manifestation of normalized domination against both the people and the earth. We argue that climate change is a matter of injustice, and as such, it is a political, moral, and ethical issue. As such, it is also a civil matter, which requires everyone to take moral actions. First, we approach the environmental justice movement and show the ways in which climate change, racial issues, and social inequities are connected. Second, we explain how religious and philosophical concepts have aided in justifying racism and environmental destruction. Third, we highlight some of the many initiatives today fighting against the destruction of the earth, as well as striving to repair severed relationships with nature, all through the lens of racism.

The Environmental Justice Movement: The Connection of Climate Injustice, Racism, and Social Inequities

Of course, there is nothing "natural" about racism, but there are reasons to connect racism and Earth's natural environments. Anthropologist Ghassan Hage argues that racism is, itself, an environmental threat: "[racism] reinforces and reproduces the dominance of the basic social structures that are behind the generation of the environmental crisis—which are the structures of its own generation" (Hage 2017: 15). Recently, Trad and Elaine Nogueira-Godsey argued that environmental racism "is faceless and insidious" (2021: 91). They argued that "Not only does racism fuel and compound the environmental crisis, but it also reproduces our racism in the environmental crisis. Worse, it depersonalizes our racism when it boomerangs back from the natural world, which makes accountability and responsibility that much easier to evade" (Nogueira-Godsey and Nogueira-Godsey 2021: 94).

To better understand how racism is an environmental threat, we need to understand the connections between environmental justice issues, anthropogenic climate change, and social economic inequities (Ahuja 2021). Although the terms environmental justice and anthropogenic climate change are intimately connected, they are often discussed as separate issues. Scholars explain that as a consequence of climate change, "Changes in temperatures and precipitation levels are shifting agricultural zones and habitats for wild and domesticated species, negatively affecting biodiversity, and creating challenges for food production" (Cuomo 2012). According to the IPCC (2021), although all of these effects have direct and indirect consequences for human communities, the most vulnerable are often poor women in developing countries, and to a greater degree, poor women of color. This makes climate change an environmental justice issue.

Environmental justice as a movement emerged from many places, such as a battle over the siting of landfills and incinerators in the city of Houston (Bullard 1983) and the early 1980s Warren County protests against a waste site for a highly toxic chemical (PCBs) that was illegally dumped on former agricultural land in a predominantly Black part of North Carolina (Perkins 2021; Roberts and Toufflon-Weiss 2001; Schlosberg 2009). The outraged local community organized a campaign of opposition, largely based in two churches, one Baptist and the other United Church of Christ (UCC). As a result, in 1987, the UCC Commission for Racial Justice statistically documented the connection between *Toxic Wastes and Race in the United States*, revealing that the most statistically significant predictor of location of a hazardous waste site is a community's race. This document was updated and the results continue revealing that "Race continues to be an independent predictor of where hazardous wastes are located" (Bullard et al. 2007: xii). Benjamin Chavis, coauthor of *Toxic Wastes and Race*, refers to this kind of injustice as "environmental racism" (Fears and Dennis, 2021).

Our takeaway from Chavis is that although international political debates have often explained anthropogenic climate change as a matter of the outcome of a history of polluting industries in developed and developing countries, the consequent global warming cannot be only framed and addressed as a matter of our need for clean air, water, and soil. We also need to recognize the interconnected reasons that have led governments and corporations to place polluting facilities in predominantly Black, native, and Hispanic communities (Nogueira-Godsey 2019b; see also Bravo et

FIGURE 7.1 *A diverse crowd of well over 150,000 at the Washington, DC People's Climate March on April 29, 2017.* Source: *majunznk—CC BY ND 2.0.*

al. 2016; Pulido 2000, 2019). First, the blind desire for economic growth and greed have manipulated "the consequences of human systems of consumption, such as polluted air and contaminated water, to affect some populations more than others" (Nogueira-Godsey and Nogueira-Godsey 2021: 91–2). Second, racism foregrounded the decision-making "to funnel vulnerabilities to specific population groups" (92). The inconvenient truth is that the human activities degrading the environment and causing climate change are "part of a deeply ingrained structure [of injustice] that affects a multiplicity of daily decisions, significantly limiting the options of the poorer, blacker neighborhoods to the advantage of a wealthier, whiter population" (Bohannon and O'Brien 2011: 177). This can particularly be seen in a wide range of health outcomes, from at least double the rates of asthma and COVID-19 related to air pollution, to rates of cancer in particular (Brender et al. 2011; United Church of Christ Environmental Integrity Project 2020; Washington 2020).

FIGURE 7.2 *A former resident visits the "Uptop" section of Altgeld Gardens in Chicago, located in an area that Hazel Johnson, the 1979 founder of the environmental justice organization People for Community Recovery (n.d.) nicknamed the "toxic donut" because they were surrounded by the highest concentration of hazardous waste sites in the United States. The wall pictured here displays the names of residents who have died, most from environmental-related issues. Photograph by Nikki Hoskins.*

The globalized dominant economic system in place is a market-oriented system (See Moe-Lobeda chapter in this volume). This means that the more people consume, the more the market-demand determines the proliferation of transnational corporations and the facilities necessary to produce consumer goods, such as industrial sites, ports, high traffic roadways, truck roads, gas stations, and the resulting toxic waste sites; all of which contribute to put high quantities of CO_2 in the atmosphere and thereby influence the warming of the planet (Story of Stuff n.d.). Living near to those sites has real and significant impacts on public health, quality of life, and life expectancy (Hoskins 2023; Mikati et al. 2018). Strategically searching for cheap manufacturing labor and weak environmental policies, transnational corporations have moved manufacturing to places such as Mexico and other developing countries, causing not only the degradation of living conditions on the planet but also the slow death of those who are seen as expendable (Nixon 2011; Pulido et al. 2019). The same is true of living near sites of extraction of fossil fuels (coal mining, fracking, tar sands oil, etc.) and concentrated animal feedlots (CAFOs), as Rev. Dr. William Barber II of the Poor People's Campaign (n.d.) points out (Barber and Yaggi 2015; Hribar 2010). This is one of the causal links behind the apparent correlations between environmental justice, climate change, racism, and economic power.

While everyone produces waste and has a carbon footprint, some produce much more and leave behind a much larger footprint. Likewise, while everyone depends on the earth for survival, it is those producing the most waste and causing the most harm to the environment that have the resources to avoid the most severe personal impacts of climate change (Tessum et al. 2019). It is not the climate or the earth that steers polluted air, extreme heat, hurricanes, floods, and other products of climate change toward Black, brown, Asian, and Indigenous communities (Renkl 2021). It is people with economic, legislative, and political power that have positioned industries and populations such that these communities will bear the most tragic and devastating effects of anthropogenic climate change (Bullard 2005; Nishime and Williams 2018; Whyte 2017).

The Normalization and Justification of Domination

Race and ethnicity, as well as class and gender, must be taken into consideration as we investigate causes of anthropogenic climate change (Eaton and Lorentzen 2003; Nogueira-Godsey 2022; Sellers 2016). Moreover, the social dynamics shaped by racism, classism, and sexism are not merely an aspect of how humans are changing the climate, but are fundamental to how we understand the environment/ nature in the first place (i.e., the environment includes humans), and therefore have been key in creating our climate problem. Scholars and activists argue that anti-racism work is a fundamental part of the very basis for the preservation of the living conditions on the planet. Ecofeminist scholars globally have asked the question of why people of color as well as poor women have been put in such positions of vulnerability (Whyte and Cuomo 2017). They have recognized that the reasons why the earth and people have been an object of domination and oppression in capitalist-driven societies are directly linked to the reason-nature dualism forming "the ideals of western culture and humanity as oppositional to nature" (Plumwood 1993: 27).

Before we continue, it is important to understand that dualisms are the tendency of making sense of the world through hierarchical binaries (e.g., reason over nature, male over female, mind over body, master over slave, rationality over animality or emotion, culture over nature, freedom over necessity, civilized over primitive, production over reproduction) (see O'Dell-Chaib chapter in this volume). Ecofeminist philosophers, such as Val Plumwood, have explained that dualism is "the construction of a devalued and sharply demarcated sphere of otherness" (1993: 41). Karen Warren refers to "unjustifiably dominated groups as 'Others,' both 'human Others' (such as women, people of color, children, and the poor) and 'earth Others' (such as animals, forests, the land)," producing a hierarchy of "less-than-human" humans (2000: 1). They explain the oppression of marginalized groups as tied to a view of nature as Other and outside the human realm of reason (Eaton 2005; see Eaton chapter in this resource).

Through analyzing the development of nature's representation in the history of rationalism in Western philosophy and culture, Plumwood explained that the view that humans' capacity to reason places them as part of a sharply separated realm, apart from the earth and above other animals, has led to an understanding of nature "as passive, as non-agent and non-subject, as the 'environment,' or the background condition for human survival" (Plumwood 1993: 4; see also Nogueira-Godsey 2022). This understanding has for centuries justified the violation of the earth's rights, and the rights of those considered less-than-human humans to conduct their lives as free subjects. The natural environment became "a field of multiple exclusion and control, not only of non-humans, but of various groups of humans and aspects of human life which are cast as nature" (Nogueira-Godsey 2022). Brazilian ecofeminist theologian Ivone Gebara (2003: 169) has demonstrated that in the history of the Americas, European colonizers justified the enslavement and treatment of Indigenous and Black African female slaves by locating Africans and Indigenous on the same level as animals, or as feminist theologian Kwok Pui-Lan has observed, as "belonging to a different species" other than human (2005: 227). They have dissected the racist and sexist motives in the ideology of colonization by demonstrating how the colonizers fused the unknown foreign land as a female body to be conquered and possessed. Womanist theologian Delores Williams discusses the "defilement, wanton desecration" of women and "othered" categories of humans, as well as the lands and oceans (1993b: 148). Black liberation theologian James Cone puts it succinctly: "The logic that led to slavery and segregation in the Americas, colonization and apartheid in Africa, and the rule of white supremacy throughout the world is the same one that leads to the exploitation of animals and the ravaging of nature" (2000: 36).

The reality of colonial histories and today's environmental racism issues raises the questions: Who is placed in the human category? What does it mean to be human? In light of these histories, it is not difficult to see how the reason-nature dualism has birthed a dominant economic global system that regard Others as objects of exploitation and manipulation. The earth and those associated with nature were backgrounded as the environmental "condition against which the 'foreground' achievements of reason or culture (provided typically by the white, Western, male expert or entrepreneur) take place" (Plumwood 1993: 4). Today the Earth, people of color, women, and the poor are still located in the sphere of material support for privileged elites.

Environmental Racism and Religion

The dualisms of which Plumwood speaks are not only supported by philosophical tenets, but also by religious ones. In the context of North America, this has meant mostly monotheistic (and mostly Christian) influences, although differences exist based on Protestant versus Catholic colonization. Take, for example, the idea of creation out of nothing. As Catherine Keller (2003) and others (see also Ruether 1994) have pointed out, this is not a biblical idea, rather it was created over time by the early church fathers (theologians) and later fed into the Catholic Doctrine of Discovery that blessed the seizing of "empty lands" by European colonizers. What is biblical is creation out of "the deep" (or the tehom). However, once you get a God that creates everything seen and unseen out of nothing, then you have an omnipotent, omniscient, omnipresent God that undermines any other religious truth claims. If the Christian God created everything out of nothing, then no other religious or truth claims have validity. This has foregrounded a colonial mentality toward "the other" (non-Christian) (Bauman 2009). At the same time, Western readings of the biblical texts have largely suggested that only human beings are created in the image of God. Humans are then "god-like" and above the rest of the natural, created world in some way. Humans are "exceptions" to the rest of the natural world (Peterson 2001). Lynn White, Jr. a historian of science, suggested that the biblical idea that humans have dominion over the rest of the natural world has helped to support environmentally destructive actions (White 1967). Of course, since that time, there has been a lot of work done to show that these somewhat popular interpretations from the Genesis stories are not the best ones (Bernstein 2021; Heibert 2008). Indeed, some have argued for an agrarian, or even kinship-based, Christian ethic, as did White with his concept of the democracy of all creatures (Levasseur 2017; McDaniel 1989; Riley 2014; Ruether 1977). The point here is that if God creates the world out of nothing, this means that God is different from (that is, above) that creation. If humans are made in the image of that God, then humans are also somewhat above the rest of the natural world. Furthermore, if humans are to have dominion over the planet, then "taming wild nature" becomes a religious command.

This monotheistic mentality is evident in the ways in which European colonizers sought to bring the "light" of this "truth" culture to "other" darker peoples they came

FIGURE 7.3 *A mural in Detroit by Brandan "bmike" Odums. The mural eventually included the Mexican proverb, "They tried to bury us. They didn't know we were seeds." Source: PunkToad/CC BY 2.0.*

into contact within India, Africa, and the Americas (Deloria 1973). It is also evident in the way that land was only seen as valuable if that land was cultivated or put to some use for human beings. Of course, as the section above points out, just who was a human being was defined by the colonizers, which meant European, mostly Christian, male, and pale skinned (Roothaan 2019). All "others" were more "like nature" and could be used like a resource by those defined as humans, in the case of slavery, or gotten rid of (in the case of the genocide of Indigenous peoples) (Gilio-Whitaker 2020).

This same mentality, from a monotheistic perspective, also played into the European Enlightenment and scientific mentality. As Carolyn Merchant has pointed out in *Death of Nature* (2019), the idea that humans were not a part of nature, and that nature is something that is "dead material" that can be transformed toward human ends, underlined the emerging of the Industrial Revolution. If God and the world are separated, all value and power lie with God and the immaterial. If the material world is changing and corrupt (an old lingering Greek idea), and humans are somehow special, made in the image of God, and "above" the rest of the natural world; then, it makes sense that humans can transform the world toward human ends in ways that the Industrial Revolution did.

Once some began to see the effects of the Industrial Revolution on the rest of the natural world and upon daily urban life, especially among the poor, a critique of the mechanism that brought about such a world was in order. Many of those we

FIGURE 7.4 *A poster advertising "Indian Territory" available for settlement, circa 1889. President Grover Cleveland recommended opening Indian Territory for settlement in his annual message to Congress on December 3, 1888. The Indian Appropriations Act of 1889 made way for mass-scale land theft from Native American communities. Source: National Archives/Public Domain.*

now call "romantics" looked to Indigenous animisms, and the relational ontologies of Buddhism and other Vedic traditions to rethink human-earth relations. This appropriation and often misappropriation was not without its problems. Again, as Merchant notes in *Reinventing Eden* (2003), there was a certain sense in which Romantics such as Thoreau wanted to "go back" to a simpler time (see also Gould 2017). Did this not imply that Indigenous animisms and Asian traditions were somehow "in the past" (which is, of course, the critique made by postcolonial scholars)? In terms of race, what did this mean for brown and Black peoples versus the white Europeans who brought the Enlightenment to the "dark masses?" Indeed slavery and servanthood were connected with skin color in a way that associated lighter skinned people more with Reason and Good, and darker skinned people with material bodies in need of controlling and educating (for many Indigenous peoples, they were eliminated and their cultures erased, through disease, massacres, relocation, and being sent away to boarding schools, where thousands died).

Today this contested legacy means that, on the one hand, environmentalism and its concepts of "nature" in North America is deeply indebted to Indigenous and Asian influences (See Kearns and Bauman chapter in this volume). On the other hand, it means that critiques of a naive romanticism can also be taken as critiques on Indigenous animisms and on the relational ontologies of Asian traditions (See Allison chapter in this volume). The complicated issues during the Romantic era, and the contemporary ways in which romanticism is critiqued mean that for many native peoples, people of Asian descent, and people of African descent, environmentalism is a double-edged sword (Oh 2011; White 2016). Critiquing those ideas that are influenced by Eastern traditions, and romanticism's ideas about which bodies were "closer to nature," all make this history very complex, especially when many are turning to reclaim those animisms (Clay 2018).

The category of nature, like the category of race, is socially constructed differently in different times, places, and cultures, as Confucian scholar Young-chan Ro explains (1989). One thing is clear, however, race and nature are always tied together in their constructions (Ko 2019; Taylor 2016). In some Euro-Western constructions, whiteness (itself a construct) is closer to Reason/God, while Black, brown, Asian, and Indigenous peoples are closer to nature (and can thus be treated as property/animals). In other constructions, such as among European and American white Romantics, as well as critics of color, the white people were corrupt and needed to learn from Indigenous, Asian, and other peoples of color about how to live in harmony with nature (See Leduc chapter in this volume). Adding in economic status, and who is "closer" to the land, and for what reasons, further complicates it. Many in more urbanized settings today romanticize a return to the land, whereas for many who have had no choice but to work the land in some fashion, there is nothing romantic or nostalgic about it because the land is filled with the blood of their ancestors' enslavement and forced labor (Carter 2021). Others want nothing to do with being seen as farmers or gardeners due to past histories of sharecropping, migrant farm or landscape work (Kyle and Kearns 2018). In addition to the systemic racisms that are tied up with environmentalism and understandings of nature that we mentioned above, race and nature are also tied together conceptually in terms of how we understand bodies (Jackson 2020). Which bodies are understood to represent "human nature" in terms of medical research, since many illnesses are mainly researched in white, often male, bodies? Which bodies are more human, or considered the norm, perhaps, in popular culture? Which bodies are docile? Which bodies are agential versus seen as servants? These are all questions that are tied up with how nature is defined and by whom (Candraningrum 2014; LaVasseur 2021; Morgan and Anzaldúa [1981] 2005; Williams 1993a).

Expanding Our Understanding of Environmentalisms

So far, we have attempted to show that the racialized experience of nature is socially constructed; connected to distinct geographies and experiences (Lipsitz 2011); and embedded in cultural, often religiously influenced, ideologies that then justify those racial, and racist, realities. There is no "one" experience of nature or of being racialized (APEN n.d.; Ialobaloca 2014; White 2016). For example, it is important to remember that while indigenous peoples often experience environmental racism in kindred ways to those of peoples of color, who involuntarily or voluntarily (recognizing that economic issues often leave little choice but to immigrate) came from elsewhere, there are vast differences in people's experiences and attitudes toward nature that are shaped by those histories and geographies of the vast and diverse lands of North America (Glave 2010; Wells 2018). Indigenous peoples' lands throughout North America were stolen by colonizers, and their nations were forced onto less desirable lands that then often became toxic dumping grounds; Mexicans and Japanese have also been displaced in the United States and their lands taken by government actions (Anzaldúa 1987; Gilio-Whitaker 2020; PBS 2009). Native lands continue to be stolen every time some valuable "natural resource" is "discovered" on it, such as the tar sands oil extraction on First Nations' lands, and in the process of obtaining it, the people are displaced and the thriving ecosystems upon which communities depend are decimated (Pagán 2020; Sacred Land Film Project n.d.). In a similar fashion, communities of color are often in urban and rural areas where the lack of government regulation and protection lead not only to the siting of hazardous sites, but also to the lack of clean water or the impact of concentrated animal feeding operations (CAFOS) on those who endure the hazardous excess of the meat industry (De La Torre 2021; Hribar 2010). As environmental justice has often come to be connected with urban areas, Rev. Dr. William Barber II, Catherine Flowers, and others remind us of its rural character (Flowers 2020).

These histories have often meant that environmental issues were, and are, seen as white issues about nature as wilderness and endangered animals, and that environmentalists did not see the connection with issues of racism: this is the history that shaped the First National People of Color Environmental Leadership Summit in

FIGURE 7.5 *The Athabasca Chipewyan First Nation claims that the vast mining operation in the Athabasca Tar Sands, Alberta, Canada, and the resulting destruction is a violation of Treaty 8 signed with the Canadian government.* Source: *Jason Woodhead/CC BY 2.0.*

1991 and related challenges to the whiteness of the big environmental groups (Rakia and Mair 2016; Taylor 2015). That history is what the environmental justice movement has worked to change, as James Cone challenged:

> People who fight against white racism but fail to connect it to the degradation of the earth are anti-ecological, whether they know it or not. People who struggle against ecological injustice but do not incorporate in it a disciplined and sustained fight against white supremacy are racists, whether they acknowledge it or not. The fight for justice cannot be segregated but must be integrated with the fight for life in all its forms.
>
> (2000: 36)

As already described, many of the roots of the environmental justice movement are religious, for example, the Christian justice impetus of care for the neighbor and the least of these that motivated the UCC, and other members of the National Council of Churches Eco-Justice Working Group in the 1980s onward (Kearns 2013). Religion has shaped the leaders and tactics of grassroots groups such as Charlotte Keys and Jesus People Against Pollution (founded in 1992) in Mississippi, or the Newtown Florist Club in Georgia (Spears 2020), or more recent examples such as Green The Church

(Milman 2016). Religious groups have been invaluable in grassroots organizing, acting as movement midwives by providing space to meet; funding; ways to disseminate information; connections and networks that expand beyond the local; and ways to frame a message in moral terms that resonate deeply by turning environmental issues into the moral justice issues that they always are in some way (Baugh 2016; Betancourt 2018; Hay 2009; Immergut and Kearns 2012).

Other religious roots of the environmental justice movement can be seen in the Indigenous perspectives that shaped the articulation of the Principles of Environmental Justice at the First National People of Color Environmental Leadership Summit (1991), and then influenced the goals and vision of the emerging movement, as the First Principle states: "the sacredness of Mother Earth, ecological unity and the interdependence of all species." Reclaiming the first principle has been transformational in breaking free of dominant cultural constructs, and rekindling connections to nature and ancestors, whether through Indigenous, or African diaspora traditions such as Yoruba, Santeria and, Candomble (see Gray chapter in this volume; Harris 2017b; Kimmerer 2015; Perez 2016; Pinto and Harding 2016). Elonda Clay's challenging essay, titled "How Does it Feel to Be an Environmental Problem?" (2011), reminds us how important it is to remember that not all racialized experience/connectedness to nature is as negative as the lens of environmental injustice might seem to indicate. Many of African, Latinx, and Indigenous descent are exploring the foods of their traditions, such as African American chef Michael Twitty's Afroculinaria (n.d.) explorations of how enslaved Africans transformed southern food ways, or the Pawnee and Athabaskan Hillel Echo-Hawk's focus on precolonial Indigenous food traditions, Rich Francis's of Tetlit Gwich'in and Tuscarora Nations championing of the sovereignty of Indigenous hunting, and the I-collective of Indigenous chefs cofounded by Oaxaqueño Neftalí Durán, in an assertion of principles of food sovereignty and food justice (Civil Eats n.d.; Sherman 2017; Whyte 2018). Others, such as Rowan White of Sierra Seeds, or Leah Penniman (2018) of SoulFire Farm, are nurturing seed stewards and "rescuing" seed varieties, historically cultivated by Indigenous, Black, and brown peoples, which the dominant "agribusiness" model of monoculture and patented seeds are displacing (PBS 2012; see also Briggs-Cloud chapter in this volume). The nurturing of urban gardens and food security, and the challenge to systems of food apartheid, such as the Sankofa Community Farm in Philadelphia, or the Black Church Food Security Network (n.d.) and the work of Rev. Heber Brown III, are reconnecting urban people with the land, health, and heritage of sustainable farming (Alkon and Agyeman 2011; Betancort 2018; BTS Center 2020; Reynolds and Cohen 2016; Vox 2021; White 2018).

Although growing food does intimately connect us with the land, others are connecting with land and the earth through the deep spirituality of someone like Howard Thurman, or Alice Walker and other ecowomanists, or Indigenous traditions (Baker-Fletcher 1998; Harris 2017a; Marcos 2009; Robinson 2021). Many are wrestling with the "nature deprivation," or the racialized experiences of those who love "nature"

FIGURE 7.6 *Veronica Kyle of Faith and Place, co-visionary and cofounder of the Eco Womanist Institute, leading a story circle concerning food and migration and helping Black and brown southside Chicago residents feel more comfortable in "nature."* Source: *Courtesy Faith in Place/used with permission.*

in terms of hiking, fishing, camping, but are often seen as "out of place" in "white spaces" because of normative images of white people doing these things (Finney 2014), and as a result are establishing a myriad of organizations, networks, and blogs working to reclaim access and comfort in "nature" for racialized others under memes such as "hiking while black" (Rowland-Shea et al. 2020). Indeed, these complex histories add up to shape attitudes toward the acceptance of climate change and the need to respond, now. Studies show consistently that it is white Euro-Americans who are less likely to be concerned or to accept the scientific evidence, although there is differentiation, of course, within groups based on country, religious identity, political party, class, and levels of education (Kearns 2018). This insight is grounded in the realization of who will be the most unjustly impacted by climate change. This work of reconnecting to "nature" and nurturing alternative life-giving relationships with the earth is also part of the work on resilience, resistance, and adaptation that lies ahead in the face of the brutal realities of global warming (Carvalhaes 2019).

The relationship between race, religion, and nature is a complex one, as this chapter has shown. Though at times it seems that environmentalism and critical

FIGURE 7.7 *A Latinx Chicago congregation on a Nature Outing through Faith in Place, as a way to help heal broken relations with the creation that is part of the often forced migration story of so many, and to help see the beauty of nature rather than feeling fear over the dangers that "nature" might hold as part of land restoration efforts.* Source: *Faith in Place/used with permission.*

understandings of race have not overlapped, the past few decades have brought these issues together, with the help of environmental justice movements, and with critical studies of how racism has been justified by both religious authority and the understanding of race as "natural." In addition, studies showing how human relationships with the Earth are influenced by different cultures, languages, and intersectional embodiment in the world, have enriched our understanding of "nature," including human nature. These, and the many ways in which systemic racism leads to the inequitable distribution of environmental costs and benefits, have brought into focus the dire intersectionality of climate justice and related movements of racial and economic justice. The future of any type of environmentalism (religious or nonreligious) has to take into account these complex issues and the variety of perspectives expressed by different peoples' understandings and experiences of race. We might then move beyond what makes us see difference, whether human or nonhuman, as something that exists to be managed or dominated, to facing the very serious work of climate justice.

Further Reading and Online Resources

Dungy C.T., ed. (2009), *Black Nature: Four Centuries of African American Nature Poetry*, Athens: University of Georgia Press.

Intersectional Environmentalist (n.d.). Available online: https://www. intersectionalenvironmentalist.com/ (accessed September 25, 2021).

Sacred Land Film Project (n.d.). Available online: https://sacredland.org/sacred-land-film-project/ (accessed September 25, 2021).

Wilbur M., D. Small-Rodriguez, and A. Keene (2019–), *All My Relations Podcast*. Available online: https://podcasts.apple.com/us/podcast/all-my-relations-podcast/id1454424563 (accessed September 25, 2021).

Yugar T.A., S.E. Robinson, L. Dube, and T.M. Hinga, eds. (2021), *Valuing Lives, Healing Earth: Religion, Gender, and Life on Earth*, Leuven: Peeters Publishers.

References

Ahuja N. (2021), *Planetary Specters: Race, Migration, and Climate Change in the Twenty-First Century*, Chapel Hill: University of North Carolina Press.

Alkon A. and J. Agyeman, eds. (2011), *Cultivating Food Justice: Race, Class, and Sustainability*, Cambridge, MA: MIT Press.

Anzaldúa G. (1987), *Borderlands/La Frontera: The New Mestiza*, San Francisco: Spinster/ Aunt Lute.

Asian Pacific Environmental Network (APEN) (n.d.). Available online: https://apen4ej.org/ (accessed September 25, 2021).

Baker-Fletcher K. (1998), *Sisters of Dust, Sisters of Spirit: Womanist Wordings on Creation*, Minneapolis, MN: Augsburg Fortress Publishers.

Barber W.J. II and M. Yaggi (2015), "A Different Kind of Discrimination," *Charlotte Observer*, May 13. Available online: http://www.charlotteobserver.com/opinion/op-ed/article20859924.html (accessed August 13, 2021).

Baugh A. (2016), *God and the Green Divide: Religious Environmentalism in Black and White*, Berkeley: University of California Press.

Bauman W. (2009), *Theology, Creation and Environmental Ethics: From Creatio ex Nihilo to Terra Nullius*, New York: Routledge.

Bernstein E. (2021), "The Bible Does Not Validate Endless Exploitation and Domination of the Environment," *Tikkun*, September 27. Available online: https://tinyurl.com/Dominon-is-not-Exploitation (accessed October 10, 2021).

Betancourt S. (2017), "Between Dishwater and the River: Toward an Ecowomanist Methodology," in M. Harris (ed.), *Ecowomanism, Religion, and Ecology*, 59–69, Leiden: Brill.

Betancourt S. (2018), "Ethical Implications of Environmental Justice," in J. Nordstrom and M. Mishra (eds.), *Justice on Earth: People of Faith Working at the Intersections of Race, Class, and the Environment*, 37–44, Boston: Skinner House Press.

Black Church Food Security Network (n.d.). Available online: https://blackchurchfoodsecurity.net (accessed November 25, 2021).

Bohannon R. and K. O'Brien (2011), "Saving the World (and the People in It, Too): Religion in Eco-justice and Environmental Justice," In W.A. Bauman, R.R. Bohannon, and K.J. O'Brien (eds.), *Inherited Land: The Changing Grounds of Religion and Ecology*, 171–87, Eugene, OR: Wipf and Stock Publishers.

Bravo M., R. Anthopolos, M. Bell, and L. Miranda (2016), "Racial Isolation and Exposure to Airborne Particulate Matter and Ozone in Understudied US Populations: Environmental Justice Applications of Downscaled Numerical Model Output," *Environment International* 92–3: 247–55.

Brender J., J. Maantay, and J. Chakraborty (2011), "Residential Proximity to Environmental Hazards and Adverse Health Outcomes," *American Journal of Public Health*, 101 (S1): S37–S52.

The BTS Center (2020), "Unlocking Possibility: Imagine a New Church," Vimeo, November 19. Available online: https://vimeo.com/481451490 (accessed August 16, 2021).

Bullard R. (1983), "Solid Waste Sites and the Black Houston Community," *Sociological Inquiry*, 53: 273–88.

Bullard R. (2005), *The Quest for Environmental Justice: Human Rights and the Politics of Pollution*, San Francisco: Sierra Club Books.

Bullard R. and B. Wright (2012), *The Wrong Complexion for Protection: How the Government Response to Disaster Endangers African American Communities*, New York: New York University Press.

Bullard R., P. Mohai, R. Saha, and B. Wright (2007), *Toxic Wastes and Race at Twenty 1987–2007: A Report Prepared for the United Church of Christ Justice & Witness Ministries*, Cleveland, OH: United Church of Christ and Witness Ministries.

Candraningrum D., ed. (2014), *Body Memories: Goddesses of Nusantara, Rings of Fire and Narratives of Myth*, Indonesia: Yayasan Jurnal Perempuan Press (YJP) & PPSG-UKSW.

Carter C. (2021), *The Spirit of Soul Food: Race, Faith, and Food Justice*, Champaign: University of Illinois Press.

Carvalhaes C. (2019), "Why I Created a Chapel Service Where People Confess to Plants," *Sojourners*, September 26. Available online: https://sojo.net/articles/why-i-created-chapel-service-where-people-confess-plants (accessed August 15, 2021).

Civil Eats (n.d.). Available online: https://civileats.com/ (accessed August 16, 2021).

Clay E. (2011), "How Does It Feel to Be an Environmental Problem? Studying Religion and Ecology in the African Diaspora," in W. Bauman, R. Bohannon II, and J. O'Brien (eds.), *Inherited Land: The Changing Grounds of Religion and Ecology*, 148–70, Eugene, OR: Wipf & Stock.

Clay E. (2018), "Backyard Gardens as Sacred Spaces: An Ecowomanist Spiritual Ecology," in L. Hobgood and W. Bauman (eds.), *The Bloomsbury Handbook of Religion and Nature: The Elements*, 11–24, New York: Bloomsbury Academic.

Cole L. and S. Foster (2000), *From the Ground Up: Environmental Racism and the Rise of the Environmental Justice Movement*, New York: New York University Press.

Cone J.H. (2000), "Whose Earth Is It Anyway?," *Cross Currents*, 50 (1/2): 36–46.

Cook J. et al. (2016), "Consensus on Consensus: A Synthesis of Consensus Estimates on Human-Caused Global Warming," *Environmental Research Letters*, 11 (4) (April).

Cordova V.F. and K.D. Moore (2007), *How It Is: The Native American Philosophy of V. F. Cordova*, Tucson: University of Arizona Press.

Cuomo C.J. (2011), "Climate Change, Vulnerability, and Responsibility," *Hypatia*, 26 (4): 690–714.

Cuomo C.J. (2012), "Gender and Climate Change," in G. Philander (ed.), *Encyclopedia of Global Warming and Climate Change*, 609–11, Los Angeles: SAGE Publications.

De La Torre M., ed. (2021), *Gonna Trouble the Water: Ecojustice, Water, and Environmental Racism*, Cleveland, OH: Pilgrim Press.

Deloria V., Jr. (1973), *God Is Red: A Native View of Religion*, New York: Putnam.

Eaton H. (2005), *Introducing Ecofeminist Theologies*, New York: T&T Clark.

Eaton H. and L.A. Lorentzen, eds. (2003), *Ecofeminism and Globalization: Exploring Culture, Context, and Religion*, Lanham, MD: Rowman & Littlefield.

Fears D. and B. Dennis (2021) "This is Environmental Racism" Washington Post (April 21).

Faith in Place (n.d.). Available online: https://www.faithinplace.org (accessed October 9, 2021).

Finney C. (2014), *Black Faces, White Spaces: Reimagining the Relationship of African Americans to the Great Outdoors*, Chapel Hill: University of North Carolina Press.

First National People of Color Environmental Leadership Summit (1991), "Principles of Environmental Justice," October 24–27, Washington, DC. Available online: https://www.ejnet.org/ej/principles.html (accessed September 25, 2021).

Flowers C. (2020), *Waste: One Woman's Fight against America's Dirty Secret*, New York: New Press.

Gebara I. (2003), "Ecofeminism: An Ethics of Life," in H. Eaton and L.A. Lorentzen (eds.), *Ecofeminism and Globalization: Exploring Culture, Context and Religion*, 163–76, Lanham, MD: Rowman and Littlefield.

Gilio-Whitaker D. (2020), *As Long as Grass Grows: The Indigenous Fight for Environmental Justice, from Colonization to Standing Rock*, Boston: Beacon Press.

Glave D. (2010), *Rooted in the Earth: Reclaiming the African American Environmental Heritage*, Chicago: Chicago Review Press.

Gould R. (2017), "Thoreau, Race and Environmental Justice: Deepening the Conversation," *Concord Saunterer: A Journal of Thoreau Studies*, 25 (December): 172–84.

Green The Church (n.d.). Available online: https://www.greenthechurch.org (accessed September 25, 2021).

Hage G. (2017), *Is Racism an Environmental Threat?*, Malden, MA: Polity Press.

Harris M. (2017a), *Ecowomanism: African American Women and Earth-Honoring Faiths*, Maryknoll, NY: Orbis Books.

Harris M., ed. (2017b), *Ecowomanism, Religion and Ecology*, Boston: Brill.

Hay A. (2009), "A New Earthly Vision: Religious Community Activism in the Love Canal Chemical Disaster," *Environmental History*, 14 (3): 502–27. Available online: http://dx.doi.org/10.1093/envhis/14.3.502.

Hiebert T. (2008), "Air: The First Sacred Thing," in N. Habel and P. Trudinger (eds.), *Exploring Ecological Hermeneutic*, 9–19, Atlanta, GA: Society of Biblical Literature.

hooks b. (2014), *Sisters of the Yam: Black Women and Self-Recovery*, Florence, KY: Routledge.

Hoskins N. (2023) "Environmental Justice" in Bauman, W., R. Bohannon, and K. O'Brien, (eds.), *Grounding Religion: A Field Guide to the Study of Religion and Ecology*. 3rd edition New York: Routledge.

Hribar C. (2010), *Understanding Concentrated Animal Feeding Operations and Their Impact on Communities*, Bowling Green, OH: National Association of Local Boards of Health.

I-Collective (n.d.). Available online: https://www.icollectiveinc.org (accessed September 25, 2021).

Immergut M. and L. Kearns (2012), "When Nature Is Rats and Roaches: Religious Eco-Justice Activism in Newark, NJ," *Journal for the Study of Religion, Nature & Culture*, 6 (2): 176–95. Available online: https://doi.org/10.1558/jsrnc.v6i2.176.

IPCC (2021), *Climate Change 2021: The Physical Science Basis. Contribution of Working Group I to the Sixth Assessment Report of the Intergovernmental Panel on Climate Change*, ed. V. Masson-Delmotte et al., Cambridge: Cambridge University Press.

Jackson Z. (2020), *Becoming Human: Matter and Meaning in an Antiblack World*, New York: New York University Press.

Keel T. (2018), *Divine Variations: How Christian Thought Became Racial Science*, Palo Alto, CA: Stanford University Press.

Kearns L. (2007), "Cooking the Truth: Faith, the Market, and the Science of Global Warming," in L. Kearns and C. Keller (eds.), *Eco-Spirit: Religions and Philosophies for the Earth*, 97–123, New York: Fordham University Press.

Kearns L. (2013), "Religion and Environmental Justice," in R. Bohannon (ed.), *Religions and Environments: A Reader in Religion, Nature and Ecology*, 297–312, New York: Bloomsbury.

Kearns L. (2018), "Conspiring Together: Breathing for Justice," in L. Hobgood and W. Bauman (eds.), *The Bloomsbury Handbook of Religion and Nature: The Elements*, 117–32, London: Bloomsbury.

Keller C. (2003), *Face of the Deep a Theology of Becoming*, New York: Routledge.

Kimmerer R. (2015), *Braiding Sweetgrass: Indigenous Wisdom, Scientific Knowledge and the Teachings of Plants*, Minneapolis, MN: Milkweed Editions.

Ko A. (2019), *Racism as Zoological Witchcraft: A Guide to Getting Out*, Brooklyn, NY: Lantern Books.

Kwok P. (2005), *Postcolonial Imagination and Feminist Theology*, Louisville, KY: Westminster John Knox Press.

Kyle V. and L. Kearns (2018), "The Bitter and the Sweet of Nature: Weaving a Tapestry of Migration Stories," in M. Krasny (ed.), *Grassroots to Global: Broader Impacts of Civic Ecology*, 41–64, Ithaca, NY: Cornell University Press.

Lalobaloca (2014), "Reclaiming Abuelita Knowledge as a Brown Ecofeminista," *Autostraddle*, March 20. Available online: https://www.autostraddle.com/reclaiming-abuelita-knowledge-as-a-brown-ecofeminista-213880/ (accessed August 15, 2021).

Levasseur T. (2017), *Religious Agrarianism and the Return of Place: From Values to Practice in Sustainable Agriculture*, Albany: State University of New York Press.

Levasseur T. (2021), *Climate Change, Religion, and Our Bodily Future*, Lanham, MD: Rowman & Littlefield.

Lipsitz G. (2007), "The Racialization of Space and the Spatialization of Race," *Landscape Journal*, 26: 10–21.

Lipsitz G. (2011), *How Racism Takes Place*, Philadelphia: Temple University Press.

Local Science Engagement Network (LSEN) (n.d.), "AAAS Help LSEN Bring Science to Climate Solutions." Available online: https://lsen.quorum.us/campaign/34052/?et_rid=754120396&et_cid=3854998 (accessed July 24, 2021).

Marcos S. (2009), "Mesoamerican Women's Indigenous Spirituality: Decolonizing Religious Beliefs," *Journal of Feminist Studies in Religion*, 25 (2): 25–45.

McDaniel J. (1989), *Of God and Pelicans: A Theology of Reverence*, Louisville, KY: Westminster/John Knox.

McKittrick K. and C. Woods (2007), *Black Geographies and the Politics of Place*, Cambridge, MA: South End Press.

Merchant C. (2003), *Reinventing Eden: The Fate of Nature in Western Culture*, New York: Routledge.

Merchant C. (2019), *The Death of Nature: Women, Ecology, and the Scientific Revolution Reprint Edition*, New York: HarperOne.

Mikati I., A. Benson, T. Luben, J. Sacks, and J. Richmond-Bryant (2018), "Disparities in Distribution of Particulate Matter Emission Sources by Race and Poverty Status," *American Journal of Public Health*, 108 (4): 480–5.

Milman O. (2016), "'World Can't Afford to Silence Us': Black Church Leaders Address Climate Change," *The Guardian*, July 24. Available online: https://www.theguardian.com/environment/2016/jul/24/african-methodist-episcopal-church-climate-change-letter (accessed August 13, 2021).

Moe-Lobeda C. (2013), *Resisting Structural Evil: Love as Ecological-Economic Vocation*, Minneapolis, MN: Fortress Press.

Morgan C. and G. Anzaldúa, eds. ([1981] 2005), *This Bridge Called My Back Writings by Radical Women of Color*, Albany, NY: State University of New York Press.

NASA (n.d.), "Scientific Consensus: Earth's Climate Is Warming." Available online: https://climate.nasa.gov/scientific-consensus/ (accessed August 9, 2021).

Nishime L. and K.D. Hester Williams, eds. (2018), *Racial Ecologies*, Seattle: University of Washington Press.

Nixon R. (2011), *Slow Violence and the Environmentalism of the Poor*, Cambridge, MA: Harvard University Press.

Nogueira-Godsey E. (2019a), "Beyond 'Mother Goddess and God the Father'," *The Immanent Frame: Secularism, Religion, and the Public Sphere*, July 1. Available online: https://tif.ssrc.org/2019/07/01/beyond-mother-goddess-and-god-the-father/ (accessed August 14, 2021).

Nogueira-Godsey E. (2019b), "Towards a Decological Praxis," *Horizontes Decoloniales*, 1: 73–98.

Nogueira-Godsey E. (2022), "A Decological Way to Dialogue: Rethinking Ecofeminism and Religion," in E. Tomalin and C. Starkey (eds.), *The Routledge Handbook on Religions, Gender and Society*, 365–84, London: Routledge Press.

Nogueira-Godsey T. and E. Nogueira-Godsey (2021), "Environmental Racism in the 'True' America: A Reflection on Race, the Earth and Moral Action after Trump," in M. De La Torre (ed.), *Faith and Reckoning After Trump*, 85–97, New York: Orbis Books.

Oh J. (2011), *A Postcolonial Theology of Life: Planetarity East and West*, Upland, CA: Sopher Press.

Pagán M. (2020), "Cultivating a Decolonial Feminist Integral Ecology: Extractive Zones and the Nexus of the Coloniality of Being/Coloniality of Gender," *Journal of Hispanic/Latino Theology*, 22 (1): Article 6. Available online: https://repository.usfca.edu/jhlt/vol22/iss1/6 (accessed September 25, 2021).

PBS (2009), "The National Parks—Manzanar: 'Never Again'." Available online: https://www.pbs.org/video/the-national-parks-untold-stories-manzanar-never-again/PBS (accessed August 16, 2021).

PBS (2012), "Food Forward: Urban Farming," April 3. Available online: https://www.pbs.org/video/food-forward-pilot-episode-urban-farming/ (accessed October 10, 2021).

Penniman L. (2018), *Farming While Black: Soul Fire Farm's Practical Guide to Liberation on the Land*, Hartford, VT: Chelsea Green Publishing.

People for Community Recovery (n.d.). Available online: http://www.peopleforcommunityrecovery.org (accessed October 10, 2021).

Pérez E. (2016), *North American Religions*, vol. 9: *Religion in the Kitchen: Cooking, Talking, and the Making of Black Atlantic Traditions*, New York: New York University Press.

Perkins T. (2021), "The Multiple People of Color: Origins of the US Environmental Justice Movement: Social Movement Spillover and Regional Racial Projects in California," *Environmental Sociology*, 7 (2): 147–59.

Peterson A. (2001), *Being Human: Ethics, Environment and Our Place in the World*, Berkeley: University of California Press.

Pinto V. and R. Harding (2016), "Afro-Brazilian Religion, Resistance and Environmental Ethics: A Perspective from Candomblé," *Worldviews*, 20: 76–86.

Plumwood V. (1993), *Feminism and the Mastery of Nature*, London: Routledge.

Poor People's Campaign (n.d.). Available online: https://www.poorpeoplescampaign.org (accessed October 10, 2021).

Pulido L. (2000), "Rethinking Environmental Racism: White Privilege and Urban Development in Southern California," *Annals of the Association of American Geographers*, 90 (1): 12–40.

Pulido L., T. Bruno, C. Faiver-Serna, and C. Galentine (2019), "Spectacular Racism, Environmental Deregulation and the White Nation," *Annals of the Association of American Geographers*, 109 (2): 520–32.

Rakia R. and A. Mair (2016), "My Neighborhood Is Killing Me," *Sojourners*, June. Available online: https://sojo.net/magazine/june-2016/my-neighborhood-killing-me (accessed August 14, 2021).

Renkl M. (2021), "How to Fight the Poison of Environmental Racism," *New York Times*, August 16. Available online: https://www.nytimes.com/2021/08/16/opinion/environmental-racism-memphis-pipeline.html (accessed August 16, 2021).

Reynolds K. and N. Cohen (2016), *Beyond the Kale: Urban Agriculture and Social Justice Activism in New York City*, Athens: University of Georgia Press.

Riley M. (2014), "A Spiritual Democracy of All God's Creatures: Ecotheology and the Animals of Lynn White, Jr," in S. Moore (ed.), *Divinanimality: Animal Theology, Creaturely Theology*, 241–60, New York: Fordham University Press.

Ro Y. (1989), *The Korean Neo-Confucianism of Yi Yulgok*, Albany: State University of New York Press.

Roberts J.T. and M. Toffolon-Weiss (2001), *Chronicles from the Environmental Justice Frontline*, New York: Cambridge University Press.

Robinson T. (2021), "He Talked to Trees! 'Thinking Differently' about Nature with Howard Thurman," *Spiritus: A Journal of Christian Spirituality*, 21 (1) (Spring): 1–19.

Roothaan A. (2019), *Indigenous, Modern and Postcolonial Relationships to Nature*, New York: Routledge.

Rowland-Shea J., S. Doshi, S. Edberg, and R. Fanger (2020), "The Nature Gap," *Center for American Progress*, July 21. Available online: https://www.americanprogress.org/issues/green/reports/2020/07/21/487787/the-nature-gap/ (accessed August 16, 2021).

Ruether R.R. (1977), *New Woman New Earth: Sexist Ideologies and Human Liberation*, Maryknoll, NY: Orbis Books.

Reuther R.R. (1994), *Gaia and God: An Ecofeminist Theology of Earth Healing*, San Francisco: HarperOne.

Ryan-Simkins K. and E. Nogueira-Godsey (2010), "Tangible Actions Toward Solidarity: An Ecofeminist Analysis of Women's Participation in Food Justice," in T. Yugar, S. Robinson, L. Dube, and T. Hing (eds.), *Valuing Lives, Healing Earth: Religion, Gender, and Life on Earth*, 203–22, Leuven: Peeters Publishers.

Sankofa Community Farm at Bartram's Garden (n.d.). Available online: https://www.bartramsgarden.org/farm/ (accessed September 25, 2021).

Schlosberg D. (2009), *Defining Environmental Justice: Theories, Movements and Nature*, New York: Oxford University Press.

Sellers S. (2016), "Gender and Climate Change: A Closer Look at Existing Evidence," *WEDO and Global Gender and Climate Alliance*, November. Available online: https://wedo.org/wp-content/uploads/2016/11/GGCA-RP-FINAL.pdf (accessed January 12, 2021).

Sherman S. (2017), *The Sioux Chef's Indigenous Kitchen*, Minneapolis: University of Minnesota Press.

Spears E. (2020), *Rethinking the American Environment Post-1945*, New York: Routledge.

Story of Stuff (n.d.). Available online: https://www.storyofstuff.org (accessed September 25, 2021).

Taylor D. (2014), *Toxic Communities: Environmental Racism, Industrial Pollution, and Residential Mobility*, New York: New York University Press.

Taylor D. (2015), "Gender and Racial Diversity in Environmental Organizations: Uneven Accomplishments and Cause for Concern," *Environmental Justice*, 8 (5): 165–80.

Taylor D. (2016), *The Rise of the American Conservation Movement: Power, Privilege and Environmental Protection*, Durham, NC: Duke University Press.

Tessum C., J. Apte, A. Goodkind, N. Muller, K. Mullins, D. Paolella, S. Polasky, N. Springer, S. Thakrar, and J. Marshall (2019), "Inequity in Consumption of Goods and Services Adds to Racial-Ethnic Disparities in Air Pollution Exposure," *Proceedings of the National Academy of Sciences*, 116 (13) (2019): 6001.

Twitty M. (n.d.), *Afroculinaria: Exploring Culinary Traditions of Africa, African America, and the African Diaspora*. Available online: https://afroculinaria.com (accessed August 14, 2021).

United Church of Christ Commission for Racial Justice (1987), *Toxic Wastes and Race in the United States: A National Report on the Racial and Socio-Economic Characteristics of Communities with Hazardous Waste Sites*, New York: United Church of Christ Commission for Racial Justice. Available online: https://www.ucc.org/wp-content/uploads/2020/12/ToxicWastesRace.pdf (accessed September 25, 2021).

United Church of Christ Environmental Integrity Project (2020), *Breath to the People: Sacred Air and Toxic Pollution*, Cleveland: United Church of Christ. Available online: https://www.ucc.org/what-we-do/justice-local-church-ministries/justice/faithful-action-ministries/environmental-justice/breaththepeople/ (accessed September 25, 2021).

Veldman R. (2019), *The Gospel of Climate Skepticism: Why Evangelical Christians Oppose Action on Climate Change*, Oakland: University of California Press.

Vox (2021), "How Radical Gardeners Took Back New York City," YouTube, June 7. Available online: https://www.youtube.com/watch?v=_g2CaF12xxw (accessed August 18, 2021).

Walker A. (1982), *The Color Purple*, New York: Harcourt Brace Jovanovich.

Warren K. (2000), *Ecofeminist Philosophy: A Western Perspective on What It Is and Why It Matters*, Oxford: Rowman & Littlefield.

Washington H. (2020), "How Environmental Racism Is Fueling the Coronavirus Pandemic," *Nature Research Journals*, May 19.

Wells C., ed. (2018), *Environmental Justice in Postwar America*, Seattle: University of Washington Press.

White C. (2016), *Black Lives and Sacred Humanity: The Emergence of an African-American Religious Naturalism*, New York: Fordham University Press.

White L. (1967), "The Historical Roots of Our Ecological Crisis," *Science*, 155: 1203–7.

White M. (2018), *Freedom Farmers: Agricultural Resistance and the Black Freedom Movement*, Chapel Hill: University of North Carolina Press.

Whyte K.P. (2017), "Is It Colonial Deja Vu? Indigenous Peoples and Climate Injustice," in J. Adamson, M. Davis, and H. Huang (eds.), *Humanities for the Environment: Integrating Knowledges, Forging New Constellations of Practice*, 88–104, London: Earthscan Publications.

Whyte K.P. (2018), "Food Sovereignty, Justice and Indigenous Peoples: An Essay on Settler Colonialism and Collective Continuance," in A. Barnhill, T. Doggett, and A. Egan (eds.), *Oxford Handbook of Food Ethics*, 345–66, Oxford: Oxford University Press.

Whyte K.P. and C. Cuomo (2017), "Ethics of Caring in Environmental Ethics: Indigenous and Feminist Philosophies," in S. Gardiner and A. Thompson (eds.), *The Oxford Handbook of Environmental Ethics*, 234–47, New York: Oxford University Press.

Williams D. (1993a), "Sin, Nature, and Black Women's Bodies," in C. Adams (ed.), *Eco-Feminism and the Sacred*, 24–9, New York: Continuum Publishing Company.

Williams D. (1993b), *Sisters in the Wilderness: The Challenge of Womanist God-Talk*, Maryknoll, NY: Orbis Books.

Yusoff K. (2018), *A Billion Black Anthropocenes or None*, Minneapolis: University of Minnesota Press.

8

African American Religious Naturalism in the Novel *Sula* by Toni Morrison

Tyson-Lord Gray

Much has been written about African American environmental experiences in the rural South. Historians have noted that African Americans were forced into an intimate relationship with the environment through slave labor and share cropping, yet alienated from the land due to their inability to reap the benefits of their toil (Smith 2007). During the *Great Migration* nearly six million African Americans fled the South and moved north relocating to urban centers in the Northeast, Midwest, and West.

Environmental literature covering this period primarily focuses on the transition from the natural and landscaped environment of the South to that of urban industrial life. Consequently, little has been written about the rural environmental experiences of African Americans in the Midwest.

Within this chapter, I examine African American rural experiences in the Midwest through an ecocritical reading of the novel *Sula* by Toni Morrison.

As opposed to asking how the experiences faced by the characters shaped their environmental perspectives, I explore the impact of these experiences on their religious beliefs. *Sula* depicts an African American community struggling to connect with nature, hindered by racism and segregation. In addition to these social challenges, at times nature itself appears hostile to African Americans' pursuit of happiness. I argue that these social and environmental conditions not only affected African American's environmental views but also their religious perspectives. In contrast to Southern African American Christianity, which was often tethered to *The Black Church*, in the Midwest, religious naturalism is also a primary authority on God.

FIGURE 8.1 *An African American family leaving Florida during the Great Depression.* Source: *MPI/Stringer/Getty Images.*

FIGURE 8.2 *Toni Morrison.* Source: *Angela Radulescu/Wikimedia.*

By religious naturalism, I rely on Jerome Stone's definition. He writes,

> On the topic of God I find that religious naturalists tend to fall into three groups:
> (1) those who conceive of God as the creative process within the universe, (2) those
> who think of God as the totality of the universe considered religiously, and (3) those
> who do not speak of God yet still can be called religious.
>
> (Stone 2008: 6)

More specifically, I argue that African American religious naturalism as depicted in *Sula*
reflects what Victor Anderson refers to as pragmatic naturalism. That is,

> a particular way of construing reality which is the undifferentiated totality of
> experience. For pragmatic naturalists, all conscious differentiations of reality
> are related to the ways in which human beings identify the various qualities of
> world experience. Reality is the world in its concrete actuality and transcendent
> potentiality. The world and its processes are contingently related, and the world
> processes are open to the novelties that arise from the transcendent potentialities
> of reality. Pragmatic naturalists do not see reality as fixed or closed. Rather, it is
> fluid, dynamic, processive, and exhibits the possibilities of tragedy and irony in
> human experience.
>
> (Anderson 1998: 111)

Drawing from Stone, I suggest that although residents in the Bottom use God-
language and theological terms, these concepts ultimately reflect their belief in God as
the creative process within the universe. In contrast to African American Christianity in
the South, residents in the Bottom (see below) do not speak of God as being "on their
side" nor do they express belief in being rescued from their earthly conditions for a
heavenly home. Rather, as Anderson notes, they see God as being present in both the
good and evil in their lives, they believe human transcendence is possible on Earth, and
they understand uncertainty in life as a reflection of the uncertainty they see in nature.
Although not essential, the reader would benefit from reading the novel *Sula* prior to
or in conjunction with this chapter.

Sula

Set in the early twentieth century, *Sula* takes place in Medallion, Ohio, in an area of
town known as the Bottom. Local folklore has it that the Bottom received its name from
a trick a white farmer perpetrated against a formerly enslaved man when he promised
him freedom and a piece of "bottom land" if he completed some difficult tasks. When
the time came for the farmer to pay up, he told the formerly enslaved man that the
bottom land wasn't in the valley, as he had presumed, but rather that it was up in the
hills because that's the bottom of heaven. Consequently, Blacks ended up with hilly

FIGURE 8.3 *African American sharecropper boy plowing.* Source: *Universal History Archive/Getty Images.*

land, "where planting was backbreaking, where the soil slid down and washed away seeds, and where the wind lingered all through the winter" (Morrison 1982: 5), while whites lived on the rich valley floor where farming was easy.

Morrison introduces readers to the Bottom in the future. She writes,

> In that place, where they tore the nightshade and blackberry patches from their roots to make room for the Medallion City Golf Course, there was once a neighbourhood. It stood in the hills above the valley town of Medallion and spread all the way to the river. It is called the suburbs now, but when Black people lived there it was called the Bottom.
>
> (Morrison 1982: 3)

This framing of the Bottom's past and future, as being characterized by environmental hardship, is significant in that it foreshadows the role of religious naturalism in the lives of the residents.

God as the Source of Good and Evil

As predicted in the Introduction, the Bottom is perpetually plagued with strange and erratic ecological happenings. One night the wind tears through the town breaking windows, destroying trees, and shaking the very foundations of buildings. Residents wait up half the night frightened and expecting rain but nothing comes. One year a plague of robins covers the town for days disrupting everything from yard work to leisure with no explanation other than the fact that a similar occurrence has happened before. And in 1941, a blanket of ice covers the town destroying the harvest, confining everyone to their home, and resulting in all manner of sickness and illnesses. These events only affect Medallion's Black residents and twice Morrison writes, "the hills protected the valley where the white folk lived" (Morrison 1982: 72).

Yet, in spite of nature's seeming hostility toward Blacks, we see instances of environmental intimacy. Nel is struck by the smell of gardenias from the magnificent garden in the back of her grandmother's house when she and her mother travel to New Orleans. The smell of gardenias lingers in the air as Helene's mother Rochelle enters the room. Later, when Helene returns to Medallion, she establishes the practice of having seasonal altar flowers in the town's Black church.

Eva Peace also has a garden of forsythia bushes, sweet peas, and clovers along the side of her house. In a twist of irony, we learn of this garden when she jumps from her third-floor window and lands in it attempting to save her daughter, Hannah, who catches on fire in the front yard. In spite of their bad fortune however, African American residents in the Bottom view tragedy and aberrations as much a part of nature as grace. Morrison writes, "They lived with various forms of evil all their days, and it wasn't that they believed God would take care of them. It was rather that they knew God had a brother and that brother hadn't spared God's son, so why should he spare them?" (Morrison 1982: 118).

Here, the language of God and God's brother are references to good and evil experiences within nature. A similar refrain is echoed at Chicken Little's funeral. Morrison writes, "when they thought of all that life and death locked into that little closed coffin they danced and screamed, not to protest God's will but to acknowledge it and confirm once more their conviction that the only way to avoid the Hand of God is to get in it" (Morrison 1982: 66).

African Americans in the Bottom did not separate nature from God nor did they separate good from evil. Rather, they maintain that reality is an undifferentiated totality of experience. Morrison notes, "There was no creature so ungodly as to make them destroy it. They could kill easily if provoked to anger, but not by design, which explained why they could not 'mob kill' anyone. To do so was not only unnatural, it was undignified" (Morrison 1982: 118). For them it was not the presence of evil that was unnatural but, rather, the attempt at destroying it.

Human Transcendence on Earth

Morrison notes that even while living with the challenges of racism, environmental aberrations, death, and evil, Blacks in the Bottom still believed that human transcendence was possible. By transcendence, however, I do not mean an outer body experience.

Instead, I rely on what Stone refers to as "situation transcendence," which is both imminent and episodic. For Stone, transcendence is not necessarily a theological category. He writes, "Situational transcendence has been defined [...] as referring to resources of growth and renewal which are transcendent, that is, unexpected, uncontrollable, and superior in power and worth to the antecedent ingredients of the situation as perceived by an individual or group" (Stone 1992: 33). In this regard, transcendence is inclusive of virtues such as openness, courage, and hope in moments of defeat and despair.

Without doubt African Americans in the Bottom faced their fair share of defeat and despair. Yet, Morrison writes,

> They [residents of the Bottom] did not believe Nature was ever askew—only inconvenient. Plague and drought were as "natural" as springtime. If milk could curdle, God knows robins could fall. The purpose of evil was to survive it and they determined (without ever knowing that they had made up their minds to do it) to survive floods, white people, tuberculosis, famine and ignorance.
>
> (Morrison 1982: 90)

In addition to ecological aberrations, African Americans in the Bottom also faced ecological alienation. The only economic hope for the town was the work being undertaken building New River Road. Yet, African American men were continually passed over in favor of less fit white men. African Americans in the Bottom longed for the opportunity to contribute to the landscape and to be able to say they had built the New River Road but they were denied.

It was in this absence of any viable connection to the land that Blacks chose to develop deeper relationships and build communities as a means of cultivating a sense of belonging. Rather than resigning themselves to *environmental determinism*, Blacks in the Bottom responded to their environmental limitations with an openness to the possibilities of courage, love, and joy. For example, when Jude is unable to gain work on the New River Road it results in his openness to marriage.

Morrison writes,

> It was while he was full of such dreams, his body already feeling the rough work clothes, his hands already curved to the pick handle, that he spoke to Nel about getting married. She seemed receptive but hardly anxious. It was after he stood in lines six days running and saw the gang boss pick out thin-armed white boys from the Virginia hills and the bull-necked Greeks and Italians and heard over and over, "Nothing else today. Come back tomorrow," that he got the message. So it was rage, rage and a determination to take on a man's role anyhow that made him press Nel about settling down. He needed some of his appetites filled, some posture of adulthood recognized, but mostly he wanted someone to care about his hurt, to care very deeply.
>
> (Morrison 1982: 82)

As Stone notes, one type of situational transcendence is moments of extremity. These are moments of despair or jubilation when one becomes aware of their human limitations. He writes, "Often in these moments the good which comes to the self comes through some form of personal meeting. Often there is an unexpected and powerful good which moves in acts of love or forgiveness [...] the appreciation of the preciousness of another human can at any time be vehicles of transcendent renewal and resource" (Stone 1992: 34).

This is depicted as Nel learns of Jude's despair, "His fears lest his burst dream of road building discourage her were never realized. Nel's indifference to his hints about marriage disappeared altogether when she discovered his pain. Jude could see himself taking shape in her eyes. She actually wanted to help, to soothe" (Morrison 1982: 83). Ironically, Jude's experience of situational transcendence is only made possible by his environmental and social conditions.

Uncertainty in Life

Finally, the environmental conditions in the Bottom serve as a reminder to residents that nature and thus life is constantly in process, developing, fluid, and dynamic. Shadrack faces this reality when Sula dies. As a distraught young girl, he had once said to her "always" to convince her of permanency and that things would be okay. Yet, seeing her body lying lifeless on the table after her death revealed to him that he had been terribly wrong. There was no such thing as "always." Death and tragedy were as unpredictable in the Bottom as the weather, which explained the unexpected sunshine on January 3, 1941. Each year Shadrack had chosen this day to carry out his annual Suicide Day march through the city, but that year was different.

"By the time Shadrack reached the first house, he was facing a line of delighted faces. Never before had they laughed. Always they had shut their doors, pulled down the shades and called their children out of the road" (Morrison 1982: 159). But that year, the sun literally beckoned them to come out and play. Little by little the crowd grew as they marched through the city, down New River Road, and found themselves at the mouth of the abandoned river tunnel where their broken dreams and promises lay. It was there, for the first time, that the residents of the Bottom disobeyed their own rule and attempted to destroy evil. Yet, as the earth gave away at their feet they found themselves in a chamber of water, deprived of the sun that had brought them there, and many died (162).

As *Sula* ends, the town's river is polluted, the fish have been killed, and nature is being destroyed to give way to a golf course. Although we are not told what happened to its remaining residents, we can assume that their removal was no worse than their occupancy. For residents in the Bottom, life was difficult. They faced environmental racism and ecological alienation. Ironically, Morrison foreshadowed much of the same environmental injustices prevalent today in the *Environmental Justice movement.*

FIGURE 8.4 *Social and Environmental Justice March through Harlem, New York.* Source: *M. Stan Reaves/Alamy Stock Photo.*

Yet, it was these environmental experiences that informed Bottom residents' understanding of God. Unlike religious life in the South, we do not see this Midwest African American community attending church services or singing African American spirituals. Yet, they speak of God, acknowledge the struggle between good and evil, and experience transcendence. As I have argued, these perspectives are informed by their experiences in nature and best understood through the lens of religious naturalism.

Further Reading and Online Resources

Blocker J.S., Jr. (2008), *A Little More Freedom: African Americans Enter the Urban Midwest, 1860–1930*, Columbus: Ohio State Press.

McCammack B. (2017), *Landscapes of Hope: Nature and the Great Migration in Chicago*, Cambridge, MA: Harvard University Press.

Sernett M.C. (1997), *Bound for the Promised Land: African American Religion and The Great Migration*, Durham, NC: Duke University Press.

White C.W. (2016), *Black Lives and Sacred Humanity: Towards an African American Religious Naturalism*, New York: Fordham University Press.

References

Anderson V. (1998), *Pragmatic Theology*, Albany: State University of New York Press.
Morrison T. (1982), *Sula*, New York: Penguin Books.
Smith K. (2007), *African American Environmental Thought*, Lawrence: University Press of Kansas.
Stone J. (1992), *A Minimalist Vision of Transcendence*, Albany: State University of New York Press.
Stone J. (2008), *Religious Naturalism Today: The Rebirth of a Forgotten Alternative*, Albany: State University of New York Press.

Glossary Terms

Black Church The institution of churches that currently or historically have ministered to predominantly African American congregations in the United States, as well as their collective traditions and members.

Environmental determinism The belief that the environment, most notably its physical factors such as landforms and climate, determines human culture and societal development.

Environmental Justice movement A movement started in the 1980s by individuals, primarily people of color, who sought to address the inequity of environmental protection in their communities.

The Great Migration The movement of six million African Americans out of the Southern United States to the Northeast, Midwest, and West that occurred between 1916 and 1970.

9

Religion, Nature, and Critical Materialisms

Courtney O'Dell-Chaib

At times we humans like to think of ourselves as discrete and self-directed entities. Enclosed in our flesh, we fantasize that we are in control of how we interact with the world—how much we will engage, with whom, who we are intimate with, who we are influenced by, how much we have "control" over our own minds and bodies not to mention the environment around us. Writing from the middle of a global pandemic, immersed in a worldwide protest movement illuminating state violence perpetrated on Black people and communities, and shaken by the disturbing beginnings of our environmentally unstable futures, control over anything seems a bit farcical. In fact, in my most vulnerable moments I feel overwhelmed by the troubling press of being so open to others: to contagion, to sentiment, to influence, to the unraveling of any certainties. What does it mean to be human in these moments? Furthermore, who gets to decide what it means to be human and what the future for humans should be?

In this chapter, I will introduce you to a conversation at the intersections of environmental and critical theory that is beginning to reshape religion and nature scholarship, one I term critical materialisms. Critical materialisms reconsider what it means to be human within a universe of diversity. They also compellingly suggest that our twenty-first-century horrors are all related in that they were birthed by historical projects to define what is and is not human and the normative ways humans should relate to nonhuman others. This conversation is a methodological approach to the humanities and part of what is called the *nonhuman turn* in the humanities and social sciences. It might seem counterintuitive for me to center the "human" within a movement to decenter humans but, importantly, critical materialisms argue that to rethink human-nonhuman relationships, we must interrogate what we mean by "human" in the first place by tracing who, historically, had the power to define it.

Before I move to this conversation, there are two important framing points to keep in mind. First, the "nonhuman turn" is not a singular nor homogenous theoretical approach to the humanities and social sciences, rather it is an umbrella term that covers a collection of intellectual projects that revolve around thinking about nonhuman others including: animal studies, new materialism, object-oriented ontologies, actor-network theory, science and technology studies, affect studies, and non-representational theory, among others. Often these terms identify parts of a larger conversation or similar conversations stirring within different academic disciplines (for example, media studies, gender, race, and sexuality studies, philosophy, English, film studies, and environmental studies) so it is important to keep in mind that the scholarship I discuss does not encompass all the thinking we might identify as part of the nonhuman turn and, as with all scholarship, these conversations are continually evolving.

Second, these various intellectual projects (an element they share) are all critical responses to the many *dichotomies* or dualisms that haunt Western thought like subject or object, culture or nature, mind or body, rationality or emotion, human or nonhuman, male or female. While philosophers historically used these dichotomies to attempt to make sense of our material world and human "natures," our more fluid contemporary realities are very difficult to fit into these tidy definitional boxes. The implications of this form of thinking are incredibly damaging. Scholarship within the nonhuman turn illuminates the tremendous material tolls these dichotomies extract from particular bodies, communities, and environments.

An example, and one I will return to, is that Western philosophy has historically tended to shape nature and culture as diametrically opposed—there are things created by humans through resolute conquest, marshaling, and ordering of nature that we can call "culture," and then there is everything else which is "nature." This dichotomy, through value and investments, celebrates "culture" while it regards "nature" as just the raw material we humans can wrestle into objects and experiences of value. It is not too difficult to imagine how dichotomous thinking contributed to our environmental crisis. Viewing nature as solely the "raw" materials, "natural resources," used to make culture and to separate humans so much in value from nonhuman others, makes it easier to exhaustively take from nature and to devalue the infinite ways there are to exist on this planet other than our own human experiences.

Furthermore, Western thinkers did not interrogate their own biases in the construction of these dichotomies. While shaping the human/nonhuman dichotomy, philosophers (consciously and unconsciously) had a particular *kind* of human in mind as the norm in the human/nonhuman division. Critical race (Karera 2019; Sharpe 2016), feminist (Braidotti 2013; Butler 1993), ecofeminist (Gaard 2017), and queer theorists (Jackson 2015; Kafer 2013) argue that while assumed to be universal, these dichotomies are always raced and gendered. The valued part of the dichotomy is attached to the type of human these thinkers most valued. Consequently, historically Christian, able-bodied, heterosexual, males of European descent were celebrated as rational masters of nature and thus, ideal culture producers and leaders. While everyone else—women, Indigenous peoples, people of color, immigrants, the poor, those with disabilities and illnesses, religious minorities, and queer communities—were seen as more governed by their "nature" than governors of nature.

These marginalized others, particularly throughout North American history, are all positioned in numerous ways as less rational and more emotional, more animalistic or "natural," and in need of the same conquest, control, and management as unruly nature. I will explore these concepts more later but it is important to understand that the nonhuman turn, in part, is a project of progressively chipping away at the normativity of dichotomous thinking by arguing that we cannot separate our perceptions or claims about the "natural world" from human conceptions, constructions, limitations, and desires. After all, even the parts of North America we claim are wilderness spaces are still mapped, funded (or defunded), protected, fenced, and idealized by humans.

The most compelling scholarship in the nonhuman turn is writing from the perspectives of marginalized communities that demonstrate how we defined "human," "nature," and normative relationships between the two, always came at the expense of particular communities and environments. If white males are the environmental norm, their experiences in nature and ideas about how nonhuman others should be treated remain the norm. But what does it mean to be human if you are female, a person of color, queer, Indigenous, or disabled? What is "nature" from these perspectives and how should it be treated?

Critical Materialisms

Whether we are familiar with René Descartes's name or not, much of what humans claim to understand about the material world was shaped by the seventeenth-century French mathematician and philosopher. Descartes's tremendous advancements in math and science, a tradition later called Cartesianism, were rooted in his ontological understanding of the material world as a division between mind and matter. Descartes (1986) resisted prevailing conceptions of nature that suggested matter could possess magical forces. He argued only humans and God possess wills or spirits and he separated existence into three substances: (1) matter, (2) mind or thought/spirit/soul, and (3) God. Human beings were imbued by God with matter in the form of body, *and* mind. On the other hand, Descartes proposed that material objects were "identifiably discrete," that they "move only upon an encounter with an external force or agent," and they do so according to a rational logic that humans, possessing minds, could come to understand (Coole and Frost 2010: 7). Thus humans, as thinking subjects, could determine laws or truths about the material world through observation of and experimentation with natural objects.

Cartesianism fuels, in part, an explosion of scientific inquiry as it emboldens humans with the sense that they themselves have the ability to puzzle out mysteries about their universe. However, ontological conceptions always have ethical implications. Critical materialisms tie the ethical problems facing our planet to Descartes's understanding of matter and they examine the many troubling dichotomies that follow. For Descartes, humans, the active thinking subject, are "rational, self-aware, free, and self-moving" while nonhuman objects are acted upon and can/should be manipulated according to human desires (Coole and Frost 2010: 8). Unfortunately, this understanding of matter as inert and passive led to the "conceptual and practical domination of nature" by instilling humans with a "sense of mastery" over the nonhuman world (8).

Furthermore, Descartes regarded nonhuman animals as purely reflexive in their behavior because they did not possess souls or reason. Cartesianism argued nonhuman animals were incapable of suffering or feeling complex emotions and of little ethical consequence. The human/animal, culture/nature, subject/object dichotomies entrenched in Western philosophy and science through Cartesianism, materialist theorists argue, encouraged solely *anthropocentric* beliefs about our material world. You might also encounter this perspective titled "human exceptionalism" or "human supremacy," but it centers human experiences of the material world as the only point of reference for knowledge and practice. In fact, materialist theorists argue, anthropocentric perspectives are so ingrained in human interaction with the material world that they remain hidden—an unrecognized background to how we perceive and move in the world. Consequently, to change our behaviors on the planet, for humans to rethink their ethical ideals, critical materialisms argue we must first reconsider our ontological conceptions.

In her 1989 book *Primate Visions: Gender, Race, and Nature in the World of Modern Science*, foundational feminist science and technology studies scholar Donna Haraway asked:

> How are love, power, and science intertwined in the constructions of nature in the late twentieth century? What may count as nature for late industrial people? What forms does love of nature take in particular historical contexts? For whom and at what cost? [...] How do the terrible marks of gender and race enable and constrain love and knowledge in particular cultural traditions, including the modern natural sciences? Who may contest for what the body of nature will be?
>
> (1989: 1)

In many ways we can think of critical materialisms as perpetually trying to address Haraway's questions. What counts as nature, particularly as new technologies continually shift human capabilities beyond what we thought was possible? What counts as nature when our impact on nonhuman others moves well beyond what we ever anticipated? What does it mean to love and care for nature and who gets to decide what that love looks and feels like? How do human constructions of race, sexuality, and gender inhibit us from seeing, imagining, and encouraging all the different forms of care for nature that are possible? Can we fix a broken relationship with nature if we cannot fix broken relationships with one another?

Critical materialisms relocate humans from the center of our conceptual universes and into the messy diversity of our human and more-than-human world to reconsider knowledge about ourselves, other creatures, and the planet we inhabit in a complex, twisted, and intimate relationship. This work is heavily indebted to ecofeminist scholarship that began to puzzle through how *anthropocentrism* was tied to androcentrism, or beliefs and practices that center male perspectives as the most important. Ecofeminists such as Vandana Shiva and Maria Mies (1993), Val Plumwood (1993), Catriona Sandilands (1999), Noel Sturgeon (1997), Stacy Alaimo (2000), Karen Warren (2000), and Greta Gaard (2017) as well as ecowomanists like Karen Baker-Fletcher (1998), Shamara Shantu Riley (2003), and Melanie L. Harris (2016) realized that conceptions about nature were not just shaped around anthropocentric views but numerous human inequalities within social constructions of gender, sexuality, race, and ability. Consequently, beliefs and practices that oppress, devalue, and deplete the bodies, perspectives, and interests of marginalized humans, ecofeminists and womanists argued, were the same beliefs and practices that devalued and depleted nonhuman nature. Essentially, these forms of violence are so linked that any social liberation project hoping to expand the abilities of humans to move, think, and choose freely in the world, must also include concern for the environment and vice versa. Environmental justice advocates such as Robert Bullard (1983, 2000), Dorceta E. Taylor (1997), and Steve Lerner (2005) have perpetually demonstrated that environmental projects that do not also address human inequalities and hierarchical politics are incomplete and ineffective. How might paying attention to human constructions of race, sexuality, and gender open up new possibilities for caring for nature?

Building on this scholarship in an attempt to push our ontological conceptions, work from theorists such as Stacy Alaimo (2010), Mel Chen (2012), Jane Bennett (2010), Andrew Pickering (1995), Elizabeth Grosz (2005), Rosi Braidotti (2013), Catriona Mortimer-Sandilands (1999), and Karen Barad (2007) turns our attention to the *agency* of nonhuman nature. Followers of Descartes only recognized humans as possessing agentic capacity and the mythos of human progression throughout history is a story of human technology subduing or controlling both the inert and chaotic tendencies of nature to extract resources for human endeavors. Put plainly, humans have the capacity to act and create, nonhuman nature is the base material with which we create.

As much as human animals might be uncomfortable admitting this truth, however, humans are not the only creatures with agentic capacity. Nonhuman others are agentic beings. Nonhuman animals also create, have cultures, build structures, reshape landscapes, care for families, defend their homes and loved ones, go to war, adapt to troubling circumstances, mourn, celebrate, and even participate in elaborate rituals that we might call "religious" (Schaefer 2015). Many plant life-forms have languages to communicate with one another and a resiliency that is difficult for any human to replicate. And, something as miniscule as a virus can *through its actions* bring the human world to its knees. Positioning humans as singularly creative, powerful, and purposeful is a convenient fantasy that makes the use and abuse of nonhuman others more ethically acceptable but it does little to help us understand the true complexity of the material world. Nature acts—often in ways we cannot predict and potentially with the ability to threaten human existence. Critical materialisms not only uncover how tendencies to view nonhuman others as passive inert matter have contributed to our environmental crisis, but they also propose the troubling question: what happens when nature "punches back" in ways we have not predicted (Alaimo and Heckman 2008: 7)? How and why have we ignored clever and compelling resistance to human mastery at our own peril and how can we reimagine ethical relationships with nonhuman others that truly consider their agentic potential? I will walk us through three creative responses to these questions and then think about the opportunities they offer for religion and environmental studies.

One, critical materialisms welcome us to reconsider scientific inquiry as not about uncovering "Truths" about how to represent nature (facts and observations about "how the world really is") but rather a struggle to relate to the tremendous material agency of the world that always slips beyond human abilities to represent or control it (Pickering 1995: 5). Philosopher of science Andrew Pickering argues that "scientists are human agents in a field of material agency which they struggle to capture in machines" (21). Pickering resists ontologies that separate human/nonhuman, mind/matter by arguing our realities are truly a mixing up of everything together. He calls this mixing *the mangle* or a jumble of human and nonhuman, body and thought, matter and language, that produces unpredictable results. "Human and material agency," Pickering writes, are "reciprocally and emergently intertwined [...] their contours emerge in the temporality of practice and are definitional of and sustain one another" (21). The mangle is an "impure" mixing that highlights that the "contours" themselves of "material and social agency are mangled in practice" (23). We see the agential resistance of nature when technological instruments, human scientific concepts, and nonhuman nature meet and mingle with unintentional consequences, setbacks, and results. Human intention, practice, machines, nonhuman material, philosophies of science, conceptions of nature, all are "emergently intertwined" as the material world "leaks into and infects our representations of it in a nontrivial and consequential fashion" (183).

Two, as examples of the material world "leaking" into the language and concepts we might use to represent it, critical materialisms use our contemporary environmental emergencies as evidence that there is no clear ontological divide between human and nonhuman. How do we make divisions between nature/culture, human/nonhuman with things such as lead poisoning, nuclear waste, or environmental cancers? Even the "natural" phenomena humans attempt to study always emerge from the interplay of human and nonhuman elements. Nancy Tuana in her essay "Viscous Porosity: Witnessing Katrina," uses Hurricane Katrina and its truly catastrophic impact on the US Gulf Coast and particularly low-income Black communities in Louisiana as a prime example. While Katrina came into being, Tuana remarks, through a "concatenation of phenomena— low pressure areas, warm ocean waters, and perhaps swirling in that classic cyclone pattern are the phenomena of deforestation and industrialization" the problems of Katrina and its disproportionate impact on Black communities are not so easily separated into "natural" or "human-induced" (2008: 193). Humans may believe they subdued the landscape through technology but if superstorms teach us anything, it is that these interconnections have agency.

FIGURE 9.1 *People waiting to enter the Superdome during Hurricane Katrina.* Source: *Marty Bahamonde/FEMA/Wikimedia Commons.*

Regarding the "toxic soup" that the destruction of Katrina left behind, Tuana employs a porous *ontology* to convey that this "dance of agency between human and nonhuman agents also happens at a more intimate level" as the "boundaries between our flesh and the flesh of the world we are of and in" are porous (2008: 198). "While porosity is what allows us to flourish—as we breathe in the oxygen we need to survive and metabolize the nutrients out of which our flesh emerges—this porosity," she writes, "often does not discriminate against that which can kill us. We cannot survive without water and food, but their viscous porosity often binds itself to strange and toxic bedfellows" (198). These toxins settle in bodies, disproportionately impacting poor communities of color through materialized racial discrimination, belying "any effort to identify a natural divide between nature/culture" (Tuana 2008: 201).

Three, realizing humans are all jumbled up with/in the tremendous diversity of material in the world around us, critical materialisms argue we must be attentive to the material consequences of our theory by rethinking our *ethics*. How should humans live in the world, with the knowledge that "nature" or the "environment" is not some place "out there," outside ourselves, a location to visit or pieces of land to protect, but the very substance of our beings? We must remember ontological conceptions always have ethical consequences so as we go about the project of reconceptualizing the human and nonhuman, materialist theorists argue we must attend to the social construction of the sciences via asking how scientific knowledge is produced, upon whose bodies it is built, and what histories it illuminates and erases. Reconceptualizing material in these ways forces us to "relinquish mastery" over nature as we find ourselves "inextricably part of the flux and flow of the world that others would presume to master" (Alaimo 2010: 17). What critical materialisms offer, however, is a shift away from ethical principles rooted in dichotomous thinking and toward ethical practices that are attentive to the "needs, the significance, and the liveliness of the more-than-human world" (Alaimo and Hekman 2008: 8) as well as the diverse human communities struggling with environmental degradation. Who gets to be the shapers and teachers of what it means to be human in the future and how humans should treat the environment?

Religion, Nature, and Critical Materialisms

At this point you may be wondering, *but what does this all have to do with religion*? I want to focus on two particular intersections that fundamentally shape North American religion and ecology. The first intersection is the growing awareness that through attachments to dichotomous thinking many religious traditions are intricately implicated in the environmental crisis facing our planet. Significantly for North American religious studies, the Christianity of white European settlers was heavily invested in nature/culture, nonhuman/human dichotomies from their initial colonial presence on the shores of the Americas. Two fifteenth-century papal bulls, the "Law of Nations" (1452) and "Inter Caetera" (1493), gave religious and political authority to Spanish and Portuguese colonizers to claim sovereignty, supreme authority, or power over all "discovered" lands and peoples in the name of the Catholic Church.

Later termed the "Doctrine of *terra nullius*" and the "Doctrine of Discovery," these public decrees from the pope legitimized the conquest, resource extraction, and enslavement of non-European territory by declaring the sovereign authority of the church over land and peoples that were not Christian. While the Americas were populated with millions of Indigenous people at the time of the arrival of Christopher Columbus, because they were not European Christians, they were deemed inhuman, inferior, uncivilized, and part of the landscape. If the land was unpopulated by humans, then it was *terra nullius*—empty land—and colonial projects for the church had the sovereignty to take land and its resources and enslave people who would not convert to profit the *sacred* mission of the church to spread Christianity across the globe.

These bulls clearly divided the world into Christian and non-Christian, human and nonhuman, European and "other" in ways that still shape our perspectives today as the Doctrine of Discovery continues to be referenced in legal decisions on land disputes. Furthermore, as scholar of law and religion Dana Lloyd argues in her article "The Coloniality of Wilderness" (2020) that conceptualizing land itself as *property*, a fundamental American value, is directly tied to the Doctrine of Discovery. However, the idea that lands can be "discovered" and "acquired" was certainly not the only relationship humans had with nonhuman nature during colonization. The Doctrine of Discovery granted supremacy to Euro-Christian relationships with the land by essentially erasing both Indigenous peoples and their own complex relationships with nonhuman nature, which includes the stance that nonhuman others cannot be owned as property (Lloyd 2020).

For example, in her book *Braiding Sweetgrass: Indigenous Wisdom, Scientific Knowledge, and the Wisdom of Plants* (2015) Native American botanist Robin Wall Kimmerer traces how Indigenous people cultivate reciprocal (not subject/object or owner/owned) relationships with nature and position humans within an enmeshed world with plants that they regard as tremendous teachers of knowledge. One of the questions Kimmerer's work encourages is, how might shifting away from the Christian colonial subject/object dichotomous relationship to land as property and toward Indigenous ways of knowing and relating to nonhuman others shift human spiritual and ecological relationships with nature and one another? Unsettling these histories within their own communities and reconsidering the legacies of Christian colonization in the Americas, many religious groups and Indigenous communities have called for actions similar to Kimmerer's line of inquiry. In 2016, a gathering of 524 clergy in North Dakota joined the Standing Rock oil pipeline protests by publicly burning copies of the Doctrine of Discovery and demanding a unified religious rejection of its troubling dichotomies (Jameson 2016). Indigenous, environmental, and other Christian groups continue to ask for the Vatican to rescind the Doctrine and publicly recognize its harmful history.

FIGURE 9.2 *A water protector at Standing Rock.* Source: *Revolution Messaging/Flickr.*

The second intersection is the work of religion scholars that begins to unpack how the American environmental movement *is itself* inherently intertwined with certain forms of Christianity (Stoll 2017). For example, in his incredibly detailed historical research *Devoted to Nature: The Religious Roots of American Environmentalism*, Evan Berry (2015: 20–1) argues that "American environmentalism was grounded in a vision that linked nature with spiritual redemption," or a "particular approach to human flourishing" that attempted to address the increasing exploitation of nonhuman nature but still continued some of the troubling dichotomous thinking that haunts our relationships with one another. Progressive era conservation and nature organizations held up "pristine" nature or wilderness as the ideal source of "moral vitality," a space for encounters with the divine, and the prime location for American Protestant conceptions of goodness, hard work, and salvation to be explored (63–71). Through vigorous activities in wilderness, humans could recapture many of the "basic virtues cherished in particular by Americans," such as "self-sufficiency, ingenuity, camaraderie, and fortitude" (74) that many white Protestants felt were being destroyed by growing urbanization.

Foundational environmental thinkers such as Aldo Leopold, John Muir, and Robert Marshall advocated for "the protection of those landscapes by which Americans could continue to cultivate the 'spirit of the wilderness'" (Berry 2015: 77) shaping many Americans' conceptions of what "nature" and "nature experiences" should be or look like: grand expanses of land that are free from development and the presence

FIGURE 9.3 *Yosemite National Park.* Source: *Carol M. Highsmith/Library of Congress.*

of people. However, while these movements somewhat unsettled American comfort with nature/culture dichotomies by championing the inherent value of nature, this growing environmental movement maintained other divisions by investing, through policy, discrimination, and intimidation, in nature spaces as the salvific playground for only white, Christian, heterosexual males. These movements to protect areas of "pristine" nature as *sacred,* as Lloyd (2020) details, were always in contention with Indigenous habitation and relationship with the land and often used as arguments to displace native peoples in the name of public land use or nature preservation.

Furthermore, cultural geographer and environmental justice advocate Carolyn Finney argues that during the birth of contemporary environmental thought, significant events impacting African Americans shaped a very different Black environmental experience. Finney traces how the Emancipation Proclamation and Homestead Act initially allowed former slaves to own confiscated or abandoned Confederate land (2014: 36). In 1866, however, "former white owners of the land, who were pardoned after the war, began to pressure President Andrew Johnson to allow their land to be returned to them," fearful that "black landowners and farmers would start to accumulate wealth and power in the South" (37). In response to their requests, in 1866 Congress forced the freedmen "off their newly acquired land, and it was returned to former white plantation owners" (37).

While Muir was giving influential lectures in the 1870s on forest preservation and revering pristine nature, Black men and women were forced to continually renegotiate their relationships with the landscapes they were once forced to cultivate, owned for a brief moment, and then had torn from them. In the 1880s, Muir's conservation ideologies influenced President Theodore Roosevelt to take an interest in forestry and eventually sanction the creation of the National Park Service establishing nature reserves that many Americans consider sacred spaces.

However, at the same time significant pieces of legislation were enacted to "limit both movement and accessibility" of these spaces for "African Americans, as well as American Indians, Chinese, and other nonwhite peoples in the United States" (Finney 2014: 37). As American environmentalism was forming its identity, this legislation coupled with numerous race-related massacres of African Americans (37) shaped natural spaces and wilderness as unsafe and unwelcome for many Americans. These histories complexify many of the foundational ideas environmentally conscious people have about environmental projects in the Americas. What is nature? How do we define and protect it? Whose voices and experiences are included in its definition? Who are we protecting nature for and from? For the intersections of environmental and religious studies: What sorts of places, spaces, and landscapes do we continue to revere as sacred nature? How might dichotomous thinking shape which spaces we value, protect, and celebrate? Is all nonhuman nature sacred? Are some religious groups' sacred landscapes recognized and protected at the expense of others? Finally, are sacred nature encounters only possible for a particular kind of human? Who is truly allowed to worship in/with nature? (Glave 2010).

FIGURE 9.4 *Theodore Roosevelt with John Muir.* Source: *Wellcome Collection Gallery.*

FIGURE 9.5 *Muir Woods.* Source: *The Jon B. Lovelace Collection of California Photographs/ Library of Congress.*

Religion and nature, like the *nonhuman turn*, is a complex conversation involving many different kinds of scholars and religious leaders with very different backgrounds, investments, and agendas. However, in his helpful framing of the past few decades of work in religion and nature broadly defined, Bron Taylor suggests that they all seem to work from an agreement that "nature is sacred (in some way); and this conviction appears to be tethered to ethical concern about the environmental decline" (2004: 995). While critical materialisms have wisdom to offer all environmental conversations, concluding we can ask: How do critical materialisms encourage religion scholars to consider the more-than-human world ethically in new and challenging ways? How does this work encourage religion scholarship to become more aware of our reliance on white conceptions of and encounters in nature? While the field of religion and nature attempt the difficult task of bringing religious studies and environmental science into conversation, critical materialisms encourage religion scholars to remain critical of scientific narratives that do not recognize our own biases, or social inequalities, or the ways people of color have been marginalized by environmental movements. By seriously considering the contributions from critical materialisms, we can work to understand the political implications of how "the sacred" is defined, produced, reproduced, and protected, and draw attention to the communities, occluded, excluded, and abandoned by dichotomous thinking.

Further Reading and Online Resources

Hazard S. (2013), "The Material Turn in the Study of Religion," *Religion and Society: Advances in Research*, 4: 58–78.

O'Dell-Chaib C. (2019), "The Shape of This Wonder? Consecrated Science and New Cosmology Affects," *Zygon*, 54 (2): 387–95.

Shotwell A. (2016), *Against Purity: Living Ethically in Compromised Times*, Minneapolis: University of Minnesota Press.

Sideris L.H. (2017), *Consecrating Science: Wonder, Knowledge, and the Natural World*, Oakland: University of California Press.

Taylor D. (2016), *The Rise of the American Conservation Movement: Power, Privilege, and Environmental Protection*, Durham, NC: Duke University Press.

References

Alaimo S. (2000), *Undomesticated Ground: Recasting Nature as Feminist Space*, Ithaca, NY: Cornell University Press.

Alaimo S. (2010), *Bodily Natures: Science, Environment, and the Material Self*, Bloomington: Indiana University Press.

Alaimo S. and S. Hekman (2008), "Introduction: Emerging Models of Materiality in Feminist Theory," in S. Alaimo, and S. Hekman (eds.), *Material Feminisms*, 1–19, Bloomington: Indiana University Press.

Baker-Fletcher K. (1998), *Sisters of Dust, Sisters of Spirit: Womanist Wordings on God and Creation*, Minneapolis, MN: Fortress Press.

Barad K. (2007), *Meeting the Universe Halfway: Quantum Physics and the Entanglement of Matter and Meaning*, Durham, NC: Duke University Press.

Bennett J. (2010), *Vibrant Matter: A Political Ecology of Things*, Durham, NC: Duke University Press.

Berry E. (2015), *Devoted to Nature: The Religious Roots of American Environmentalism*, Oakland: University of California Press.

Braidotti R. (2013), *The Posthuman*, Cambridge, UK: Polity.

Bullard R. (1983), "Solid Waste Sites and the Black Houston Community," *Sociological Inquiry*, 53: 273–88.

Bullard R. (2000), *Dumping in Dixie: Race, Class, and Environmental Quality*, Boulder, CO: Westview Press.

Bullard R. and B. Wright (2007), *Race, Place, and Environmental Justice after Hurricane Katrina: Struggles to Reclaim, Rebuild, and Revitalize New Orleans and the Gulf Coast*, New York: Routledge.

Butler J. (1993), *Bodies That Matter: On the Discursive Limits of "Sex,"* London: Routledge.

Chen M. (2012), *Animacies: Biopolitics, Racial Mattering, and Queer Affect*, Durham, NC: Duke University Press.

Coole D. and S. Frost (2010), "Introducing the New Materialisms," in D. Coole and S. Frost (eds.), *New Materialisms: Ontology, Agency, Politics*, 1–43, Durham, NC: Duke University Press.

Descartes R. (1986), *Meditations on First Philosophy with Selections from the Objections and Replies*, trans. and ed. J. Cottingham, Cambridge: Cambridge University Press.

Finney C. (2014), *Black Faces, White Spaces: Reimagining the Relationship of African Americans to the Great Outdoors*, Chapel Hill: University of North Carolina Press.

Gaard G. (2017), *Critical Ecofeminism*, Lanham, MA: Lexington Books.

Glave D. (2010), *Rooted in the Earth: Reclaiming the African American Environmental Heritage*, Chicago: Lawrence Hill Books.

Grosz E. (2005), *Time Travels: Feminism, Nature, Power*, Durham, NC: Duke University Press.

Haraway D. (1989), *Primate Visions: Gender, Race, and Nature in the World of Modern Science*, New York: Routledge.

Harris M. (2017), *Ecowomanism: African American Women and Earth-Honoring Faiths*, Maryknoll, NY: Orbis Books.

Jackson Z. (2015), "Outer Worlds: The Persistence of Race in Movement 'Beyond the Human,'" *GLQ: A Journal of Lesbian and Gay Studies*, 21: 215–18.

Jameson N. (2016), "Clergy Repudiate 'Doctrine of Discovery' as Hundreds Support Indigenous Rights at Standing Rock," *Baptist News*, November 4. Available online: https://baptistnews.com/article/clergy-repudiate-doctrine-of-discovery-as-hundreds-support-indigenous-rights-at-standing-rock/#.XzL2RJNKjhb (accessed July 16, 2020).

Kafer A. (2013), *Feminist, Queer, Crip*, Bloomington: Indiana University Press.

Karera A. (2019), "Blackness and the Pitfalls of Anthropocene Ethics," *Critical Philosophy of Race*, 7: 32–56.

Kimmerer R.W. (2015), *Braiding Sweetgrass: Indigenous Wisdom, Scientific Knowledge and the Teachings of Plants*, Minneapolis, MN: Milkweed Editions.

Lerner S. (2006), *Diamond: A Struggle for Environmental Justice in Louisiana's Chemical Corridor*, Cambridge, MA: MIT Press.

Lloyd D. (2020), "The Coloniality of Wilderness," *Political Theology Network*, June 18. Available online: https://politicaltheology.com/the-coloniality-of-wilderness/ (accessed May 2, 2021).

Mies M. and V. Shiva (1993), *Ecofeminism*, London: Zed Books.

Pickering A. (1995), *The Mangle of Practice: Time, Agency, and Science*, Chicago: University of Chicago Press.

Plumwood V. (1993), *Feminism and the Mastery of Nature*, London: Routledge.

Riley S. (2003), "Ecology Is a Sistah's Issue Too: The Politics of Emergent Afrocentric Womanism," in R. Foltz (ed.), *Worldviews, Religion, and the Environment: A Global Anthology*, 472–80, Belmont, CA: Wadsworth.

Sandilands C. (1999), *The Good-Natured Feminist: Ecofeminism and the Quest for Democracy*, Minneapolis: University of Minnesota Press.

Schaefer D.O. (2015), *Religious Affects: Animality, Evolution, and Power*, Durham, NC: Duke University Press.

Sharpe C. (2016), *In the Wake: On Blackness and Being*, Durham, NC: Duke University Press.

Stoll M. (2017), *Inherit the Holy Mountain: Religion and the Rise of American Environmentalism*, New York: Oxford University Press.

Sturgeon N. (1997), *Ecofeminist Natures: Race, Gender, Feminist Theory and Political Action*, New York: Routledge.

Taylor B. (2004), "A Green Future for Religion?," *Futures*, 36: 991–1008.

Taylor D. (1997), "Women of Color, Environmental Justice and Ecofeminism," in K. Warren (ed.), *Ecofeminism: Women, Nature and Culture*, 38–82, Bloomington: Indiana University Press.

Tuana N. (2008), "Viscous Porosity: Witnessing Katrina," in S. Alaimo and S.J. Hekman (eds.), *Material Feminisms*, 188–213, Bloomington: Indiana University Press.

Warren K. (2000), *Ecofeminist Philosophy: A Western Perspective on What It Is and Why It Matters*, Lanham, MD: Rowman & Littlefield Publishers.

Glossary Terms

Agency The capacity of an entity to act or influence other entities.

Anthropocentrism The belief that humans are the most important entities on the planet.

Dichotomy A division between two entities or concepts that asserts they are mutually exclusive and opposed or contradictory. Dichotomies attribute more value to only one set of the division or binary.

Ethics The process of questioning and prescribing how to live in our material world. For example, *how should humans treat nonhuman others* (?), is an ethical question.

Nonhuman turn An intellectual movement that seeks to decenter the human as the conscious and unconscious focus of scholarship by turning concerns to the agency of the nonhuman world.

Ontology The study of existence or the nature of being. For example, *what does it mean to be human* (?), is an ontological question.

Sacred Describes places, spaces, events, and objects that are set apart from every day or "profane" objects, places, etc. as deserving of veneration and of ultimate importance.

10

Bodily Beings: Sex, Sexuality, and Gender at the Intersection of Religion and Nature

Heather Eaton

Sex, Sexuality, and Gender

The topics of sex, sexuality, and gender are vast and complex, as well as being personal, relational, and lived. The meaning of gender, the ideological, cultural and political tenets surrounding sexuality, and the purposes of sex are often discussed and debated, and they are often highly influenced by religions. Social controls of people according to their gender, sexuality, and sexual practices can be rigid and unforgiving. These most intimate aspects of a person are often influenced, or controlled, by rules and regulations, beliefs and biases, and cultural and religious traditions. This chapter is divided into subtopics of being "natural"; the body; sex; sexuality; gender; and gender roles, rules, and repressions.

Being Natural

Many adherents of Christianity and other religions like to make claims about what is "natural," a term whose many meanings are framed in terms of being derived— or distinct—from nature and natural processes (Warren 1997). Thus, adherents of the same religious tradition can make different claims, as the relationship of these meanings to science is often confusing and conflicting. They may use, or refute, theories of evolution, animal behavior, reproduction, biology, physiology, and more to make their points. Biblical or other scriptural texts are often used to support patriarchal views of biological determinism and gender essentialism as a way to claim that this is how the creator designed humans. Using religious claims to guide the selective use of science, religious leaders often "teach and preach" on what is natural and, of course, what is not. These positions usually support heteronormativity. This shows how easy it is to make claims about sexuality and identity based on a muddled mixture of partial facts, beliefs, and bias. These are then used to secure gender, sex, and sexuality norms, and present them as "natural." It should also be noted that some religious leaders overtly resist heteronormativity, and their voices are important in changing views of sexuality and sexual identities, and what is deemed to be "natural" (Bauman 2018).

The Body

What does it mean to live with, in, and be "a body"? When we look around, we see a variety of bodily shapes and sizes, with different meanings and expressions. We are embodied creatures, and there is no escape from our bodylines (Butler 2011). We dress up or down, decorate, expose or cover, massage, modify, love or loathe, or try to ignore our bodies.

We play with/in our bodies. Dancing, playing sports, praying, eating, bathing, and touching are everyday bodily practices. Sex and sexual expressions are bodily activities, and they perform a variety of functions. In a patriarchal and puritan setting, sex is mainly about reproduction. Yet this is only one, even a minor, purpose of sexuality. Affection, comfort, desire, arousal and pleasure, and love are nurturing sexual/bodily expressions.

Bodies are also interpreted. For example, clothing the body is a zone of interpretation, sending a plethora of signals and meanings to others. What women should and should not wear, where and when, and what they must cover and why, often based on religious norms, is a disturbing reality many women must face regularly. Women's bodies are a frequent social topic and have been interpreted in ways that have altered both individual and collective histories. The differences between women's and men's bodies have been a popular research field, which frequently resulted in women being considered to be less capable due to their brain mass, bone density, hip size, foot length, menstruation, child-bearing, and on and on. These are the arguments used why women should not learn to read and write, be politicians or religious leaders, have their own bank accounts, own land, or drive cars or become pilots.

Bodies are also sites of oppression. Sexual and physical assaults are common in North America, as elsewhere. Judith Butler's influential book, *Gender Trouble* (1990), reminds us to take bodiliness seriously, as a site of empowerment, oppression, and performance. She is adamant that being embodied is also nonlinear with sex, sexuality, and gender identity, but is implicated in all of these.

Sex

Most cultures and religions have patriarchal traditions, with strongly held views on sex. At a basic level, sex, as a biological category, means there are males (penis, XY chromosomes, testosterone), females (vagina, XX chromosomes, estrogen), and sometimes, in about 1–1.5 percent of the population, intersex (combinations of reproductive sex organs, chromosomes, and hormones) (Intersex Society of North America 2008). Sex, in this sense, has a largely biological base. The long history of assuming that biological sex determines sexual preferences and gender identity has been upended in the past fifty years. Bodies matter, and considerations of differences in sex organs, hormones, chromosomes, and even genes are important, making the current understanding of sex more interesting and relevant to the sexual diversity that exists.

An assumption of patriarchy is that one's biological sex determines one's sexuality and gender identity. It is important to consider that most religions are patriarchal in origins, texts, teachings, and leadership (Ruether 1992). Many remain entrenched in

FIGURE 10.1 *Gender Unicorn, "Trans Student Educational Resources, 2015."* Source: *https://transstudent.org/gender.*

patriarchal beliefs, structures, and views on gender, sexuality, and sexual controls, especially of women. Further, many religions are still inflexible around homo-, trans-, and fluid sexuality, in identity or expression. Ann Taves traces a history of sexuality and religion in the United States, noting how beliefs about the body, sex, and sexual acts have shaped the country's history. She reveals that notions of marriage, the family, and reproduction contain distinct cultural biases (Taves 1997). For example, the United States and Canada were initially colonized by Catholic and Protestant missionaries and settlers. Some came with Puritan beliefs that became part of the colonizing practices. The encounters between various Indigenous peoples, Christians, and the state were often destructive and denigrating to the Indigenous communities. The efforts to establish a Christian culture and state structure included strict views on sexuality, which were imposed by state and religious institutions. Taves notes that if we consider "the body" as a colonizing site, we see how the rigid views of patriarchal Christianity were another way to oppress and control people.

Sexuality

In contemporary North America, terms of ethnicity, race, religion, gender, and sexuality have become central to the ways that people consider their personal and political identities. However, sexual identities are often seen as the most significant identifier, and research into sexuality and sexual identities is relatively recent. Such research has also revealed the contentious and repressive history of sexuality in North America. For example, public and respectful conversations on homosexuality have occurred only in the last fifty years or so in North America. Decriminalizing homosexuality is an ongoing process, which started in the 1960s, and there is still plenty of denigrating public discourse and discrimination. Discussing being intersex, bisexual, or trans is even more recent (Vakoch 2020). There are ongoing debates in some conservative, usually religious, settings, as religions are more ambivalent on these issues, and change slowly. Conflicts between religions and the state regularly occur on matters of sexuality. There are frequent court cases in North America, ruling on conflicts between religious freedom, sexuality, and the law, including on LGBTQ rights, conversion therapies, women's reproductive rights, and sexual expressions (Rimmerman and Wilcox 2007).

There are histories to all these topics. For example, in 1969 Canada decriminalized homosexual acts between consenting adults, indicating the importance of the state in sexuality (Rayside and Wilcox 2011). The Stonewall Riots in New York in 1969 were a watershed for gay rights and strengthened resistance to stop police persecuting gay communities (Editors of the Encyclopedia Britannica 2021). In the United States, the first pride parade was Saturday, June 27, 1970, organized by the Chicago Gay

FIGURE 10.2 *US Supreme Court protest for LGBTQ equality, Washington, DC, 2019.* Source: *Ted Eytan/CC BY-SA 2.0.*

Liberation group, as part of gay rights movements and in response to systematic oppression. In 2021, Pride parades are increasingly common, representing and celebrating sexual diversities, although they continue to be met with opposition in some settings.

In terms of definitions, sexuality usually means one's sexual desires, activities, expressions, identity, and relationships. Yet, as Butler noted, these are not always connected for a person, as there are numerous sexual desires and expressions. Sexual identity, a relatively recent concept, is how one chooses to describe or define one's sexuality. Cultures that are homophobic (negative attitudes toward homosexuality) and heteronormative (assumes that heterosexuality is the natural, normal, proper, and only type of sexual orientation) draw a direct line between biological sex and sexuality. In spite of endless historical and contemporary evidence that biological sex and sexuality are nonlinear, these heteronormative beliefs and constraints endure. Nonetheless, it is now clear that there are multiple sexualities within human communities. Many terms now exist, such as: homosexual, bisexual, heterosexual, asexual, pansexual, queer, trans, questioning, and more (see Abrams

2019). Thus sexuality and sexual expressions are broad, diverse, personal, flexible, and not determined by ones sex or gender. Furthermore, they are constructed, meaning that cultures—power, knowledge, beliefs, biases, and choices—create and influence sexual identities. In 1990, Michel Foucault in *The History of Sexuality* explained how social, political, economic, and religious powers manipulate and construct sexual identities.

Gender

Gender has historically been regarded in terms of the binaries of women/men, female/male, and feminine/masculine. Within patriarchal religious settings, gender, sex, and sexuality together are an ontology—a defined way of being—within strict boundaries. In traditional terms, gender then means the biological sex and role one is ascribed in society: male or female. They may argue that this connection is natural, normal, virtuous, or even divine, and inflate the significance of biological sex, which assumes, incorrectly, that gender roles stem from biological differences or sexual expressions.

Gender roles are personal, social, and cultural, and shaped by countless factors. These roles are lived, or performed, every day in every culture. Gender is best understood as the role one plays personally and socially, as a key aspect of one's sense of self, as an identity one presents, and as one's manner of social participation. These are assumed to be interconnected. Yet, the social role one performs may not be in sync with one's sense of self, or desired sexuality. As gender awareness increases, and social movements challenge gender stereotypes, it is clear that some people are cisgender (identity that corresponds with their birth sex), transgender (identity or expression that differs from the sex that they were assigned at birth), or gender fluid or nonconforming (gender identity is flexible, not fixed, and not constrained by assigned sex or gender roles). There is no inherent or "natural" connection between one's sex, gender, and sexuality, and these things change over time in individuals and across cultures.

Gender Roles, Rules, and Repressions

Gender is one, if not the, most pressurized aspect of being human. From infancy onward, we are constantly being trained in, and compelled to conform to, prescribed gender roles (Eckert and McConnelle-Ginet 2013). The obsession with gender roles has been a key facet of patriarchal cultures, which means virtually all cultures. In North America, gender roles are taught, often under the guise that this is natural, normal, and prescribed by God. There are cross-cultural differences in the specifics, but all cultures maintain gender stereotypes and detailed training. Although there

FIGURE 10.3 *Promise Keepers rally in Washington, DC, 1997, which promoted godly manhood and fatherhood.* Source: *Elvert Barnes Photography/CC BY 2.0.*

are some spaces, usually urban, where gender fluidity and a multiplicity of gender roles and sexual expressions are accepted, there are still more spaces where these remain rigid.

In North America it is becoming common to have gender reveal parties before a child is born. What does this mean, other than indicating that labeling the sex/gender of a baby is decisive? Most people assume sex means gender, and as soon as a child is born, gender training begins. It is termed "gender lore" by some. As Eckert and McConnell-Ginet argue:

> Gender is embedded so thoroughly in our institutions, our actions, our beliefs, and our desires, that it appears to us to be completely natural. The world swarms with ideas about gender – and these ideas are so commonplace that we take it for granted that they are true, accepting common adage as scientific fact.
>
> (2013: 1)

From a theoretical viewpoint, there is a key difference between theories of gender essentialism—that there are biological, psychological, character, or other essential differences between women and men—and theories of social construction. The former is part of patriarchal cultural tenets. The latter sees that gender training is so strong, that until there are significant efforts to dismantle gender lore, it is best to assume that what we consider to be gender differences are socially constructed. Of course, gender is neither constructed in a cultural vacuum nor determined solely by "nature," namely, biology, sexual organs, or hormones. Both nature and cultural/religious beliefs and practices influence gender formations.

There is no culture or religious community where gender is not an active factor in determining large parts of personal identity, sexual expressions, life choices, and security. These elements involve lifelong training in gender: clothing, gestures, posture, communication, and all the minutiae of daily living. The governing gender binary separates "women" from "men," creating a gender stratification where, usually, most women have fewer privileges than most men. This is similar to racism: ethnic or racialized systems that benefit some over others. Not everyone will experience the full force of racism, while others will, but racism intersects with gender expectations and heteronormativity to further prescribe one's experience. Furthermore, those who benefit from such systems can be unaware that their advantages are simply granted to the privileged sectors of that society. The terms structural oppression or structural violence are often used to show that these gendered norms are part of social systems held in place by ideological, often religious, and economic practises. These practises are promoted and maintained by the society as a whole and are often legally and/or religiously enforced. Individuals can rarely change these gender lore ideologies and structures; it requires social transformations.

Societies manifest gender stratifications within overarching systems that benefit those viewed as men more than women, and can restrain women's and trans lives through limiting education, nutrition, life choices, reproductive autonomy, financial independence. This may include prescribed purity norms and a range of physical, emotional, and sexual violence. There is a sexual division of labor in most cultures that separates the realms of work for women and men, usually with women relegated to the domestic sphere. There are other systems of oppression that place limits on people's lives—outside of their control—such as ethnicity, race, class, abilities, poverty, religious affiliation, etc. These realities intersect and shape people's lives in terms of opportunities, health, employment, education, geographical options, and life-span (see "Race, Religion, and Environmental Racism in North America," in this volume). The terms intersectionality or intersectional analysis are used to understand how factors intersect to compound discriminations. Intersectionality is widely used in gender studies to expose and assess how domination and privilege operate, and identify multiple ways that advantages and disadvantages, and benefits and burdens, are distributed and imposed in a given culture.

Given that gender roles are operative in every culture, it is necessary to consider the damaging elements of these systems, since people do not fit the mold, in the stories of how men and women should be, behave, think, and develop. What is labeled as masculine and feminine rarely corresponds fully to men and to women. Furthermore, to label any trait—being beautiful, intelligent, emotional, strong or weak—as belonging to a woman or a man is mistaken. These are human traits, although as we are taught to be a woman/feminine or a man/masculine, this training encourages the development of some traits over others.

One of the most difficult topics concerning gender, sex, and sexuality is the ubiquitous continuum of violence, primarily against women, and GLBTQI. The United Nations defines violence against women as "any act of gender-based violence that results in, or is likely to result in, physical, sexual, or mental harm or suffering to women, including threats of such acts, coercion or arbitrary deprivation of liberty, whether occurring in public or in private life" (World Health Organization 2021). The World Health Organization notes that violence against women is the most significant health threat most women face. For example, on average, nearly twenty people per minute are physically abused by an intimate partner in the United States, over ten million women and men per year. In general this means that one in four women and one in ten men experience severe intimate partner violence, with women victims sustaining injuries three times more often than male victims. Also, the Femicide Accountability Project notes that in the United States over two thousand women are killed each year by intimate partners (Women Count USA 2021). In Canada, one woman or girl is killed every 2.5 days (Canadian Feminist Observatory for Justice and Accountability 2020). Six women are killed by men every hour in a "global pandemic of femicide" that is being partly hidden by COVID-19—and the United Nations is calling for urgent action. Most countries now keep statistics on femicide. Those who are trans, gay, bisexual, or men labeled as "feminine" can also be subject to violence. These gender-based acts of violence are now considered to be systemic human rights violations.

FIGURE 10.4 *A Missing and Murdered Indigenous Women (MMIW) Task Force rally in Minnesota to bring attention to the intersection of racism and sexism in the lack of law enforcement response and prosecution for the hundreds of missing and murdered Indigenous women.* Source: *MN Senate DFL/Public Domain.*

These gender issues are changing. Heterosexism, homo- or transphobia, and gender identity restrictions are being challenged and lifted around the world, even when such challenges bring violent and restrictive backlash. Incredible gains in understanding, legal protection, and public acceptance have been made in the past few decades, albeit unevenly. Childcare is increasing, freeing parents to pursue other work. Legal rights for LGBTQ+ are expanding, as is medical and psychological assistance. Yet, abortion rights, while difficult to gain, are again under threat in the United States, with fifteen states putting more restrictions on abortions since January 2021 (Guttmacher Institute 2021). These rights can be secured, and then lost, depending on the cultural and religious ethos and who has political power.

While in most places the spectrum of gender identities is becoming more recognized, and social movements for gender equality and autonomy are gaining traction, there remains a hierarchy that privileges some men over women, and is overall heterosexist. These discriminations are often upheld by what some consider to be religious values and/or by suggesting they are "natural." Thus, it is important to challenge those understandings of both religion and nature together. Nonetheless, what is understood to be sex, sexuality, and gender is undergoing significant transformations, and liberations in North American and around the globe.

Ecofeminism

The approach of ecofeminism brings gender, sexuality, religion, and nature together into a single focus. Ecofeminism refers to connections between ecological and feminist concerns: discerning multiple associations between feminist and ecological movements, and between the historical and contemporary oppression and domination of women and the natural world, a women/nature nexus. It examines a long history of ideas, found in most religions and cultures, that claim there are specific associations between women and nature. While at times such essentialist connections are revered, under patriarchy, a women/nature nexus (described below) places bodies, women, animals, and the earth as less valuable than men, reason, spirit, and culture. The ideological and historical legacies of associating women with nature coalesced into a devaluation of both. The term *ecofeminism* is thought to have originated with French feminist Françoise d'Eaubonne in *Le Féminisme ou la Mort* (1974).

Today ecofeminism is an umbrella term including distinct and multiple links between feminism and ecology, and women and the natural world. It includes a vast area of research and activities, perhaps as a third wave of feminism. Much has been written about the emergence and development of ecofeminism and its many forms (Eaton 2005; Eaton and Lorentzen 2003; Gaard 1997, 2017). Here is a synopsis of some of the key aspects, noting that some who focus on ecology-feminist connections prefer concepts such as feminist ecology, feminist social ecology, feminist green socialism, feminist environmentalism, feminist ecocriticism, ecowomanism, women and environment, feminist green philosophy, and so on.

FIGURE 10.5 *Ecofeminism, Ritual Venus de Primavera, part of the Tiempo de Mujeres, Festival por la Igualdad, Mexico.* Source: *Andrea Herrera/Secretaría de Cultura CDMX/CC BY 2.0.*

Eco-womanism adds a lens of race, along with the critique that feminism was too often by and about white women (Harris 2017). Also, some are more interested in feminism than ecological issues. It is advantageous here to consider a broad, flexible, and inclusive use of the term.

Historical connections between women and nature are deep-rooted, and formed within patriarchal and Christian dogmas, systems, and customs. Women and the natural world are seen as interrelated, namely, women are considered to be close to nature, and nature was deemed to be feminine (Adams 1993; Plumwood 1993). Discovering the extent of these ideas and practices sparked a range of ecofeminist academic work, especially in North America in the fields of philosophy, theology, and religious studies.

Theologians such as Rosemary Radford Ruether were instrumental in showing how Christianity incorporated and promoted this association of women with nature, and their joint inferiority to men and culture (1992). Religious/spiritual activists and academics contributed from many standpoints, such as from Wiccan, Goddess, Jewish, Christian, Hindu, Buddhist, Indigenous, and Islamic traditions. Case studies revealed that while culturally distinct, a woman/nature nexus is common around the world (Eaton and Lorentzen 2003; Kirk and Hall 2021; Ruether 2005). The exposure of hierarchical dualisms—ways of perceiving the world in opposites, binaries, or dualisms, such as heaven/earth, culture/nature, men/women, masculine/feminine, reason/emotion, spirit/matter, and mind/body—provided a vital catalyst for ecofeminist cultural analyses. These dualisms are deeply embedded in Christian, Jewish, and Islamic worldviews, and the related logic of domination evidenced in social patterns, in economic, political, and spiritual relationships, and in a denigration of the natural world. Thus, the linked dominations of women and nature became justified, normalized, *natural*, accepted, reinforced, and perpetuated. Ideas that the natural world was untouched, or virgin, and empty were part of the attitudes that led colonizers to aggressively expand, rule, and oppress the Indigenous peoples as well as the land (Merchant 1990).

Ecofeminist critique also has an empirical base in contemporary societies (Nogueira-Godsey 2021). In most parts of the world environmental problems generally disproportionately affect men. Studies show how sociopolitical and economic structures compress many women's lives to poverty, ecological deprivation, and economic powerlessness. A sexual division of labor reinforces women's work in the domestic sphere, where ecological ruin is readily felt in water scarcities or contamination, crop failures, soil erosion, and food and fuel shortages. Additional problems are caused by agribusiness, deforestation, ecosystem disruption, eco-health decline, or climate change, and repairs or remedies are challenging.

From the beginning, the associations between women/nature and feminism/ecology were made by environmental, peace, and animal rights activists, as well as by farmers, artists, teachers, theologians, and more throughout North America and beyond. Eventually ecofeminism incorporated intersectionality as a cornerstone, as well as including approaches from critical race, queer, ethnicity, identity, disability, and numerous contextual-cultural and postmodern and postcolonial theories (Bauman 2018; Chen 2012; Kirk and Hall 2021).

Ecofeminism is multifaceted, encompassing different forms of knowledge, and has provided enormously useful and flexible insights and analyses. The purpose is always to dismantle what is oppressive and to propose liberating alternatives.

Religions have considerable social power to influence what is acceptable on the topics of sex, sexuality, and gender and the relationship to nature. Much work is occurring to reevaluate patriarchal positions and shift the emphasis to human flourishing, nurturing relationships, justice, and social support for all genders (Hultman and Pule 2018). The intersection of sex/gender ideologies and cological devastation is an additional and most difficult challenge of this era.

Religion, Nature, and Culture: A Planetary Approach

What would it mean to situate sex, sexuality, and gender in evolutionary, ecological, and planetary perspectives? To ponder these topics from such approaches means that we must consider planetary dynamics as well as realizing human lives are integrated in an Earth community of life: a biosphere. The most important part for understanding this framework is the scientific evidence which claims that life has evolved over billions of years. Life emerged, developed, and evolved on planet Earth some 3.7 billion years ago, with microorganisms that replicated molecules to reproduce. It took over a billion years for sexual reproduction to become the main mode of the expansion of life. Sexual reproduction began approximately two billion years ago with single-celled life-forms, which were infinitely more complex than the first microorganisms (Margulis 1998; Margulis and Sagan 1991).

Most life-forms procreate by sexual reproduction: algae, plants, insects, and most animals. This is done by releasing sperm into the wind or the water, and carrying it to eggs, or using other species to carry male gametes to female ones, such as with pollinators and flowers. Further evolutionary processes involved the development of male and female sexual organs, and sex meant maneuvering two bodies so that the openings to the internal reproductive organs are close enough together for fluid exchange, such as with most insects and birds.

Sexual intercourse evolved. This is the kind of reproductive sex that humans and other mammals, as well as some birds, reptiles, amphibians, and fish have: an external male penetrating organ and an internal female "reception" area. The evolution of sex is a fascinating topic of study! Given that the drive to establish a successful species requires propagating, sex and sexuality can be seen to be mainly about reproduction. However, for many animals, sexuality serves multiple purposes. One is to attract an appropriate mate, with elaborate courtship and mating rituals performed by eels, peacocks, penguins, whales, and many other birds, insects, and mammals. Some have songs and calls, others have extravagant plumage, puff their chests, change colors, emit strong scents, display great dance moves, or indicate nest/cave-building skills. Some bring food, beautiful stones or sticks, or make themselves look, sound, or smell lovely to lure a mate. The variety is endless. This is where sexual attraction is key to the success of a species. It is noteworthy that beauty, abundance, health, and the ability to construct a safe home are key indicators to successful sexual mating (Rosenthal 2017). This is true for animals that mate for life, and for the majority of animals that mate with many.

In some species it is the male who nurtures, feeds, raises, and educates their offspring. Gender stereotypes cannot be seen in animal behaviors. It is also important to note that sexual coercion in animals is rare, other than in human males. However, harassment, intimidation, aggression, grabbing, and at times sexual force can exist in males of several species such as guppies, some birds, spider monkeys, and dolphins, to name a few. The main theory used to explain this behavior is that often there are more males than females, and the males are pressured, instinctually, to procreate. Females in some species have also coevolved with strategies of resistance: male avoidance, habitat relocation, alliances with other females, and escape. Although this topic is important to mention, it is crucial to understand that sexual coercion is not the norm in the biosphere, and furthermore, it is unacceptable and immoral in human communities.

Attraction, or sexuality, plays a role in mating: the expressing of desire, desirability, availability, and charm. Even sex itself is not just about procreation. Many animals engage in sex for pleasure, or to establish themselves in social hierarchies. Many animals engage

FIGURE 10.6 *A greater sage-grouse* (Centrocercus urophasianus) *with its gular sacs inflated to attract mates during its courtship display.* Source: *Bureau of Land Management/Public Domain.*

in heterosexual, homosexual, asexual, and other relations. This brings us to humans. We share the impulse to reproduce and engage in elaborate attraction rituals that involve being eye-catching through dress, smell, gift-bringing, and appealing skills. Humans also have sex for pleasure, comfort, status, or procreation. Sex and sexuality have coevolved to have intrinsic connections to each other. Yet, from the earlier descriptions of sex, sexuality, and gender, it is evident that while these behaviors are common throughout the biosphere, humans have added layers of meaning and interpretation that influence our actions.

Of course, humans are entangled within natural as well as diverse cultural systems. Furthermore, if we look at these activities in the larger Earth community, it becomes clear that a patriarchal emphasis on heterosexism is an ideological, not a biological, imperative. Through this evolutionary lens we can see that the constraints and controls surrounding human, particularly women's, sexuality, purity, sexual freedom, choices, and reproductive rights can be seen for what they are: oppressive mechanisms of patriarchal domination.

An added layer of meaning and interpretation of sex, sexuality, and gender will always be part of human cultures, narratives, identities, and social norms. Humans live within worldviews that make claims about these dimensions of existence. Both science and religion have a lot to say about sex, gender, sexuality and what is natural and normal. Neither are without bias, and either can be used for liberating or oppressive purposes (Bardon 2019). We will always live within narratives about the roles and rules surrounding sex, sexuality, and gender, and in North America, and elsewhere, these patriarchal narratives are being challenged. Ecofeminism is challenging the meanings associated with gender, nature, and culture by reinterpreting the human-nature connection and should not be underestimated in importance or impact.

If human communities were seen within a planetary biosphere, or Earth community, there may be new insights to consider. When sex and sexuality are seen as activities of all species, for procreation or pleasure, it normalizes and deemphasizes these. Western societies are saturated with normative ideas about sexuality and sex. They saturate virtually all media, often with sexualized portrayals of women coupled with hyper-masculine rhetoric and images. Sexuality is used to promote, sell, control, or influence desires. This needs to change. Perhaps with a greater understanding of evolution and the dynamics of the biosphere, and the sex lives of other animals, human sex and sexuality could be defused, and reconceptualized with less toxic and dangerous cultural narratives.

Some groups, at times on the margins, are imagining and creating living together in new configurations. Some of these groups are lesbian separatist or polyamorous communities, or radical faeries who for decades have lived in intentional communities without strict social regulations. Others create welcoming space for trans or intersex individuals, or challenge homophobia, and it is particularly important when these are spiritual or religious communities that are often seen as the oppressor. From more traditional sectors are the green Catholic nuns, who have, again for decades, reformed their communities to live within the parameters of the natural world. All these are examples of people living outside of patriarchal strictures, reducing their ecological footprint, and founded upon renewed human–Earth relations (for an example, see communities of Radical Faeries n.d.; Sisters of the Earth n.d.; or other intentional efforts for sustainable living).

Religions and spiritualities also have themes of human communities that are thriving, mutually supportive, just, kind, and generous, and where autonomy and choice are appreciated. These values are important in the needed transformations that are occurring on the topics of sex, sexuality, and gender. In tandem, religions are being transformed to be more responsive to ecological issues, from rituals to resistance, retrieval, and innovation. They are encouraged to make bold claims for sustainability, climate justice, ecojustice, and ecological literacy. Together all these efforts are transforming the intersections of religion, nature, gender, and identity.

Further Reading and Online Resources

Frank G.A., B. Moreton, and H.R. White, eds. (2018), *Devotions and Desires Histories of Sexuality and Religion in the Twentieth-Century United States*, Chapel Hill: University of North Carolina Press.

Hunnicutt G. (2020), *Gender Violence in Ecofeminist Perspective: Intersections of Animal Oppression, Patriarchy and Domination of the Earth*, London: Routledge.

Rayside D. and C. Wilcox (2014), *Faith, Politics, and Sexual Diversity in Canada and the United States*, Vancouver: UBC Press.

References

Abrams M. (2019), "46 Terms That Describe Sexual Attraction, Behavior, and Orientation," Healthline, December 10. Available online: https://www.healthline.com/health/different-types-of-sexuality#why-it-matters (accessed September 25, 2021).

Adams C. (1993), *Ecofeminism and the Sacred*, New York: Continuum.

Bardon A. (2019), *The Truth About Denial: Bias and Self-Deception in Science, Politics, and Religion*, Oxford: Oxford University Press.

Bauman W., ed. (2018), *Meaningful Flesh: Reflections on Religion and Nature for a Queer Planet*, Santa Barbara, CA: Punctum Books.

Butler J. (2011), *Gender Trouble: Feminism and the Subversion of Identity*, New York: Routledge.

Canadian Feminist Observatory for Justice and Accountability (2020), "Femicide in Canada." Available online: https://www.femicideincanada.ca (accessed July 23, 2021).

Chen M.Y. (2012), *Animacies: Biopolitics, Racial Mattering, and Queer Affect*, Durham, NC: Duke University Press.

Cooey P.M. (1991), *After Patriarchy: Feminist Transformations of the World Religions*, Maryknoll, NY: Orbis Books.

Eaton H. (2005), *Introducing Ecofeminist Theologies*, New York: T&T Clark.

Eaton H. and L.A. Lorentzen (2003), *Ecofeminism and Globalization: Exploring Culture, Context, and Religion*, Lanham, MD: Rowman & Littlefield Publishers.

Eaubonne Françoise d' (1974), *Le féminisme ou la mort*, Paris: P. Horay.

Eckert P. and S. McConnell-Ginet (2013), *Language and Gender*, Cambridge: Cambridge University Press.

The Editors of Encyclopaedia Britannica (2021), "Stonewall Riots," *Encyclopedia Britannica*, June 21. Available online: https://www.britannica.com/event/Stonewall-riots (accessed September 25, 2021).

Foucault M. (1990), *The History of Sexuality*, vol. 1: *An Introduction*, New York: Vintage Books.

Gaard G. (1997), "Toward a Queer Ecofeminism," *Hypatia*, 12 (1): 114–37.

Gaard G. (2017), *Critical Ecofeminism*, Lanham, MA: Lexington Books.

Guttmacher Institute (2021). Available online: https://www.guttmacher.org (accessed July 23, 2021).

Harris M. (2017), *Eco-Womanism: African American Women and Earth-Honoring Faiths*, Maryknoll, NY: Orbis Books.

Hultman M. and P.M. Pulé (2018), *Ecological Masculinities: Theoretical Foundations and Practical Guidance*, London: Routledge.

Intersex Society of North America (2008). Available online: https://isna.org (accessed July 23, 2021).

Kirk G. and K.M.Q. Hall (2021), *Mapping Gendered Ecologies: Engaging with and Beyond Ecowomanism and Ecofeminism*, Lanham, MD: Lexington Books.

Lerner G. (1986), *The Creation of Patriarchy*, Oxford: Oxford University Press.

Margulis L. (1998), *Symbiotic Planet: A New Look at Evolution*, New York: Basic Books.

Margulis L. and D. Sagan (1991), *Mystery Dance: On the Evolution of Human Sexuality*, New York: Summit Books.

Maseno-Ouma L. and E.S. Mligo (2020), *Women within Religions: Patriarchy, Feminism, and the Role of Women in Selected World Religions*, Eugene, OR: Wipf & Stock.

Merchant C. (1990), *The Death of Nature: Women, Ecology, and the Scientific Revolution*, San Francesco: HarperCollins.

Nogueira-Godsey E. (2021), "A Decological Way to Dialogue: Rethinking Ecofeminism and Religion," in E. Tomalin and C. Starkey (eds.), *The Routledge Handbook of Religions, Gender and Society*, New York: Routledge.

Plumwood V. (1993), *Feminism and the Mastery of Nature*, New York: Routledge.

Radical Faeries (n.d.). Available online: http://www.radfae.org (accessed September 25, 2021).

Rayside D. and C. Wilcox (2011), "The Difference that a Border Makes: The Political Intersection of Sexuality and Religion in Canada and the United States," in D. Rayside and C. Wilcox (eds.), *Faith, Politics, and Sexual Diversity in Canada and the United States*, 3–25, Vancouver: UBC Press.

Rimmerman C.A. and C. Wilcox, eds. (2007), *The Politics of Same-Sex Marriage*, Chicago: University of Chicago Press.

Rosenthal G. (2017), *Mate Choice: The Evolution of Sexual Decision Making from Microbes to Humans*, Princeton, NJ: Princeton University Press.

Ruether R.R. (1992), *Gaia and God: An Ecofeminist Theology of Earth Healing*, San Francisco: Harper.

Ruether R.R. (2005), *Integrating Ecofeminism, Globalization, and World Religions*, Lanham, MD: Rowman & Littlefield Publishers.

Sisters of the Earth (n.d.). Available online: https://www.sisters-of-earth.net (accessed September 25, 2021).

Taves A. (1997), "Sexuality in American Religious History," in T. Tweed (ed.), *Retelling US Religious History*, 27–56, Berkeley: University of California Press.

Vakoch D.A., ed. (2020), *Transecology: Transgender Perspectives on Environment and Nature*, New York: Routledge.

Warren K., ed. (1997), *Ecofeminism: Women, Culture, Nature*, Bloomington: Indiana University Press.

Women Count USA (2021), "Women Count USA." Available online: https://womencountusa.org (accessed July 23, 2021).

World Health Organization (2021), "Violence against Women." Available online: https://www.who.int/health-topics/violence-against-women#tab=tab_1 (accessed July 23, 2021).

11

Religion, Nature, and Disability

Roger S. Gottlieb

Definition

Since childhood I have been dreadfully near-sighted. But in a society in which corrective lenses are plentiful and well within my economic means, my limited ability to see has meant comparatively few limitations on my life. I could not, as I once wished, have piloted a jet fighter or played first base for the Yankees; in rain or snow my lenses get coated and my vision diminishes. While I wish these realities were different, they have not prevented me from working, fathering children, enjoying friendship, and doing extensive rugged traveling in wilderness. My limited ability is not a *disability*.

In a society without lenses, or in which I could not afford them, I would have been unable to drive, needed constant daily help, and been unable to pursue an academic career. There I would have a disability: a physical, psychological, or cognitive condition that limits or prevents (variously) normal, necessary, average, essential, basic, or highly desirable activities and functions.

Disability—like birth, aging, and death—is an essential, irremovable part of our human condition as natural beings, one of the realities of our human nature. As we shall see later on in this chapter, however, the naturalness of disability is now joined by the effects of human-caused environmental pollution.

Considerations

Disabilities vary greatly: blindness or overly brittle bones; inability to walk or walk very far; difficulty in speaking, handling anxiety, digesting food, registering pain, or comprehending social cues. We can distinguish between temporary disabilities—severe limitations that recede when the illness or accident heal; and permanent disabilities that last a lifetime. Identifying someone as a "person with disabilities" does not obviate the fact that for the first several years of life—and very often for the last—every human being lacks significant capacities: to feed or dress oneself, hear or see, and to move very well. Even so, the vast majority of people between, say, the ages of nine and seventy (depending on the society) can do all such things reasonably well.

While there are only the shadiest of boundaries between who is or is not disabled, once we are well into the category there is some clarity. In today's society being in a wheelchair or having intellectual deficits that make it impossible to live independently, for example, are significant disabilities.

Technological changes can remove some disabilities or create new ones. Widespread cataract surgery can bring millions back from the brink of blindness; a failure of elevators would make many currently employed people too disabled to work above the lower floors of office buildings. An inability to read is a severe handicap in today's world. Five hundred years ago, when the vast majority of the population was illiterate, it would not even be recognized as a problem. Therefore, the social factors determining many disabilities should remove any sense that the lack of limitations involved indicate some absolute or purely individual fact about a person. However, a

FIGURE 11.1 *Protesters at a rally outside a courthouse.* Source: *Erik McGregor/Getty Images.*

particular historical and social situation is where we all live. To have one's life restricted, one's ability to function limited, and to need comparatively unusual amounts of support, remains a reality, however much that reality is socially and historically constructed.

In the connections among religion, nature, and disability, religions are called on to confront a number of moral and spiritual challenges having to do with the strains these realities place on human existence. I will review some of them below, and in particular offer reflections on how "nature," always having been part of our human condition from the outset, has now in some respects been replaced by "environment." That is, by an encompassing world in which living and nonliving bodies have been deeply affected by human action.

Religion and Disability

Moses, the leading figure in Torah's account of the formation of Jewish peoplehood, had a speech impediment (Exod. 4:10, 6:12).[1] He needed his brother Aaron to speak for him.

Jesus instructed his followers: "When you give a luncheon or a dinner, stop inviting only your friends, brothers, relatives, or rich neighbours [...]. Instead, when you give a banquet, make it your habit to invite the poor, the crippled, the lame, and the blind. Then you will be blessed because they can't repay you. And you will be repaid when the righteous are resurrected" (Lk. 14:12–14).

The *Qur'an* tends to assimilate disability into other forms of social and physical "disadvantage." Its emphasis is on the moral demand that the existence of such disadvantages places on the advantaged: people who are not in poverty, sick, blind, ill, and the like (Bazna 2005).

Insofar as traditional religions offer clear moral instruction about care for the vulnerable and suffering (the "widow, stranger, and orphan" so often referred to in the Torah), it would seem an easy step to extend this to the "crippled, the lame, and the blind." And we are directly forbidden to "mock the deaf or put a stumbling block in front of the blind" (Lev. 19:14). In other words: do not take advantage of those who cannot protect themselves. Comparable lessons abound in Buddhism, particularly the Mahayana form, which emphasizes caring for all sentient beings.

To be clear: the "we" in the previous paragraph includes—to the extent that particular disabilities allow for it—those with serious special needs as well. The blind must not mock the slow of speech, the physically abled but intellectually challenged must not take advantage of the constitutionally weak and frail. As with other moral rules, by their life condition some people will be exempt from following them; for example, those with dementia, or those whose intellectual challenges are so severe that they cannot comprehend moral relationships. And the same provision holds for the more complicated political and economic issues that arise. Those who can be included are part of the decision-making and obligated "we" who must make laws about disability rights and decisions about allocating funds for support—and those who cannot do so are not part of the "we."

The brief account so far suggests at least three central dimensions of religion's response to disability. There is the question of demarcation. When we discuss "people with disabilities" of whom are we talking? There is the question of care—of how people with disabilities should be treated. And there is what we might term the "existential" question of what our encounter with disabilities reveals about the human condition in absolute terms and what, we shall see, it reveals about our own particular present. Here are brief examples of the latter.

It is a cliché of the Western religious tradition that all people are made in the image of God (Gen. 1:27) and thus have an immeasurable value. Can we treat those suffering from major impairments as if they too fit that description? For we typically evaluate *ourselves* in social and/or religious terms on the basis of characteristics that people with extreme physical or intellectual limits often cannot manifest. If physical beauty and strength, intelligence, intellectual or artistic creativity, hard physical or mental labor, do not prove *our* value to other people and God, how can we be sure we have such value? And if these characteristics are what make us of value, of what value are the disabled?

As well, people with severe disabilities can arouse difficult feelings, such as insecurity about how to communicate with someone who has intellectual deficits; distaste for people who wear colostomy bags; irritation with communicative styles that are repetitive, unusual, or hard to understand. Above all, there is the fear of the stark human vulnerability the disabled embody. In a moment, any of "us" could become one of "them."

Claims that "we are all disabled" or "I just see regular people" are disingenuous at best and at worst an evasion of the emotional work that needs to be done for full inclusion in the religious community to be possible. We may all be equal in the sight of God, but humans tend to see things in human ways, not divine ones. Often people with disabilities are not easy to deal with, require far more care than others, and do not fit into the typical structures of social interaction. While all people may be made in the image of God, some of those images require considerably more effort on our part to be experienced as divine. It does no good to deny this reality, for then the effort is not likely to be made.

Finally, consider the way the very notion of disability can obscure the failings of the dominant, "normal" society. While many people with intellectual disabilities may not be able to graduate from high school, they generally know enough not to excrete wastes in their bedrooms or living rooms. Yet we of (supposedly) much higher intelligence have been fouling our air, water, and earth with toxins for several decades. Men who have great financial, technical, or political skills are lauded as models, even though they may lack compassion, empathy, or the ability to recognize and express their emotions. By contrast, some people with intellectual disabilities are emotionally intelligent. Who then is the most disabled?

Religion, Suffering, Nature

To be a creature of nature is to be vulnerable to suffering. As religions offer moral instruction about our social relationships, they also respond to the seemingly undeserved distribution of disabilities. This may be particularly difficult when this "natural" affliction besets someone of complete innocence or great virtue.

So, when your child is born with half a brain; your wise and loving spouse develops early Alzheimer's; or a seemingly healthy teenager becomes schizophrenic even the most devoutly religious person must wonder why. And the wonder may coexist with anger from the suffering person's loved ones and the person him or herself. I remember my daughter Esther—whose disabilities include high anxiety, weak muscles, poor balance, moderate hearing loss, digestive weakness, frequently broken bones, curved spine, and intellectual limits—struggling to learn how to shoot a basketball, shaking her fist at the sky and proclaiming: "God, I'm really angry at you. Why did you give me all these special needs? I'm sick of them!"

FIGURE 11.2 *My daughter Esther takes a shot. Photograph by the author.*

A variety of religious responses are offered to sooth the believer's difficulty in combining belief in an all-powerful, wise, and good God with the reality of undeserved suffering.

- While the child seems innocent, s/he is actually the reincarnation of someone who was quite sinful in a previous life. The suffering in this life is a morally justified punishment.

- The overall consequences of this particular child's disability lead to the best possible outcome for the child, for the human community (or this particular religious community) as a whole. God can see why this is, but we—with our limited perspective—cannot.

- Suffering is simply a part of the human experience, and God's role is not to prevent it, but to be a source of compassion and comfort (Kushner 2004).

- Our grief and anger over disability make perfect sense. However, we could pay at least as much attention to all that we have been given. Almost everyone has much to be grateful for.

- We are *all* limited and we all have spiritual and moral gifts to offer. Given human frailty and mortality, distinctions between able and disabled, normal and abnormal, make little sense. We should simply seek to meet each person's physical, emotional, and spiritual needs as best we can.

Each one of these justifications can be questioned. However, people of faith attached to traditional views of God may at least find some comfort in them.

More broadly, we may notice that Abrahamic religions offer two seemingly opposed attitudes toward our existence as natural beings and the disabilities to which such existence gives rise. First, they preach gratitude for what we have; the need to focus on the ultimate value of love and faith no matter how difficult our lives; and the importance of accepting what we are given and making the best of it. Simultaneously, however, religions also offer belief systems that deny the ultimate reality of our vulnerability and mortality and thus reject the notion that we are essentially natural. Life may be hard here and now, but virtue will earn you an eternity of heaven where disability and mortality do not exist; or, when the Messiah comes your actual dead body will be resurrected; or spiritual discipline can lead you to a form of existence in which pain is banished or your particular soul will, once again, be joined with God. Thus, both an acceptance of our natural condition *and* its rejection are cornerstones of dominant theistic religions. (Attitudes toward nature are, not surprisingly, quite different in most Indigenous traditions.)

Religion and Disability Inclusion

In the last few decades much has been written about various Western religions' responses to disability (see Belser and Betcher 2015). And a good deal of that has been criticism combined with passionate demands for change. Stories have been told of exclusion, insensitivity, blaming the victim ("God must be punishing you"), denial of the experience of second-class status, and fundamental contradiction between general religious teaching ("we are all children of God; every soul is precious") and the manner in which those with disabilities are ignored, devalued, and literally unseen.

When it was time for Esther to have her Bat Mitzvah we were casually told by the clergy of the very large Reform Temple we attend that "Of course you'll want to do it on Thursday rather than Saturday." "Why is that," we asked, shocked and hurt. "Well, of course, you see, she couldn't quite, you know, match up to what's expected," the clergy continued, embarrassed at never having had to justify this routine, hurtful exclusion from the "normal" celebration.

We insisted on Saturday, and Esther's splendid Bat Mitzvah paved the way for later families whose children had disabilities. But the clergyman's unthinking assumption that there was an intellectual standard that justified exclusion was precisely the discrimination that the disability rights movement—an initially and essentially secular movement—has attempted to overcome (Pelka 2012).

The good news is that in the last twenty years or so religious communities in the United States have taken steps to overcome prejudice against and marginalization of those with disabilities, although many continue to ask for exemptions from the American Disabilities Act's requirements. Here are excerpts from statements by leading religious institutions, statements that hopefully are reflected in changing attitudes and practices.

From the United States Council of Catholic Bishops:

The Church continues to affirm the dignity of every human being, and to grow in knowledge and understanding of the gifts and needs of her members who live with disabilities. Likewise, the Church recognizes that every parish community includes members with disabilities, and earnestly desires their active participation. All members of the Body of Christ are uniquely called by God by virtue of their Baptism. In light of this call, the Church seeks to support all in their growth in holiness, and to encourage all in their vocations.

(US Council 2020)

From the Protestant United Church of Canada:

The United Church is committed to becoming an open, accessible, and barrier-free church, where there is full participation of people with disabilities [...]. God invites all human beings to rely on and participate in the ministry of the church. God continually empowers each member of the Body of Christ to reflect the divine image in ways that will serve and benefit the church and the broader community.

(United Church 2020)

The Islamic Society of North America has also committed itself to "Promoting the Rights of People with Disabilities, to speak out and take action on disability policy issues with Congress, the President and Administration, and society at large."

Its "core spiritual values affirm the rights and dignity of people with disabilities" (Islamic Society 2020). There are also numerous attempts to form spiritually-oriented communities around the tasks of caring for—and learning from—people with serious intellectual and physical disabilities. The dozens of L'arche ("ark") communities in North America, for example, rely on volunteers enabling the disabled to be integrated into a heterogeneous community rather than being shunted into limited and limiting institutional settings. The volunteers typically—though not always—understand their participation in explicitly religious or spiritual terms (Greig 2015). The comparatively recent statements of religious institutions reflect serious soul-searching on the part of the religious community. However, like supposed commitments to loving enemies or eschewing wealth, they are not easily honored.

Among other things, integrating people with disabilities can take a good deal of money. Wheelchair ramps, signers for services, one-on-one support for children in religious school—none of these are cheap. In a social context in which there never seems to be enough money for all the important causes and concerns, full inclusion of the disabled can become yet another, according to some, tangential issue.

Is disability inclusion as important as helping the poor? Supporting Israel? Advocating for tax-exempt status? Anti-racist organizing? Who has sex with whom? How does the

FIGURE 11.3 *A sign indicating the location of the wheelchair ramp and entrance.* Source: *Mark Buckawicki/Wikimedia Commons.*

money for the aide of the autistic boy in fifth grade compare to these? Answers to such questions define religions' response to disability. Despite the moral complexity here, at least one thing is certain: just saying "we are all limited" will not make real tensions over resources go away.

Disability and the Environmental Crisis

While in earlier times someone might suffer from war, malnutrition, or from a tannery or mining accident, throughout the world now a host of chronic illnesses and special needs stem in whole or part from global environmental causes. Life-shortening cancers, intellectual deficits, respiratory problems responsible for millions of premature deaths per year, bodies that don't have all their limbs—these and countless other conditions have been traced to the vast array of chemicals in the air, water, earth, and food; and to the health effects of climate change. In particular, a wide range of birth defects and debilitating childhood illnesses reflects the fact that pregnant women and young children, especially people of color and the poor, are highly susceptible to being damaged by pollutants (Shabecoff 2019). As well, the trillions of dollars of global damage done by environmental catastrophes consume resources desperately needed for health care and disability support. This reality raises difficult moral issues.

FIGURE 11.4 *Flint, Michigan water crisis.* Source: *Bill Pugliano/Stringer/Getty Images.*

First, despite the wide range of information easily available in this internet age, far too many people—religious and secular alike—avoid informing themselves about what is going on. I am not aware of any traditional religious teachings that require us to be informed. Yet now there should be. Certainly for most of humanity's history getting information about global realities was simply not an option—and it is not appropriate to instruct people to do things they cannot do. Since the nineteenth-century newspapers have been plentiful, and in many communities a commitment to awareness of moral issues outside their immediate settings was common. Now, of course, anyone with internet access can consult countless news sources, of every possible political, religious, and ethical perspective. Also, while the technical details of environmental problems might prove daunting it is not hard to find the issues explained in lay terms.

Yet despite the availability of vast amounts of information about environmental issues, people's ignorance remains at a very high level. Vague generalities about climate change and pollution may be known, but the details of species loss, lead in the water supply, and toxins in everyday objects are generally unknown. Especially, the needed connection between pollution and disability is rarely made (Nixon 2011). Further, a good deal of this lack of knowing results from avoidance. As the information appears on our mental screen, we turn away, repressing the part of us that recognizes this deep and growing threat. We glance at headlines or email subject lines about polluted rivers or pesticide residues on food, and quickly glance away, a dismissal often fed by fake news and alternative facts.

FIGURE 11.5 *Alaska climate change erosion village refugee.* Source: The Washington Post/ *Getty Images.*

The situation is complicated by the fact that environmental issues often lack the immediacy of other threats. War and rape, starving children, and violent political repression have an obviously menacing character. But the danger posed by a simple ingredient in the plastic water bottles holding our spring water and seltzer, and which may (or may not) increase one's chances of getting cancer by some not fully known percent, is much less clear—though, in the end, it may well be just as lethal. So, if a member of your congregation is the CEO of the company making this particular chemical—BPA—and happens to spend some money lobbying for regulations that allow it to be used, it is not so easy to see just how violent his actions are.

It thus takes considerable effort to develop an awareness of environmental problems and a moral perspective that can comprehend them. But, far too many people, including far too many people of faith, do not make that effort. Until environmental awareness becomes a commonly mandated and expected part of religious life—along with financial contributions to religious organizations, charitable giving, following the community's sexual mores, reading sacred texts or mandated practices—the dominant religions will continue to be insufficiently aroused on environmental issues. Illness and disability from preventable environmental causes will continue to increase. It should be remembered that the consequent limitation and suffering afflicts not only individuals, but their families as well. Having a significantly or severely disabled child can lead to a far more emotionally, physically, and financially challenging and isolating experience of family life.

Second, the people who produce, profit from, and defend the polluting chemicals are not the type of people whom religious ethics typically critiques. They are not racists (though they might take advantage of racial minorities to site their facilities), warmongers, atheists, or blasphemers. They are among the best dressed and the most respectable members of society, perhaps even of the local church, synagogue, or mosque. They might be "big givers" to the parish fund and because of their wealth be welcomed to the board of trustees. Yet while few, if any, religious groups would allow, say, a well-known pornographer to be on the board of directors or put his name on a new church building built with his donation, there has yet to be a committed and public rejection of those who produce and lobby for the chemical deluge that has made so many people ill, disabled, or dead. There is a refusal to reckon with the ultimate consequences of environmental damage: millions of deaths per year, tens of millions of climate refugees, countless other species eliminated. To say of the people with power—the CEOs, the lobbyists, the kept politicians and scientists—that they are "just doing their job" is, as we have known since the Holocaust, no excuse. At the very least, religious leaders and local clergy could make clear and forceful moral denunciations of environmental crimes an essential and widely broadcast part of their public message. The consequences of these crimes are simply too dire to do anything else.

But the moral guilt at the heart of the environmental crisis is not restricted to those with the most power, even though it rests most heavily there. To the degree to which any particular religious group contains people enjoying a middle-class form of life—house, car, vacation, travel, consumer goods—they too are a source of environmentally caused disability. The very ordinariness of using fossil-fuel powered electricity or buying any of the myriad toxic consumer products—from dry cleaning to steak to cotton T-shirts—casts a shadow on the moral status of the most devout. The way so much of our "normal" lives is dependent on these products and activities challenges the moral status of every single religious community. It will require a great deal of moral courage and personal honesty for people of faith, who all too often pride themselves on their moral virtue, to admit that they are part of this terrible problem. As with disability inclusion, a serious reckoning with environmental issues can be expensive. Solar collectors on the roof, electric cars, and fully insulated houses of worship, for example, are expensive.

Thankfully, over the last forty years or so religious communities have begun to recognize this new moral challenge. Statements, rituals, and above all actions from religious sources are now integral to the environmental movement (Gottlieb 2009; Yale Forum on Religion and Ecology n.d.). And an awareness of the special vulnerability of children to environmental damage has emerged. For example, the US Council of Catholic Bishops for a time had a special committee focusing on environmental pollution and children. In a statement on "Church and Children" the National Council of Churches asserts that we are "called to treat our children as sacred" (Mt. 18:2–4) and to provide for future generations. Sadly, studies have found that children carry a disproportionate toxic burden. Research indicates that newborns in the United States have an average of 200 toxic chemicals in their umbilical cord blood (Goodman 2009). As well, the environmental justice movement has clearly shown how race and class are factors in a dramatically unequal distribution of both environmental toxins and health care, leading to higher rates of environmentally caused disabilities (Sze 2020).

The Moral Present

Despite the good intentions and important strides that have been made, I believe that a full realization of the tasks of religious disability liberation has not occurred. Nor are the connections between disability and environmental pollution sufficiently prominent features of religious moral awareness. We can only hope that as religions have risen to other challenges—for example, slavery, male domination—they can rise to the complex moral demands of both disability and the environmental crisis.

One significant obstacle to meeting this challenge is that much in today's culture demands oversimplified either/or responses to complex issues—whether they be racial oppression, women's rights, war and peace, vast income inequality, environmental crisis, or disability. For example, we *are* all clearly finite creatures, subject to all sorts of ills, and virtually guaranteed a time in life when our faculties decline and our abilities lessen. Therefore, a rigid and prejudicial distinction between abled and disabled is not justified. Yet at the same time there are crucial differences in needed support, accommodation, and relationship. For North American religions to fully comprehend and respond to the challenge of disabilities, they will have to integrate responses that include *both* of these truths.

Also, a theologically based acceptance of our human limitations and the need to make our peace with suffering is a wisdom built into virtually all religious traditions— and surely that acceptance is essential if we are to face our own disabilities or those of loved ones with a modicum of equanimity and spiritual grace. Yet it is just as true theologically that immoral behavior—for example, polluting our environment—that causes unjustified suffering should be named and opposed, lest we become bystanders or accomplices to injustice. Therefore, spiritual acceptance and political activism must be joined, not seen as opposed alternatives.

Thus any simple, one-sided response to these theological and moral challenges will virtually always be inadequate, for it will necessarily ignore how equally valid concerns and demands lead in an opposing direction. Is this particular situation one that requires spiritual acceptance and a trust in God or political activism to right correctable wrongs? Do we have sufficient resources to fully include this particular disabled person—or in this case is there something else that should take priority? How much are we willing to change our personal lives and our society as a whole to up the chances that the earth will be liveable for people in a hundred years—or in twenty-five? Do we really think our faith will survive a world made chaotic and dangerous by an altered climate? Clearly there is much serious work to be done here, but as the Talmud reminds us: "It is not your duty to finish the work, but neither are you at liberty to neglect it" (Pirke Avot 2:16).

Note

1   All references to the Bible are from *HarperCollins Study Bible: Fully Revised and Updated* (2006).

Further Reading and Online Resources

Belser J.W. and S.V. Betcher, eds. (2015), "Religion, Disability, and the Environment," special issue, *Worldviews: Global Religions, Culture, and Ecology*, 19 (1) (January): 1–82.

Betcher S. (2014), *Spirit and the Obligation of Social Flesh: A Secular Theology for the Global City*, New York: Fordham University Press.

Carter E. (2007), *Including People with Disabilities in Faith Communities: A Guide for Service Providers, Families, and Congregations*, Baltimore: Brookes Publishing.

Clifton S. (2018), *Crippled Grace: Disability, Virtue Ethics, and the Good Life*, Waco, TX: Baylor University Press.

Eiesland N.L. and D.E. Saliers, eds. (1998), *Human Disability and the Service of God: Reassessing Religious Practice*, Nashville, TN: Abingdon Press.

Gaventa W. (2018), *Disability and Spirituality: Recovering Wholeness*, Waco, TX: Baylor University Press.

Gottlieb R.S. (2015), *Political and Spiritual: Essays on Religion, Environment, Disability, and Justice*, Lanham, MD: Rowman and Littlefield.

Greig J.R. (2015), *Reconsidering Intellectual Disability: L'Arche, Medical Ethics, and Christian Friendship*, Washington, DC: Georgetown University Press.

Journal of Disability, Religion & Health (2014–), "Publication History." Available online: https://www.tandfonline.com/loi/wrdh21 (accessed March 29, 2021).

Schumm D., ed. (2011), *Disability in Judaism, Christianity, and Islam: Sacred Texts, Historical Traditions, and Social Analysis*, London: Palgrave McMillan.

Shabecoff P. and A. Shabecoff (2019), *Poisoned for Profit: How Toxins Are Making Our Children Chronically Ill*, White River Junction, VT: Chelsea Green Publishing.

References

Bazna M.S. and T.A. Hatab (2005), "Disability in the Qur'an: 'The Islamic Alternative to Defining, Viewing, and Relating to Disability'," *Journal of Religion, Disability & Health*, 9 (1): 5–27.

Goodman S. (2009), "Tests Find More Than 200 Chemicals in Newborn Umbilical Cord Blood," *Scientific American*, December 2. Available online: https://www.scientificamerican.com/article/newborn-babies-chemicals-exposure-bpa/ (accessed April 21, 2021).

Gottlieb R.S. (2009), *A Greener Faith: Religious Environmentalism and Our Planet's Future*, New York: Oxford University Press.

Islamic Society of North America (n.d.), "Rights of People with Disabilities." Available online: https://isna.net/rights-of-people-with-disabilities/ (accessed September 1, 2020).

Kushner H. (2004), *When Bad Things Happen to Good People*, New York: Anchor.

National Council of Churches (1998), "NCC Policy." Available online: http://www.nationalcouncilofchurches.us/common-witness/1998/disabilities.php (accessed September 1, 2020).

Nixon R. (2011), *Slow Violence and the Environmentalism of the Poor*, Cambridge, MA: Harvard University Press.

Pelka F. (2012), *What We Have Done: And Oral History of the Disability: An Oral History of the Disability Rights Movement*, Amherst: University of Massachusetts.

Schumm D., ed. (2011), *Disability in Judaism, Christianity, and Islam: Sacred Texts, Historical Traditions, and Social Analysis*, London: Palgrave McMillan.

Shabecoff P. and A. Shabecoff (2019), *Poisoned for Profit: How Toxins Are Making Our Children Chronically Ill*, White River Junction, VT: Chelsea Green Publishing.

Sze J. (2020), *Environmental Justice in a Moment of Danger*, Berkeley: University of California Press.

Taylor S. (2019), "Disabled Ecologies: Living with Impaired Landscapes," YouTube, May 3. Available online: https://www.youtube.com/watch?v=_OOEXLylhT4 (accessed March 29, 2021).

United Church of Canada (n.d.), "Disability and Inclusion." Available online: https://www.united-church.ca/community-faith/being-community/disability-and-inclusion (accessed September 10, 2020).

US Council of Catholic Bishops (2017), "Guidelines for the Celebration of the Sacraments with Persons with Disabilities," June 15. Available online: https://www.usccb.org/committees/divine-worship/policies/guidelines-sacraments-persons-with-disabilities (accessed September 9, 2020).

Yale Forum on Religion and Ecology (n.d.), "About the Forum." Available online: https://fore.yale.edu/ (accessed March 29, 2021).

12

Prayerful Living with Animals in the Ancestral Skills Movement

Sarah M. Pike

Woniya Thibeault, dressed in hand-stitched buckskin clothes, stroked her rabbit-fur scarf as she described her experiences on the 2018 season of the History channel reality survival show, *Alone* (2015–). Thibeault was the runner-up, lasting seventy-three days in the Arctic as winter descended. Rabbits were her saving grace, as she put it, "offering themselves" to her wire snares when she was starving. Before *Alone*, Thibeault had spent two decades learning ancient skills, attending ancestral skills gatherings, taking wilderness survival trips, and teaching classes. Her rabbit-fur scarf was the fruit of her skills, embodying her ability to survive *with* rather than *against* the land. Because of her ritual work and her deep intimacy with the place, she believed the land, and its rabbits, looked after her.

A dozen of us were assembled under a leaky tarp at Rabbitstick Gathering (n.d.), the oldest ancestral skills gathering in North America, trying to stay dry while we listened to Thibeault describe her ritualized relationships with the Arctic landscape. Every day on the shores of the Great Slave Lake in Canada's Northwest Territories, she made offerings to the ancestors. She explained to the land why she was there: to "show a better way to live," because "we all long for these connections" to the rest of the natural world and that we can find them in a "prayerful" way.

The "ancestral skills movement" (also known as "primitive skills" or "bushcraft"), is a worldwide network of people that yearn to live more closely with the rest of nature, beyond the human, by learning and practicing ancient skills such as fire-making (Pike 2018). Every year, hundreds of gatherings, workshops, and classes are held throughout the United States and Europe. For many participants it is the center of meaning in their lives and they often refer to ancestral skills gatherings as "home," "family," and even "church." They share a focus on skills and tools and an orientation to the natural world around them as a site of sacred connections, but participants in ancestral skills

FIGURE 12.1 *Rabbitstick organizers' trailer. Photograph by author.*

come from varied spiritual and religious backgrounds. They are Mormons, Pagans, Buddhists, atheists, and so on. Peter Michael Bauer, who writes a blog on "*rewilding*" called "Urban Scout," notes that at many gatherings, "you may find yourself between a Mormon and a Rainbow child" (Bauer n.d.). Although not allied with any particular religion, some aspects of this movement are imbued with spirituality. It is an important contemporary site at which to observe the creation, maintenance, and expression of spiritually meaningful human relationships with the nonhuman natural world and especially the ritual practices around these relationships.

The ancestral skills movement is primarily made up of middle-class white Americans, though people of other classes and ethnic backgrounds are involved with the movement as well. My neighbors at Rabbitstick's camp included an Inuit truck driver from Alaska and a biochemist of European-American ancestry from northern Utah. At gatherings I met retired engineers living in cities and teaching ancestral skills classes, as well as hermits living off the grid in remote woods and deserts. As Rabbitstick organizer Dave Westcott put it during an interview, "A dumpster diver and retired dentist are learning from each other" (TJack Survival 2016). In the same interview, David Holladay, a long-time ancestral skills teacher, observed that "skills and respect for the natural world are the common denominators" that unite many participants in this movement (TJack Survival 2016). Knowledge, such as how to use "Stone Age" methods to prepare and cook nonhuman animals, or preserve their skins for various uses, is at the center of the ancestral skills movement.

FIGURE 12.2 *Handmade hunting tools. Photograph by author.*

The turn to ancestral skills is sometimes a reaction against the non-prayerful ways most contemporary Americans live with nature. A number of ancestral skills practitioners express dissatisfaction with consumer-driven lifestyles and a kind of paleo-nostalgia for older, more direct ways of interacting with other species. As teacher Lynx Vilden put it in a blog: "Come live wild and help make the world a better place" (Vilden 2014). In this way, the ancestral skills movement involves both a reaction to the climate crisis, overconsumption, ill health, etc. and a process of practicing other ways to live on Earth, with plants, stones, and other animals. For ancestral skills practitioners, this means challenging what they see as a legacy of domestication that has alienated humans from the rest of nature and led to the environmental and societal crises we find ourselves in.

Ritualized actions involving tools and the skills needed to use them properly are central to the movement. Ritual has been largely disregarded in studies of religion and nature, outside of publications about Indigenous and Asian religions. Yet many Americans who grew up Christian, Jewish, atheist, and so on, are creating and rediscovering ritualized, spiritually powerful ways of interacting with the rest of the natural world. In this chapter, I understand ritualization as a distinctive way of enacting and constituting relationships among humans, as well as between humans and nonhuman animals, plants, rocks, and landscapes (Houseman 2006). These focused and intensified relationships that are expressed in and emerge from learning and practicing ancestral skills call into question the lines dividing us from other species and things, and express ancestral skills practitioners' orientation to the world.

In his essay/performance piece "Performance Is Currency in the Deep World's Gift Economy: An Incantatory Riff for a Global Medicine Show" (2019), ritual theorist Ronald L. Grimes asks, "What actions, rightly performed, can save the planet?" Grimes argues that any serious response must be embodied "radically, to the bone, to the quick," that we must nurture an attitude of interconnectedness. This means an identification with other animals, becoming them, knowing their worlds. When I asked Woniya Thibeault how she maintained her connection to the Arctic landscape now that she was home, she held up her rabbit scarf. She explained that her body *was* the land, that the berries and rabbits she ate were *her*. Through self-consciously ritualized practices of hunting, gathering, processing, and eating, she had taken these other beings deeply into "the bone." Even "when those cells are replaced," she said, she would still have the rabbit-fur scarf. Like wearing buckskin, that scarf is for her "a reminder, a link to our human past [...]. It speaks to that place inside us that remembers what it feels like to know the world around us intimately." Particular interactions with nonhuman animals—hunting, killing, processing, eating animals, using their inedible parts—are among the most important ritualized practices that connect humans to the rest of the world around them and to their ancestral past.

FIGURE 12.3 *Hunting bows and handmade brooms at Rabbitstick. Photograph by author.*

Eating Animals

One of the most central areas in which ancestral skills practitioners diverge from and counter broader American cultural norms is food. Ancestral skills practitioners gather, kill, and eat in ways that emphasize intimacy with rather than distance from food. Dylan, a featured speaker at an online workshop about "eating wild" year-round, "never bought meat from a grocery store" and urged his audience to take responsibility for where their food comes from (Eyers n.d.). Lynx Vilden observes that in ancestral skills, animal deaths are close up and personal. They are a part of that animal's life story: "The story of the sheep you killed, and ate, and wear, and made tools from, is a much richer and more durable story than the story of the piece of meat wrapped in cellophane that you bought from the grocery store and knew nothing else about" (Vilden n.d.-a).

From Vilden's perspective, in contrast to shopping at a grocery store, hunting connects us to the forces of life and death and involves processing as much of the animal's body as possible: "We used the brains for tanning, the hooves and connective tissue for glue, and the bones for tools and jewelry and even musical instruments. Every part of the animal becomes precious" (Vilden n.d.-a). As Thibeault puts it, "We are so desperately divorced from the things that feed us," meaning that many Americans are repulsed by seeing what goes into the butchering of meat that feeds us, so for her, "if we choose to eat animals, then it's important for us to recognize the reality of what taking life means and doing that responsibly" (Buckskin Revolution Online Gathering n.d.). Relations with other animals, such as hunting, processing animals for food and materials, and wearing their skins are where the sacralization of relationships with nature becomes most visible.[1]

Lynx Vilden teaches students to hunt and kill other animals in her "Living Wild" workshops. Yet she acknowledges that, "I don't enjoy killing but it is a necessary skill that I keep working on … I do not want to kill the deer, I want to BE the deer" (Vilden n.d.-b). Like other teachers, she observes that tracking and hunting create intimacy and identification with other animals through ritualized practices in which mind and body are focused and habituated to their tasks: "there is something magical about gliding through the forest, all senses tuned with a hand made weapon poised for that moment of expectation. Sublime" (Vilden n.d.-b). Vilden also prays when hunting and killing other animals. She speaks to the deer: *"Deer People I thank you. I would that your flesh be my own. Is there one amongst you willing to sacrifice your life, your body? I ask with humility, ready to accept your answer, whatever it may be"* (Vilden n.d.-a). She cautions students that killing an animal is "life-changing … To hold a warm, living, breathing animal in your hands, to pull back its fur or feathers prior to slitting its throat … it's very humbling. It really commands your attention, too—the realization that another being is going to give its life so that you can eat" (Vilden n.d.-a). Intimacy, respect, sacred slaughter, prayer, these are all ways of expressing and constructing important relationships with other living beings. Hunting and killing nonhuman animals is one of the ways that ancestral skills practitioners participate in what anthropologist Gisli Palsson calls "the ensemble of biosocial relationships" (Palsson 2013: 22).

Not everyone involved with ancestral skills focuses on hunting and trapping other animals. In this ensemble of biological and sociocultural relationships, eating roadkill especially symbolizes the convergence of the wild and civilization. Some Rabbitstick gathering participants discussed putting to good use the dead animal bodies left on the roadside. I was shown pelts and skins of roadkill decorating a hood and sewn into a buckskin skirt. Many participants I met described themselves as "opportunistic" eaters. If they came across roadkill they knew how to tell if it was good to eat and how to process as many parts of its body as possible.

Trading in the Deep World's Currency

Another aspect of that biosocial relationship is the process of preparing a dead animal's body for food or other purposes. Tanning a hide by hand is long, hard work that engages the senses of smell and touch as well as sight. It is all done by hand, with knives and other simple tools, close up and personal. What is it like to work the brains into the skins, bare-handed? Does the tanner ever think about what that animal's history is? What was its life like? A leather worker who was a relative newcomer to primitive skills explained how classes on "wet scrape brain tanning" (using the animal's brains to process a skin) helped her "learn to honor the animal." In the ancestral skills world, for many practitioners, honoring means praying, leaving offerings, being aware of the ecosystems where you find your food, taking only what you need, using the whole animal in such a way as to minimize waste, and taking care to ensure the health of other species.

As some ancestral skills practitioners see it, they are profoundly changed by relations with the plants and animals they harvest/kill, prepare, and eat, just as these other beings are changed (processed) by them. Woniya Thibeault, for example, was transformed by rabbit relations. Thibeault's relationships with the more-than human world were expressed and constituted through her intentions voiced to ancestors, her hunting practices, working with and wearing animal bodies. In a sense she was becoming other animals through acts of radical porosity at the same time that she shored up her human survival abilities by killing and eating. The rabbits encircled her neck, no longer alive but symbols of her human accomplishments and the merging of her body with another animal's body. Clothing, like knives and fire-making tools, expresses and constitutes relationships with the more-than-human world and bestows meaning on things (buckskin and furs that represent being wild and closeness to nonhuman animals), even within a worldview that in other ways tends to be anti-materialistic.

What does it mean to wear furs and skins now, not by necessity but by choice? What is it to become another animal in this way? To absorb that other's flesh into our own? In one of her classes, Thibeault describes the process of making a new dress out

FIGURE 12.4 *Skins for sale at Rabbitstick. Photograph by author.*

of a roadkill deer, weaving seams together, both sorrow and the joy of creation moving in and out with the awl in her hand. Feeling connection can be painful. We cannot live without causing death.

Some ancestral skills teachers who hunt and process other animals for food and skins were once vegans or vegetarians. Thibeault was a vegan animal rights activist before becoming deeply involved with ancestral skills. Natalie Bogwalker, founder of the Wild Abundance primitive skills and permaculture school in North Carolina, was a vegetarian for many years. Now Bogwalker runs a "sacred and humane" slaughter workshop (Burrows 2016). The mission of her school is to connect students with "the sacred process of taking animal life to provide meat for one's family and community" (Burrows 2016). Many animal species suffer and die for my vegetarian diet, as philosophers Lori Gruen and Robert Jones (2015) point out in "Veganism as an Aspiration." The industrial growing and harvesting of fruits and vegetables results in immense losses of animals' habitats. Instead of being the opposite of veganism, hunting and killing wild animals is more in continuity with it.

The treatment of our own dead bodies, not just those of other animals, was also a concern at ancestral skills gatherings I attended. A few tents away from the hide-tanning at the Winter Count gathering in Arizona, Dani, one of the gathering teachers, instructed her audience on how to prepare a dead body at home for a green burial without chemicals. Ancestral skills teacher Peter Bauer wants his body to be eaten by other animals, just as he has eaten them. He hopes his body will be buried in the ground, without a coffin or embalming, a tree planted to mark its resting place. If that is not possible, he would prefer a "sky burial" in which his body is "placed high atop a mountain and eaten by vultures." Eating animals and being eaten by them is a kind of ritualized reciprocity, coming full circle in the deep world economy of ancestral skills. Interacting with dead animals and deciding how to treat one's own dead body are ways of creating meaning around some of our most fundamental experiences and life passages.

Note

1   At the three different gatherings I attended there were food lines for both vegetarians and non-vegetarians.

Further Reading and Online Resources

Alone (2015–), [TV Series], USA: History.

Buckskin Revolution (n.d.). Available online: https://www.buckskinrevolution.com (accessed February 7, 2021).

Kochanski M. (2016), *Bushcraft: Outdoor Skills and Wilderness Survival*, Edmonton, Canada: Lone Pine.

Pike S.M. (2017), *For the Wild: Ritual and Commitment in Radical Eco-Activism*, Oakland: University of California Press.

Watts S.M. (2005), *Practicing Primitive: A Handbook of Aboriginal Skills*, Layton, UT: Gibbs Smith.

Westcott D. (2001), *Primitive Technology II: Ancestral Skill from the Society of Primitive Technology*, Layton, UT: Gibbs Smith.

References

Bauer P.M. (n.d.). Available online: https://www.petermichaelbauer.com (accessed February 7, 2021).

Buckskin Revolution Online Skills Gathering (n.d.). Available online: https://www.buckskinrevolution.com/online-skills-gathering.html (accessed February 19, 2021).

Burrows S. (2016), "Vegan Group Threatens Primitive Skills Teacher over Humane Slaughter Class," *Return to Now*, November 16. Available online: https://returntonow.net/2016/11/16/vegan-group-harasses-primitive-skills-teacher/ (accessed September 15, 2020).

Eyers D. (n.d.), [Video] "Seasons of Eating Wild," talk at Outdoor Adventure Summit. Available online: https://outdoor-adventure-summit.heysummit.com/talks/seasons-of-eating-wild-a-conversation-on-the-opportunities-and-barriers-to-sourcing-wild-food-throughout-the-year/ (accessed February 7, 2021).

Grimes R.L. (2019), "Performance is Currency in the Deep World's Gift Economy: An Incantatory Riff for a Global Medicine Show," *Circling The Deep*, September 26. Available online: https://circle.twohornedbull.ca/performance-is-currency-in-the-deep-worlds-gift-economy-an-incantatory-riff-for-a-global-medicine-show/ (accessed February 7, 2021).

Gruen L. and R.C. Jones (2015), "Veganism as an Aspiration," in B. Bramble and B. Fischer (eds.), *The Moral Complexities of Eating Meat*, Oxford Scholarship Online. Available online: https://www.wellbeingintlstudiesrepository.org/cgi/viewcontent.cgi?referer=https://www.google.com/&httpsredir=1&article=1001&context=diecfaori (accessed November 11, 2020).

Houseman M.J. (2006), "Relationality," in J. Kreinath, J. Snoek, and M. Stausberg (eds.), *Theorizing Rituals,* vol. 1, *Issues, Topics, Approaches, Concepts*, 413–28, London: Brill.

Palsson G. (2013), "Ensembles of Biosocial Relations," in T. Ingold and G. Palsson (eds.), *Biosocial Becomings: Integrating Social and Biological Anthropology*, 22–41, Cambridge: Cambridge University Press.

Pike S.M. (2018), "Rewilding Hearts and Habits in the Ancestral Skills Movement," *Religions*, 9. Available online: https://www.mdpi.com/2077-1444/9/10/300 (accessed September 15, 2020).

Rabbitstick Gathering (n.d.), "Honoring Our Shared Heritage." Available online: https://www.rabbitstick.com (accessed February 7, 2021).

TJack Survival (2016), "Rabbitstick 2016 with Cody Lundin, Dave Wescott, and Dave Holladay," YouTube, October 8. Available online: https://www.youtube.com/watch?v=Q7pIlksEzWs (accessed February 7, 2021).

Vilden L. (n.d.-a), "The Call of the Wild," *Moon Magazine*. Available online: http://moonmagazine.org/lynx-vilden-the-call-of-the-wild-2013-09-01/5/ (accessed November 10, 2020).

Vilden L. (n.d.-b), "Living Wild." Available online: https://www.lynxvilden.com (accessed February 7, 2021).

Vilden L. (2014), "Rewild-Education! With Lynx Vilden (Reconnexion with Our Primitive Nature)," [Blog] *Paradiso Trovato*, May 17. Available online: https://paradisoritrovato.wordpress.com/2014/05/17/reconnexion-with-our-primitive-nature/ (accessed February 7, 2021).

Glossary Terms

Rewilding The idea and scientific approach of *rewilding* was developed by Michael Soulè in the mid-1990s. Rewilding is "the scientific argument for restoring big wilderness based on the regulatory roles of large predators" (Buckskin Revolution Online Skills Gathering n.d.). For some ancestral skills practitioners "rewilding" may also refer to personal lifestyle choices such as eating wild foods and choosing natural burial. Both of these are ways of rewilding the individual human body.

PART THREE

Themes and Issues

13

Globalization and Planetary Ethics Related to Religion and Nature in North America

Cynthia D. Moe-Lobeda

What does it mean to think about globalization and planetary ethics *in relationship to religion and nature in North America* now, in the twenty-first century's early decades?

The first and most crucial step in ethics is perceiving with searing honesty "what is going on." This means facing the most salient realities at play in any given situation, especially those social dynamics and power relationships that endanger or devalue some groups of people while advantaging others. These dynamics tend to remain invisible to those who benefit from them. For North Americans, considering planetary ethics and globalization, two overarching morally defining realities that must be faced are the climate crisis and the vast inequity between those who have too much and those whose lives are threatened or destroyed by having too little. In both—climate injustice and economic violence—white supremacy is a corrosive factor. By "morally defining realities" for North Americans, I mean realities that determine life or death around the globe, and in which North Americans are morally implicated. Said differently, these two realities determine whether many people will live or die, and they determine the quality of our moral lives.

Both the climate crisis and the crisis of a racialized wealth gap are intricately intertwined with globalization in at least two senses: (1) the impacts of both crises are global in scope, and (2) the systems that generate both crises are global. In fact, both crises are caused in significant part by a centerpiece of globalization, the reigning global economic and financial architecture. (Later we discuss the ambiguities and dangerous deceptions residing in the term, "globalization.")

What do I mean by claiming that these two defining realities "determine life and death?" Through climate change, humankind—or rather the high consuming members of humankind—are destroying the climate conditions for life on Earth. Through the systems that generate and maintain the racialized wealth gap (both within and between societies), a tiny percentage of people accumulate massive wealth; a few (including many US citizens) consume exorbitantly through exploitation of both Earth and its impoverished people; and a vast majority of people suffer that exploitation and impoverishment. As declared by Jesuit Priest Jon Sobrino (1986), for many of the world's impoverished people "poverty means death." African American theologian Peter Pero described this well: "In ecclesiological terms, if the church is the one universal body of Christ, this body of Christ is divided among active thieves, passive profiteers, and deprived victims" (2001: 257).

In short, through climate change and the racialized wealth gap, North American humans are impacting the lives of people around the globe in terribly destructive ways. From an ethical perspective, something is clearly wrong with the way we are living— wrong in a moral sense. By "the way we are living," I refer to the practices of daily life and to the public policies, corporate practices, and belief systems that shape and legitimate those daily practices.

FIGURE 13.1 *Electronic waste.* Source: *escrappers_pic by baselactionnetwork/CC BY-ND 2.0.*

The question of ethics, "how then shall we live," is at the core of being human. In the repository of human ethical wisdom, religion holds a particular place. Religion is understood to be a main source of ethical wisdom, guiding people in how to live rightly. Buddhism, for example, teaches compassion as a central guide for living. Judaism may be seen as a theologically rooted and practiced moral code. Christianity—along with Judaism and Islam—claim that life is to be guided by God's commandment, heard first in the Hebrew scriptures, to "love your neighbor as yourself" (Lev. 19:18).

Religious ethics, then, ought to offer invaluable guidance to the anguishing question of: How are we to live rightly in the midst of these two crises in which we are implicated? That is, how are we to live in ways that enable us to address both the climate catastrophe and the morally reprehensible impoverishment of many by systems that enrich others? Wherein lies the moral-spiritual power to do so? What forms us toward ways of life that are more equitable and ecological, and what malforms us away from them?

The obvious irony is that religions often have done the opposite of providing moral guidance. Some forms of various religions have led people *en masse* to commit terrible crimes against humanity and the Earth. As argued by countless religious scholars and activists, many religions have contributed to the mindsets and practices that bred and continue to support climate change, economic exploitation, and white supremacy.

The Question

With this groundwork laid, we arrive at this chapter's central question: "Given two defining realities of the twenty-first century—climate change and profound inequity—how are North Americans to do religious ethics in ways that serve planetary flourishing and that dramatically lessen the gap between those who have too much and those who have far too little?" Asked differently, "How are North Americans to bring the resources of religious ethics to bear on developing an ethic capable of guiding life today in the face of these seemingly insurmountable moral travesties?" (Moe-Lobeda 2013).

The outcome of ethical inquiry is determined by the "method" employed and by the interrogation and meaning of central concepts engaged. Often key concepts that mystify ecological and social devastation, hide them from people who benefit materially from them, and reinscribe dominance in many forms go unquestioned and undefined. (Examples of such concepts are "development," "sustainability," "democracy," "globalization," and "ethics.") Likewise, method itself often remains unacknowledged, and hence its power to reinforce oppressive social relations and exploitative Earth-human relations remains hidden. This has been the great error of the academy in North America and Europe—to presuppose the meaning of terms as defined by the dominant culture, to presuppose that the standard Eurocentric approach to intellectual inquiry is the only valid approach, and to assume that concepts and methods are morally and politically neutral. These tendencies obstruct power for moving from "the way things are" into more socially just and ecologically sane alternatives.

The response to our question, therefore, in this chapter takes the form of conceptual clarification and guideposts to a viable method in ethics (Moe-Lobeda 2013).

Conceptual Clarifications

Ethics

Ethics is commonly understood to be the discipline that brings self-consciousness, method, intentionality, and sensitivity to the task of discerning what is morally good and right for any given situation and context. I would argue that this is a deficient understanding of ethics and will not enable morality capable of meeting the intersecting moral crises of climate change and racialized economic inequity. Many people understand that living in ways that catapult us into climate catastrophe and that base the material well-being of some on the exploitation of others is morally wrong, yet continue with them. Therefore, to the aforementioned task of ethics (discerning what is morally good and right for any given situation and context), must be added two others: (1) finding the moral-spiritual power to act on that discernment, and (2) discovering what forms individuals and society toward the good and what malforms us away from it.

Globalization

"Globalization" is a multifaceted term with myriad shifting and contested connotations and denotations. The word is used by different people to mean different things. Confusion and miscommunication ensue when people who assume they are talking about the same set of dynamics—because the same word is used—actually are not.

This confusion presents two dangers. I will point to them presently. But first, note two common referents of the term. One is the increasing interconnectedness between people throughout the world through transportation, the internet, and other advances in technology and communications. Second is the currently prevailing architecture of global economic and financial relationships and the power arrangements that determine them, widely known as neoliberalism. Identifying defining characteristics of neoliberal economic globalization, the presuppositions undergirding it, and its long-term consequences for varied social groups and for Earth's broader web of life is a vitally important task before citizens of the United States today. Six defining features of neoliberal economic globalization are: (Moe-Lobeda, 2002)

1   A rapid increase in the movement of goods and services as well as capital—trade and investment—across international borders.
2   Privatization, which gives ownership and control of basic goods and services such as water, seeds, electricity, education, and health care to corporations

or individuals usually not accountable to the communities impacted. To illustrate, the privatization of water allowed a foreign corporation to purchase the water supply in an impoverished area of Bolivia and export it for sale at whatever price the global market would bear (Barlow 2000). The original users of the water could not afford it and were left without clean water until public organizing reversed this case of privatization.

3   The commodification of money. Increasingly buying and selling money for the purpose of high short-term gain outpaces trade in other goods and services, and long-term investment in production. Together with the revolution in communications technology, this development enables huge amounts of money to be bought and sold across national borders instantly by investors unaccountable for social and environmental impacts of their investments, and unregulated by national or international entities. The impact may be devastating.

4   The accelerating commodification of life experiences and life forms (such as human genetic material or seed strains that may have been developed over generations by a particular people). "Commodification" refers to placing a monetary value on something and marketing it.

5   The strategic marketing of Western consumer-oriented ways of life around the world.

6   The increasing power of unaccountable economic players relative to more or less democratic governments (local and national) to enable the aforementioned developments. A significant portion of the world's largest economies are planned and directed in ways unaccountable to the public as a whole. Fifty-one of the world's 100 largest economies are corporations, comparing gross sales of a corporation to the gross domestic product (GDP) of a nation (Anderson and Cavanagh 1996).

At the intersection and the heart of these six trends is the movement to "free" international and transnational trade and investment from regulations or other political constraints that might diminish profit. This form of economic life shapes the conditions of life for people the world over, and the terms of humankind's relationship to our fragile planetary home. In this chapter, "globalization" is used in the latter sense: the prevailing global financial and economic architecture.

The distinction between these two uses of "globalization" is vitally important from a moral perspective for two reasons. First, people claim that global interconnectedness is inevitable given the realities of communication, technology, and transportation in today's world. Thus, globalization is inevitable and, therefore, unchangeable. This may well be true for globalization in the first meaning of the term noted above. The problem comes when the two meanings are conflated. The result is that the prevailing economic and financial arrangements also then are perceived as inevitable and unchangeable. That is, when globalization as interconnectedness is not distinguished from economic-financial globalization, then the inevitability of the former is projected on to the latter.

FIGURE 13.2 *Deforestation.* Source: *crustmania/CC 2.0 Generic.*

The second reason to distinguish between the two referents for the term globalization is equally consequential. People often claim that interconnectedness between peoples is a good thing, that it is mainly beneficial, and is to be applauded. Most of us would in general agree. If interconnectedness is good, and globalization is interconnectedness, then globalization is good. Again, the problem comes when the two referents for globalization are conflated. Both then are presupposed to be "good."

Together, these two assumptions (that neoliberal economic globalization is inevitable and is definitely beneficial) have enormous implications on public policy formation but even more important on society's sense of what is possible and what is not, and what is good. We come almost unconsciously to believe that what *is*, is what *should* be, *has* to be, and *will* be: the currently reigning form of global economy and finance is both good and inevitable. Lost is the critical ethical impulse to question its moral validity, and the critical social analysis to recognize that it is a system constructed by human decisions and actions and therefore may be reconstructed by other human decisions and actions.

Method in Ethics

Recall the question at hand: given two defining realities of the twenty-first century—climate change and profound inequity—how are North Americans to do religious ethics in ways that serve planetary flourishing and diminish the gap between those who have too much and those who have far too little? How are North Americans to bring the resources of religious ethics to bear on developing an ethic capable of guiding life today in the face of these seemingly insurmountable moral travesties? Our first step was to clarify key terms. The next step is to interrogate method.

Method in any discipline refers to the disciplined and intentional way in which we go about an inquiry using the resources of that discipline. Method in ethics then is the way in which we answer the basic questions of: (1) how ought we to live or what is morally good and right for any given situation and context? (2) where will we find the moral-spiritual power to act on that discernment? and (3) what forms individuals and society toward the good and what mal-forms us away from it?

The elements or variables of method are many. Here we consider just seven, given the limited space of a single chapter.

Seeing the Eyes through Which We See

The first element of method is the extent to which one commits to "see the eyes through which we see." This means identifying the assumptions and ideological frameworks through which our perceptions, feelings, thoughts, actions, and decisions are filtered. This is the extent to which we dare to become aware of the unintentional and often unconscious or unacknowledged assumptions that frame our relationship to the world around us. Human beings "breathe in" a worldview or belief systems as we grow and are socialized in our subgroups, and larger society. We take on a prevailing set of assumptions about reality. These assumptions shape our sense of meaning and purpose, our identity, our sense of self-interest, our understanding of what ways of life are good and what power arrangements are normative, our sense of what people and things are inherently more valuable than others, and our everyday actions. In terms of the moral life, these are enormously influential formative processes. They shape our sense of morality; our understanding of what is good, right, and true; our assumptions regarding how we ought to live. They shape our judgments of other people.

Most significantly, these processes go on largely beneath our consciousness. Education theorist Stephen Brookfield refers to these as "culturally produced assumptions, taken-for granted values, common-sense ideas, stereotypical notions about human nature and social organization" (1987: 16), and as "unquestioned givens that to us have the status of self-evident truth" (44). To the extent that we fail to "see the eyes through which we see," they run our lives. Ethics to serve planetary flourishing and social equity will open eyes to the culturally produced assumptions that undergird both climate change and the racialized wealth gap in order to refute and replace such assumptions.

Moral Vision

How is it possible that good, compassionate, caring North Americans have accepted ways of life that are destroying the conditions for life on Earth and that require brutal forms of ongoing systemic economic violence wed to white supremacy? What explains our complicity in causing the two defining crises of climate catastrophe and a racialized gap between the high-consuming classes and those who are profoundly impoverished? One key is moral vision—the presupposed vision of the good (Moe-Lobeda 2019).

Vision of the moral good in any society is established by dominant sectors to uphold the power arrangements that maintain their dominance. Thus, the established moral vision rationalizes itself and is ill-equipped to assess itself. In colonial North America, for example, a moral vision was established by Northern European men who owned property. Slavery, therefore, was seen by slave-holding society as moral, and primary sources of moral authority such as the Bible sanctioned it. In a similar manner, morally valuing maximizing profit—seeing it as good—makes extractive industries that maximize their own profit appear to be good despite the devastation to workers, water systems, land, species, and climate conditions that result from the profit-maximizing moves.

The fact that a socially constructed moral vision is established to preserve dominant sectors' privilege has yet another shadow side: its dangers tend to be relatively invisible to those who are advantaged by the vision. Thus, for example, in a society in which the moral vision is constructed on the unacknowledged myth of white supremacy, such as the United States, white people tend not to realize that this myth exists. They do not see that whiteness is "normalized," engenders privilege, and colonizes white people's vision of the good. In like manner, the dangers inherent in a vision of the good embraced by a society that is, in fact, engaged in an ongoing consumption orgy are not evident to people engaged in that consumption orgy.

The point here is not that we who have lived according to these moral visions are morally bad. In many aspects of our lives we may be tremendously compassionate, honest, generous, and caretaking of others and the Earth. The point, rather, is that the moral vision of a people who have claimed as good a structure of life that devastates Earth's life systems and multitudes of people is suspect. Such a moral vision must be transformed with careful critical consciousness that cracks through the blinders of privilege. Moral vision, if it is to live up to its charge of enabling planetary flourishing and social equity will reveal uncritically held assumptions regarding moral visions that sanction "the way things are."

Hermeneutical Lenses

A third element of method in ethics is the hermeneutical lens—the guiding lens or set of perceptual and analytical commitments—that we bring to ethics. In the context of globalization, climate change, and economic violence, three appropriate lenses are structural, critical theoretical, and eco-critical.

A structural lens asks not simply what *individuals* need to do to mitigate climate change, but what are the social structures—public policies, corporate practices, cultural norms, etc.—that contribute to climate change and how can we change them. In reading scripture, a structural lens examines the social structural factors at play in the texts and the moral implications for how we structure society. This is in stark contrast to widespread practice in Christianity of reading biblical texts as conveying primarily interpersonal or intrapersonal dynamics. The story of Jesus' death illustrates that pervasive tendency. An interpersonal interpretation might claim that Jesus died to save individuals from their sin. A structural reading might see Jesus as having been executed by imperial Rome as a threat to imperial power since crucifixion was in fact a form of public torture and humiliation reserved for rebels to the empire.

A critical theory lens interrogates social realities as well as religious texts and traditions for the dynamics of race, class, gender, and colonialism at play. A critical lens changes one's view of climate change from assuming that "we are all in this together" to recognizing that the world's people of color and impoverished people are far more likely to be killed or displaced by climate change than are people of European descent or with economic resources. The concepts of "climate debt" and "climate colonialism" are useful in making that distinction. Both terms arise from the Global South to describe the imbalance between nations and communities likely to suffer first and worst from climate change and those contributing most to it. These terms refer to the disproportionate per capita use of the atmospheric space for carbon sinks by industrialized countries in the past and present. "Climate debt" entails: (1) inter-generational climate debt, the debt owed by current generations to future generations due to climate change; (2) inter-species climate debt, the debt owed by humankind to other-kind for the ecological damage wrought now and in centuries to come by climate change; and (3) intra-generational, the debt owed by high greenhouse gas emitting countries, sectors, and specific corporations—for example, corporations in the fossil-fuel industry—to climate vulnerable people and peoples.

Recognizing climate debt and climate colonialism is morally significant because determining the ethical response to a moral dilemma depends upon what the problem is understood to be. Inadequate analysis leads to inadequate diagnosis and remedies. Responses to the perilous reality of climate change frequently are framed around the principle of sustainability—reducing carbon emissions and adapting to deal with the impacts. These moves are crucial, to be applauded and supported. If climate change were not connected, historically and contemporarily, to the power imbalances that have rendered climate debt, then this response—together with assistance to the victims of climate change—would be ethically adequate. It is, however, an inadequate and deceptive moral response for affluent societies and sectors if we: (1) are disproportionately responsible for climate change, (2) could choose sustainability measures that have adverse impact on impoverished people and peoples, (3) are material beneficiaries of the fossil-fuel economies that generated the climate crisis, and (4) have produced economic orders that impoverished vulnerable peoples, thus rendering them less able to survive climate change-related disaster (Moe-Lobeda 2020).

A response organized around sustainability alone allows the world's high-consuming societies and people to address climate change in ways that do not take moral responsibility for these factors and for the disproportionate impact that climate change and efforts to mitigate it have on people of color and economically impoverished people. The probable consequences are sinister. Vulnerable people without resources to flee from or adapt to the storms, disease, food and water shortages, and other impacts of climate change would be left to suffer and die. If climate change—on the other hand—is seen not only as a problem of sustainability but also of climate debt or climate colonialism, then more is required in response. For example, climate debt theory posits that the costs of adapting to climate change and of mitigating it are primarily—though not singularly—the responsibility of the countries that historically have been far more responsible for creating the crisis, the industrialized world. In other words, "the polluter pays." Article 3(1) of the 1992 United Nations Framework Convention on Climate Change (UNFCCC) addresses this responsibility by obligating the Global North to take the lead on efforts to combat climate change. Here we see clearly the moral and material significance of a critical theory lens.

The third hermeneutical lens, *an eco-critical lens,* resists the anthropocentrism currently manifest in nearly all of Earth's great faith traditions. Eco-criticism locates the human *within* the Earth's economy rather than *outside* of it, acknowledges the moral standing including moral subjectivity of the other-than-human, and includes eco-systems in the analysis of reality.

FIGURE 13.3 *Three men braving the flood waters on a tractor in Sri Lanka.* Source: *Amantha Perera/CC BY 2.0.*

Purpose of Ethics

Method in ethics also includes an understanding of the purpose of ethical inquiry. The purpose of religious ethics—if they are to meet the moral crises of our day—is not to learn what a given religious tradition has said is right and good, and then simply repeat it. Rather, religious ethics are in the service of enabling people to draw critically upon their traditions' teachings and practices, put them in dialogue with other sources of moral wisdom, and read contemporary and historical circumstances clearly to craft ways of living, from personal lifestyle to influencing public policy and social structures, that are consistent with the profound goodness at the heart of the particular religious tradition. But that is not all. The purpose of religious ethics is also to offer the moral and spiritual resources of religion to efforts in the broader public to address the moral issues of our day.[1]

Epistemological Assumptions and Sources of Moral Wisdom

What are claimed as valid sources of moral wisdom determine what is perceived as moral. Religious ethics for planetary well-being will question what has counted traditionally as valid sources. Christian ethics, for example, has upheld four categories of moral wisdom: scripture (be it the Bible, Torah, Qur'an, Upanishads, etc.); the other teachings of the religious community throughout history (referred to in ethics as "tradition"); human experience; and other bodies of human knowledge such as science, philosophy, the arts, and so on. This traditional understanding or four categories of moral wisdom bears two significant flaws. First, as made clear by liberation theologies and post-colonial theologies, these sources have been developed, interpreted, and passed on primarily by people on the upper side of power and privilege. Their particular perspectives have shaped interpretation of scripture's moral meaning, and have been seen as universal and objective rather than particular and subjective. To address this distortion, people may pivot to reading scripture, tradition, and other bodies of human knowledge as interpreted by people on the underside of dominant power structures. The second flaw in the traditional understanding of four sources is that it ignores the other-than-human aspects of Earth's web of life as sources of moral wisdom. Thus, humankind fails to access the vital wisdom that may be gained by listening to the waters, trees, eco-systems, other-than-human animals, and other aspects of the Earth community. As I have said elsewhere,

> Recent decades prove the folly of this truncated and anthropocentric perspective. Called for is a modification in the centuries-old quadrilateral of moral wisdom (scripture, tradition, other bodies of knowledge, and experience). A fifth source [...] will join the traditional four; it is *other-than-human voices of the Earth* [...]. Human creatures are invited to learn—from the other-than-human parts of creation that now groan under our weight—wisdom for living in sync with Earth's well-being.
>
> (Birch et al. 2017: 170; emphasis added)

FIGURE 13.4 *Voices of the Earth.* Source: *Mary Elise Lowe/used with permission.*

This modification is joined with another: to "read" the initial four traditional sources through the lens of the other-than-human. The challenge, while likely to yield priceless insight, is daunting. How shall we, who may never have imagined such a move, learn even to glimpse the Bible, Christian beliefs and practices, scientific knowledge, or human experience from perspectives that are not human-centered? One foray into this challenge is the five-volume *Earth Bible* series that seeks to read the Bible from different perspectives of the Earth.

Theological Underpinnings

Theology matters. A sixth element of ethical method is theological underpinnings. While not all religions claim to have theologies, all do have systems of belief. Loci of theology (or of belief systems) particularly relevant for ethics include cosmologies (beliefs about the origins, purpose, nature, and destiny of the cosmos), anthropologies (beliefs about the origins, purpose, nature, and destiny of humankind), theologies of the human predicament and resolution to it (in Christianity, to illustrate, this refers to theologies of sin and salvation), and theologies regarding faith (is faith a matter of belief, or practice, or both). What people believe in these and other theological categories impacts the moral life. We illustrate this power of beliefs by looking at Christian traditions. Consider, for example, a theology of sin. One theology of sin considers sin to be acts of individuals; individual people sin. Another sees sin not only as individual but also as structural. Thus, systemic racism, systemic economic violence, and economic systems that fuel climate change without seeking to change would be sins. If sin is something that only individuals do, then people are not accountable for structural sin. Thus, if I am not personally racist in my behaviors and thoughts, then I am not a part of the systemic sin of racism and white supremacy that pervade US society. Likewise, if I am not personally exploiting others economically, I am not culpable of contributing to and benefiting from systems that exploit others brutally. I am not accountable, for example, for the fact that my mutual fund may be invested in a company that has terrible ecological impacts or pays its workers so little that they cannot afford shelter and must live on the streets. I am not accountable for my material gain from a salary paid by an institution invested in fossil fuels that contribute to climate change.

Similarly, cosmologies shape the moral life. If the created world is an inconsequential or bad material state to be left behind by those who are raptured to heaven (endtimes theology), then I am not motivated or obligated to honor creation and tend to well-being. In contrast, if I understand creation to be "good," and to be beloved by God and destined for ultimate union and communion with divine love, then I may seek ways of life that love creation as God does.

Primary Moral Norms and What They Mean

Yet another element of method is the primary moral norms embedded in a religion's ethics, and how they are interpreted. In Christian, Jewish, and Muslim traditions, arguably, the primary moral norm is the call to love neighbor as self. Neighbor-love, according to their scriptures, includes serving the well-being of the "neighbor," and one's neighbor refers to whomever one's life impacts. In Christianity, neighbor-love typically has been privatized; it has been individualized or reduced to its implications for interpersonal relationships, and has not been seen as applying to the structural dimensions of life. However, in the world of globalization and climate change, our lives have far more impact on neighbors through the systems in which we are intimately involved than through our interpersonal relationships. The examples are endless: the wars funded by my tax dollars, the police department norms produced by public policies and assumptions, the climate change caused by fossil fuels that pervade every moment of my life, the farmworkers in ill-paid and dangerous working conditions producing my food, all are impacted by my role in these systems. Yet, if love applies only to private interpersonal relationships, then these systems are exempt from the demands of neighbor-love to serve the well-being of the neighbor. These seven elements of method in ethics are not alone. Other elements also impact the outcome of ethics (e.g., communities of accountability and theory of justice, theory of social change, and theory of moral agency used). These seven are meant to be illustrative, not comprehensive. They illustrate that planetary ethics related to religion and nature in this age of globalization must attend to method in the doing of ethics.

In Sum

What does it mean to view globalization and planetary ethics in *relationship to religion and nature in North America* now? Doing ethics requires identifying morally defining

FIGURE 13.5 *Climate change protesters march in Paris' streets.* Source: *Jeanne Menjoulet/ CC BY-ND 2.0.*

realities at play in any given situation. Considering planetary ethics and globalization, two such defining realities are the climate crisis and the vast and racialized inequity between those who have too much and those whose lives are threatened or destroyed by having too little. We claimed at the outset that religious ethics ought to offer guidance as human beings seek to live in ways that counter both the climate catastrophe and the morally reprehensible impoverishment of many by systems that enrich others. We posed the questions: Given these two globalized and defining realities of the early twenty-first century, how are North Americans to do religious ethics in ways that enable Earth's fragile climate and other life systems to flourish and that build social equity within and among societies? How are North Americans to bring the resources of religious ethics to bear on developing ethics capable of guiding life in the face of these seemingly insurmountable and literally deadly moral travesties?

We arrived at a twofold response that, while not comprehensive, illuminates a path forward. Religious ethics can help clarify terms and concepts that mystify ecological and social devastation and that hide exploitation from those who benefit materially from it. And method in religious ethics will pivot in powerful ways that build moral-spiritual power for the most daunting moral challenge yet to face our young and dangerous species. It is the challenge of forging ways of living together—our public policies, economic and political structures and practices, cultural norms, ideological assumptions, and daily practices—that enable Earth's climate and community of life to flourish and that build justice with joy for all people.

Note

1   This paragraph restates for religious ethics what I previously wrote about Christian ethics in Birch et al. (2017: 94).

Further Reading and Online Resources

Birch B., J. Lapsley, C. Moe-Lobeda, and L. Rasmussen (2017), *The Bible and Ethics in the Christian Life: A New Conversation*, Minneapolis, MN: Fortress Press.

Lustgarten A. (2020), "The Great Climate Migration Has Begun," *New York Times*, July 23. Available online: https://www.nytimes.com/interactive/2020/07/23/magazine/climate-migration.html (accessed March 29, 2021).

Moe-Lobeda, C. (2002), *Healing a Broken World: Globalization and God*. Minneapolis, MN: Fortress Press.

Moe-Lobeda C. (2013), *Resisting Structural Evil: Love as Ecological-Economic Vocation*, Minneapolis, MN: Fortress Press.

National Climate Assessment (2014), *Climate Change Impacts in the United States*. Available online: https://nca2014.globalchange.gov/ (accessed March 29, 2021).

World Bank (2012), "Turn Down the Heat: Why a 4 Degree C Warmer World Must Be Avoided," Washington, DC: World Bank. Available online: http://documents.worldbank.org/curated/en/865571468149107611/Turn-down-the-heat-why-a-4-C-warmer-world-must-be-avoided (accessed March 29, 2021).

References

Anderson S. and J. Cavanagh (1996), *The Top 200*, Washington, DC: Institute for Policy Studies. Available online: http://www.rrojasdatabank.info/top200.pdf (accessed March 29, 2021).

Barlow M. (2000), *Blue Gold: The Global Water Crisis and the Commodification of the World's Water Supply*, San Francisco: International Forum on Globalization.

Birch B., J. Lapsley, C. Moe-Lobeda, and L. Rasmussen (2017), *The Bible and Ethics in the Christian Life: A New Conversation*, Minneapolis, MN: Fortress Press.

Brookfield S. D. (1987), *Developing Critical Thinkers: Challenging Adults to Explore Alternative Ways of Thinking and Acting*, San Francisco: Jossey-Bass.

Habel N.C., S. Wurst, and V. Balabanski, eds. (2000–2), *Earth Bible, Volumes 1–5*, Sheffield, UK: Sheffield Academic Press.

Henwood D. (1998), *Wall Street: How It Works and for Whom*, London: Verso.

Moe-Lobeda C. (2006), "Religious Claims in Public: Lutheran Resources," *Dialog: A Journal of Theology*, 45 (4) (Winter): 322–37.

Moe-Lobeda C. (2013), *Resisting Structural Evil: Love as Ecological-Economic Vocation*, Minneapolis, MN: Fortress Press.

Moe-Lobeda C. (2019), "Finding Common Ground on Moral Vision for the Good Society," in H. Koster and E. Conradie (eds.), *T&T Clark Handbook of Christian Theology and Climate Change*, 157–73, London: T & T Clark.

Moe-Lobeda C. (2020), "Climate Change as Race Debt, Class Debt, Climate Colonialism: Moral Conundrums, Vision, and Agency," in K. Hughes, D. Martin, and E. Padilla (eds.), *Ecological Solidarities: Mobilizing Faith and Justice for an Entangled World*, 61–80, University Park: Pennsylvania State University Press.

Moe-Lobeda, C. (2002), *Healing a Broken World: Globalization and God*. Minneapolis, MN: Fortress Press.

Pero A., Jr. (2001), *Between Vision and Reality: Lutheran Churches in Transition*, ed. W. Grieve, 257–65, Geneva: The Lutheran World Federation.

Sobrino J. (1986), "Poverty Means Death to the Poor," *CrossCurrents*, 36 (3): 267–76.

Sparr P. (1993), "United Methodist Study Guide on Global Economics: Seeking a Christian Ethics," New York: General Board of Global Ministries, The United Methodist Church.

United Nations Research Institute for Social Development (UNRISD) (1995), "States of Disarray: The Social Effects of Globalization: A Report by the UNRISD for the World Summit for Social Development.

Vallianatos, M. with A. Durbin (1998), *License to Loot*, Washington, DC: Friends of the Earth.

14

Religion and Climate Change

Kevin J. O'Brien

Introduction

In a 2018 study, the Yale Program on Climate Communication found that 70 percent of people surveyed in the United States are convinced that global warming is a real and serious threat. However, only 30 percent of them reported that they even occasionally talk to anyone else about the issue (Marlon 2018). Climate change is real, it is threatening, and most of us do not know how to talk about it.

The reality of climate change is all too present in contemporary life. Coverage of severe weather events—droughts, hurricanes, floods—is prominent, and it is widely understood that these events are increasing in frequency because the average temperature of the planet is warming. That warming is largely the result of industrial activity, as gases such as carbon dioxide and methane are released through the consumption of fossil fuels, linger in the atmosphere, and trap heat. That heat then changes weather patterns and acid levels in the ocean, and increasingly impacts all life on Earth.

Beyond the bare facts of *anthropogenic climate change*, most of us have little practice in talking about it. This chapter attempts to make that talking easier in two ways: First, the more clearly we can frame what is going on, the more possible it will be to start conversations. And so, the chapter is structured with five questions about the challenges posed by the changing atmosphere: Should something be done about climate change? Can it be solved by science alone? How unprecedented is the problem? What stories help to make sense of it? How do we attend to the injustices of climate change?

The second approach this chapter takes is less intuitive: it argues that it becomes easier to talk about climate change when people understand that religion plays a powerful role in how we understand and respond to the issue. Many of us have been encouraged to avoid public discussions of religion since it can be so contentious, or personal, or complicated. But I hope to show by exploring religious responses to each of the five questions above that religious ideas and religious studies are incredibly helpful in thinking about this issue, that connecting climate change to religion will enhance rather than hinder conversations.

What Should Be Done about Climate Change?

The most common stories in the North American media about the intersection of religion and climate change concern the *climate skepticism* of evangelical Christians in the United States. These stories are too often simplistic or overblown, ignoring the diversity within Christianity as a whole and evangelicalism within it. Contrary to what is frequently said in the media, many evangelical Christians are profoundly concerned about climate change, and some have devoted their lives to working on the issue.

Nevertheless, climate skepticism is higher among white evangelicals in the United States than in virtually any other demographic group. White US citizens who identify themselves as evangelicals are statistically less likely to believe that any personal or political change is required by the issue than any other group. Scholar of religion Robin Globus Veldman studies this trend, and she argues that this skepticism is a result of the particular place Evangelicals understand themselves to occupy in US society and the ways their leaders have made their faith synonymous with right-wing political positions (2019).

Veldman explains that evangelical leaders in the United States have spent the last three decades connecting their faith to conservativism by arguing that increasing liberalism in the wider culture is a threat to Christian faith, that changing laws about issues such as sexuality and abortion are replacing traditional ways of life, and that Christian ideas and biblical morality should be more central in public life. Environmentalism has been understood in many of these communities as a secular and left-wing political concern, and so Veldman notes that many of the Evangelicals she talked with explicitly defined their own beliefs *against* those of environmentalists. They framed "environmentalists as an out-group" and thereby made opposition to environmentalism a test of who "belongs" in their own community (2019: 219). For example, a group of conservative Evangelicals called the Cornwall Alliance asserts that "without a doubt one of the greatest threats to society and the church today is the multifaceted environmental movement." They see environmentalism as the "cult of the green dragon," a secular religion that competes against Christianity with "deceptions" about a false sense of crisis (Cornwall 2010).

These Evangelicals understand environmentalism as a false religion that seeks to replace Christianity, and they therefore believe that they are called to defend traditional culture and Christian faith against such threats. Climate change is, for them, a dangerous tenet of a misguided faith. So, the key problem of climate change, from their perspective, is the fact that so many people are worried about the issue. They believe that people with faith in God, those who practice genuine Christianity, have nothing to worry about from the climate. So, their response to climate change is to defend and lift up true faith.

Canadian climate scientist Katharine Hayhoe, who also identifies as an evangelical Christian, sees the problem very differently. She argues that climate change should not be understood as a matter of "belief" at all, insisting that her understanding is based on facts: "We know the earth's climate is changing thanks to observations, facts and data about God's creation that we can see with our eyes and test with the sound minds that God has given us" (Hayhoe 2019). For her, the question "do you believe in climate change?" is inappropriate, comparable to the question "do you believe in gravity?"

The world Hayhoe observes, which she believes God made and gave humanity the tools to understand, includes a rapidly changing climate. The response to this reality, for Hayhoe, is not denial but compassion. Evangelical Christianity as she understands it should be defined by love for neighbors, and climate change is threatening neighbors all over the world. The changing atmosphere is already "amplifying hunger and poverty, and increasing risks of resource scarcity that can exacerbate political instability, and even create or worsen refugee crises" (Hayhoe 2019). So, she calls on fellow Evangelicals to recognize that if they care about their neighbors, they need to do something about climate change.

FIGURE 14.1 *Evangelical climate scientist Katharine Hayhoe, speaking about climate change at the LBJ Presidential Library in Texas in 2018. Photograph by Jay Godwin.*

From both of these perspectives, climate change calls for an urgent response, it is a test for evangelical Christians. For the first group, the test is about rejecting and opposing a false belief system that threatens the true faith. For others, such as Katharine Hayhoe, climate change is a fact, and the test is whether Christians will respond compassionately to the poor and marginalized who are endangered by it. These are two very different views of the intersection of climate change and religion, emerging from two very different interpretations of the same religious tradition.

Can Climate Change Be Solved by Science?

Katharine Hayhoe, like many other scientists, believes that her faith is entirely compatible with scientific findings, and she insists that a faith in God can in fact inspire a profound commitment to understand God's creation in scientific terms.

Others who want to address climate change fear that the approach of the Cornwall Alliance is a better representation of religious responses to climate change, and so hope to banish religion from the conversation altogether. For example, oceanographer and former White House science advisor Jeff Schweitzer unequivocally states: "We will not effectively address the issue of global warming if we appeal to religion." Climate change, he insists, requires people to develop "the most cogent, fact-based, scientifically-sound argument possible given the evidence in hand." Religion as Schweitzer understands it always emphasizes faith over reason, and has participated too often in irrational prejudices and anti-scientific protests to be trusted (Schweitzer 2009).

Schweitzer and many who think like him tell a story about climate change that centers science and rationality. The climate is changing in complex ways, and scientific thinking is both the best way to understand the problem and the best way to develop a response. Schweitzer asserts that "religious morality has failed." So, he seeks a new moral system based on science and reason, "divorced from god and religion" that will emphasize rational rather than spiritual thought (Schweitzer and Sciar 2010: 17–19). For him religion is, at best, an obstacle to be overcome in the development of a rational response to the climate crisis.

Christian ethicist Larry Rasmussen disagrees. He studies science carefully, learning from the reports of the Intergovernmental Panel on Climate Change and other scientific experts. But he argues that while science is equipped to explain reality, it cannot interpret that reality nor inspire people to act in response. He writes: "few people will die for a pie chart. Data, even the good data of sound science, do not of themselves upend habitual and cherished ways." If scientific findings are suggesting that people need to change behavior and social systems, then people need to think ethically about those findings. Rasmussen argues that religions are a key source of ethics for billions of adherents, and that religious traditions have developed "millennia of fluency in the arts of life instruction and renewal." So, he draws from his own Christian tradition in conversation with other religions to highlight "Earth-honoring faiths," religious ideas that train people to transform themselves and the world (Rasmussen 2013: 6).

While Jeff Schweitzer understands the problem at the root of climate change as a failure to be rational, Larry Rasmussen understands it as a failure to be properly religious. He argues that those who deny climate change are frequently motivated far more by a commitment to industrial economies than by religion, and calls the belief in economic growth and development "the world's secular religion since the Industrial Revolution." This secular religion teaches an ethic of "life, liberty, and the pursuit of shopping," and contributes to the economic and political systems that exacerbate climate change (Rasmussen 2013: 77, 244). The best response to this misguided religion, for Rasmussen, comes not only from rational, scientific analysis of its consequences, but also from the teachings of religious communities. The best religious traditions, he believes, call people to live for something bigger than themselves, something more meaningful than simple wealth. From this perspective, climate change is inherently a religious as well as a scientific problem.

Rasmussen and Schweitzer agree that science is essential to any climate response. Both would certainly support more research into renewable energy sources, more basic science to understand the workings of the climate, and more behavioral research

FIGURE 14.2 *Aerial view of a solar power plant station in Nevada, United States. Solar power is widely seen to be an important technology to produce energy without exacerbating climate change. Courtesy of Getty Images.*

to understand human motivations and how they might change. The difference is that Rasmussen insists such scientific work is not sufficient by itself, that those who learn from science should also learn from spiritual insights, religious traditions, and faith communities.

How Unprecedented Is Climate Change?

Every religion in North America has climate advocates such as Hayhoe and Rasmussen. Among Muslims, one public effort to respond to climate change culminated in 2016 when the Islamic Society of North America (ISNA) divested from fossil fuels, deciding that putting money into "companies whose operations and products cause such grave harm to humanity and to Creation" defied the basic principles of Islam. "According to Islam's most basic and fundamental teachings," ISNA President Azhar Azeez asserted, "human beings have been uniquely charged with the great responsibility of being Guardians and Caretakers of the Earth" (Catovic 2016).

ISNA also developed a campaign called "Greening Our Ramadan," bringing environmental themes into the most holy time of year by asking members to pledge sustainable practices such as reducing waste and conserving food and water while fasting and providing for those in need. This, too, was justified by an appeal to basic Islamic principles, quoting the Qur'an's command to "Eat and drink but waste not by extravagance. Certainly Allah loves not the wasters" (ISNA n.d.).

FIGURE 14.3 *The Qur'an, the holiest book in Islam, which many Muslims believe contains clear directions for sustainable living. Courtesy of Getty Images.*

ISNA's leaders are confident that their communities can respond to the challenges of climate change by learning from long-standing moral traditions. It is true that human beings have never experienced global climatic shifts as rapid as those now going on, and the earth has never before seen such substantial atmospheric change through the activities of a single species. But these Muslims—like the Christians discussed above—nevertheless emphasize that the moral challenge of climate change is familiar. The big challenges of learning to care for other people, avoiding wasteful extravagance, and caring for the created world are issues with which religious traditions have wrestled for thousands of years.

Others, however, believe that inherited religious traditions are not equipped to deal with a problem as severe and unprecedented as climate change. Scholar Bron Taylor advocates for new religious thinking in response to environmental degradation, arguing that our times call for a different kind of religion, which he describes as "dark green." *Dark green religions* emerge from "a deep sense of belonging to and connectedness in nature, while perceiving the earth and its living systems to be sacred and interconnected." These new forms of religion integrate Indigenous and Eastern traditions with contemporary science, forming "an amalgamation of bits and pieces of a wide array of ideas and practices, drawn from diverse cultural systems, religious traditions, and political ideologies" (Taylor 2010: 13–14).

Taylor spends very little time with traditional religious teachings, believing that the moralities of the past are too focused on human beings and too disconnected from contemporary science. "Most of the world's major religions have worldviews that are antithetical to and compete with the worldviews and ethics found in dark green religion" (Taylor 2010: 178). Jeff Schweitzer might agree, but unlike him, Taylor does not entirely reject faith. Instead, he calls for religious innovation: In the face of a changing climate, people should develop new spiritualities designed to respond to the world we live in and its contemporary threats. He calls people to "let go of ancient dreams" and to instead work dark green spiritualities into "a sensible religion, one that is rationally defensible as well as socially powerful enough to save us from our least-sensible selves" (221–2).

Both Bron Taylor and the leaders of the Islamic Society of North America treat climate change as a religious issue, calling for a moral and spiritual response. But they disagree on how much that response should emerge from existing traditions or new innovations. The question at the root of this disagreement is how new the problem of climate change is. Is the moral challenge of our time completely unlike what has come before? Are our inherited ideas still relevant? This conversation is not unique to religion; for example, we can find the same argument between those who advocate giving up technology to reduce our carbon footprints and those who believe that engineering can create climate solutions (Clingerman and O'Brien 2017). Still, understanding that this argument is in part about religious traditions and moralities helps to demonstrate, again, that attitudes about religion shape the ways people understand climate change and the best responses to it.

What Stories Can Help Make Sense of Climate Change?

The three questions above have focused on debates, identifying two-sided disagreements about the relationship between climate and religion. The final two questions are different, highlighting questions that invite many possible answers and highlight the diversity of possible religious responses to climate change, many of which complement rather than contrast one another.

The first has to do with what stories help to make sense of climate change. Human beings are storytelling creatures, and in the face of a complex problem, new or remembered narratives help us to make sense of where we are, how we got here, and where we might go. As novelist Amitav Ghosh argues, storytelling "makes possible the imagining of possibilities. And to imagine other forms of human existence is exactly the challenge that is posed by the climate crisis: for if there is any one thing that global warming has made perfectly clear it is that to think about the world only as it is amounts to a formula for collective suicide" (2016: 128). For Ghosh, if we are to respond to climate change, we need better stories.

Religious traditions have many stories, and religious people think deeply about how these stories can orient believers in the midst of climate change. For example, ethicist Nancy Menning argues that the Hebrew Bible's story of Exodus offers a helpful way to understand the first half of the twenty-first century as a "rite of passage," a "fundamental transition" that is "both dangerous and powerful." The Exodus story narrates a passage from slavery to freedom, with the Israelites escaping bondage in Egypt, enduring hardships and confusion on a long trip through the desert, and finally arriving in the "promised land" of Israel. Similarly, Menning argues, humanity has left a period of stability, is now suffering from uncertainty and depravation, and hopes for a more sustainable future with a new way of relating to both one another and the land (Menning 2018). If we understand ourselves to be in the midst of a transition, then we can have realistic hopes.

Menning also argues that the story of Exodus trains people to think about issues of justice in two ways. The narrative of Israelites escaping slavery is commonly interpreted by Jews and Christians to mean that God is always on the side of the oppressed. But Exodus has a more questionable approach to justice when it comes to driving the existing inhabitants out of the promised land. Wrestling with the story of Exodus helps people to think critically about fairness and justice across history and in our own time. This will encourage us to "condemn the inequities associated with ongoing climate change" while also taking "a critical-constructive approach" to challenge simplistic stories about justice (Menning 2018: 352, 350).

Another more contemporary story comes from Kyle Powys Whyte, a Potawatomi activist and scholar of religion who argues that the broad issue of climate change can be helpfully captured within a more historic understanding of the mistreatment of the

FIGURE 14.4 *Water protectors and protesters march at Standing Rock to protest the Dakota Access Pipeline in 2016. Courtesy of Getty Images.*

Standing Rock Sioux. In 1868, the Sioux were granted exclusive rights to most of what we know today as South Dakota. But the Great Sioux Reservation was broken up thirty years later when settlers found gold, and then again in the 1960s when the Army Corps of Engineers built a dam that flooded 200,000 acres of remaining reservation land. So, it is sadly no surprise that the Standing Rock Sioux's objections were ultimately dismissed when the Federal Government permitted the Dakota Access Pipeline on the tribe's traditional lands in 2017. Whyte argues that a theme of this story is "a lack of indigenous consent," a disregard for the desires and traditions of the peoples who have lived with the land the longest (2017: 168–9).

The story of Standing Rock, for Whyte, sheds light on the broad issue of climate change, which he believes is best explained as the result of white settler colonialism's tendency to believe that the desires and plans of a dominant culture are more important than the desires and well-being of other peoples and the natural world. The story of Standing Rock teaches that climate change is "colonial déjà vu," simply the latest expression of the erasure of Indigenous peoples and their sacred relationships to the land (Whyte 2016). This history then helps Whyte to argue that the best response to climate change is to cede authority to Indigenous peoples, to trust that decisions about managing ecosystems will best be made by cultures that are intimately tied to places rather than industrial economics.

Still a third story told about climate change comes from the Buddhist activist and scholar Joanna Macy, who insists that, among stories of denial and climate catastrophe, it is important to also tell a story of "the Great Turning," a "transition from a doomed economy of industrial growth to a life-sustaining society committed to the recovery of our world" (2012: 26). This story is built on Buddhist ideas about the cyclical nature of time and the inevitability of change, frequently expressed as "the turning of the wheel." Working from a Buddhist teaching that the best response to suffering is expanded awareness, Macy tells a global story that "a new view of reality is emerging, where spiritual insight and scientific discovery both contribute to our understanding of ourselves as intimately interwoven with our world" (26). She encourages her readers to consciously choose this story and live in way that makes it true: "When we find a good story and fully give ourselves to it, the story can act through us, breathing new life into everything we do" (32–3).

These three perspectives relating stories to climate change demonstrate some of the options available in narratively understanding the problem. Menning seeks to give people a realistic hope by acknowledging that our time of transition will have complicated results. Whyte emphasizes that the story of a specific Indigenous community should be highlighted to understand which sacred traditions are best equipped to respond to climate change. Macy seeks to orient people to a positive future by narrating a new global vision. What these thinkers all have in common is an understanding that climate change is an occasion for storytelling, that making sense of the dramatic and catastrophic changes to the atmosphere requires the narrative impulse inherent in human beings and their religious traditions.

How Do We Attend to the Injustices of Climate Change?

Another broad and generative question asks about how we should understand the injustice associated with climate change.

It used to be that the most prominent images to represent climate change were polar bears on ice floes and graphs comparing average temperatures to CO_2 levels. In recent years, though, climate change has been more commonly depicted with flooding cities, refugees making their way across deserts, and angry young people protesting. Climate change used to be thought of a primarily an issue about the natural world, but it is increasingly understood to be a fundamental threat to human life.

This trend has fueled the growth of a global *climate justice* movement. The human threats of climate change are not evenly distributed. Poorer people, those in less economically developed countries, people of color, Indigenous peoples, women, and children bear a disproportionate burden. The flooding, drought, scarcity, and homelessness caused by climate change and climate-related extreme weather tend to

FIGURE 14.5 *A resident in her damaged home in Puerto Rico in the aftermath of Hurricane Maria, which struck the island in October 2017. Electrical power was not fully restored to all residents for eleven months. Photograph courtesy of Oxfam East Africa.*

be most severe for those who are already most vulnerable (Shue 2014). Thus, climate change exacerbates inequalities and injustices, and any reasonable response to the problem must attend to this fact.

Episcopalian activist Jill Rios argues that one important way for Christians to attend to the injustices of climate change is to care for their neighbors who have fled hostile conditions and seek refuge in their communities. The Christian teaching to welcome strangers and care for neighbors is crucial in a time of climate change, she argues, because rising seas and extreme weather events are driving more and more people—particularly those in poor countries—to flee their homes. Rios belongs to La Capilla de Santa Maria, a Hispanic Mission church in Hendersonville, North Carolina, which primarily ministers to migrants who work multiple jobs and send money home to support their families in Mexico and Latin America. These migrants need immediate help, which Rios and her fellow congregants seek to provide. Inspired by this work, she offers a "hope and challenge" for religious communities to "provide a prophetic voice to welcome strangers into our communities in ways that reflect our Christian values and protect God's Earth" (Rios 2012: 168).

Rios's work with migrants also inspires her to call for political change. Seeing how her friends and neighbors are treated and learning from them that climate change is making life harder in their countries of origin inspires her to advocate for more hospitable immigration laws that will welcome climate refugees. She has also been inspired to advocate for more aid to be sent directly to less wealthy nations: "Because the developed world bears the brunt of responsibility for climate change, Christians especially should honor a moral obligation to the developing world for the adverse effects those countries will suffer" (Rios 2012: 179). For Jill Rios, wealthy and privileged Christians should attend to the injustices of climate change by supporting their neighbors and learning from them about the needs of the wider world.

Ethicist Melanie Harris argues that the most important perspectives on injustice come from those who have themselves suffered oppression. So, Harris develops an ecowomanist response to environmental problems that draws primarily on the specific experiences of African American women like herself. A key source for her ethics is her own "ecoautobiography," learning from her experiences, those of her family, and their specific relationships to places and environments (Harris 2017: 23). This approach includes attention to Christian traditions that have shaped Harris's family as well as to the indigenous African traditions that her ancestors brought to North America and sustained for centuries.

Harris highlights the "parallel oppressions that black women and the earth face" (2016: 18), including the overuse of human labor and natural resources that has been ongoing since agricultural practices that were developed with slave labor. Her ancestors' experience of slavery included being forced to harvest in an unsustainable way, overproducing cotton "for the sake of profit, thus robbing the soil of nutrients in Mississippi and causing soil erosion in Alabama" (7). The particular experience of enslaved people is thus a way to understand how deep the roots and the violence of climate change run.

Rios emphasizes that climate change is a way for privileged people to understand the reality of human suffering among our neighbors. Harris emphasizes that the voices of oppressed people themselves can also demonstrate the depths of destructiveness in a changing climate. Both offer sustained attention to climate change as a problem of injustice, and call on their readers to do the same, to understand that the changing atmosphere threatens human lives and threatens them in uneven, unjust ways. Many other perspectives—religious and otherwise—would emphasize these issues differently, but all agree that conversations about climate change must include attention to justice.

Conclusion: Talking about Climate Change

The questions raised in this chapter are difficult. It is challenging to wrestle with injustice, to make sense of the world with stories, to learn from or reinvent traditions, to balance science and faith, and to ponder a response to climate change. The argument of the chapter has been that religion makes these difficult questions a bit more approachable, offering perspectives that help us to explore possible answers and to bring them into dialogue with one another.

The chapter has also sought to offer conversation partners by citing a diverse range of people and organizations who are working on climate issues in North America today.

This demonstrates the variety of religious responses to climate change. Dialogue partners here have included Muslims, Buddhists, Christians, Indigenous activists, and people who reject traditional religious categorization; the differences between them have revealed diversity within as well as between faith communities. Climate change does not relate to religion in any single way. To the contrary, the diversity of religion helps us to grasp the complexity of climate change and the myriad possible responses to it.

As noted in this chapter's Introduction, most people do not discuss climate change often. This is a problem, because the changing climate is reshaping life on Earth and it will continue to do so for the foreseeable future. We need to learn to talk about the issue well enough to make productive progress on disagreements, change the minds of those with bad ideas, and inspire action in all who can make positive changes. There are no easy answers, and there is a great deal of complexity to master. This is a reason to talk more, not less. An understanding of religion and its varieties can help to support these much-needed conversations.

Further Reading and Online Resources

350.org (n.d.), "Stop Fossil Fules." Available online: https://350.org/ (accessed December 27, 2020).
Earth Ministry (n.d.), "Welcome to Earth Ministry." Available online: https://earthministry.org/ (accessed December 27, 2020).
Hulme M. (2009), *Why We Disagree about Climate Change: Understanding Controversy, Inaction and Opportunity*, New York: Cambridge University Press.
Stephenson W. (2015), *What We're Fighting for Now Is Each Other: Dispatches from the Front Lines of Climate Justice*, Boston: Beacon Press.
Yale Project on Climate Communication (n.d.), "What We Do." Available online: http://climatecommunication.yale.edu (accessed December 27, 2020).

References

Catovic S. (2016), "Islamic Society of North America (ISNA) Divestment from Fossil Fuel Announcement." Available online: https://parliamentofreligions.org/videos/islamic-society-north-america-isna-divestment-fossil-fuel-announcement (accessed March 1, 2020).
Clingerman F. and K.J. O'Brien (2017), "Is Climate Change a New Kind of Problem? The Role of Theology and Imagination in Climate Ethics," *WIREs Climate Change*, 8 (5). Available online: https://doi.org/10.1002/wcc.480.
Cornwall Alliance (2010), "Resisting the Green Dragon: A Biblical Response to One of the Greatest Deceptions of Our Day." Available online: https://www.resistingthegreendragon.com/ (accessed March 1, 2020).
Ghosh A. (2016), *The Great Derangement: Climate Change and the Unthinkable*, Chicago: University of Chicago Press.
Harris M.L. (2016), "Ecowomanism: An Introduction," *Worldviews*, 20 (1): 5–14.
Harris M.L. (2017), *Ecowomanism: African American Women and Earth-Honoring Faiths*, Maryknoll, NY: Orbis Books.

Hayhoe K. (2019), "I'm a Climate Scientist Who Believes in God. Hear Me Out," *New York Times*, October 31. Available online: https://www.nytimes.com/2019/10/31/opinion/sunday/climate-change-evangelical-christian.html. (accessed January 18, 2021).

ISNA. (n.d.), "Greening Our Ramadan." Available online: http://www.isna.net/greenramadan/ (accessed December 27, 2020).

Macy J. and C. Johnstone (2012), *Active Hope: How to Face the Mess We're in without Going Crazy*, Novato, CA: New World Library.

Marlon J., P. Howe, M. Mildenberger, A. Leiserowitz, and X. Wang (2018), "Yale Climate Opinion Maps 2018," Yale Program on Climate Change Communication, August 7. Available online: http://climatecommunication.yale.edu/visualizations-data/ycom-us-2018/?est=happening&type=value&geo=county (accessed December 27, 2020).

Menning N. (2018), "Narrating Climate Change as a Rite of Passage," *Climatic Change*, 147: 343–53.

Rasmussen L. (2013), *Earth-Honoring Faith: Religious Ethics in a New Key*, New York: Oxford University Press.

Rios J. (2012), "Faith and Flight: Immigration, the Church and the Climate," in M. McDuff (ed.), *Sacred Acts: How Churches Are Working to Protect Earth's Climate*, 167–81, Gabriola Island, BC: New Society Publishers.

Schweitzer J. (2009), "Climate Change and Christian Values," *Huffington Post*, June 10. Available online: http://www.huffingtonpost.com/jeff-schweitzer/climate-change-and-christ_b_198047.html (accessed December 27, 2020).

Schweitzer J. and G. Notorbartolo-Di Sciar (2010), *A New Moral Code*, Los Angeles: Jacquie Jordan.

Shue H. (2014), *Climate Justice: Vulnerability and Protection*, New York: Oxford University Press.

Taylor B.R. (2010), *Dark Green Religion: Nature Spirituality and the Planetary Future*, Berkeley: University of California Press.

Veldman R.G. (2019), *The Gospel of Climate Skepticism*, Oakland: University of California Press.

Whyte K.P. (2016), "Is It Colonial Déjà Vu? Indigenous Peoples and Climate Injustice," in J. Adamson, M. Davis, and H. Huang (eds.), *Humanities for the Environment: Integrating Knowledges, Fording New Constellations of Practice*, 88–104, New York: Earthscan Publications.

Whyte K.P. (2017), "The Dakota Access Pipeline, Environmental Injustice, and U.S. Colonialism," *Red Ink*, 19 (1): 154–69.

Glossary Terms

Anthropogenic Climate Change Shifts in global weather patterns created by increasing emissions from industrialization and consumption by human beings.

Climate Justice Attention to the ways that marginalized peoples tend to suffer the most consequences of anthropogenic climate change.

Climate Skepticism An approach to climate change that emphasizes the issue as a matter of politics, personal belief, and group membership rather than a set of facts about the natural world.

Dark Green Religions New religious movements developed in response to environmental crisis, based on earlier traditions, scientific tradition, and reverence for the natural world.

15

Petrocultures and Christianity in the United States

Terra Schwerin Rowe

Among the vast range of pressing environmental concerns, scholars of religion and ecology as well as religious environmental ethics have long recognized the urgency of addressing climate change and, with the scientific consensus, have acknowledged its primary anthropogenic causes in fossil fuel consumption (Conradie and Koster 2020). At least since John B. Cobb's 1972 text *Is It Too Late?: A Theology of Ecology* and Dieter Hessel's 1979 *Energy Ethics: A Christian Response,* significant scholarship has focused on the religious ethics of energy use and policy (Peppard et al. 2016).

What has escaped scholarly and common attention until relatively recently, though, are the key historical and symbolic resonances between Christianity and fossil fuels, particularly in the United States. This research has been influenced by the rise of the environmental humanities and its subdisciplines, energy humanities and *petroculture* studies. These discourses emphasize that the causes of and mitigation strategies for climate change require a broader response than what a solely techno-scientific strategy can offer (Holm et al. 2015). One finds, for example, that a rise in greenhouse gases is inextricably entwined with cultural and socio-economic habits, practices, affects, beliefs, assumptions, future expectations, values, and desires (Boyer and Szeman 2017).

Petro-religious scholarship emphasizes the importance of religious perspectives in these cultural approaches to environmental issues. Such a focus on religiopolitical-economic values, symbols, and meaning production reveals that the United States has not just made significant technological, economic, scientific, and infrastructure investments in fossil fuels but also significant emotional, identity constructing religio-spiritual investments as well. Such a perspective offers valuable insight into the powerful resistance to alternative energy futures in the twenty-first century.

Petro-apocalypse: The Late Nineteenth-Century Religious Symbolism of Oil

While the term "apocalypse" is commonly used to signal a destructive end, it originally referred to an unveiling or revealing (Keller 2021). From this perspective, petro-apocalypse turns out to be quite an apt description of the early religious framing given to oil in the United States. Starting in Titusville, Pennsylvania, in 1859 and continuing when oil was discovered in Texas and California decades later, writers framed oil as a revelation of divine providence, an unveiling of God's gifts for humanity. For example, in *Petroleum* (1866) Rev. S.J.M. Eaton describes oil as lying in wait since the beginning of creation until the divinely prescribed moment: "And now here, in this remote county of Western Pennsylvania, so humble and so poor in agricultural resources, God's treasure has been concealed for ages [...] awaiting the time of need, and accomplishment of the eternal purposes of Omnipotence" (1866: 61). Oil made its apocalyptic appearance when the nation was floundering, divided, and heading toward civil war. In this context, petroleum emerged as a redemptive gift sent to reunify the stumbling nation, providing crucial economic stability to replace cotton and eventually offering a substitute for enslaved labor (Dochuk 2019; Nikiforuk 2012). At times, oil was even given Christ-like figuration, as in the case of John J. McLaurin's 1896 *Sketches in Crude Oil*. Here oil, the "star of the East," is known of and foretold by authors of the Hebrew Bible, only revealed as "the full orb of day" (McLaurin 1896: 60–1) in the West (particularly in the United States, the "Lord's darling" [70]). McLaurin's portrayal resonates with an already entrenched narrative of the United States as a "redeemer nation" (Tuveson 1968) such that oil and the United States emerge conjoined, together playing a key role in the salvation history of all creation (Schwerin Rowe 2023).

Spiritual and Religious Methods for Finding Oil

Beyond the redemptive agency granted oil, religion and spirituality also played a significant role in early methods employed to find petroleum. Reports from newspapers such as Pennsylvania's *Oil City Register* (1865), for example, suggest divining rods and spiritual oil guides were regularly relied on even if some remained skeptical (Sabin 1999). More than seeking mere wealth, the late nineteenth-century Spiritualist movement promoted spiritual oil guides and even created their own oil companies such as the Chicago Rock Oil company to demonstrate the validity and practicality of Spiritualism (Zuck 2014). The assertion of a connection between oil and the spiritual world was understood within Spiritualist frameworks such as Andrew Jackson Davis's harmonial interpretation of electricity (Caterine 2014). Such "harmonial religions" (Ahlstrom 1972) sought consonance between human and cosmic energies for improved spiritual, physical, and even economic well-being. Certain Spiritualists became famous for their ability to

FIGURE 15.1 *Spindletop Lucas Gusher, Texas, 1901.* Source: *Library of Congress, public domain.*

successfully find oil by engaging the spirit world. Abraham James, for example, gained a reputation of something of an oil prophet after he reportedly became possessed by a "spirit guide," fell unconscious on the ground, and then woke to accurately predict that oil could be found directly below the place where he fell (Zuck 2014). This was the case also with more biblically based believers such as Texas Baptist Patillo Higgens, the "prophet of Spindletop," who claimed biblical guidance for reading the earth to discover what became the most productive oil discovery seen yet (Dochuk 2012).

Oil Culture and Contemporary Religious Divides

While oil and methods for finding it were invested with spiritual and redemptive qualities, petroleum also shaped the twentieth- and twenty-first-century US religious landscape. Historian Darren Dochuk has written the first comprehensive history of US oil and religion, emphasizing the lasting implications of the religious beliefs of key oil figures such as the Rockefellers, Lyman Stewart, and the Pew family. These influential personalities infused their oil pursuits, business models, and advertisement schemes with religious values and then bolstered their preferred religious institutions—many newly created by them—with oil money (Dochuk 2019).

Like Eaton, Baptist John D. Rockefeller believed US oil was a divine blessing for the whole world. Shaped by *progressive millennial*, or postmillennial, beliefs, his philanthropy and business models emphasized methodical, systematic improvements of human and social conditions and—particularly later and with John D. Rockefeller Jr.—embraced economic, labor, and eventually environmental regulations.

Presbyterian Lyman Stewart also believed that oil was a divine blessing for humanity, but was strongly influenced by the libertarian spirit of wildcat oil and the urgency of Christian *dispensational premillennialism*. For him, wildcat-style oil extraction and religion coordinated beautifully: oil, like the spirit of Protestantism, should not be regulated by any human institution or authority, but left up to the individual conscience and individual efforts. Both required freedom from the impositions of regulating authorities (Pietsch 2013).

The theological differences of the Rockefeller and Stewart camps were buttressed with oil riches and solidified into institutions that have come to shape the divided landscape of twentieth- and twenty-first-century US Christianity. Influenced by the gradual progress narrative of Christian millennialism, the Rockefellers helped found the University of Chicago, which the Stewart camp viewed as aggressively liberal and dangerously leading the way toward secularization and atheism. In response, Stewart helped found the influential California Bible college, now BIOLA University. Resisting Rockefeller's style of theological liberalism, Stewart also funded and organized the distribution of *The Fundamentals*, a series of religious tracts that sparked the now profoundly influential religious fundamentalist movement. In response, Rockefeller funded the distribution of Harry Emerson Fosdick's sermon "Shall the Fundamentalists Win?" He also helped found the *National Council of Churches* and Interchurch World movement, which spurred the Sun Oil Pew family—more in line with Stewart's conservative evangelical concerns than the Rockefellers' progressive vision—to start the National Association of Evangelicals, Fuller Theological Seminary, and the popular magazine *Christianity Today* (Dochuk 2019; Pietsch 2013).

FIGURE 15.2 *While it was a common belief early on in the oil rush that very little oil would be found west of Pennsylvania, significant oil discoveries in Texas and then California soon turned the oil hungry nation's attention to the West. In 2019 the top producing states were North Dakota and Texas. (https://www.eia.gov/dnav/pet/PET_CRD_CRPDN_ADC_MBBLPD_A.htm.)* Source: *John Ciccarelli, public domain.*

The significance of this newly emerging work in petro-religious studies can be framed broadly in terms of public sentiment and more narrowly in terms of academic scholarship. By highlighting the ways religion and spirituality have influenced US oil culture while simultaneously outlining the ways oil has infused the landscape of Christianity in twentieth- and twenty-first-century US petro-religious scholarship sheds light on the commonly unconscious and often unexamined affective, intellectual, economic, and institutionalized alliances between oil and religion in the United States. These under-analyzed alliances continue to inform US attitudes, values, practices, and public policy around energy and environment.

Petro-religious studies are also making important academic contributions. Environmental humanities scholarship introduces new methodologies and critical perspectives that have not been fully explored by or integrated into religion and ecology studies. And while the historical convergences of oil and religion have generally been overlooked among religion and ecology and religious energy ethics scholars, they have also gone widely unexamined within energy humanities and early petroculture studies. Consequently, petro-religious studies fill a religious gap in environmental humanities scholarship and an environmental humanities gap in religious (both religion and ecology as well as religious environmental ethics) scholarship.

Further Reading and Online Resources

LeMenager S. (2014), *Living Oil: Petroleum Culture in the American Century*, New York: Oxford University Press.

Szeman I. and D. Boyer, eds. (2017), *Energy Humanities: An Anthology*, Baltimore: Johns Hopkins University Press.

Szeman I. and Petrocultures Research Group (2016), *After Oil*, Edmonton, AB: Petrocultures Research Group.

Wilson S., A. Carlson, and I. Szeman, eds. (2017), *Petrocultures: Oil, Energy and Culture*, Montreal: McGill-Queen's University Press.

References

Ahlstrom S.E. (1972), *A Religious History of the American People*, New Haven, CT: Yale University Press.

Boyer D. and I. Szeman (2017), *Energy Humanities: An Anthology*, Baltimore: Johns Hopkins University Press.

Caterine D. (2014), "The Haunted Grid: Nature, Electricity, and Indian Spirits in the American Metaphysical Tradition," *Journal of the American Academy of Religion*, 82 (2): 371–97.

Cobb J.B. (1995), *Is It Too Late?: A Theology of Ecology*, rev. edn., Denton, TX: Environmental Ethics Books.

Dochuk D. (2012), "Blessed by Oil, Cursed with Crude: God and Black Gold in the American Southwest," *Journal of American History*, 99 (1) (June): 51–61.

Dochuk D. (2019), *Anointed with Oil: How Christianity and Crude Made Modern America*, New York: Basic Books.

Eaton S.J.M. (1866), *Petroleum: A History of the Oil Region of Venango County, Pennsylvania*, Philadelphia: J.P. Skelly & Co.

Hessel D.T., ed. (1979), *Energy Ethics: A Christian Response*, New York: Friendship Press.

Holm P. et al. (2015), "Humanities for the Environment—A Manifesto for Research and Action," *Humanities*, 4: 977–92.

Keller C. (2021), *Now Facing Apocalypse: Climate, Democracy and Other Last Chances*, New York: Orbis.

Koster H.P. and E.M. Conradie (2020), *T&T Clark Handbook of Christian Theology and Climate Change*, New York: Bloomsbury.

McLaurin J.J. (1896), *Sketches in Crude Oil: Some Accidents and Incidents of the Petroleum Development in All Parts of the Globe*, Harrisburg, PA: Published by the author.

Nikiforuk A. (2012), *The Energy of Slaves: Oil and the New Servitude*, Vancouver: Greystone Books.

Peppard C.Z., J. Watts Belser, E. Lothes Biviano, and J.B. Martin-Schramm (2016), "What Powers US?: A Comparative Religious Ethics of Energy Sources, Power, and Privilege," *Journal of the Society of Christian Ethics*, 35 (1): 3–25.

Pietsch B.M. 2013. "Lyman Stewart and Early Fundamentalism," *Church History*, 82 (3): 617–46.

Sabin P. (1999), "'A Dive into Nature's Great *Grab-bag'*: Nature, Gender and Capitalism in the Early Pennsylvania Oil Industry," *Pennsylvania History*, 66 (4): 472–505.

Rowe, T. S. (2023), *Of Modern Extraction: Experiments in Critical Petro-theology*, New York: T&T Clark, Bloomsbury.

Tuveson E.L. (1968), *Redeemer Nation: The Idea of America's Millennial Role*, Chicago: University of Chicago Press.

Zuck R.R. (2014), "The Wizard of Oil: Abraham James, the Harmonial Wells, and the Psychometric History of the Oil Industry," in R. Barrett and D. Worden (eds.), *Oil Culture*, 19–42, Minneapolis: University of Minnesota Press.

Glossary Terms

Dispensational premillennialism
Dispensationalism refers to a belief that God has divided history into different eras characterized by different ways God chooses to deal with humanity and particular divine aims for each time period. Premillennialism refers to a belief in Christ's imminent return to begin his thousand-year rule (millennium).

National Council of Churches A US Christian ecumenical organization with thirty-eight member bodies including Protestant, Anglican, Orthodox, historic African American, and Evangelical denominations. The organization began in the early twentieth century as the Federal Council of Churches in response to economic and racial justice concerns. The organization remains active into the twenty-first century as a way for diverse US Christian denominations to work together publicly on issues of social concern while seeking greater unity and mutual understanding between the partner denominations.

Petroculture The humanistic and cultural impact of fossil fuels on a society or the interconnections of multiple societies around petroleum. Petroculture analysis examines the ways that petroleum influences not just industrial infrastructure and technological aspects of a society, but has shaped basic philosophical concepts, worldviews, common ideals, values, beliefs, and gender norms, racialized distinctions, aesthetics from high art culture and design to pop culture. Petroculture studies and the Energy Humanities are overlapping branches of the Environmental Humanities, which focuses on cultural or humanistic aspects of environmental problems, emphasizing that alongside the sciences the humanities disciplines have key insights to offer on environmental issues such as climate change.

Progressive millennialism The belief that human history is aiming toward divine redemption. It is characterized by optimism about human capacity, often in concert with divine agency, to make progressive improvements and work toward divine aims of salvation for all creation. Also referred to as postmillennialism.

16

Is Extinction Religious?

Willis Jenkins

The great dwindling and unwinding of nonhuman life that is sometimes called "mass extinction" may not, on first consideration, seem a religious matter. Named in reference to precedents long before humans existed, this sixth mass extinction seems to be an event unanticipated in any of the human stories and traditions that arose in the late *Holocene*. Moreover, because it does not seem to imperil humans as acutely as climate change, extinction does not receive nearly the same attention from major religious communities and representatives.

And yet, the lexicon of religion often appears in discussion of mass extinction. Reference to "apocalypse" is especially prevalent. An ancient Christian term for a revelation of how God will transform the world, in popular discourse the apocalypse is nearly always a catastrophic end. In writing about mass extinction, it refers to how humans are bringing a catastrophic end to other species and communities of life. Recent papers on declining animal numbers refer to an "insect apocalypse" or "amphibian apocalypse," and the adjective "apocalyptic" is commonly used to convey the magnitude of fear or doom that the writer perceives. Writers seem drawn to the genre of apocalyptic as more than a synonym for cataclysmic change; it names a cluster of feeling and evaluation.

One does not have to be religious in any conventional way to experience mass extinction as apocalyptic. One may share in the feelings and responses of witnessing the end of days for communities of earthly life and find that the best available concept for it is "apocalyptic." The knots of grief, responsibility, anger, helplessness might come together in other ways analogous to historically religious clusters: mourning in need of ritual observance, damning judgment upon those empires causing the diminishment, incurment of existential debt, or wrongdoing that requires propitiation. Even if people do not believe in divine judges or karmic debt or propitiating rites, the religious precedents may seem appropriate to interpreting mass extinction.

In other words, mass extinction may evoke the density of mood and scale of interpretation common to religion. Different kinds of time collide here as so many evolutionary lines of life come to an end in the short space of cultural history that it becomes a geological event, marked as one of a few in the billions of years of Earth's history. Mass extinction seems to beg for cosmological interpretation. Wonder about the story and purpose of the planet, and of humans, seems appropriate. Questions about the visions and values organizing the most powerful politics may make one uneasy or angry, and therefore motivated to find alternative sources of values.

But isn't religion really about beliefs, group identities, scriptures? The theorist Donovan Schaefer argues that religion is not only about texts and beliefs but also "about *the way things feel*, the things we want, the way our bodies are guided through thickly textured, magnetized worlds" (2014: 4; my emphasis). On that view, it matters less what subjects say they believe, or how they identify with groups; religion has to do with affect: "the flow of forces through bodies outside of, prior to, or underneath language" (4). Schaeffer's opening example is an ecstatic response to a waterfall by chimpanzees, whose dancing and excitement he takes to exemplify the way environments can evoke affective response that may be seen as proto-religious. The recognized religions of human history are made possible by those feelings, argues Schaeffer, and usually develop practices to work with them.

Consider mass extinction as something like the opposite of a waterfall: a dread phenomenon of death and world-ending. Inasmuch as this different form of ecological falling evokes proto-religious affective response, practices from recognized religious traditions could possibly offer resources for naming and working with the felt experience of extinction. For example, Nancy Menning (2017) examines mourning rituals from West African Dagara, Tibetan Buddhism, Shi'ite Islam, and Judaism to develop rituals appropriate to mourning extinction. Such adaptations must beware the perils of appropriation, of distortion and disrespect; yet that kind of search for rituals appropriate to extinction indicate the cultural stress and inarticulacy here. The diminishment of life's swarming *feels* like the kind of problem that religious traditions were constructed to address.

If we think of mass extinction in that way, as the kind of cultural event with dimensions that feel religious, then the recognized religious traditions may offer needed vocabularies (Swinarski 2017). Working with those inheritances, one might name many more ways to think and feel about mass extinction: negligence of a trust, apocalyptic anticipation, compassionate identification with nonhuman life, incitement of hungry ghosts, annihilation of nonhuman peoples, lamentation for wrongdoing, atonement for sin, alienation from the sacred, flouting of original instructions, hope in resurrection, Mother Earth's anger, Creator's punishment, desecration, failed obligations to one's kin, withdrawal of relatives, and more. Opened to religion, extinction evokes worlds of affect.

That list is of course full of contradiction and friction. Religious interpretations of mass extinction are not likely to tutor the same feelings or converge on a policy. However, the very proliferation might open cultural space for recognizing how significant is this moment for human ways of being with Earth. Where the imperatives of contemporary economies require not noticing the dwindling of nonhuman life, or where premises of

FIGURE 16.1 *1556 painting by Aurelio Luini of the story of Noah's Ark from the book of Genesis.* Source: *Wikimedia Commons.*

modern law in settler societies require not acknowledging reciprocal responsibilities with nonhuman persons, then religious expressions can have the irruptive effect of invoking alternative moral worlds. Religious thought may offer nonmodern *cosmovisions* through which to interpret relations of Earth. Indeed, in the few political movements to directly address mass extinction, scholars observe implicit and explicit religious behaviors, from multiple traditions and new inventions, coming together in a shared space (Skrimshire 2019). Religion, it seems, helps them give expression to what is happening.

While the multiplicity may not converge on a single interpretation, the proliferation can contribute to this consequence: in the turn to religion, modern *settler colonialism* is confronted, called to accountability by realms of otherwise possibility. Where Indigenous cosmovisions enter into this space, the confrontation is intensified. For what settler people describe as "non-human extinctions" often involves the unravelling of Indigenous relations, ways of life in which those "other" species are known as kin, involved in reciprocal relations and mutual responsibilities (Mitchell 2016). Moreover, as Kyle Powys Whyte (2017) observes, many Indigenous peoples have already lived through apocalypse in several versions, and are already imagining and constructing future worlds with their more-than-human relations.

Could the multiplicity of imagination and affect around extinctions give rise to new religious futures? With a different model of religion, it may be possible to see that already happening. Political theorist William Connolly (2017) suggests the possibility of a "politics of swarming." While the actions available to individuals and collectives may not seem adequate to a planetary crisis, if people experiment with fitting patterns of interaction, they might begin to flock together with other experiments, each free and yet collectively a swarm of response. If we suppose that religious responses to extinction include senses of care and reciprocity, moods of love and mourning, practices of attentiveness and interpretation, then religious response to mass extinction, I am suggesting, might be understood on the model of swarming. Imagine religions as "lines of flight," suggests Whitney Bauman, to bring into view forms of meaning-making that emerge from planetary relations and attempt to "move life into ever new and creative ways of becoming" (2014: 10). Now imagine those lines of flight converging, influencing one another, moving together as a swarm.

Mass extinction may be thought of as proto-religious phenomenon, I am suggesting, and new religious formations may be taking shape—however disparately, faintly, contradictorily—in ways not yet understood as new assemblies or tradition. On this view of religion and extinction, the deepest and most important conflicts do not stand between the identified "world religions" but rather those questions run through them. Does one move with those who care or those who are indifferent? How is the dying or fraying meshwork of life felt in one's body? How is loving attentiveness sustained amidst dwindling?

Acknowledgments

This chapter reproduces with permission some material from Willis Jenkins, "Loving Swarms: Religious Ethics Amidst Mass Extinctions," in Jeremy H. Kidwell and Stefan Skrimshire (eds.), *Religion and Extinction* (Bloomington: Indiana University Press, 2023).

Further Reading and Online Resources

Heise U.K. (2016), *Imagining Extinction: The Cultural Meanings of Endangered Species*, Chicago: University of Chicago Press.

O'Brien K.J. (2010), *An Ethics of Biodiversity: Christianity, Ecology, and the Variety of Life*, Washington, DC: Georgetown University Press.

Skrimshire S. and J. Kidwell (2021), *Religion and Extinction*, Bloomington: Indiana University Press.

Syons K. and B. Garlick (2020), "Geographies of Extinction," special issue, *Environmental Humanities*, 12 (1). Available online: https://read.dukeupress.edu/environmental-humanities/issue/12/1 (accessed March 14, 2021).

Links to Datasets

Brondizio E. S., J. Settele, S. Díaz, and H. T. Ngo, eds. (2019), *Global Assessment Report on Biodiversity and Ecosystem Services of the Intergovernmental Science-Policy Platform on Biodiversity and Ecosystem Services*. Bonn, Germany: IPBES secretariat. https://doi.org/10.5281/zenodo.3831673

Intergovernmental Science-Policy Platform on Biodiversity and Ecosystem Services (IPBES), Available online: https://www.ipbes.net/assessing-knowledge (accessed March 14, 2021).

International Union for Conservation of Nature and Natural Resources Red List, Available online: https://www.iucnredlist.org/ (accessed March 14, 2021).

IPBES (2019), Global Assessment Report on Biodiversity and Ecosystem Services of the Intergovernmental Science-Policy Platform on Biodiversity and Ecosystem Services, E.S. Brondizio, J. Settele, S. Díaz, and H.T. Ngo (edS.), Bonn, Germany: IPBES secretariat, 1148 pages. https://doi.org/10.5281/zenodo.3831673

References

Bauman W.A. (2014), *Religion and Ecology: Developing a Planetary Ethic*, New York: Columbia University Press.

Connolly W.E. (2017), *Facing the Planetary: Entangled Humanism and the Politics of Swarming*, Durham, NC: Duke University Press.

The Editors (2019), "The Extinction of Whales, Birds, and Other Creatures that Once Praised God," *The Christian Century*, May 20. Available online: https://www.christiancentury.org/article/editors/extinction-whales-birds-and-other-creatures-once-praised-god (accessed March 14, 2021).

Menning N. (2017), "Environmental Mourning and the Religious Imagination," in A. Cunsolo and K. Landman (eds.), *Mourning Nature: Hope at the Heart of Ecological Loss and Grief*, 39–63, Montreal: McGill-Queen's Press.

Mitchell A. (2016), "Beyond Biodiversity and Species: Problematizing Extinction," *Theory, Culture & Society*, 33 (5): 23–42.

Schaeffer D. (2014), *Religious Affects: Animality, Evolution, and Power*, Durham, NC: Duke University Press.

Skrimshire S. (2019), "Extinction Rebellion and the New Visibility of Religious Protest," *Open Democracy*, May 12. Available online: https://www.opendemocracy.net/en/transformation/extinction-rebellion-and-new-visibility-religious-protest/ (accessed May 12, 2019).

Swinarski C. (2017), "When We Lose Endangered Species, We Lose God's Creation," *America Magazine*, August 29. Available online: https://www.americamagazine.org/politics-society/2017/08/29/when-we-lose-endangered-species-we-lose-gods-creation (accessed August 29, 2017).

Whyte K. (2017), "Our Ancestors' Dystopia Now: Indigenous Conservation and the Anthropocene," in U.K. Heise, J. Christensen, and M. Niemann (eds.), *The Routledge Companion to the Environmental Humanities*, 206–15, London: Taylor & Francis.

Glossary Terms

Cosmovisions Particular worldviews or ways of making sense of the universe, around which societies are formed. The term cosmovision often refers to Indigenous worldviews, particularly Mesoamerican worldviews.

Holocene The present geological epoch, which began about 11,650 years ago. It is the epoch that follows the Pleistocene epoch. The Holocene began after the last glacial period.

Settler colonialism A type of colonialism where Indigenous populations are replaced or suppressed through domination by settlers for the invading group to claim the land and resources of Indigenous communities.

17

Animals and Religion

Laura H. Hobgood

What do animals and religion have to do with each other? After all, religion is just about and for humans, right? Are all animals included in religions or just some animals? Do some religions respect or think about animals while others do not?

These are just some of the many questions that are often posed when considering the broad topic of animals and religion. Many people grew up in the various religions in North America without ever pondering animals, at least animals other than humans (since humans are, indeed, animals). But other people think about animals in relationship to or as part of their religions with some frequency. Still other people who are not part of a "traditional" religion (such as *Judaism*, Buddhism, *Christianity*, Native or Indigenous traditions, etc.) or consider themselves secular or non-religious might experience connections to animals that border on being sacred in some way. Following a brief history of the complicated, intertwined lives of humans and animals, a few examples from different traditions and from the secular world will be examined as this chapter explores the various ways that animals and religion intersect, or do not intersect, in North America.

The Field of Animals and Religion

The subfield of "Animals and Religion" is quite interdisciplinary and exists at the intersection of several other fields including History of Religions, Philosophy, Critical Animal Studies, and to a lesser extent, Ethology (or Animal Behavior). "Animals and Religion" is also sometimes considered a subfield of the broader field of "Religion and Nature," but the two fields do not overlap completely and "Animals and Religion" is not contained completely within that broader field of "Religion and Nature." Arguably the most important intersecting field is "Critical Animal Studies." This relatively new area of research and teaching is defined variously and is still under significant theoretical and methodological formation. According to the Institute for Critical Animal Studies, the field is:

> rooted in animal liberation and anarchism, is an international intersectional transformative holistic theory-to-action activist led based scholarly think-tank to unapologetically examine, explain, be in solidarity with, and be part of radical and revolutionary actions, theories, groups and movements for total liberation and to dismantle all systems of domination and oppression, in hopes for a just, equitable, inclusive, and peaceful world.
>
> (Institute for Critical Animal Studies 2021)

Some who count themselves as working within the field would not include such an activist component in the definition, thus that aspect continues to be debated with some intensity. Even the naming of the field is debated with some preferring "*Human-Animal Studies*" and constructing it differently. Margo de Mello suggests this definition for human-animal studies: "The study of the intersections and relationships between human and nonhuman animals" (2012: 5). De Mello, and some others, actually distinguishes between these various subfields and describes them differently.

Regardless, there is a radical component to animal studies since it does place animals at the center, a deviation even from the study of animals in the natural sciences, which is frequently looking at animals to learn about humans (for instance, in medical research, comparative psychology, ecology, etc.). Indeed, many of the first works in the area did include such a radical, ethical component. Peter Singer's *Animal Liberation*, published first in 1975, is widely recognized as the founding ethical and philosophical statement of the animal rights movement. The 1980s saw the growth of a significant contribution from ecofeminists, including Harriet Ritvo's *The Animal Estate* (1987) and Donna Haraway's *Primate Visions* (1989). This growth of what would come to be known as "Critical Animal or Human-Animal Studies" contributed significantly to the founding of the more specific field of animals and religion. Though it bears keeping in mind that this mushrooming field is still a contested one and, as Wolfe wrote, "trying to give an overview of the burgeoning area known as animal studies is, if you'll permit me the expression, a bit like herding cats" (2009: 564).

Animals in Religion Scholarship and Pedagogy

In religion scholarship, animals formally entered the picture in the last decade of the twentieth century. Though some historians of religion and theologians had studied them before that time and a series of scholarly pieces emerged starting in the 1970s, the official "Animals and Religion" group of the American Academy of Religion met for the first time in 1998. Then, following and drawn from a major conference on Animals and Religion in 1999, the edited volume *A Communion of Subjects: Animals in Religion, Science, and Ethics* was published. It was a major effort with contributions from over forty-five scholars. Following these events and publications, research into animals and religion expanded dramatically and courses in the subject appeared at increasing rates in college curricula across North America. As stated by Aaron Gross, some of the main issues considered are "the importance of attending to actual animals, the presence of a religious dimension of human-animal relations, the probability that fraught human-animal relationships generate much of what we deem religious, and the manner in which traditional views on animals tend to be conflicted and marked by internal tensions" (2017: 1).

Animal and Animals

Before delving specifically into the role of animals in religions and religious practices in North America, the very word "animal" needs to be considered. What or who does one think of when one hears that word? It is broad ranging indeed and covers myriad living beings with little in common except for the fact that they are not human animals. One could say it is even a gerrymandered category. Animals can be whales or snails, frogs or hogs, bats or cats, a goose or a moose, a shark or a lark, owls or fowls. The range is uncanny. So how does this category of "animal" even work? Psychologist Ken Shapiro frames it this way, human-animal studies is "as incoherent as saying 'carrots and vegetables'" (2008: 7).

And the social construction of animals impacts how humans envision, think, and converse about other animals. A cow, for example, can be divided into parts and called a filet or a hamburger. A chicken can become nuggets, a breast, and wings. Embedded in this construction of animals is the deeply ingrained idea of a human-animal binary, which is based on and continues to promote *speciesism*. This ultimate divide between humans and animals, this speciesism, is one of the main assumptions questioned by animal studies. Just as feminist studies questions the assumed superiority of males over females (and questions those simplistic gender categories) and as race/ethnicity studies interrogates the assumed superiority of white people over people of other races/ethnicities (and, again, questions those categories at all), so does animal studies question speciesism. In doing so animal studies rethinks who animals, and indeed who humans, truly are.

As various religious traditions in North America are considered, it will become apparent that not all religious traditions think of other animals in the same way. It seems that speciesism arose with agriculture and the domestication of animals (with the exclusion of dogs) for agricultural purposes. Pastoral societies and hunter/gatherer cultures tend to have a different spiritual/cultural/religious relationship with other animals, as at least one of our examples below will illustrate. And these religious relationships with animals are in constant flux, as are relationships with different species of other animals. But it is imperative to keep in mind that the term "animal" itself is quite problematic.

Animals in Indigenous North American Traditions

There are literally dozens of Indigenous traditions spread throughout North America and they are quite varied. This study will look at two of these traditions to give a sense of some of the specificities within them and to give something of a broader overview of the relationship of humans with other animals: *Yup'ik* Eskimos (Southwestern Alaska) and *Buffalo* People (Northern Plains). At present the Yup'ik of the Yukon-Kukokwim delta are "the largest indigenous group still occupying their traditional lands, speaking their native language, and living a subsistence lifestyle" (Kuntz 2007: 14). For the purposes of this piece, the Intertribal Bison Cooperative, made up of sixty-nine tribes over nineteen states, is the basis for those included among the contemporary Buffalo People. Ellam Yua, Spirit of the Universe or Unseen One, "gave life to the Yupiit [...] as well as to all the animals who live on the land or in the water" (Ayunerak et al. 2014: 92). Yup'ik Inuit culture considers animals as persons and the relationship between humans and other animals is central both for spiritual and subsistence purposes. As stated by Ann Fienup-Riordan: "The on-going relationship between humans and animals is central to the Yup'ik view of the world. For the Yupiit, society included both human and nonhuman members. They extended personhood beyond the human domain and attributed it to animals as well" (2001: 543).

The Yup'ik believe that "each person and animal has a spirit given to it [...] and [...] inhabit a sentient world infused with spirit" (Ayunerak et al. 2014: 94). Ellam Yua is the one who granted a similar to spirit to all beings. Because of this there are also very particular rules that must be followed in relationship with other animals (particularly those you hunt or fish) to show them due respect. If one does not maintain these signs of respect, the animals could choose not to come back. Thus, animals are believed to have agency in their relationship with humans. For example, just as humans would select where and what to hunt, a hunter's success was dependent on the fact that animals control their own destinies. So, "when they are treated in ways they do not like, they do not return:"

> All the animals or birds decrease or increase when they want to. Although many are killed, they increase again. Many years ago we used to kill many geese. Geese don't decrease to extinction, they become plentiful again when they want to. Even the mink or any living creature that lives on the land decreases and increases when they want to.
>
> (Fienup-Riordan 2001: 544)

In addition, animals are central to Yup'ik ritual. Various masks were made to honor animal spirits, sometimes honoring an animal that had already been caught, other times requesting the spirit of an animal who was going to be hunted (Ayunerak et al. 2014: 97). The dances and masks were also considered a way to "maintain harmony between the human, animal, and supernatural realms for the coming year" (Metropolitan Museum of Art n.d.).

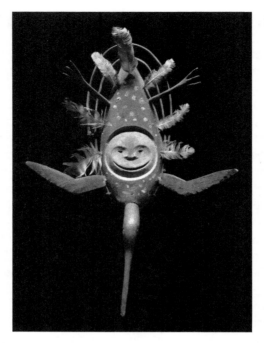

FIGURE 17.1 *Yup'ik ceremonial mask.* Source: *Universal History Archive/Getty Images.*

Of course, Yup'ik life changed significantly in the last half of the twentieth century and continues to change because of the impacts of global warming. Many Yup'ik youth no longer learn the traditional languages, particularly since Christian missionaries ran many of the schools. Hunting technologies mean that dog teams and kayaks are no longer needed so the relationship with animals and subsistence hunting are very different. As one Yup'ik elder stated, "Our disrespect of the animals and the environment where we pursue our food has led to our becoming wasteful of life" (Ayunerak et al. 2014: 99). But the Yup'ik are responding by reinvigorating traditional ways of living and oftentimes these still include recognizing the spirit of animals. For example, one very interesting adapted ritual that is used for suicide prevention encourages younger people to "think about the way of the musk ox." The adults encircle the children who have come for protection, "just as the musk ox do with their young to protect them" (100). And, since hunting (though it has changed) is still a primary part of Yup'ik survival, the belief that animals are guests and have spirits, just as do humans, is very much central to their worldview.

Buffalo People have a complicated, frequently tragic and violent, history with white people in the United States. Throughout the second half of the nineteenth century it was official US Army and government policy to try to wipe out the buffalo of the great plains to wipe out Native Americans as well. In 1875, after almost forty million buffalo had been slaughtered on the North American plains, General Philip Sheridan, Commander of the Armies of the West, made these remarks at the Texas legislature:

> These men (the buffalo hunters) have done [...] more to settle the vexed Indian question than the entire regular army has done in the last thirty years. They are destroying the Indians' commissary [...]. Send them powder and lead if you will, but for the sake of lasting peace let them kill, skin, and sell until the buffalo are exterminated. Then your prairie can be covered with the speckled cattle and the festive cowboy who follows the hunter as the second forerunner of an advanced civilization.
>
> (LaDuke 1999: 141)

In many ways, this horrific policy was effective as numerous humans were also slaughtered or lost their lifeways with the demise of the buffalo. By the end of the nineteenth century, white hunters and settlers had killed over fifty million buffalo and taken tens of millions of acres of tribal land. Shockingly, at the turn of the century, there were only twenty-six buffalo left in the United States and approximately five hundred in Canada (LaDuke 1999: 149).

Indeed, historically buffalo were central to the lives of myriad tribes of Native North Americans spanning from Texas to Canada and from the Mississippi River to the Rocky Mountains. Not only were they a primary source of sustenance for everything from clothing to food to housing, but they were also a grounding source of ceremony and belief structures. "Buffalo Bull was the spirit master and chief of the Buffalo People" (Posthumus 2017: 389). The all-important Buffalo Kill Ceremony, which communicated the inherent respect and relationship between the human and the buffalo, was one of the most revered moments in the spiritual lives of the buffalo people.

For most of the Plains Indians, there is a conviction that all life forms are sacred and are related. As a matter of fact they understand humans to be the "younger brothers" of other peoples. In describing nineteenth-century beliefs, Vine Deloria, a member of the Standing Rock Sioux, states that "American Indians" understood "that the universe consisted of living entities" and they were "interested in learning how other forms of life behaved, for they saw that every entity had a personality and could exercise a measure of free will and choice. Consequently, Indian people carefully observed phenomena in order to determine what relationships existed between and among the various 'peoples' of the world" (Posthumus 2017: 386).

But the buffalo were not only sacred "big brothers" and a major source of sustenance but also the makers of the great prairie lands. As LaDuke states, "buffalo determine landscapes" (1999: 143). Monoculture dominates this same huge ecosystem now with millions of cattle and pigs, fences, industrialized crops (corn and soy) where once there had been amazing species diversity. Buffalo made that species diversity possible for complex reasons. Without them, other Indigenous species plummeted in number.

FIGURE 17.2 *Bison at Ekvn-Yefolecv. Photograph courtesy of Ekvn-Yefolecv.org—ekvn-yefolecv.org.*

For all of these reasons, in the late twentieth and early twenty-first centuries, a collective of tribes is working to bring the buffalo back to the great plains. The Intertribal Buffalo Council (ITBC) states its purpose: "Restoring Buffalo to Indian Country, to preserve our historical, cultural, traditional, and spiritual relationship for future generations" (ITBC 2019). The ITBC was officially founded in 1992 and its work has not been easy. But as of 2020 the herd is thriving and the Buffalo people, both the human ones and the bison ones, are once again becoming a central part of religious culture in North America.

North American Blessings of Animals

Every January 17 on the feast day of Saint Anthony Abbott, Mexican animals get their blessing. This tradition was established by Franciscan monks and priests during the colonial period and it has retained its popularity, with a few twists. Congregants arrive at the Catholic churches dressed in their best Sunday attire. But it is not only the human congregants who wear fancy clothing, they have often dolled up their pets as well. The selection of this particular saint's day is because Saint Anthony Abbott, a fourth-century

Christian from Egypt, is the patron saint of animals and has been understood as such since early medieval times. In his iconography, Saint Anthony is usually accompanied by a pig, a rooster, or a dog. Churches in Rome, Italy, also recognize this saint's day with animal blessings every January.

People gather at Mexico City's Metropolitan Cathedral to pray for the health and well-being of these important members of their families. They also gather in other cities throughout Mexico, including Zapopan, Oaxaca. Usually a priest will splash the dogs, guinea pigs, cats, iguanas, birds, goats, horses, and even cows with holy water as part of the ceremony.

Churches across the United States and Canada celebrate similar blessings, though on a different day. The Saturday and Sunday closest to October 4, the Feast of Saint Francis, is when these blessings occur in Catholic, Episcopalian, and Protestant churches. Though the number varies annually, there are as many as five hundred or more of these blessings across the two countries, and that is likely an underestimate since there is no official tally. Amelie Wilmer suggests why these blessings have become increasingly important in North American culture, particularly in the United States:

> As human families become smaller, animals often become significant sources of affection and intimacy. Some people feel a spiritual dimension in that bond—one that religion has traditionally not recognized. Animal blessings provide a way to affirm and sanctify this experience, renewing a religious interest in ancient traditions where animals held a revered position.
>
> (2019: 280)

One of the most spectacular is the Blessing of the Pets at the Cathedral of St. John the Divine in New York City. For well over thirty years, this has been an annual celebration. Thousands of people and pets line up in front of the church early in the morning to await entry. The cathedral is usually full to overflowing for the high Eucharistic service. Amazingly the animals (the majority of whom are dogs) all get along very well as they sit under or on the pews with their people. The service comes to a dramatic conclusion, as described by the author in one of her books:

> The final event of the formal liturgy is "The Living Earth: Opening of the Great Bronze Door and the Silent Procession." At the entrance to the sanctuary stand two massive bronze doors. According to the dean, these doors are only opened three times a year: Christmas, Easter, and the Procession of the Animals [...]. The congregation was asked to remain silent and not take flash photographs in order to keep the animals in the procession safe and calm. A camel, adorned with a wreath on her hump, an eagle, a beehive, two llamas, and many more animals moved into the sanctuary through the bronze doors and gathered at the altar.
>
> (Hobgood-Oster 2009: 114–15)

FIGURE 17.3 *Blessing of animals, First Christian Church, Alexandria, Virginia. Photograph by the author.*

The animals were all blessed with words attributed to Saint Clare: "Live without fear: your Creator loves you, made you holy and has always protected you. Go in peace to follow the good road and may God's blessing be with you always." Outside in the park on the church grounds, each animal could also receive an individual blessing.

This spectacular blessing of the pets motivated others to follow their example. For instance, after the death of her bulldog Buddy twenty years ago, a member of the Catholic Church of the Redeemer in Calgary, started the tradition in that Canadian city. She was "inspired by the video I saw once from Saint John the Divine Cathedral in New York. It's an extravaganza, unbelievable [...] I thought it would be really nice to have something like that here" ("Calgary Church Welcomes Pets for Blessing of the Animals" 2016).

Animal blessings also happen in Mexico. One of the oldest recorded *blessings of animals* in Mexico (though part of it is now in Los Angeles, so officially in the United States) is the annual Olvera Street Blessing. This area of contemporary Los Angeles was once part of Mexico, originally developed by Indigenous people and then Spanish settlers. The Olvera Street blessing takes place on the Sunday before Easter most years and is still a central part of Mexican-American culture there. It has melded with Catholic blessings of animals and the archbishop of Los Angeles frequently participates.

FIGURE 17.4 *Blessing of animals, First Christian Church, Alexandria, Virginia. Photograph by the author.*

In addition, there are animal blessings connected to Dia de los Muertos in Mexico with shrines erected to animal spirits.

These various blessings of animals invite animals back into the sanctuary. For centuries animals were (and are) in the sanctuary of Christian churches. Sometimes they are found in the artwork, other times they entered to literally "take sanctuary" in Europe, when cathedrals were also fortresses, and with the influence of Saint Francis of Assisi they entered as part of Nativity celebrations at Christmas. Now with many blessings of animals emerging, they have returned to the Christian sanctuaries in North America.

But animal blessings in North America are not confined to Christian communities. At Temple Isaiah in Los Angeles, Cantor Evan Kent decided to introduce a blessing of animals to his congregation. After an interesting encounter with his cat, Merlin, on Shabbat one evening, Kent described his decision to improvise this blessing: "May you be blessed to be all the cat that you are capable of, and may you always know you have a warm safe home with plenty of food and a comfortable place to sleep" (2019). Kent and the rabbis at the temple then created together a communal blessing to accompany the Torah reading of the story of Noah.

And it is not just at Temple Isaiah, blessings of animals in conjunction with Parshat Noah are becoming increasingly common. Since 2001 Rabbi Eddie Sukol has been leading blessing ceremonies for his congregation. He initially started this as a way of connecting elementary age children in his Hebrew school to blessings and then expanded it to his congregation. For quite some time Sukol, who was serving in Ohio, was unaware of other such blessings but eventually found congregations in Michigan, New York, California, and Florida who were doing the same (Meiser 2013).

While blessings of animals in religious settings have sometimes been critiqued, scholars who study the history and sacred texts in these traditions raise valid points about the centrality of animals that tends to support such ceremonies. For example, Richard Kool argues that there "is a rich literature within the Jewish tradition, both from biblical exegesis and Talmudic and Midrashic commentary, of concern for animals" (2010: 83) and, in my research, it becomes clear that animals "surround Jesus at his birth, he spends forty days in the wilderness with the wild beasts, he tells parables articulating God's care for the birds of the air, he instructs his followers to break the rules of the Sabbath in order to pull a sheep from a pit" (Hobgood-Oster 2010: 5). Blessings of pets seem to be quite appropriate and seem to be growing in popularity.

Animals in the Religion of Market Capitalism

Arguably, the religion of *market capitalism* dominates the interconnected cultures and economies of North America. In his seminal article, David Loy concludes that "the market is not just an economic system but a religion, yet not a very good one" (1997: 289). Unfortunately in this, probably the single most all-encompassing religion of North America, animals do not fare well (neither do many humans). All animals are commodified from those who are pets to those who are food to those who are still living in the few remaining wild areas. Granted, there are exceptions such as the bison cooperative and some who consider animal rights as a religion, but they are few and far between.

Furthermore, in the midst of market capitalism as a religion, animals are considered as food (though it is certainly not the only place in this economics-religion that animals are consumed). In the United States alone, according to the United States Department of Agriculture (USDA), over ninety-four million cattle and calves were in feedlots or on ranches in January of 2020 (USDA 2020). Pigs, chickens, turkeys, cows, and other animals are *factory (confined) farmed* throughout North America. Mexico and Canada are also filled with intensive animal agricultural production. For example, in 2018 Mexico recorded 17.2 million pigs in intensive farming productions (Hermida 2019). And, while Canada sometimes denies massive industrial farming, in 2017 the official country statistics reported that "half of all farms that reported pigs held 99.7 percent of the 14.1 million pigs in Canada" ("Livestock in Canada" 2017). Animals are purely commodities in much of North America's primary religious ideology—market capitalism.

As Carol Adams states in her book, *Burger*: "Are we ever just eating? We are consuming interspecies history, environmental history, national history, and gender politics. A hamburger is never just a hamburger, even in a dream. What are we giving ourselves that we do not want?" (2018: 133). So much of religion has to do with what one eats as it points to what one values and how one lives day to day. Examining what we eat and the meaning we give to that food is central to who we are and what we believe. Thus many religious traditions have rituals that include eating. From the Eucharist in the Christian tradition to kosher food in the Jewish tradition to the sacred status of cows in Hinduism to the place of the buffalo or salmon in different Indigenous traditions to fasting during Ramadan in Islam, food is an outward expression of the sacred and religious practices. In the religion of market capitalism, animals are to be consumed and have no inherent value of their own.

Death, Dying, and Companion Animals

The National Institute of Statistics and Geography reported in 2019 that at least 70 percent of households in Mexico have pets, which makes it the second most pet-owning nation in the world ("Mexico is No. 2 in the World for the Most Household Pets" 2019). According to the *2017–2018 AVMA Pet Ownership and Demographics Sourcebook*, over forty-eight million households have dogs and over thirty million have cats (American Veterinary Medical Association [AVMA] 2019). The Canadian Animal Health Institute reports that in 2018 there were 8.3 million cats and 8.2 million dogs in Canadian homes (CAHI). With such a significant presence of pets, and with a decreasing number of households who have human children, these other animals seem to hold an increasingly important place emotionally for humans (Spain et al. 2019).

For thousands of years humans have practiced burial and mourning rituals for dogs and some other animals (Hobgood-Oster 2014: ch. 2). In contemporary culture one of the ways that pets are memorialized on an international scale, including throughout North America, is through the idea of the Rainbow Bridge. Since pets generally live much shorter lives than humans, grieving for them and ritualizing this grief is something that people might experience numerous times throughout their lives. It is a "virtual memorial home and grief support community for your departed fur baby" (Rainbows Bridge 1997–). The poem on the site is translated into a number of languages to help globalize this phenomenon.

There are other ways of memorializing pets as well. Pet cemeteries and cremation services dot the maps of Canada, Mexico, and the United States. The International Association of Pet Cemeteries and Crematoriums lists members in all three countries as well (IAOPCC 2018). Many pet owners retain their pets' ashes in a type of home memorial. In Mexico these memorials can take the form of a traditional home shrine. In his study of death memorials in Mexico City, Marcel Reyes-Cortez describes a young woman who keeps her "late parrot and dogs […] in a flower pot she keeps in her bathroom and carries with her every time she moves." She told him that the "spirits of her animals look after her and are part of her extended family" (2012: 146).

Conclusion

Of course, this is a small sampling of the ways that religion and animals are related in North America. An additional resource is provided by the Humane Society of the United States, which started a Faith Outreach program in the early years of the twenty-first century. Their website includes "Religious Statements on Animals" from a variety of religious groups including Judaism, Buddhism, Christianity, Islam, Hinduism, and Unitarian Universalism. And, within each of these, there are statements from each of a number of more specific variations. For example, under Judaism there are perspectives from Orthodox, Conservative, and Reform traditions.

While there is not space to include them all here, a couple of examples do help to show the wide array of positions. In 2011 Unitarian Universalists approved a statement of conscience on "Ethical Eating: Food and Environmental Justice" that included this statement:

> Ethical eating is the application of our Principles to our food choices. What and how we eat has broad implications for our planet and society. Our values, Principles, and integrity call us to seek compassion, health, and sustainability in the production of food we raise or purchase and end the inhumane treatment of animals.
>
> (Humane Society of the United States 2020)

Included under the statements from Islam are both a list of places where animals are mentioned in the Qur'an and sayings from the Prophet Muhammed.

In sum, there are various ways animals are included in and impacted by religion in North America. Additional considerations of animal rights as a religion, kosher eating in Jewish traditions, halal preparation in Islamic traditions, various pagan or earth-based spiritualities that include animal spirits, and more could be elaborated. It is a rich area of research and practice.

Further Reading and Online Resources

Herzog H. (2010), *Some We Love, Some We Hate, Some We Eat: Why It's so Hard to Think Straight about Animals*, New York: Harper.

Humane Society of the United States (2020), "Facts and Faith." Available online: https://www.humanesociety.org/resources/facts-and-faith (accessed May 2, 2021).

Intertribal Buffalo Council (ITBC) (2019), "Who We Are." Available online: https://itbcbuffalonation.org/ (accessed May 2, 2021).

Nelson R. (1983), *Make Prayers to the Raven: Koyukon View of the Northern Forest*, Chicago: University of Chicago Press.

Rainbows Bridge (1997–), "Welcome to Rainbows Bridge." Available online: https://www.rainbowsbridge.com/ (accessed May 2, 2021).

References

American Vetinary Medical Association (AVMA) (2019), *2017–2018 AVMA Pet Ownership and Demographics Sourcebook*. Available online: https://www.avma.org/sites/default/files/resources/AVMA-Pet-Demographics-Executive-Summary.pdf (accessed June 20, 2020).

Adams C. (2018), *Burger*, New York: Bloomsbury.

Applebaum P. (2015), "Why Blessing Animals Has Become Popular in Recent Decades," *The Christian Century*, October 27.

Ayunerak P., D. Alstrom, C. Moses, J. Charlie Sr., and S. Rasmus (2014), "Yup'ik Culture and Context in Southwest Alaska: Community Member Perspectives of Tradition, Social Change, and Prevention," *American Journal of Community Psychology*, 54: 91–9.

"Calgary Church Welcomes Pets for Blessing of the Animals" (2016), *CBC News*, October 1. Available online: https://www.cbc.ca/news/canada/calgary/blessing-animals-cathedral-church-redeemer-calgary-1.3787846 (accessed June 16, 2020).

Canadian Animal Health Institute (2019), "Latest Canadian Pet Population Figures Released," January 28. Available online: https://www.cahi-icsa.ca/press-releases/latest-canadian-pet-population-figures-released (accessed June 28, 2020).

DeMello M. (2012), *Animals and Society: An Introduction to Human-Animal Studies*, New York: Columbia University Press.

Fienup-Riordan A. (2001), "A Guest on the Table," in J. Grim (ed.), *Indigenous Traditions and Ecology*, 541–58, Cambridge, MA: Harvard University Press.

Humane Society of the United States (2020), "Facts and Faith." Available online: https://www.humanesociety.org/resources/facts-and-faith (accessed June 12, 2020).

Gross A. (2017), "Religion and Animals," in *Oxford Handbook Topics in Religion*, Oxford: Oxford University Press. Available online: https://doi.org/10.1093/oxfordhb/9780199935420.013.10 (accessed November 17, 2023).

Haraway D. (1989), *Primate Visions: Gender, Race, and Nature in the World of Modern Science*. New York: Routledge.

Hermida F. (2019), "Global Market Report Mexico," The Pig Site, March. Available online: https://thepigsite.com/news/2019/04/global-market-report-mexico-march-2019 (accessed July 1, 2020).

Hobgood-Oster L. (2008), *Holy Dogs and Asses: Animals in the Christian Tradition*, Urbana: University of Illinois Press.

Hobgood-Oster L. (2010), *The Friends We Keep: Unleashing Christianity's Compassion for Animals*, Waco, TX: Baylor University Press.

Hobgood-Oster L. (2014), *A Dogs History of the World: Canines and the Domestication of Humans*, Waco, TX: Baylor University Press.

Institute for Critical Animal Studies (2021), "About." Available online: http://www.criticalanimalstudies.org/about/ (accessed June 25, 2020).

International Association of Pet Cemeteries and Crematoriums (IAPCC) (2018), "Member Directory." Available online: https://www.iaopc.com/search/custom.asp?id=5419 (accessed June 20, 2020).

Intertribal Buffalo Council (ITBC) (2019), "Who We Are." Available online: https://itbcbuffalonation.org/ (accessed June 15, 2020).

Kent E. (2019), "How Blessing Our Pets Brought Holiness to Our Community," ReformJudaism.org, October 30. Available online: https://reformjudaism.org/blog/how-blessing-our-pets-brought-holiness-our-community (accessed May 2, 2021).

Kool R. (2010), "Worldviews: Global Religions," *Culture & Ecology*, 14 (1): 83–95.

Kuntz B. (2007), "Hunters in the Garden: Yup'ik Subsistence and the Agricultural Myths of Eden," MA diss., *Graduate Student Theses, Dissertations, and Professional Papers*, 534. Available online: https://scholarworks.umt.edu/etd/534 (accessed May 2, 2021).

LaDuke W. (1999), *All Our Relations: Native Struggles for Land and Life*, Cambridge, MA: South End Press.

Loy D. (1997), "The Religion of the Market," *Journal of the American Academy of Religion*, 65 (2): 275–90.

Magliocco S. (2018), "Beyond the Rainbow Bridge: Vernacular Ontologies of Animal Afterlives," *Journal of Folklore Research*, (May): 39–68.

Meiser R. (2013), "The Rabbi Who Blesses Jewish Pets," *Tablet*, October 10. Available online: https://www.tabletmag.com/sections/news/articles/the-rabbi-who-blesses-jewish-pets (accessed June 20, 2020).

Metropolitan Museum of Art (n.d.), "Dance Mask: Early Twentieth Century, Yup'ik." Available online: https://www.metmuseum.org/art/collection/search/313313 (accessed June 19, 2020).

"Mexico is No. 2 in the World for the Most Household Pets" (2019), *Mexico New Daily*, February 15. https://mexiconewsdaily.com/news/mexico-is-no-2-for-the-most-household-pets/ (accessed June 20, 2020).

"Pets Received Traditional Church Blessing in Mexico" (2016), *Parent Herald*, January 19. Available online: http://www.parentherald.com/articles/16410/20160119/pets-traditional-church-blessing-mexico.htm (accessed June 15, 2020).

Posthumus D. (2017), "All My Relatives: Exploring Nineteenth Century Lakota Ontology and Belief," *Ethnohistory*, 64 (3): 379–400.

Rainbows Bridge (1997–), "Welcome to Rainbows Bridge." Available online: https://www.rainbowsbridge.com/ (accessed May 2, 2021).

Reuters (2007), "Mexican Animals Get Their Blessing," *Banderas News*, October. Available online: http://www.banderasnews.com/0710/nr-petsgetblessing.htm#:~:text=Mexican%20Animals%20Get%20Their%20Blessing&text=Mexicans%20bring%20their%20pets%20to,of%20St%20Anthony%20the%20Abbott.&text=Every%20January%2017%2C%20Mexicans%20celebrate,Mass%20for%20an%20annual%20blessing (accessed June 16, 2020).

Reyes-Cortez M. (2012), "Living with the Dead: Cremating and Reburying the Dead in a Megalopolis," in N. Hinerman and A. Glahn (eds.), *The Presence of the Dead in Our Lives*, 139–64, Amsterdam: Rodopi.

Ritvo H. (1987), *The Animal Estate*, Cambridge, MA: Harvard University Press.

Schwartz R. (2003), "18 Reasons Jews Shouldn't Be Vegetarians (And Why They're Wrong)," *Tikkun*, 18: 3.

Shapiro K. (2008), *Human-Animal Studies: Growing the Field, Applying the Field*, Ann Arbor, MI: Animals and Society Institute.

Spain B., L. O'Dwyer, and S. Moston (2019), "Pet Loss: Understanding Disenfranchised Grief, Memorial Use, and Posttraumatic Growth," *Anthrozoos*, 32 (4): 555–68.

Statistics Canada (2017), "Livestock in Canada," May 24. Available online: https://www150.statcan.gc.ca/n1/pub/11-627-m/11-627-m2017011-eng.htm (accessed June 28, 2020).

United States Department of Agriculture (USDA) (2020), "Cattle," January 31. Available online: https://downloads.usda.library.cornell.edu/usda-esmis/files/h702q636h/rb68xv24k/76537h73d/catl0120.pdf (accessed June 27, 2020).

Waldau P. (2003), "Religion and Animals: A Changing Scene," in D. Salem (ed.), *The State of the Animals II*, 85–98, Washington, DC: Humane Society Press.

Waldau P. and K. Patton, eds. (2006), *A Communion of Subjects: Animals in Religion, Science, and Ethics*, New York: Columbia University Press.

Wilmer A. (2019), "In the Sanctuary of Animals: Honoring God's Creatures through Ritual and Ceremony," *Interpretation: A Journal of Bible and Theology*, 73 (3): 272–87.
Wolfe C. (2009), "Human, All Too Human: 'Animal Studies' and the Humanities," *PMLA*, 124 (2): 564–75.

Glossary Terms

Blessings of animals Rituals that are part of various religious traditions that recognize the significance of, and even the sacredness of, other than human animals.

Buffalo The popular name for *bison bison*, a North American mammal belonging to the same family (Bovidae) as domesticated cattle.

Christianity A monotheistic religious tradition that emerged in the first century CE in the Mediterranean world. At the beginning of the twenty-first century, the various denominations of this tradition counted over 2.4 billion adherents.

Factory farming One of the primary means of the mass production of animals for consumption in the economic system of market capitalism. It requires intensive confined animal feeding operations to produce at the scale necessary for profit.

Human-animal studies An interdisciplinary field of study that critically analyses the relationships between humans and other animals.

Judaism The oldest known monotheistic religious tradition in the world, dating back at least three thousand years. At the beginning of the twenty-first century, this tradition counted over fourteen million adherents.

Market capitalism An economic system in which individuals and corporations are the owners of capital goods, including ownership of other animals.

Speciesism The idea that humans are superior to all other species on Earth and can, therefore, have preference over all other species in terms of needs and wants.

Yup'ik A group of Indigenous people who live in the southwestern area of coastal Alaska and eastern Siberia.

18

Sacred Water of Florida: Ceremony and Spirituality in the Sunshine State

Victoria Machado

Broadly speaking, the water rituals described below and, more specifically, the emphasis on the sacredness of water expresses larger themes of connectivity. Leaders and participants in these rituals view the environment as holistic and they view humanity as one part of what constitutes the natural world. In many ways they are both within the natural world while also recognizing disconnection from it. Identifying such disconnections allows participants to deepen their quest to establish closer ties with the water as they find water impacts every part of life, including their own personal bodies. Such connectivity reinforces holistic understandings of healing. While these rituals occurred on a regular monthly basis on both the east and west coasts of Florida for several years, the blue-green algae that covered Florida's water largely impacted these ceremonies, expanding their reach as people began recognizing the importance and sensitivity of Florida's water.

In 2016, South Florida experienced a series of extensive toxic algae blooms that wreaked havoc on waterways, harming marine life and severely damaging local livelihoods such as water-related tourism, recreation, and fishing. During this time, the blue-green algae bloom, otherwise known as cyanobacteria, proved particularly harmful. Concentrated heavily in Lake Okeechobee, Florida's largest lake, the overwhelming amount of cyanobacteria caused the water to turn slime green accompanied by an overbearing stench.

Common in freshwater, while cyanobacteria date back billions of years, recent human activities have led to compounded amounts, creating lengthy and catastrophic

FIGURE 18.1 *Fueled by fertilizer, sewage, and manure, slime coated the Caloosahatchee River at Cape Coral, Florida, in July 2018. Photograph by John Moran.*

outbreaks. Such was the case in the summer of 2016, when so much cyanobacteria led state officials to declare a state of emergency. By 2017, the blooms nearly covered Lake Okeechobee causing another state of emergency declaration by July 2018. Paired with a red-tide outbreak in the Gulf, the conditions continued to worsen as the cyanobacteria seeped out of the lake through local waterways producing widespread fish and marine kills that plagued both coasts. The compounded *harmful algae blooms* resulted in the loss of more than 400 sea turtles, roughly 200 manatees, over 40 dolphins, and tons of fish.

Humans both caused the problem and were severely impacted by the issue as industry, agriculture, and storm runoff as well as septic tanks and rampant development led to high nutrient loading and an accumulation of bacteria. In turn, such conditions severely impacted tourists and visitors who kept their distance, causing businesses to feel the brunt of the impact in terms of tens of millions of dollars. The sludge that brutally damaged local economies and presented a slew of respiratory problems for

FIGURE 18.2 *At the offices of* Florida Sportsman *magazine in Stuart, staff complaints of headaches and nausea caused by the toxic algae bloom on the adjacent St. Lucie River prompted publisher Blair Wickstrom to temporarily close the office in July 2018. "It smells like death," he said. Photograph by John Moran.*

those living near the water caused many Floridians to realize just how interconnected they are with the natural world.

During the cyanobacteria outbreaks, environmental groups and forums on social media were faced with the task of making sense of this problem in the midst of their work, figuring out how to best take action to clean up the state's most vital resource: its water. While many groups turned to petitions and protests, a handful of individuals turned to prayer.

One such collective began viewing the state's water problems as both a physical and spiritual crisis, approaching this problem through prayer, ritual, and mindfulness. Created in 2014, Kristin Bauer convened the Sacred Water Tribe, a handful of spiritually inclined people praying for the healing of Florida's water. Even prior to the severe 2016 outbreaks, the Sacred Water Tribe recognized the importance of water as they hosted monthly sacred water ceremonies consisting of rituals on beaches, banks of rivers, and dikes of lakes on the east coast. Holding such events in close proximity to water bodies, the group hoped to raise awareness about the sacredness of water while further connecting to the water through positive energy forces to promote healing efforts. The group drew from the power of thoughts and actions to support restoration for both the water and the individual through the creation of a clean, loving, and peaceful planet for future generations. While the ceremonies usually attracted a handful of people, at times some rituals hosted a couple of dozen attendees. The ceremonies eventually found their way to the west coast of Florida, as residents around Fort Myers began hosting similar events.

In South Florida, the sacred water ceremonies draw from *hado* instruction as well as knowledge from Native American elders and a range of other earth-based belief systems to honor and bless the water thereby promoting holistic spiritual healing. This is achieved through collective song, prayer, and reflection as participants send kind words, healing energy, and positive thoughts to the water. The ceremonies seek to promote such energy connections. Key have been the hado teachings of Masaru Emoto, a holistic healer of alternative medicine, known for professing the power of consciousness as best explained through his experiments with water. Emoto stated that water crystals can physically change based on the positive or negative words spoken to them. Sending negative energy causes the water crystals to harmfully change, while sending positive thoughts helps promote clean water. Trained hado instructors who studied under Emoto, such as Bauer, have since brought the practice of healing water and the importance of subtle vibrational energy from Japan to the rest of the world, including Florida.

Prior to the start of such events, an altar composed of sacred materials, often crystals, shells, and stones is established on the sand or on colorful blankets. Such items are arranged in a circular or spiral configuration to make up a *mandala*. The pattern leads to a large vessel filled with water that is placed in the center. The water is usually borrowed from a local body of water and returned at the end of the ceremony. Participants gather in a circular formation around the outside of the mandala. Sometimes crystal bowls or other instrumental sounds commence such gatherings as participants are asked to center themselves by taking a few deep breaths and prepare mentally for the ceremony.

The vibrational nature of sound cultivates a space in which music is a common and important aspect of the rituals. Songs from a range of cultures, often sung in a variety of languages, are usually introduced as call-and-response in an effort to teach the words to newcomers. Some of those more involved with the ceremonies bring musical instruments such as drums, shakers, and other handheld percussion instruments. In some cases, participants pass a drum around the circle, each having a turn at sending prayers with the strike of the drum.

Another shared aspect of the ceremonies is the acknowledgment of the natural world. In the case of the September 2018 Delray Beach gathering, the four cardinal directions were invoked and explained alongside their symbolic meanings. Each direction was paired with other living entities, namely animals, reflecting a particular creature and general stage of life. Such acknowledgments offer honor to life outside the self. Not only are participants asked to orient themselves spatially but also to listen deeply to the natural world. Leaders highlight the songs of birds, feel of the wind, and rush of the water. In some instances, participants are encouraged to place their hands on the ground, recognizing the connection of the self and the earth as similar living beings.

FIGURE 18.3 *A mandala created in the sand at the Sacred Water Tribe ceremony, September 2018. Delray Beach, Florida. Photograph by author.*

FIGURE 18.4 *Adam Ingham calls participants into reflection with the beat of a drum at the Sacred Water Tribe ceremony. Delray Beach, Florida. Photograph by author.*

In between songs and acknowledgments of the natural world is a deep sense of respect and care for the water. Water is viewed as sacred, a source of life, and the lifeblood of Mother Earth. Hado and other similar concepts of positive vibrations and energy are often woven throughout the ceremony as leaders explain the water as an active agent with the capacity to record, store, and transmit information. In this sense, water is viewed as an authoritative living entity, giving it the power to impact and transform the world in which it flows. Similar to many Indigenous worldviews, such *animistic* perspectives create a relational bond between humans and nature, uniting the two in a familial context. In this sense, participants gravitate toward the notion that Mother Earth cares for and loves the human, plant, and animal life within her.

Such ideas follow *Gaia*-like notions of the earth as alive or as mother to all humanity and all life. In many ways, these ceremonies follow the Lakota call, *mni wičoni*, "water is life," which came to the forefront of the 2016 Standing Rock demonstrations. With these viewpoints, it is easy to see why ceremony leaders and participants alike draw parallels between water and the human body, recognizing both the planet and the humans are composed of similar percentages of water (Earth's surface composed of roughly 71 percent water and humans composed of 60–78 percent depending on age). The ceremonies emphasize these connections, providing for meditative silence or silent prayers as participants take a moment to remember their reliance on water for every living process as well as human-nature connections to water.

It is important to keep in mind that a variety of cultures are also acknowledged and often play central roles. This is particularly evident with the emphasis on Native American traditions. Some leaders identify their connections to Native American tribes in other parts of the United States, as they have been adopted into various traditions, in which case, water ceremony leaders ask permission from tribal members to use specific songs or prayers.

Apart from the Sacred Water Tribe, local Indigenous leaders draw from generational wisdom, hosting prayers such as the November 2018 "Healing Our Relationship With Water" held on the dike of Lake Okeechobee, which was cohosted by a Miccosukee grandmother of the Panther Clan, Betty Osceola. Recognizing the water in a feminine lens, Osceola explained that this ceremony looked to heal relationships with water by "understanding water is not the enemy but the victim." In this sense, water is viewed within a familial context, most notably as a mother or sister that has been harmed by humans. In response to such hurt, Osceola listens to the guidance offered by ancestors and the natural world to carry out her ceremonies. Nature guides her. Though these ceremonies are separate, when examined alongside each other, they offer similar connections to music, the natural world, culture, and water. Such ideas tie into the final stage of the two ceremonies in which participants recite *ho'oponopono*, the Hawaiian prayer for forgiveness and reconciliation. A drum beat, often signifying the rhythm of a resting heartbeat begins as one person then picks up the vessel and the water is carefully walked back to the banks or shore, where the water from the vessel is respectfully returned to its source. In January 2019, Osceola hosted a longer seven-day event called the Healing Lake Okeechobee Prayer Walk, which invited participants to journey on a week-long prayer walk around the circumference of Florida's largest lake, measuring roughly 177 kilometers (110 miles). Walking silently in pairs, the prayer walkers were asked to keep their eyes and ears open to messages from the natural world. Staying in two lines, the formation was important as it kept positive energy flowing, thereby honoring the earth and the prayers sent forth. Through both body and mind, the event acknowledged the deep holistic healing needed to reunite human relationships with all the waters that connect all life. As Osceola explained, walkers embark upon a life-altering spiritual reflection as they deepen their relationships with the natural world and emerge as changed people by the end.

Many of the participants of such events do not simply recognize changes in the environment from a spiritual realm but actively seek a more sustainable future through the personal choices they make or the various environmental initiatives in which they are involved. A lot of the participants pursue personal choices as a way of changing the tide—committing to buying organic food and avoiding harsh chemicals for both the sake of their selves and the water/environment. Others are in active conversation with water management districts as they push for more effective policies surrounding water. Still others such as Holley Rauen, founder of the *Pachamama Alliance* of Southwest Florida and cohost of the November 2018 "Healing Our Relationship With Water" ceremony, have sought to further understand the science, undergoing the training to become a local waterkeeper ranger. This particular ceremony also attracted

FIGURE 18.5 *Participants gather by Lake Okeechobee for the "Healing Our Relationship With Water" prayer ceremony in November 2018. John Stretch Memorial Park, Palm Beach County, Florida. Photograph by Lisette Morales.*

FIGURE 18.6 *After the ceremony, water is returned to its source. Happehatchee Center in Estero, Florida. Photograph by Lisette Morales.*

FIGURE 18.7 *Cohosts of the "Healing Our Relationship With Water" prayer ceremony, Betty Osceola (foreground) and Holley Rauen (background). John Stretch Memorial Park, Palm Beach County, Florida. Photograph by Lisette Morales.*

a handful of community advocates and grassroots organizers, who promote clean air and water in their communities through policy changes on both the state and local level. These ceremonies show how people are trying to reconnect to water and how they acknowledge their already existing deep connections.

On a larger level, such efforts to bridge human-nature divides remind participants that they are one part of the natural world. Viewing themselves as one part of a larger ecosystem reminds ceremony participants that it is their duty to care for other members of society including animals, plants, land formations, and ecosystems. Collectively this worldview aims to turn the tide when it comes to understanding once separate human-nature relationships. Such outlooks are not limited to the religious or spiritual realm, as environmental groups in other parts of the state are also advocating for holistic understandings of humans and nature to aid their environmental campaigns.

For example, in April 2019, about a dozen environmentalists met in Orlando to discuss what a Florida Rights of Nature (RON) movement would look like. With help from the Community Environmental Legal Defense Fund (CELDF), the activists joined the global RON movement, which has secured legal rights for ecosystems, rivers, and other nonhuman living species around the United States as well as abroad in Ecuador and New Zealand. Following the larger movement, Florida environmentalists wanted their water sources to be viewed as more than commodities. They wanted water to be legally recognized by granting it the right to exist, flourish, and evolve. Having established grassroots success, the environmentalists met resistance from the state legislature that introduced a bill prohibiting *home rule*. Such bills drastically limit cities and counties from extending local rights to water bodies.

FIGURE 18.8 *In Alachua County, clean water advocates used flyers to spread the word about the local Santa Fe River Rights of Nature campaign. Flyer by John Moran and Rick Kilby.*

Though the RON movement is not necessarily spiritually driven, such initiatives reinforce a different narrative about human-nature interactions, one that upholds holistic views similar to that of the sacred water ceremonies. In both cases, the human-nature narratives act as a way of furthering environmental conversations to encompass both the physical and the spiritual—toward how people view themselves in relation to the world. In this regard, lived narratives have the potential to challenge dominant worldviews thereby laying the foundation for larger environmental change.

Whether it is saltwater intrusion, sea-level rise, drought, red tide, or cyanobacteria, given Florida's growing population, its finite resources, and more specifically its water, these climate-related pressures will continue to experience strain. Considering such entanglements of human-nature interactions can provide a fresh outlook and may help the state further grapple with such climatic impacts. In this sense, the role of lived narratives and how we view our relationship with the water not only expresses religious and spiritual dimensions but also can provide a more holistic outlook for solving future problems concerning the intersection of humans and the natural world.

Further Reading and Online Resources

Community Environmental Legal Defense Fund (CELDF) (2015), "Champion the Rights of Nature." Available online: https://celdf.org/advancing-community-rights/rights-of-nature/ (accessed August 24, 2020).

Perkinson J.W. (2019), *Political Spirituality for a Century of Water Wars: The Angel of the Jordan Meets the Trickster of Detroit*, Cham: Palgrave Macmillan.

Ray C., ed. (2020), *Sacred Waters: A Cross-Cultural Compendium of Hallowed Springs and Holy Wells*, Abingdon, UK: Routledge.

Stone C.D. (2010), *Should Trees Have Standing? Law, Morality, and the Environment*, Oxford: Oxford University Press.

References

Community Environmental Legal Defense Fund (CELDF) (2015), "Common Sense: A Community Rights Organizing 'Primer' from CELDF," June. Available online: https://celdf.org/2015/06/common-sense-a-community-rights-organizing-primer-from-celdf/ (accessed August 29, 2020).

Florida Fish and Wildlife Conservation Commission (2020), "Cyanobacteria in Florida's Waters." Available online: https://myfwc.com/research/redtide/general/cyanobacteria/ (accessed August 24, 2020).

Florida League of Cities (2020), "The History of Home Rule in Florida." Available online: https://www.floridaleagueofcities.com/home-rule-civics-education (accessed August 24, 2020).

Gillis C. (2018), "Manatee Deaths May Set New Record This Year after Boat Collisions, Red Tide," *News-Press*, December 20. Available online: https://www.news-press.com/story/news/2018/12/20/manatee-red-tide-blue-green-algae-aglal-bloom-outbreak-caloosahatchee-fort-myers-cape-coral/2366282002/ (accessed August 24, 2020).

Hutzler A. (2018), "Florida Red Tide Has Already Killed 400 Sea Turtles and It's Expected to Last until 2019," *Newsweek*, April 8. Available online: https://www.newsweek.com/florida-red-tide-kills-400-sea-turtles-expected-last-2019-1057315 (accessed August 24, 2020).

Kramer B.J., T.W. Davis, K.A. Meyer, B.H. Rosen, J.A. Goleski, G.J. Dick, G. Oh, and C.J. Gobler (2018), "Nitrogen Limitation, Toxin Synthesis Potential, and Toxicity of Cyanobacterial Populations in Lake Okeechobee and the St. Lucie River Estuary, Florida, during the 2016 State of Emergency Event," *PLoS ONE*, 13 (5): e0196278. https://doi.org/10.1371/journal.pone.0196278.

McAnally E. (2019), *Loving Water across Religions: Contributions to an Integral Water Ethic (Ecology and Justice)*, Maryknoll, NY: Orbis Books.

Masaru Emoto's Hado World (2020), "Dear Friends and Fans of Hado and Water Crystals around the World!" Available online: https://hado.com/ihm/ (accessed August 24, 2020).

Morales L. (2019), "Sharing the Voice of the Water Photos; Narrative by Victoria Machado." Available online: https://www.lisettemorales.com/#/walk-for-mother-earth-miami/ (accessed August 24, 2020).

Pachamama Alliance (2020), "About." Available online: https://www.pachamama.org/about (accessed August 24, 2020).

Sampson Z.T. (2020), "Florida Advocacy Group Says Environmental Law Hurts Its Chance to Save Nature," *Tampa Bay Times*, August 13. Available online: https://www.tampabay.com/news/environment/2020/08/13/florida-advocacy-group-says-environmental-law-hurts-its-chance-to-save-nature/ (accessed August 29, 2020).

Staletovich J. (2018), "Mounting Dolphin Deaths in Florida's Red Tide Zone Trigger Federal Investigation," *Miami Herald*, August 31. Available online: https://www.miamiherald.com/latest-news/article217654845.html (accessed August 24, 2020).

State of Florida Office of the Governor (2018), "Executive Order Number 18-191 (Emergency Management—Lake Okeechobee Discharge/Algae Blooms)." Available online: https://www.flgov.com/2018-executive-orders/ (accessed August 24, 2020).

UF IFAS (2018), "Harmful Algal Blooms: Red Tide vs. Blue-Green Algae," [Blog] August 8. Available online: http://blogs.ifas.ufl.edu/osceolaco/2018/08/08/harmful-algal-blooms/ (accessed August 24, 2020).

Glossary Terms

Animism The belief that the natural world, namely plants, animals, geographical features, objects, and phenomena such as rocks, rivers, and weather systems, contain a spirit or soul.

Gaia The notion that planet earth is a single, self-regulating living system. In many instances, such a system is compared to those of other living organisms such as humans and animals. This concept was made popular by James Lovelock's Gaia hypothesis or Gaia theory.

Hado Japanese for vibrations, hado investigates "the intrinsic vibrational pattern at the atomic level in all matter (Masaru Emoto's Hado World 2020)." Masaru Emoto, known by many sacred water participants as Dr. Emoto, related hado to the Chinese notion of *chi*, linking it with alternative practices that engage energy forces to promote holistic healing.

Harmful algal blooms Known also as HABs, these occurrences arise from the growth or "bloom" of algae and can be found in saltwater, freshwater, and brackish water. In saltwater, many HABs are known as "tides," as with Red Tide, which is formed from *Karenia brevis*, a microscopic organism commonly found in the Gulf of Mexico. In freshwater, HABs are the result of cyanobacteria, such as blue-green algae.

Home rule Deemed the "most precious power a city in Florida has," home rule is the ability for local governments to enact ordinances, codes, plans, and resolutions without state approval. Simply put, home rule is local decision-making that allows for citizen-centered solutions. According to the Florida League of Cities, 2016–18, Florida cities experienced "the most deliberative attacks upon Home Rule in state history" many that attempted to preempt cities from introducing and passing local laws that speak specifically to local issues and concerns (Florida League of Cities 2020).

Ho'oponopono The Hawaiian prayer for forgiveness and reconciliation. This prayer is recited during sacred water ceremonies when the water is returned to its source. In unison, participants speak to the water stating: I'm sorry, please forgive me, I love you, thank you. Such phrases are collectively repeated, sometimes expressed in the personal as "I" and other times expressed in the collective form as "we"—We are sorry, Please forgive us, We love you, Thank you.

Mandala A sacred geometrical pattern. During sacred water ceremonies, this space acts as a stage or alter for the water.

Pachamama Alliance With roots in the Amazon rainforest, the Pachamama Alliance seeks to incorporate Indigenous wisdom alongside modern knowledge to create personal and collective transformation that will promote "an environmentally sustainably, spiritually fulfilling, socially just human presence on this planet" (Pachamama Alliance 2020).

INDEX

Abrahamic 56–60, 65, 70–1, 101–2, 112, 192
activism 14, 18, 61, 90, 94–5, 101, 104, 106–11, 113, 116, 199
Adams, C. 180, 264–5
African 10, 13, 129, 133, 136
African American/s 13, 133, 136, 146–54, 214, 239
   Christianity 146, 148
   religious naturalism 13, 148
African diaspora traditions 136
agency 23, 52, 102, 106, 159–61, 169, 225, 257
agriculture/agricultural 9, 15, 18–19, 47, 49, 52–3, 63–4, 68, 112–13, 125, 239, 243, 256, 264
ahimsa 88, 94–5, 103
Albanese, C. L. 67, 111
algae blooms 270
   blue-green 270
   harmful 271, 280
Allah 59, 61, 104, 233
Alone (TV series) 201
Alston, D. 65
American Academy of Asian Studies (AAAS) 89
American environmentalism 13, 164–5
American Veterinary Medical Association (AVMA) 265
ancestral skills movement 201–3, 205–8
Anderson, V. 148
animal rights 64, 94, 129, 181, 207, 255, 264, 266
animal(s) 3–6, 9–10, 13, 23, 25, 28–9, 49, 59, 64, 70, 88, 110, 118, 129, 133–4, 156, 158–9, 182–4, 201–5, 256
   as agents/people 159, 257–60
   blessings 260–4, 269
   death, dying, and companion 265
   and denigrated others 5, 10, 13, 129, 264

domestication/domesticated 125, 203, 256, 261–2, 264–5
   endangered 134
   hierarchy of value 5, 10, 13, 129
   human/animal or nonhuman 4, 10, 13, 158, 160, 202–6, 208, 223, 256–7
   in Indigenous traditions 44, 257–60
   market capitalism 264–5, 269
   as meat 49, 63–4, 79–80, 86, 104, 129, 204–8, 256–7, 264–6, 269
   and race/racism 10, 13, 129, 133
   and religions 4, 44, 59, 70, 103, 254–8, 260–6, 269, 273
   and sex/sexual reproduction 182, 184
   and women 5, 10, 180
animals and human studies 254–6, 269
animals and religion as a field 255–6
animal studies 156, 254–6
animism 23, 133, 280
Anishinaabe 31, 33–4, 43
Anthony Abbott, Saint 260–1
anthropocentrism/anthropocentric 24, 43, 58–9, 62, 69–70, 78–9, 91, 101, 104, 112, 118, 158–9, 169, 222–3
anthropogenic climate change 70, 123–6, 128, 228, 241–2
apocalypse/apocalyptic 243, 249–51
appropriation 32, 38, 40, 43, 133, 250
Art of Living Foundation 1981 114
Asian 11, 83–6, 89–93, 96, 103, 128, 133, 203
Asian religions 83–5, 90–1, 93, 96, 203
asthma 127
Athabaskan 136
ayat 60–1, 69–70, 79
Azeez, A. 233

Bal Taschit "Do Not Destroy" 81
Barad, K. 23, 159
Barber, W. 128, 134
Baskin, C. 38–9

Bauer, K. 272
Bauer, P. M. 202, 208
Baugh, A. 62, 136
Baugh, T. 95
Bauman, W. A. 3–4, 8, 11, 14, 23, 57, 59, 65, 123, 130, 133, 171, 181, 252
Bean v. Southwestern Waste Management 18
Beat poets 89, 93
Bernstein, E. 80
Berry, E. 6, 67, 87, 164
Berry, T. 14, 21, 29, 32, 37, 39, 68, 91, 108
Bible 58, 83, 220, 223–4, 235, 243, 245
biblical 60, 62–3, 130, 171, 221, 229, 244, 264
binary/dualism 102, 129–30, 156, 175, 177, 180–1, 256
biodiversity 95–6, 125
bioregional 45–6
BIPOC/people of color 8, 10, 17–18, 22, 30, 65, 124, 128–30, 133, 136, 150, 154–5, 160, 165, 167, 195, 221–2, 237. *See also* Black/s; Indigenous; Latino/Latinx; race/racism
Black Church 146, 150, 154
Black Church Food Security Network 64, 136
Black Lives Matter movement 8
Black/s 125, 129, 137, 148, 150–1, 165
    and brown 6, 13, 17, 124, 128, 133, 136–7
    communities 18, 126, 128, 155, 160
    men 13, 165
    people(s) 13, 17, 30, 124, 133, 149, 155
    Protestants 70
    religious leaders 64
    women 13, 165, 239
blessings of animals 260–4, 269
body/bodies 133–4, 171–2
    dead 207–8
    mind and 10, 129, 156, 181, 205, 276
    water 272, 278
Bogwalker, N. 207
Book of Nature 6, 60
"Bottom" residents 148–53
Bradford, W. 85
Braiding Sweetgrass (Kimmerer) 163
brain lock 36, 43
Brookfield, S. D. 219
Brown III, H. 136
Brown, J. 91

Buddhism (Buddhist/s) 79, 83–5, 87–96, 103, 133, 189, 202, 215, 237, 250, 254
Buddhist Climate Action Network (BCAN) 96
Buddhist Climate Change Statement to World Leaders 96
Buddhist Peace Fellowship 95
buffalo 49, 54, 257–60, 265, 269
Buffalo People (Northern Plains) 257–9
Bullard, R. 18, 124–6, 128, 159
Butler, J. 156, 171, 174

California Institute of Integral Studies (CIIS) 89
Callicott, J. B. 84, 92–3
Canada/Canadian/Canadien 8, 11–12, 30–1, 33–7, 39, 61, 71, 108, 135, 173, 178, 201, 230, 259, 261–2, 264–5
Candomblé 136
Canfei Nesharim 80
capital 50, 216
capitalism 6, 36, 45, 50, 52, 54, 58, 114, 116, 129
    market 128, 264–5, 269
CARE International 106
Carson, R. 14–18, 84, 89–91, 107
Carter, J. 90–1
Cartesianism 157–8
Catholic/Catholicism 8, 11, 57, 60, 62, 66, 70–1, 104, 130, 162, 173, 184, 193, 198, 260–2
ceremony/ies
    Anishinaabe 33
    appropriation 38, 43
    blessing of animals 260–4, 269
    Buffalo Kill 259, 261
    fasting 43
    ho'oponopono 275, 281
    land 41
    Maskoke 45, 50, 52
    Medicine Wheel 33, 38
    Nature Spirituality church 111
    thanksgiving 32, 39
    water 270, 272–9, 281
Chavis, B. 18, 125–6
Chicago Gay Liberation group 173–4
Chinese immigration 86–8
Christian ethics 223
Christianity (Christian/s) 3–4, 6–8, 10–13, 20, 23, 33, 38, 56–8, 60–4, 67–71,

57, 70–1, 84–5, 87, 91, 101–2, 104,
108, 130–1, 135, 146, 148, 156,
162–5, 170, 173, 180–1, 203, 215,
221, 223–5, 229–32, 234–5, 238–40,
242, 245–6, 258, 261, 263, 265, 269
civil rights 6, 13, 16–20, 90
Clay, E. 17, 133, 136
climate
    colonialism 221–2
    debt 221–2
    injustice 125–8
    justice 64, 66, 138, 241
    skepticism/denial 63, 70, 229, 241
climate change/climate crisis 21–5, 29–31,
    33, 36–7, 41, 43, 47–8, 54, 57, 62–8,
    70, 104, 138, 184, 229–31, 239–40
    anthropogenic 70, 123–6, 128, 228
    injustices of 237–9
    scientific analysis 231–3
    sense of 235–7
    unprecedented 233–4
Coalition on the Environment and Jewish
    Life (COEJL) 80
colonialism 4–13, 16, 18, 30–41, 43, 45,
    47–8, 50–2, 57, 60, 69, 130, 162–3,
    220–2, 236, 251, 260
colonization 4, 8, 10, 129–30, 163
community/communities
    of accountability 225
    activism 278
    biotic 64
    Black 18, 160
    body as 23
    Buddhist 95–6
    carbon-negative 47
    Christian 13, 56–7, 62, 153, 229, 238,
    263
    and climate change 65, 124, 229, 240
    of color 13, 18, 124–6, 128, 134,
    146–53, 155, 160–1
    disabled 190, 194
    Earth-centered 111
    eco- 47–54
    and extinction 249–52
    Hindu 84, 94, 96, 265
    human 125, 162, 174, 182, 184, 192
    Indigenous 13, 30–1, 43–5, 47–54, 71,
    108, 124, 128, 132, 163, 173, 237,
    253, 278
    intentional 184

Jewish 56–7, 59–62, 64, 69–70, 80–1,
    104, 203, 225
LGBTQ 28, 157, 173–5, 177, 184
low-income 22, 160–1
marginalized 157, 167
Muslim 56–7, 61–2, 64, 70, 223–34
narratives 56
planetary 23–4, 181–4, 226
religious 190, 192–3, 198, 223, 232,
    238, 249
rural 16
scientific 15
Sikh 95
spiritual 111, 113
white 18
Cone, J. 13, 18, 129, 135
Connolly, W. E. 251–2
conservation 4–6, 12–13, 16, 83, 87, 92–3,
    95, 104–5, 111, 164–5
consumerism (consumption) 52, 58, 64–5,
    93, 127, 203, 220, 228, 242
contemplative environmentalism 95
Cornwall Alliance for the Stewardship of
    Creation 63, 229, 231
Corrington, R. 21
cosmovisions 251, 253
COVID-19 pandemic 22, 29, 32, 41, 64–5,
    127, 178
creation 14, 17, 33, 37–8, 49, 58–60, 62–3,
    65–6, 68–71, 84, 87–8, 104, 113,
    130, 165, 202, 207, 223, 225, 230–1,
    233, 243, 273
Creation Spirituality (Fox) 68
creation story/ies 28, 59, 81–2
critical materialisms 155, 157–62, 167
critical theory lens 221–2
Cultural Integration Fellowship (CIF) 89
culture 156–7. *See also* nature dualisms/
    dichotomy, culture/nature
    as landscape 13
cyanobacteria 270–2, 279

Dakota Access Pipeline 7, 85, 102, 108, 236
dark green religion(s) 109–10, 118, 234, 241
Darwin, C. 86
Davis, A. J. 243
Dayenu: A Jewish Call to Climate Action 80
decolonial/decolonization 6, 34, 36, 39, 43,
    47–8, 52
deep ecology 89, 92–3, 106–7

Deloria, V. Jr. 6, 31–2, 34–6, 38, 41, 131, 259
de Mello, M. 255
denial 60, 70, 193, 230, 237
Descartes, R. 157–9
Devoted to Nature (Berry) 164
Dharma Gaia 93
dichotomy/dichotomous 10, 156–8, 162–5,
     167, 169. *See also* binary/dualism;
     nature dualisms/dichotomy
disability/disabled 187–90, 192–9
     and the environmental crisis 195–8
     religion and 189–90, 192–5
dispensational premillennialism 245, 247
Divine Oneness 58
Doctrine of Discovery 130, 162–3
Doctrine of *terra nullius* 162
domination 59, 65, 101, 112, 124, 128–30,
     177, 179, 181, 183
dominion/ism 20, 37, 59, 62, 65, 82, 101,
     118, 130
dualism/s 10, 35, 129–30, 156, 180–1. *See
     also* binary/dualism; dichotomy/
     dichotomous; nature dualisms/
     dichotomy

Earth First! 92, 115–16, 119
Earth Holder Community 96
Earth Spirit 111
Eaton, H. 10, 62, 128–9, 179–80
Eaton, S. J. M. 243–4
Eckert, P. 175–6
ecoautobiography 239
eco-critical lens 222
eco-criticism 222
ecofeminist/ecofeminism 35, 63, 68,
     128–9, 156, 159, 179–81, 184, 255
eco-justice 57, 62, 64–5, 67, 69, 184
ecological activism 106–10
ecology 23, 28, 91–2. *See also* deep
     ecology
economic 30, 37, 39, 47, 90, 113, 116,
     125–8, 130, 133–4, 151, 175, 177,
     181, 187, 189, 208, 213–18, 220–2,
     232, 236–7, 242–4, 246, 264
EcoSikh 95
ecotage 116, 119
ecotheology 106–10, 116, 119
ecovillage 47–52, 54, 113
ecowomanist/ecowomanism 137, 180, 239
Ekvn-Yefolecv 50–4

Emerson, R. W. 60, 84–7, 89
endangered
     animals 134
     language 45
Endangered Species Act 80
energy
     body 51–2
     budget 51
     efficiency 51–4, 66
     ethics 242, 246
     fossil fuels (*see* fossil fuels)
     healing 41, 280
     numinous 44
     positive 272–3, 275–6
     renewable 30, 54, 66, 80, 232
     spiritual 119, 272–3, 275–6
Enlightenment 7, 60, 131, 133
enslaved/enslavement 4–5, 8, 10–11, 13,
     57, 129, 133, 136, 148, 239, 243
environmental/environmentalism 5–6,
     12–14, 16, 18–19, 21–3, 25, 59, 62,
     134–8, 229
     activism/activists 90, 93, 101, 105, 108,
          111, 113, 115–16, 181, 229, 278
     catastrophes 195, 215–16, 220, 226,
          237
     crimes 197, 215
     crisis/es 20, 62, 92, 101, 103, 107, 116,
          125, 156, 160, 162, 195–8, 203, 242
     damage 195, 197–8
     degradation/destruction 4–6, 66, 93, 96,
          108, 111, 114, 116, 124, 149, 162, 234
     determinism 151, 154
     and economics 108, 111, 113, 134
     ethics 11, 88, 92–3, 95, 101, 111, 198,
          242–3, 246
     and health 16, 22, 89, 160, 188, 195–8
     history 264
     intersectional environmentalism 13–14,
          21–2, 24, 70, 155, 162, 165
     issues/concerns 20, 25, 36, 57, 66, 90,
          93–5, 102, 104, 109, 181, 196–8,
          239, 243
     Jewish 59, 80–1
     justice 14, 16–20, 57, 62, 64–6, 70, 80,
          104, 109, 124–8, 134–6, 138, 152–4,
          159, 165, 198
     movement 12, 14, 16–19, 83–5, 89–90,
          101, 107, 114, 135, 164–7, 198, 273,
          278

pollution (*see* pollution)
problems 20, 181, 196–7, 239
protection 95
queer environmentalism 22–3
racism 18, 104, 123–6, 130–4, 150, 152
sustainability 104
toxics 14, 134, 198
white 12, 24, 134
Environmental Protection Agency (EPA)
    14, 106
environmental studies 84, 146, 155–6,
    160, 164–5, 243, 264
history 12–13, 24, 264
humanities 242–6, 248
literature 146
philosophy 92–3
science 58, 105, 167
theory 155–6
thought 83–5, 165
epistemological 223–4
ethical
eating 63–4, 79–80, 266
inquiry 215, 223
perspective 196, 214
problems 157
wisdom 215
ethics 169, 216, 225–6
Christian 223
earth 104
kinship 23
method in 218–19
planetary citizenship 23, 213
purpose of 223
religious 215, 226
stewardship 23, 28
European/Euro-
American 84, 137, 202
Christian 6, 162–3
colonizers 4, 8–10, 13, 129–30
settlers 8, 9, 162
Western 16, 133
white 8, 13–14, 124, 133, 162
Evangelical Environmental Network 63
evangelicalism 63, 65, 70–1, 229–31, 245
evil (and good) 149–53
humans (particular categories) as
    sources of evil 8, 10
and nature 5, 8, 150–1
spirits 5
urban life 8

evolution/evolutionary theory 23, 59, 68,
    88, 170, 182, 184
Evolution's Rainbow (Roughgarden) 23
Exodus 61, 80, 235
extinction 47, 96, 249–52, 257
extraction 30, 37, 60, 65, 128, 134, 162, 245
extra-religious practice 87, 100

factory farming 64, 264, 269
fasting 35, 38, 43–4, 233, 265
Femicide Accountability Project 178
Feng, G.-F. 91
Fienup-Riordan, A. 257
Findhorn Ecovillage 113–14
Finney, C. 17, 67, 137, 165
First National People of Color
    Environmental Leadership Summit
    18, 134–6
First Nations 44, 71, 134–5
Florida 270–9
Flowers, C. 134
food 48–9, 52–3, 62–4, 93–4, 113, 125,
    136–7, 161, 181–2, 187, 195–6,
    205–7, 225, 233, 259, 263–6
Forum on Religion and Ecology 67, 91, 198
fossil fuel/s 65–6, 80, 128, 198, 221,
    225, 228, 233, 242, 248. *See also*
    petroculture
culture and religious divides 244–6
pipelines 22, 37, 66, 81
religious framing of 243
spiritual and religious methods for oil
    exploration 243–4
Foucault, M. 175
Fox, M. 68
Francis of Assisi, Saint 261, 263
Francis, Pope 67, 104
Fruitful Darkness (Halifax) 93

Gaard, G. 8, 13, 156, 159, 179
Gaia Theory 103, 109–11, 275, 280
Garden/garden of Eden 59–60, 69, 104,
    114, 150
The Garrison Institute (TGI) 96
Gaskin, S. 113
Gebara, I. 129
Geertz, C. 102
gender binary, hierarchy 8, 10, 35, 112,
    129, 156, 175, 198
gender roles, rules, and repressions 175–9

gender stereotypes 175, 182
Gender Trouble (Butler) 171
Genesis 59, 65, 68, 81–2, 118, 130, 251
Ghosh, A. 235
Gilio-Whitaker, D. 9, 57, 60, 88, 103, 131, 134
Ginsberg, A. 89
Glacken, C. J. 20
globalization 17, 21, 128, 213–18, 220, 225–6
global warming 24, 65, 114, 126, 137, 228, 231, 235, 258
global weirding 65
God 3, 6, 20, 57–60, 63, 65, 67, 69–70, 85, 87, 102, 104–5, 110, 130–1, 148–51, 153, 157, 190–3, 225, 230–1, 235
good and evil/good and bad 8, 10, 148–50
Goodenough, U. 21
Goodman, S. D. 83, 198
Great chain of being 10, 79. *See also* hierarchy/hierarchy of value
The Great Migration 146, 154
Green Deen 63, 105–6
Green Gulch Farm 93–4
Green the Church 135
Green Yoga Association 95
Grimes, R. L. 204
Grim, J. 20, 68, 86, 89, 91
Gross, A. 256
Gross, R. 93
Gruen, L. 207

hado 273, 275, 280
Haeckel, E. 86
Hage, G. 125
halal/eco-halal 63–4, 79–80, 266
Halifax, J. 93
haram 79
Haraway, D. 23, 158, 255
harim 80
Harris, M. 13, 136, 159, 180, 239
Haudenosaunee 29, 31, 44
    confederacy of Iroquois-speaking
        nations (Mohawk, Oneida,
        Onondaga, Cayuga, Seneca,
        Tuscarora) 44
Hayhoe, K. 65, 230–1, 233
Hazon 60–1, 80
Hebrew Bible 58–9, 81, 235, 243
hermeneutical lens 220–2

heteronormativity 8, 28, 171, 174, 177
heteropatriarchy 52
heterosexuality/heterosexism 174, 179, 183–4
hierarchy/hierarchy of value 10–11, 59, 82, 129, 179
Higgens, P. 244
Hill, J. B. 107, 109–10, 119
Hinduism 83–5, 88–9, 92, 94–6, 103, 265
Hispanic 126. *See also* Latino/Latinx; Black/s, and brown; BIPOC/people of color
    Catholics 70
    Mission church 238
The History of Sexuality (Foucault) 175
Holladay, D. 202
The Hollow Tree (Nabigon) 31, 36–7
Holocene 249, 253
home rule 278, 281
homosexuality 173–4, 183
ho'oponopono 275, 281
human-animal studies 159, 255–6, 269
human exceptionalism 4, 20, 28, 158
human transcendence 150–2

idols 58
iftar/leftar 80
immanent/immanence
    and God 57, 70, 82, 102
    and goddess 111
    and Hinduism 103, 120
Indians 33, 49, 52, 83–4, 88, 93–4, 259–60
Indigenous 4–7, 9, 13–14, 17–19, 21–2, 30–9, 41, 45, 48, 50, 53–4, 60, 66, 70–1, 103, 108–9, 124, 128–9, 131, 133–4, 136, 156–7, 162–3, 165, 173, 234, 236–7, 251, 257–60, 262, 265, 275
Indigenous Environmental Network (IEN) 108
Industrial Revolution 131, 232
Institute for Critical Animal Studies 255
Intergovernmental Panel on Climate Change 231
International Association of Pet Cemeteries and Crematoriums (IAOPCC) 265
intersectional analysis 13, 19, 21–5, 177
intersectionality 22, 138, 177, 181
Intertribal Buffalo Council (ITBC) 260
IPCC 125

Iroquois. *See* Haudenosaunee
Islam 4, 7, 58–61, 66, 68, 71, 104–6, 108,
        215, 233, 265–6
Islamic Foundation for Ecology and
        Environmental Science 105–6
Islamic Society of North America (ISNA)
        61, 193–4, 233–4

Jacobs, N. 31–2, 39
Jainism 94–5
Jesus People Against Pollution 135
Jewish Renewal movement 80
Johnson, A. 165
Johnson, E. 10, 59
Johnson, H. 19, 127
Johnson, W. 94
Jones, R. 70, 207
Judaism/Jewish 7, 56–7, 59–62, 64, 68–70,
        80–1, 104, 108, 189, 215, 225, 235,
        250, 254, 264–6, 269
Jung, C. 31–2, 34–6, 38–40
justice 6, 12–14, 16–20, 56, 62, 64–7,
        69–71, 104, 108, 112–13, 124–5,
        134–6, 138, 235

Kearns, L. 11, 18–20, 57, 62–5, 70, 124,
        133, 135–7
Keller, C. 20, 57, 59, 130, 243
Kent, E. 263
Kerouac, J. 89
Keys, C. 19, 135
khalifa/vice-regent 61–2, 67, 79, 105
Kimmerer, R. W. 32, 41, 60, 70, 108, 136, 163
King, M. L. Jr. 17
Kool, R. 264
kosher/eco-kosher 63–4, 104, 265–6

LaDuke, W. 9, 50, 60, 108, 259
language revitalization 45, 48
Latino/Latinx 19, 21, 136, 138
Laudato Si 58, 67, 104
Leopold, A. 84–5, 88, 92, 164
Lloyd, D. 162–3, 165
Lovelock, J. 110

Macy, J. 89, 93–4, 237
mandala 35, 39, 44, 273–4, 281
manifest destiny 4, 6–12
Margulis, L. 110, 182
market capitalism. *See* capitalism, market
Maskoke People 45–7, 50–4

maslahah 79
mass extinction 249–52
McConnell-Ginet, S. 175–6
McLaurin, J. J. 243
Medicine Wheel 31, 33–5, 37–40, 44
Menning, N. 235, 237, 250
Merchant, C. 4, 8–9, 11–12, 60, 69, 131,
        133, 181
Mexico/Mexican 8, 11–12, 21, 66, 71, 128,
        131, 238, 260–5
millenialism 56, 231, 244–5, 247–8
mizan 79
Moe-Lobeda, C. 10, 59, 65, 123, 128,
        215–16, 220–1
Mohawk 30, 44
monotheism/monotheistic 3, 13, 25, 58,
        104, 130–1
Moore, R. 19
moral vision 219–20
moral wisdom 223
Morrison, T. 146–7, 149–52
Mother Earth 31–2, 34, 41, 96, 103, 109,
        113, 116, 136, 250, 275
Muir, J. 84–5, 87–8, 164–6
Muslim(s) 8, 10, 56–7, 61–2, 64, 66, 69–71,
        79–80, 225, 233–4, 240
myth 56–7, 59, 220

Nabigon, H. 31–41
Naess, A. 84, 92, 107
Nasr, S. H. 20, 59, 102, 104–5, 108
National Council of Churches 18, 89, 104,
        135, 198, 245, 247
National Institute of Statistics and
        Geography 265
national park(s) 6, 12, 17, 87
        National Parks Act of 1916 88
        National Park Service 88, 165
native 8–10, 13, 41, 127, 133, 165, 257
Native American(s) 8–10, 88, 91, 93, 103,
        108, 163, 258, 273, 275
natural 3–8, 10, 13–15, 17, 20–2, 29, 33,
        36, 45–7, 49, 52, 54, 59–60, 62,
        67, 69, 84–7, 89, 92, 94–5, 102–6,
        108–14, 123–5, 129–31, 134, 138,
        146, 148–51, 153, 156–8, 160–1,
        165, 170–1, 174–6, 179–81, 183–4,
        187, 191–2, 201–3, 236–7, 239, 255,
        270, 272–3, 275–6, 278–9
natural cathedrals 86–8
natural world

appreciation of/respect for 89, 94, 103, 202, 274
humans and the rest of the natural world 3–8, 10, 13–15, 17, 20–2, 28, 59–60, 66, 79, 84, 104, 130–1, 157, 181, 201–3, 207, 236
humans as part of 7–8, 13, 21, 45–7, 52, 54, 62, 67, 69, 78–9, 90, 95, 103, 106, 108, 113, 125, 157, 184, 202, 236, 270, 278
messages from 237, 273, 275–6
relationship with 95, 106, 113, 201, 272, 276
as sacred 60, 79, 109, 114, 201, 241
and women 179–81
nature 3, 85, 124, 128–31, 133–4, 138, 150–2, 156–61, 170
agency of 159–60
book of nature 6, 58–60
dangerous exile 6
domination of 12, 159, 162
dualisms 7, 129–30
as evil 5, 8
exploitation of 59, 70, 78, 101, 105, 156
as fallen 69
as a garden 60
indigenous attitudes toward 103, 108–9, 133, 136, 163, 192
as inert/dead 131, 133, 157–8
intrinsic value 12, 78–9, 165
as natural resource(s) 8, 12, 105, 108, 134, 156, 239
nature/culture (see nature dualisms/dichotomy, culture/nature)
nonhuman 7, 24, 159–60, 163–5, 202
preservation/preserves 165 (see also conservation)
as pristine 164–5
and race 123–4, 129–31, 133–7, 146, 150, 152, 156, 159–60, 165, 167
as refuge 6
religious attitudes toward 9, 12, 179
rights of 278
as sacred 102–4, 108, 110–12, 116, 118–20, 165–7
social/cultural construction 3, 6, 13, 133, 156–60, 164–5
source of renewal 8, 12, 69–70, 85, 88, 91, 114, 136–7, 165
source of revelation 6, 8

spirituality/spiritual attitudes 13, 62, 67–9, 102–3, 109–12, 150, 163–4
untamed/wild 5, 8, 12–13, 60, 69, 130, 157
utilitarian view 70, 78, 85
as wilderness (see wilderness)
and women/gender or sexuality 10, 129, 158–9, 171, 177, 179–81, 184
nature and religion as a field of study. See religion(s), and nature as a field
nature dualisms/dichotomy 10, 85, 129–30, 156–8, 162–5, 167, 169
culture/nature 5, 7, 10, 35, 38, 129–30, 156, 158, 160–2, 165, 179–80, 184
human/nature or human/non-human 7, 10, 85, 113, 118–19, 129, 156, 158–9, 163–6, 275, 278
reason/nature 129–30
Nelson, G. 90
neoliberalism 216
neo-pagan/neo-paganism 103, 109–13, 119. See also pagan/paganism
New Age 111, 113
new materialism 23, 156
new religious movement (NRM) 101, 106, 109–11, 113–14, 116, 119
New River Road 151–2
Nogueira-Godsey, E. 11, 124–5, 127–9, 181
nonhuman 7, 21, 24, 46, 88, 110, 138, 155–65, 167, 169, 202–6, 249–51, 255, 257, 278
nonviolence 88, 92, 103
numinous 30, 32, 44

oekologie 86
oil. See fossil fuel/s
Oil City Register 243
ontology 161, 169, 175
orthopraxical 106, 113, 119
Osborn, F. 88
Osceola, B. 275–7
other-worldly 68–9

Pachamama Alliance 276, 281
pagan/paganism 10, 12, 70, 103, 119, 266. See also neo-pagan/neo-paganism
Pawnee 136
PaGaian Cosmology 110
Palsson, G. 206
pantheism/pantheistic 110, 119
Paris Climate Treaty 36–7, 66, 96
patriarchy 8, 10, 53, 111, 173, 179

People of Color Environmental Leadership
    Summit 18, 134–6
permaculture 112, 207
Pero, P. 214
petro-apocalypse 243
petroculture 242, 246, 248
Petroleum (Eaton) 243
Pickering, A. 159–60
Pike, S. 110–12, 116, 201
pipeline 22, 30, 36–7, 66, 108
planetary 181–4
    community 23–4, 184
    environmentalism 14
    ethics 23, 213, 225–6
    flourishing 91, 218–23
Plumwood, V. 10, 35, 123, 129–30, 159, 180
pollution 32, 62, 64–5, 106–7, 116, 196
    and health 22, 30, 65, 127, 187, 196, 198
postcolonial 6, 133, 181
posthumanism 23–4
pratitysampupada/dependent origination 103
preservation 4, 6, 12–13, 16, 70, 84, 87,
    111, 128, 165
The Priestly Story 58–9, 81–2
primary moral norms 225
Primate Visions (Haraway) 158
progressive millennialism 244, 248
Project Vidarbha 114
Protestant (Protestantism) 7, 58, 62, 70,
    130, 164, 173, 193, 245, 261
Pui-Lan, K. 129

queer/queer studies 5–6, 21–3, 28, 157,
    174, 181
queer studies 156–7
Qur'an 58–9, 63, 104–5, 189, 233, 266

Rabbitstick Gathering 201–2, 204, 206–7
race/racism 8, 10, 16–18, 21–2, 25, 33,
    123–8, 130, 133–5, 137–8, 146, 150,
    152, 158–9, 177, 180, 198, 224–5.
    See also religion(s), environmental
    racism and
    and colonialism 4–13, 17–21, 30, 148–50
Rainbow Bridge 265
Ramadan 61, 63–4, 233, 265
Rasmussen, L. 65, 104, 231–3
Rauen, H. 276–7
Reclaiming 111–12
regenerative agriculture 49, 53
religion(s)

and animals 64, 70, 254–6
and disability 189–90, 192–5
and ecology as a field 84, 91, 162, 242,
    246
environmental racism and 130–4
and nature as a field 3–4, 14, 20–1, 155,
    162, 167, 179, 189, 203, 226, 254
religious
    environmentalism 18, 22, 57, 61, 63–4,
        79–81, 83, 89–91, 93–5, 101–16,
        136, 198, 233, 243
    groups 114, 135–6, 163, 165, 197
    leaders 60, 64, 66, 93, 96, 108, 167,
        171, 197
    naturalism 21, 146, 148–9, 153
rewilding 202, 209
Reyes-Cortez, M. 265
Rights of Nature (RON) movement 278–9
Rios, J. 238–9
rituals. *See also* ceremony/ies
    blessing 269
    earth healing 111
    and food 265
    Hindu 96
    Indigenous 33, 38, 250, 273
    Jewish 57, 250, 265
    mating 182–3
    mourning 250, 265
    neo-pagan 111, 119
    non-human 159, 182
    Sikh 95
    water 270, 272–3
Ritvo, H. 255
Rockefeller, J. D. 244–5
Rolston, H. 93
Roughgarden, J. 23
Ro, Y. 133
Rue, L. 21
Ruether, R. R. 10, 20–1, 57, 68, 130, 173,
    180

sacred 4, 32–3, 37, 40, 44, 52, 56, 59,
    63, 70, 81, 83, 91–2, 102, 104–5,
    108–11, 113–14, 118, 120, 136, 162,
    165, 167, 169, 198, 201, 207, 234,
    236–7, 259, 265, 273, 275, 281
    food 52
    and humane 207
    land 108
    literature 59
    mission 162

nature 165
    water 96, 270–9
Sacred Mountain Sangha 96
Sacred Water Tribe 272, 274–5
Sahtouris, E. 110
A Sand County Almanac (Leopold) 88
San Francisco Zen Center (SFZC) 90
Santeria 136
Schachter-Shalomi, Z. 80, 104, 108
Schaefer, D. 159, 250
Schelling, F. W. J. 83
Schumacher, E. F. 90–1
Schweitzer, A. 14, 84, 88–9
Schweitzer, J. 231–4
Second World War 14–15
settler colonialism 45, 47, 50–2, 60, 236,
    251, 253
settler/settlers 8–9, 13, 31, 162, 173, 236,
    251, 259, 262
sex/gender 10, 13, 21–3, 25, 52, 128,
    158–9, 170–9, 181–4
sexism 10, 128–9, 178
sexuality 156, 158–9, 170–1, 173–5, 178–9,
    181–4, 229
Shankar, R. 114
Shapiro, K. 256
Sheridan, P. 259
shmita 81
Shomrei Adamah ("Keepers of the Earth")
    81
Shunryu Suzuki Roshi 90
Sikh 95
Silent Spring (Carson) 15, 89, 107
Singer, P. 255
situation transcendence 151
slavery 10–13, 129, 131, 133, 198, 220,
    235, 239
Small Is Beautiful (Schumacher) 90
Smith, H. 91
Snyder, G. 89
Sobrino, J. 214
Soule, M. 92
South Florida 270, 273
sovereignty 109, 136, 162
speciesism 256, 269
spirituality 13, 21, 62, 67–9, 102, 109–11,
    114, 136, 202, 243, 246
Standing Rock
    protest 7, 163, 236, 275
    Sioux tribe 108, 236, 259

Starhawk 111–12
stewardship (steward/s) 20, 23, 28, 47, 49,
    58, 61–4, 67, 69–70, 104–6, 108–10,
    120, 136
    ethics 23, 28
Stewart, L. 244–5
stolen land/s 57, 134
Stone Age methods 202
Stone, J. 148, 151–2
Stonewall Riots 173
structural lens 220–1
Sukol, R. E. 263–4
Sula 146, 148–9, 152
sweatlodge 38, 44
Swimme, B. T. 15, 89, 91

tawhid 79
Taylor, B. 4, 12, 20, 67, 109–10, 114–15,
    167, 234
Tent of Abraham 56
terra nullius/empty land 4, 9, 12, 162
theology 56–7, 59–62, 68–70, 106–10,
    224–5, 245
Thibeault, W. 201, 204–7
Thoreau, H. D. 60, 84–6, 88–9, 133
tikkun olam ("repair of the world") 80, 81
Tillich, P. 20
toxic soup 161
*Toxic Wastes and Race in the United
    States* 18, 65, 125–6
toxins 16, 22, 162, 190, 196, 198
Traces on the Rhodian Shore (Glacken)
    20
trading 206–8
traditional ecological knowledge (TEK)
    108
transcendence (transcendent) 20, 57–8,
    69–70, 84–7, 102, 148, 150–3
transcendentalism 84–5
Truth and Reconciliation 31–3, 36, 44
Tuana, N. 160–1
Tubman, H. 13
Tu B'shavat 81
Tucker, M. E. 14, 20–1, 68, 86, 89, 91
Turtle Island 4, 28–9
Tuscarora 44, 136
Tzu, L. 91

UCC Commission for Racial Justice 125
uncertainty 152–3

United Church of Canada 193
United Church of Christ (UCC) 18
United Nations Framework Convention on
    Climate Change (UNFCCC) 222
United States Department of Agriculture
    (USDA) 264
utilitarian/utilitarianism 63, 70, 78, 85

veganism 64, 207
Vegan Muslim Initiative 64
vegetarianism 64, 94
Veldman, R. G. 63, 124, 229
Vhake 46
vhakv (law) 46
vice-regent. *See khalifa*/vice-regent
Vilden, L. 203, 205
violence 155, 159, 177–8
Vogt, W. 88

Warren, K. 129, 159, 170
water ceremony. *See* ceremony/ies and
    rituals
water of Florida 270–9
web of life 58, 110, 216, 223
Wendat 31
Wet'suwet'en 30
White. *See also* environmental/
    environmentalism
    Americans 8, 124, 137, 202, 229
    Christians (included Catholic,
        evangelical, Protestant) 8, 20, 162,
        164, 165, 229
    communities 18

    male/men 8, 11, 13, 17, 130, 134, 151–2,
        157
    people 13, 22, 47, 124, 133, 137, 150–1,
        220, 256, 258
    settlers/hunters 259
    supremacy 10, 13, 129, 135, 213, 215,
        220, 225
    women 13, 180
White, L. Jr. 3–4, 13, 16, 20, 59, 84, 91–2,
    101, 130, 133–4
Wholistic Healing 31, 44
Whyte, K. P. 30, 49, 128–9, 136, 235–7, 251
Wicca/Wiccan 119, 180
Wild Church Network 67–8
wilderness 13, 60, 67, 70, 83–5, 134, 157,
    162, 164–5, 209
Williams, D. 129
Williams, K. 96
Wilmer, A. 261
Wilson, E. O. 14–15
World Health Organization 178
World Trade Organization (WTO) 112
wudu 80

Yahwist story 59, 81
Yale Program on Climate Communication
    228
yoga 84–5, 95
Yoruba 136
Yosemite National Park 6, 87, 164
Yup'ik 257–8, 269

Zell, M. G. 110–11